LIKE IT WAS

The Diaries of Malcolm Muggeridge

LIKE IT WAS

The Diaries of Malcolm Muggeridge

Selected and Edited by
John Bright-Holmes

COLLINS
St James's Place, London
1981

Muggeridge, Malcolm
  Like it was.
  1. Muggeridge, Malcolm – Biography
  2. Authors, English – Biography
  3. Journalists – Biography
  I. Title
  070'.92'4 PR6025.U5Z/

  ISBN 0-00-216468-X

Photoset in Imprint by
MS Filmsetting Ltd, Frome, Somerset
Made and Printed in Great Britain by
William Collins Sons & Co Ltd, Glasgow

Editor's Preface

All of us who have read published diaries know how destructive it can sometimes be to the unfolding of a narrative if a text is constantly interrupted by explanatory interpolations or loaded with expository footnotes.

When I was asked to edit Mr Malcolm Muggeridge's diaries, I determined as far as possible to allow them to speak for themselves. This was the natural method for an author who not only writes vividly but who, because of his training as a professional journalist, always expects to explain himself as he writes. So I hope that readers will be able to follow the events and feelings he describes and the characters he portrays as a developing story, complete in itself. Where background material has been needed it has been added in connecting passages (printed in italics) or added to the text.

I should add that I have worked not from the author's original diaries but from a typed copy transcribed from the originals – which, because of their age are sometimes faded and not easy to decipher; and I have had the benefit and the pleasure of Mr Muggeridge's help and advice. The selection I have made however, a little under a quarter, is my responsibility.

Apologia Pro Diario Suo

Over the years I have kept diaries, but only – as I have done everything else – in a desultory way, with long gaps and abortive fits and starts. I was surprised and somewhat disconcerted to find that even so they amount, in all, to something like three-quarters of a million words, covering the years from 1924, when I first went to India – actually, to teach at the Union Christian College at Alwaye, in what was then Travancore and is now Kerala – up to comparatively recent times.

In the earlier diaries the handwriting is abysmal, and the ink has faded, to the point that there was a good chance they would never be read. I decided nonetheless to get them typed, and Mrs Millicent Coker heroically undertook the arduous and often baffling task of translating my disorderly scribble into a legible typescript. One way of achieving this was for me to read the text as best I might into a Grundig machine, with Millicent standing by, notebook and pencil in hand; a procedure that, had she been a less wise and serene lady, would scarcely have been permissible. As it was, we found relief together in laughter – that most blessed of all graces whereby our misdemeanours, however odious, are seen to be absurd as well as reprehensible, and the very Fall of Man, mainspring of all delinquency, takes on the character of the old banana-skin joke.

Out of this abundance of words, John Bright-Holmes has skilfully and considerately – but not too considerately! – put together a selection, amounting to under a quarter of the total wordage, thereby providing what is, in effect, a self-portrait of the Diarist; that is to say, an account of what he has thought and said and done through the years of his adult life as recorded contemporaneously in his own words. He emerges as a true child of the twentieth century, with a sceptical mind and a sensual disposition, brought up to entertain the standard expectations of our time, based on the assumption that a more prosperous, brotherly and peaceful world is just round the corner; which expectations, as far as he is concerned, have all been shattered by, on the one hand, revolutionary convulsions, and, on the other, affluence unlimited, purporting to have realised them.

Temperamentally a man of words, the Diarist first addresses himself to captive classroom audiences, then to more numerous and widespread ones – readers of newspapers and magazines, listeners to radio, viewers of television. Thus he comes to be a purveyor of news – the ultimate fantasy of the age – and expounder of views, in the process, like Satan in the Book of Job, going to and fro in the world and up and down in it. Of the seven deadly sins, the third – lust – is evidently the one that has troubled him most, with the seventh – sloth or *accidie*, defined as 'a state of restlessness and inability either to work or to pray' – the runner-up; in true contemporary style, confusing lust and love, *eros* and *agape*, as gourmets confuse greed and hunger. Lechery and gastronomy, indeed, being subject to the same sort of confusion, tend to end up in the same vomitarium.

If carnality has been, in the Diarist's estimation, the devil's prize exhibit in Vanity Fair by virtue of having a spurious transcendental glow – like one of those electric fires whose sham logs light up but give no heat – his other offerings have proved to be more obviously fraudulent. For instance, celebrity, amounting to no more than being recognized in restaurants and other public places, and asked to sign autographs and open garden fetes. Or money, so passionate my and universally loved that the presses are kept turning it out ever more abundantly, to the point that it becomes a digit in a stupendous, non-existent total. Or success, registered in a burgeoning *Who's Who* entry and obituary. Or power, a public rather than a private pursuit, an attribute of eminence; its language rhetoric, proclaimed from rostrums and pulpits and TV studios; with its own emblems and *apparatchiks*, its Highnesses and Excellencies and Eminences, its Comrades and Honourable Members and Noble Lords, constituting the great soap-opera of authority, presented mute in Madame Tussaud's waxworks, and in sinc-sound in the Kremlin, in the White House, in the Houses of Parliament, on Capitol Hill, and along Whitehall, wherever two or more are gathered together to imbibe, or just sniff, the strongest poison ever known – from Caesar's laurel crown. In any case, Theatre, not Life.

Wandering disconsolately through this glamorous, neon-lighted, noisy wasteland, the Diarist succumbs to hypochondria and despair, and often wishes he was dead – or at least writes repeatedly in his diary to this effect, and looks with a baleful eye on the world he lives in and its future prospects, feeling himself, as he has from his earliest memories, to be a displaced person, a stranger in a strange land. Yet somehow he manages to be on the look out for Blake's Golden String:

> I give you the end of a golden string,
>   Only wind it into a ball.
> It will lead you in at Heaven's gate
>   Built in Jerusalem's wall.

from time to time catching a glimpse of it – a glint in a sea of mud, a firefly in a dark night, a sparkle at the bottom of a deep well – picking it up, winding it into a ball, on and on interminably. So why not snip it off and make off with the golden ball? Somehow, though, he staggers on, confident that, if he can only keep going, the Golden String really will guide him to Heaven's gate.

For me, re-living my life in my own dusty sentences dredged up from the past, was a far from happy experience, though perhaps edifying. Memory, the ego's creature, is a complaisant sub-editor, and blurs over or totally erases behaviour calculated to give rise to excessive pain and remorse. Hence the disconcertment and worse that I had to endure was in some degree unexpected. All the same, I have to admit that what the diaries record is truly like it was, and the Diarist like I was – if not, alas, me.

Even when he was learning vain things, and losing himself among many vanities, St Augustine of Hyppo writes, God disciplined him and forgave him; and if in his *Confessions* he calls to mind these cruel corruptions of his soul, it is not for love of them, but rather for love of God's love, and in thankfulness that he has been forgiven. Recalling in the very bitterness of his remembrance his most vicious ways, he goes on, no comfort was to be found 'save in Thee who teachest by sorrow, and woundest to heal'. Aware of the enormous disparity between a saint in the fifth century and a knockabout journalist in the twentieth, I still, in utter humility, venture to echo his words.

1932–1933

Russian Diary 1932–1933

In 1932 Kitty and I were living in Manchester, having come there from Cairo, where I was teaching at the University, and in my spare time I got into the way of sending articles to the Manchester Guardian. *This led to my being asked to join the paper's editorial staff – an offer I eagerly accepted. Thus I found myself writing leading articles, and doing other occasional chores such as book reviewing, theatre notices and obituaries. The economic depression then in full swing had hit Lancashire particularly hard, confirming my strongly held opinion that Capitalism had irretrievably broken down. As I surveyed the world scene, the Soviet regime seemed the only convincing alternative, and I had a great longing to go to Russia, not just to look round, but to stay and bring up my family there. As it happened, circumstances favoured my departure ; Ted Scott, who had succeeded his famous father, C. P. Scott, as editor, was tragically drowned while sailing on Lake Windermere, and his successor, W. P. Crozier, readily agreed to my going to Moscow to stand in for the* Guardian *correspondent there, William Henry Chamberlin, who planned to go on extended leave. Chamberlin, an American, was the* Christian Science Monitor's *regular staff correspondent in Moscow, and covered for the* Guardian *as a useful sideline. No formal agreement was made with Crozier, but it was understood that I should receive space rates for whatever I sent that got into the paper. This casual and, for me, decidedly hazardous arrangement, did not trouble me at the time ; all my thoughts were of making a gateway from Manchester, and starting a new life in the New Civilization proclaimed so ardently by, among others, Kitty's Aunt Bo, and her consort Sidney Webb.*

September 16, 1932—Moscow

Today I arrived in Moscow. Already I have made up my mind to call this the *Diary of a Journalist* and not the *Diary of a Communist*. Moscow is an exquisite city. All the time I alternate between complete despair and wild hope. Walking by the Kremlin, and seeing the Red Flag float over the golden domes, I reflected that what made the revolution so attractive to a certain type of person was that, like revivalist religion, it exalts the humble and meek.

The currency question is at the moment exercising the Government considerably, and it appears that Sokolnikov will be recalled to deal with it. Paper roubles are almost valueless, though still nominally seven and a half to the pound, and the only stable value in the first Communist State is the currency of Capitalism. Food, they say, is getting scarcer and scarcer. Obviously the logical-minded professional revolutionaries, who constitute still the chief personnel of the administration, have little understanding of peasant mentality. They institute sweeping changes after sweeping changes – often conflicting – and the peasants just get sulky. This year's harvest is well below expectation on the Government's own showing. William Henry Chamberlin, the Moscow correspondent of the *Christian Science Monitor* and the *Manchester Guardian*, said that there had been no meat on the ration cards all summer. All the same, the streets feel good; and six years in the East convinced me that mere inefficiency, even mere brutality, are not in themselves a condemnation of anything.

This hotel echoes with just the kind of voice I had romantically hoped never to hear in Russia. The Soviet Intourist organisation spoils the high-brows and incidentally does them rather well. It may bring the loot into the country, but, in view of the millions of people undoubtedly going hungry in Russia at this moment, there is something slightly disgusting about it.

September 17, 1932

I paid a series of tiresome visits to Government Departments and slowly lost my temper.

Lenin's tomb is remarkable. For the two hours that it is open daily a constant procession of people file past the embalmed body. They take off their hats when they go in and do not talk; otherwise there is no ceremonial. No one kisses the glass round him, or makes the sign of the Hammer and Sickle, or anything like that. They just stare. And there he is – a little man with a neat beard and a determined mouth and a well-shaped, but not memorable head. Altogether the effect is austere, at the same time theatrical.

What do the thousands upon thousands of Russians who wait, sometimes a considerable time, to see him, make of the spectacle, I wondered. Their faces, quite blank, give away nothing. Here, I thought, is the one successful, even convincing, piece of ceremonial devised in modern times. But I had a queer conviction that one day an enraged mob would tear him from his place and trample him under foot. Lenin did not look a fanatic, but, as far as appearances are concerned, is quite in the Russian saintly tradition.

Coming away from the tomb I looked into a church and saw four or five old crones and a half-witted priest blessing one another indiscriminately. Christianity at least is over in Russia, and it is difficult to see how it will ever be revived.

September 18, 1932

Cholerton, the *News Chronicle* correspondent, is very bitter. It appears that a number of his wife, Katerina Georgevna's relations have been treated by the Government with savage cruelty for no other reason than that they are connected with a Russian married to a foreigner. He obviously enjoys describing their misfortunes and, for that reason, his point of view is not to be taken too seriously. The only thing to do is to learn Russian and try to see for myself.

We met Wicksteed in the hotel lounge. He came to Russia with the Quakers in 1920, or even earlier, and stayed on liking the place; especially the notion of free-love and no collar. Poor devil, I doubt if he's found much love of any sort; and though he continues collarless and faithful to his first enthusiasms, no one listens to him.

Hunting for a lodging is no joke. Unless we can get a room soon, we shall have spent all the £90 we possess, since I can't earn much yet awhile. Also there is my novel, barely begun, that has to be ready by January 1st, or, at the latest, by the end of January.

We went into the Red Square yesterday evening. It seems to me perfect. Kremlin; St Basil's – fantastically irregular; Lenin's tomb, and the Red Flag shining out like a flame. Some things in this country are done splendidly. The Red Square is one such. But I wondered what the rest of Russia was like – the feverish (and, it seems, often incompetent) developing industrial area; peasants; Collective Farms and Mongolia. Has it all any real connection with Moscow? Or was it just, as in India, an administrative theory working in a capital and having no growth outside; just imposed by force and kept going by means of an alien personnel?

September 19, 1932

Chamberlin and his wife dined with us yesterday. He eats, he told me, his own weight in chocolate a year. His wife Sonia is Russian. Obviously she is responsible largely for his success as a journalist. She knows everyone, she goes here and there, she makes plans. One of her plans is that we should take their flat and pay £90 for the furniture it contains. The first part is so agreeable that I have written for the wherewithal to deal with the latter part. Chamberlin knows a lot about Russia, yet his conversation on the subject is curiously uninteresting. It seems to have nothing to do with Russia or any place in the world unless, say, an American University Literary Society.

I've met with surprising difficulties in getting a Russian teacher. First we asked Intourist – no good; then we went to the Foreign Languages Institute run by Borodin, but no one was very helpful. Then Wicksteed told us of a girl, Klavdia Lvovna, who is eager to exchange Russian for English. We went to see her in her tiny room in a closely crowded flat. She was very enthusiastic, hurried us off on a long tram ride, and to a pine wood where we walked about in the sun and suffered under the direct method. She has ideals about language teaching; all the same she is a good teacher and I shall go on with her.

September 20, 1932

Our teacher, it appears, works at the university. She used, she said, to enjoy her work until she fell under the suspicion of 'indeterminate idealism'. She has an icon in her room and is very religious; amiable in that curious, and not altogether pleasing, Christian way.

I went to the Foreign Office and then had a stormy interview with the hotel manager. Somehow or other we shall have to leave here tomorrow. Seeking a temporary lodging we called on a man in Amtorg, the Soviet trade agency. He was a Rumanian, one of the younger veterans and I thought the most charming and intelligent Soviet official I had met. 'Conditions are bad, admittedly,' he said, 'but the comparison should be with an oriental country.' It is a good point. 'After all,' he went on, 'we have no cares for the morrow. No one owes anyone anything, no one has to save.' As he had himself been imprisoned since the Revolution for Trotsky sympathies and narrowly escaped being shot, I felt it difficult to believe that the life of a Soviet official was entirely carefree. He might not be economically insecure, but then nor was a soldier in the last war. Again, the general population. They also have a kind of security not enjoyed by the workers in capitalist countries. On the other hand, one might argue that though they need not worry about money, they do have to worry about bread. The Communists would answer that the present poor conditions are transitory and that when Russia has made herself independent of the capitalist world, the Russian worker will enjoy a standard of life and leisure hitherto undreamt of. That is to be investigated. Also, whether a Collective State is less menaced by war. If so it would of course be an enormous gain.

September 21, 1932

It looks as though we shall lodge for the time being with a barber and his wife. Andreychin, a Bulgarian whom I had met at the Cholertons', gave us a note to Markovitz, and he arranged with the barber, his colleague. Markovitz is a Macedonian. He was for seven years in Chicago but unable to get American citizenship. He got bitten with the desire to see Communist Russia, went to Moscow with a party of 28 others from America, got work and settled here. All of the 28 that had American passports, he said magnificently, had gone home. The work was not bad but he lived six in a room and had little to eat, especially lately. We had him to supper with us. You could see he was very hungry by his white gums and sunken cheeks. His speech was broken American. His overcoat and suit were still flashy – relics of his Chicago days – but his shoes had gone to bits and, he said, he had no prospect of getting others. He was paid on a commission basis – between 200 and 300 roubles a month, and he got one meal a day at the shop. With the purchasing power of the rouble at 10 kopecs, this is mighty little.

Rhea Clyman has been expelled for her articles in the *Express* on the treatment of political prisoners. The articles were pretty poor, but expelling her is the surest way to make them telling. The people we see at the Foreign Office – Podolski and so on – are nobodies. Orders are given, as in the Rhea case, by the police.

September 22, 1932

Yesterday was a bad day. I lost my head; grew full of obsessions; tortured by indecision; all the usual petulance. Kit was like an angel. The barber kept us waiting three-quarters of an hour. Then his room turned out to be a sort of cabin with just space for two beds, his and ours. It was like India all over again. Why, I wondered angrily, had I left Manchester and my nice safe job where I'd established myself?

We're both very bewildered together. There's the money question; and what am I to write about this country? Chamberlin and the others spill hate of it; and I just listen. The old enthusiastic stuff I used to write for the *Manchester Guardian* seems quite beside the point in any case. I'm glad of that. It wasn't much good. After all, I thought, I've had a bourgeois education and I've got a bourgeois, that is, critical mind. I cannot but exercise this mind. Perhaps the next great civilization will be Collective; perhaps, to belong to it, one will need a different kind of mind – capable of and susceptible to continual propaganda. So let it be. For myself I can't put across propaganda, and when it's put across to me – of whatever sort – I feel just bored.

These people are starving – that's a fact; they're building up, with some measure of success and a great deal of waste – a number of great industries; the country is governed by the stiffest dictatorship I've ever come across so there is no way of estimating what measure of popular support this grandiose Five Year Plan has – entailing terrible sacrifices, particularly on the part of the poorest people (the peasants) – however to find out I must learn Russian.

September 24, 1932

At last we are settled for a bit. The Chamberlins put us on to a Herr Freunde, who has a house, a dacha, in Kliasma – about 35 kilometres from Moscow, and who was delighted to have us share it with him. We shall of course, share the expense. It's a wooden house, very comfortable, and in the country. The air is dry and exhilarating, and we look over a lovely wide plain covered with pine trees. Herr Freunde, a Viennese, drove us down, along with a flaxen Russian girl who is, presumably, his occasional mistress.

We looked in on Rhea Clyman. With her wooden leg and half bald head and story of being arrested by the GPU, she seems a battered little person, and brave. She's struggled along. Her dingy little littered apartment (Kit sat on a box) was rather like her life. She's sick to be leaving Russia, partly because in Moscow she's a personality, and partly because she believes things are going to happen this winter, and partly because in her heart she loves the place.

September 25, 1932

We find Kliasma and Herr Freunde delightful; and I have arranged with him to share the Chamberlins' flat and this house so we shall be able to come here often, and let Pan and our new child be here all the summer.

Yesterday was a free day, and the crowds in the Moscow streets – crowding far into the roadway – were gay and, for once, well fed. In the suburban train from Kliasma everyone was smiling. A Jew spoke with us in broken German. 'Aren't there,' he said, 'thirty million unemployed in England?' I said there weren't, but he seemed sceptical. Looking at the crowd of faces in the train, I marvelled at their diversity and distinction. The mere brute is not much in evidence here, as he is, for instance, in Germany. There is a prevailing sensitiveness, as in India. Suffering and a low standard of life are not unmixed evils; they drive human beings to the inwardness of things.

For us food is very cheap and we can buy as much as we like. The special foreigner's food shop is hidden from the street lest hungry passers-by should be enraged at the sight of such plenty. I feel uneasy about this. But scrupulosity is only admirable when it is complete; and even then is one of the lesser brands of genius. Klavdia Lvovna said the peasants believe that their old masters are letting the present ones continue in order that Russia may be cured once and for all of Communism.

September 26, 1932

We called at the Embassy to see William Strang. He told me a thing or two about Manchuria that will be useful for an article I am writing. The Embassy itself, like all such places, is utterly English. Heavy furniture; competent service; full-length portraits of George and Mary. There was a little photo of the Tsar on a side table. Strang is at least not cocksure in disliking Russia.

We went to the opera house. Stalin and most of the leading members of the Government were on the platform. Stalin looked pretty tough, but forceful, even benign. You could not call him European. His simplicity – in dress, in manner, everything – was unaffected and attractive. I have never seen a man in the full enjoyment of power so little outwardly conscious of it. The speeches in praise of Gorky – who has always seemed to me a rather bogus person – were interminable and, of course, incomprehensible.

In our box was a man called Macmillan, a Conservative Member of Parliament belonging to the Young Men's Christian Association group. He knew my father. He seemed pretty hopeless about British politics, and had all sorts of good views about national planning and what not.

September 27, 1932

Klavdia Lvovna came for a lesson. She has agreed to translate the newspapers for me. She is Communist in sympathy; Christian in religion and romantic in disposition. A kind of Jane Austen. She told me a good story. A Peasant visiting Moscow went about asking what was meant by 'Tempo'. His guide took him to a large building and said: 'Before the Revolution that building would have taken twelve years to build, now we finish it in one year'. Back in his village, the peasant wanted to explain what he had learnt to his father, but in the village there were no buildings large enough for him to illustrate his point – only miserable huts. At last he thought of an idea. He took his father to the cemetery and said: 'You want to know what "Tempo" is – well, before the Revolution it would have taken us twelve years to fill that cemetery, now we fill it in one year'.

Hearing a man singing as he went along the road, it struck me that Communist Russia was singularly joyless. If so, it must be, I think, a consequence of the lack of religion. Russians seem to be lost without a religion. They are not, like French and English people, utter materialists and so naturally irreligious. Their faces suggest prayer, and, having had the occasion for prayer taken away from them, they are a little dazed. In the country the little coloured churches are exquisite. As we pass nearly every day one whose front is paved with blue and white tiles, occasionally the bell rings. It must now, I think, be a school.

September 28, 1932

On the station platform, going into Moscow to see the Chamberlins, we got into conversation (much broken Russian!) with a peasant woman who said she came from Kiev where bread was three roubles the pound and other food unobtainable. She had come here in search of work and now could only find a room at 100 roubles a month. She told her story, not bitterly, not even in despair – just told it smilingly as though it was all in the nature of things.

Bernard Shaw had told Mrs Chamberlin that everyone was well fed in Russia. She explained to him that if her child had only had the milk to which she was entitled by virtue of her food card she would, to all intents and purposes, have had none. 'Why don't you feed the child yourself?' he asked. Mrs Chamberlin pointed out that the child was four years old. 'That's nothing,' he replied, 'Eskimos feed their children till 14 years.' He is a preposterous old fool.

September 29–30, 1932

We stayed in Kliasma. In the early morning we went for a walk. Though it was bright and warm, there seemed an air of depression everywhere. In Moscow one feels only that people are hungry; there is plenty of movement and vitality. Here in the country a kind of blight has settled on everything. After all, the Kremlin bosses are all of the town. They see Russia's progress in terms only of industrial development. For the sake of that they have smashed up the countryside. Perhaps they are right. In fifty years time the ruthlessness may be seen to have been justified. The industrial revolution in England must have seemed as grim. For instance, Cobbett's reaction to it. At the moment, though, it is impossible not to feel a heavy hand everywhere – not so much of tyranny, GPU (secret police), or anything like that – but of iron theory crushing out the lives of people.

There is a vile kind of sentimentality in my whole reaction to Russia. But what I hate in it is just what I expected not to hate – the plan and all that doesn't conform, that's not mediocre, crushed out of existence. To me, tyranny and cruelty are little things. I thought today that if Klavdia Lvovna was sent to prison for talking to me I shouldn't really mind – even find a kind of aptness in her being sent to prison. But the plan is ghastly. The idea of my life being part of God's plan was bad enough, but the idea of my life being only important or significant as a part of Stalin's plan is ghastly. But, first, it's not Stalin's plan, but a collective plan, arising out of the communal consciousness. So they say. At the moment it seems to me to be the characteristic product of the minds of a number of revolutionaries, intent men, mad to impress themselves on their times, mad to be somebodies.

In the afternoon we went to see Louis Fischer, who writes for the *Baltimore Sun*. My impression was that he had grown doubtful about things, but that he was putting a good face on it.

October 1, 1932

A free day. Klavdia Lvovna came here and I got in a fury because I seem not to be learning any Russian. The usual business. I idle away months and months, and then try to do five things in a week or so. For instance, now I have my novel to finish, an exceptionally difficult language to learn and my living to earn by articles on Russia.

October 2, 1932

Kit was not well so I went in for my lesson alone. On the train a man asked me if I was a Communist. I said I wasn't. 'Why?' he asked. He was the new type of man that Soviet Russia has produced – factory workman; educated up to a point; sure of himself; in a way belonging to a ruling class and conscious of it; well fed and attractive. Also on the train I saw a dingy little priest. He was obviously starving – clutching in his hand a lump of stale black bread; face quite battered; hair and sparse beard overgrown. No one took any notice of him. He might have been a sort of dingy ghost on the train. This is to me one of the fascinating features of Soviet Russia – seeing the tables really turned. And what an influence for bad such a dingy little priest might have been fifteen years ago (perhaps, too, an objectionable saint). And now – the most wretched and most miserable member of society. I did not pity him. I must go to some churches when I know Russian.

In the evening we translated a child's reader. It was all propaganda – about a little Indian boy called Tert who was kicked about by a sahib.

October 3, 1932

The train back to Kliasma was even worse than usual. First the station was packed – mostly with peasants carrying bundles. The timetable had been taken away. A horrible radio voice bellowed out, and no one understood. We rushed – perhaps a thousand strong – on to the platform from train to train frantically asking which was which. At last, packed beyond belief, people sitting on the buffers, the steps, everywhere – we steamed out of the station. A little man with an exquisitely amiable face, slightly drunk, perched himself on a suitcase between two carriages and swinging dangerously with the motion of the train and chatting as though he were sitting safely at home.

Russians are angelic but the conditions of life and of transport available for them are bad beyond belief. They suffer their lot without complaint. It struck me that if they were fed moderately and did not have to go to war they would tolerate any sort of Government. But sometimes I feel the instability of things in Russia so acutely that I am afraid and wish that Kit were safely in England to have the baby there.

Cholerton has got to go to the Crimea – lung trouble.

October 4, 1932

Everything suggests that the winter will be bad. Mrs Chamberlin proposed laying in a stock of food.

I ran into Mirsky at the New Moscow Hotel. He is a fanatical Communist, and a former Prince in Tsarist days, who is very brave indeed to come back to Russia since his father was Minister of the Interior in 1905, and since he himself fought in the Civil War against the Bolsheviks. He is to work at the standard life of Lenin.

I have been realising lately the cruelty that can be involved by planning. A set of men plan and get absorbed in their plan – have such and such an industry – then, the biggest power station in the world – such and such sacrifices necessary for all this to be achieved. No butter, etc, no milk, no new houses built – and so on. It seems reasonable – even heroic to the planners (who don't, by the way, make personal sacrifices). But what about the others? It constantly reminds me of the Pyramids.

For Stalin to feel himself bound in a short space of time to make Russia industrialized (economic Empire-building) may have very serious consequences indeed; and, if his project quite fails to come off may be more awful than plagues and famines as far as the population is concerned. There is now a Plenum of the Communist Party. Cholerton knows a janitor in the Kremlin. The other day for the first time this man refused an offer of a snack. 'When the Plenum is on,' he said, 'we get more than we can eat in the Kremlin.' There must be a lot going if some of it trickles through to janitors.

October 5, 1932

We did Russian nearly all day. The significance of life to me (typical bourgeois trick) is not, in the last resort, connected with social systems but rather with observing men and women. They alone interest me. It is interesting in this respect, that the only really sustained thing for me ever has been words because these are the key to men and women. Without knowing a people's language one is a stranger in their midst.

October 6, 1932

We looked in on Strang at the Embassy and he said: 'It's all a pretty barbarous show.' – Socialism against Russia. I've suddenly realized that, after all, I'm civilized and that certain obvious kinds of cruelty are unexpectedly abhorrent. For instance this torturing people for *Valuta*.[1] They do it. You may say, of course, that this happened under Capitalism or in the course of war, but all the same just taking a man or a woman and torturing them to get gold or foreign currency out of them is particularly disgusting.

I thought today that I'd write a book called *Winter in Moscow*, with just the preface serious, pointing out that the only thing not true of Russia is that any single liberal principle of tolerance or reasonableness is observed there; that Christianity is ruthlessly

---

[1] Valuta – a generic term for foreign currency – in great demand then in the USSR and having a much greater purchasing power than its official exchange rate with the Rouble would suggest. The shops which only sold for foreign currency – Torg Sin – had goods which were not available in ordinary shops. The window displays of Torg Sin shops acted, therefore, as a perpetual inducement to citizens to obtain foreign currency.

suppressed, private liberty non-existent, forced labour common, the population poorer, worse fed, worse housed than any other in Europe; but that these things have a purpose. The question is – does the purpose warrant them? Then I'd go on to describe in a personal way the general character of Moscow and the people who live there – English and Russian. In Japan, as far as I can see, the Government is very like here only their Plan is imperial instead of industrial. In both cases the peasants particularly suffering to the very limit, all kinds of frustration in order that the country, or a few individuals who control its Government, may have a sense of achievement.

October 7–12—The Dnieper-Stroi Trip

The Government took all the foreign Correspondents – myself amongst them – to Dnieper-Stroi. We were accommodated in wagon-lits – pre-war but very comfortable. Meals began almost at once. And then chatter. Jogging along the lovely rolling Ukraine, we, dingy cargo of seedy intellectuals, 'chauvinist' Socialists, and down-at-heel journalists were carried to Dnieper-Stroi alternately stuffing ourselves with food, chattering together, and sleeping. I looked out of the window at night and wished I was dead (more seriously than for some months). The night was hard and clear. I had no part in it; only in a warm wagon-lit wherein, two by two, slept a crew of journalists being carried, at the expense of the Soviet Government, to admire a new dam and power-station.

The next day, Saturday, Oumansky, an official in the Soviet Foreign Office, wearing an immense cloth cap, met us at Dnieper-Stroi. The dam was illuminated by searchlights; great electric letters quoted Lenin across the top of it; all round were illuminated signs. Somehow the thing was not particularly impressive, like a toy. 'The biggest power-station in the world,' Oumansky kept saying. He is characteristic of the Soviet regime; utterly mediocre, and succeeding for that very reason. In a capitalist society he would have been a tourist guide or a salesman. Cholerton says that his wife – an Austrian – beats him because she hates so much living in Russia.

We walked to a hotel and there was supper awaiting us; a

miserable band playing, and the usual tourist plant and paraphernalia. The town round Dnieper-Stroi is just beginning – a sort of Middle-West affair; blocks of flats, and a hotel, half-finished factories. Louis Fischer turned up. He said that he had been in some of the new flats and that they were well equipped. He looked less than in his own room. Is there anything in it at all, I wonder, at Dnieper-Stroi? Anything at all? A germ of sincerity? The smallest grain of hope? Do the people governing Russia – the bosses – really care about the workers any more than any other bosses? Is this dam, so lovingly and expensively advertised, primarily intended to provide power for a better kind of industrial society; or is it just a means whereby a gloomy Georgian and his friends try to be somebodies?

On the Sunday morning we went to see the dam by daylight and were lectured on its merits. 'Damn all this talk,' said one of the American Correspondents, 'we didn't come here to listen but to see.' Colonel Cooper met us. He is small and fat, with a dynamic character. If we had tried to imagine an American Colonel employed at a very large salary by the Soviet Government to build a dam it would have been difficult to hit on anything quite as fantastic as the Colonel himself. He cracked jokes with us and then hurried away, full of self-importance and happiness of a sort. He at least found the Five Year Plan congenial.

We were then taken to the chief offices of the dam construction works. A little man with a tiny moustache and a careful voice told us all about the dam. I did not try to listen but stared out of the window watching occasional processions following a Red Flag pass by the window. They moved automatically, did not shout or sing. It was all disciplined. Perhaps, after all, I thought, it is only the vapid intellectural who kicks against the pricks. Is a Derby Day crowd with all its joviality more spontaneous in its pleasures?

Anyway, processions flowed in until an outdoor amphitheatre was quite filled. Perhaps 10,000 persons. A line of police with fixed bayonets kept them in place. There were a good number of soldiers present and several bands. These from time to time played the Internationale. We journalists – two rows of us in front of one of the stands – were a kind of spectacle; the only openly bourgeois elements present. President Kalinin and a few others mounted a raised platform. There is a legend that Kalinin is a peasant president. I never saw anyone less like a peasant, and more like a provincial lawyer. He spoke into the microphone. When the Internationale was played Colonel Cooper raised his hand.

On the Monday afternoon we were taken off to see some factories. The first one appeared to be quite deserted. We were asked to wait a little while, then admitted. The factory was obviously incomplete, but some boys in hastily put on overalls and green spectacles, all young, were pretending to work. They warmed something in a furnace, then cooled it in a trough of water, then warmed it up again. A man in a kind of trolley up above kept leaning over and grimacing at the boys. They had difficulty in preventing themselves from bursting into uncontrollable laughter. It seemed silly to try to take in a set of people in such an obvious way.

I walked back with Pat Sloan, an English leftist, who turned up from a three-months walk in the Caucasus. His enthusiasm for Communism had diminished as a result of finding himself amongst under-fed and deprived peasants. I associated him with Youth Hostels and Holiday Fellowships. Later he spoke appreciatively of these organizations. A large number of people would emigrate from Russia if they had the chance. There is a certain wastage even among the picked men sent abroad. No ordinary person is allowed to leave the country because of the Valuta difficulty. I have so far seen no creative enthusiasm. The Dnieper-Stroi celebrations were extra drab. This suggests to me that propaganda had been overdone; that the propagandists were tired, and that lack of food and bad housing conditions had neutralized any enthusiasm they might have felt for the Plan. And they were picked Party people. The rest just wandered about. A large number of workers must already have been transferred to other places. Some of the labour employed on the dam was certainly forced. But it is better than the Pyramids. Whatever happens in Russia the dam and the power-station are assets.

October 11, 1932

Andreichin, who shared my compartment, has worked in America for the Wobblies (International Workers of the World). As a result of these activities he was sentenced to twenty years imprisonment but was instructed to break his parole and come back to Russia. This he did with some difficulty.

I looked across at Andreichin while he was asleep and thought how utterly unsuitable he was to fill an important administrative post. Already he has served one term in Siberia. These adventurer revolutionaries are, in a way, aristocrats. Dashing, full of vitality, belonging nowhere in particular. They are against society because society offers them no scope for their particular talents. Now Russia has provided a home for them. But are they happy? I doubt it. Whatever they may profess, they have little or no sympathy with the tyranny and puritanical theory of the Soviet Government. They do not find the bare hard life available for them in Soviet Russia congenial. I can imagine them even sighing for the rough and tumble of the IWW agitation. Thus I felt a sudden wave of sympathy with Andreichin. What, after all, had he achieved? Where had he landed himself? He belongs to a revolutionary tradition little in favour with the Kremlin, an, as it were, Liberal revolutionary tradition. I should not, in his place, look very hopefully towards the future.

October 12, 1932

At Kharkov we were taken out to see a tractor factory. We were a little put off when they told us that the final assembly of the parts they were making would not take place till four o'clock – after we had left. Sloan asked one of the workmen privately, and was told that in fact there was a shortage of parts so that no completed tractors would be produced that day. Connected with the factory was a school. Somehow making schools and factories material for tourism demeans them. I doubted the efficiency of the school precisely because we were taken round it and invited to look at it. The whole idea of showing off what has been achieved in Russia is psychologically mistaken, for when the intelligent observer detects deceit he is inclined to be sceptical about everything.

October 13, 1932

We came back to Moscow. Altogether the expedition depressed me.
It seemed so unreal. A free trip; plenty of food and then I suppose
publicity in return. We to provide the publicity. In revulsion
against the idea of sending some telegraphed news I was ravished
by the Ukrainian countryside. The trees, the stretch of rolling
Steppes – this, I thought, and Kit, are all I've found in life to
make me really happy.

I had a nightmare on the train coming back, and frightened
poor Andreichin. As I waited in a queue for my ticket to Kliasma,
I felt the gloominess of Soviet Russia; of Marxism; of the Theory.
There is heavy gloom everywhere. Faces are gloomy – not because
of hunger but because the Theory itself is oppressive. Marx had a
heavy enough soul. You see him with Lenin and Stalin – they are a
Trinity. The Theory hangs like a cloud over Russia. Those who
believe in the Theory, and who at present have power may be able
to shape the future. They may build up a new civilization. If so,
the rest is dead wood. But should they fail, then they will leave a
desert behind them, a vast desert. Marxism may replace European
civilization; in any case, as far as Russia is concerned, it must
destroy it.

October 14, 1932

Kit is ill. I have been looking after her. When she is ill I suffer
agonies of anxiety. Then I realize how much I love her. Then I
think of the possibility of her dying with unutterable dread.
Besides, we are alone here in this gloomy country, amongst alien
people. No one here means anything to us except each other.
When the world's affairs are so bad, private affection has a greater
value than in normal times. I read in the paper of people eating
cats and dogs in Germany; around us in Moscow are millions of
gloomy faces – hungry, full of despair – everywhere it is the same.
And so this little fact that I love another individual; prefer her
interests to my own; know that whatever happens, whatever mess
I make of things, whatever follies I commit, I can count on her
sympathy and forgiveness, seems almost the single redeeming
fact in my life.

Freunde brought a German doctor here. He said it was a special kind of fever and that quite high temperatures might go on for several days. We both cheered up after the doctor had gone, and I played a game of Patience, shouting out the progress of the game to Kit to keep her interested. At night I slept on the floor near her and got up every now and again to see to her. It was a restless, unhappy night.

Chamberlin is not, after all, going away for a few months so I don't know what'll happen to us.

October 15, 1932

I had to go into Moscow to see the Chamberlins and hear, as though I didn't already know, that we shall not be able to have the apartment or his job. They were very penitent and I took a handsome line. After all, I don't care a button. My wife is pregnant; I have £70 of my own and £90 borrowed; up to now casual journalism has brought in nothing; I have a novel to finish by 1st January for which I shall get £50 on the day of publication, and not a word of it is done yet. Thus, my position is highly unsound.

When you feel mildly in relation to your fellows – unaggressive, not wanting to hurt them or to do them down – you feel yourself inferior. One ought to be assertive. It's life to be assertive. But after a point you get out of life. Then you have to write or something and express the point of view of the spectator. I find myself just now thinking more and more about my novel and less and less about Russia. I want, in my novel, to bring out the clinging together of people when everything round them is chaotic.

October 16, 1932

Kit still goes on with a temperature. I make the mistake of taking her temperature at all hours of the day and night. When it is down a little we make merry; when it is up we collapse into deep gloom. I've finished reading *Hamlet* to her, and also an article for the *New Republic*. I think this is fairly good. To write orders one's thoughts.

But in a way I hate sorting out all my experiences into words offered for sale. More and more I long to have done with political situations and settle down to my novel. About politics I'm an amateur, in regard to people's imaginative lives everything's a blank so it doesn't matter.

I believe I'm going to have this fever myself but am saying nothing to Kit in the hope that she may be more or less recovered before I sicken. She said yesterday that there was nothing in life except love and work. I agree. When I look at her face, flushed with fever, and think of my child quick in her belly, my inside melts. Mere passion is only the beginning of love. People who don't have children and don't go through troubles together can't really love. So they move like bees from one appetite to another. Promiscuity only matters when it is serious – a philosophy. Even being promiscuous on the sly is better than making a philosophy of promiscuity.

October 17, 1932

I had a note from Gerald Barry accepting an article for the *Week-End Review* and asking for another. This is the first money I have earned since I left the *Manchester Guardian*. In the evening I went for a walk in a pine wood, strolling along straight avenues with trees on either side. I thought how I would write and write, trying to attain a particular kind of perfection of language – as cool and simple and adequate as an autumn evening. This is my ambition. I shall never master any subject or language thoroughly, but I shall slowly perfect myself in making a picture of life as I have known it – like it is.

If Kit isn't better tomorrow I must get another doctor.

October 18, 1932

This illness still goes on. I feel so tired that I can scarcely write of it. Fortunately my own temperature was a false alarm. I get nervous over having a disease and then develop its primary symptoms. I know somebody who did this with clap and actually had an ejaculation.

I have to go to Moscow to get some information about the Five Year Plan. Chamberlin gave it to me but in German. It will be a sweat reading it, therefore. I hate the idea of going to live with them because I know Sonia doesn't want it. But we have no alternative. We can't go on here. And then there's the question of where Kit is to have the baby. Altogether we're in a mess. Probably she'll have to go home for it.

I sent off two articles (short) to *Reynolds News*. Going in and out of Moscow took a large part of the day. Then, when I came back and found Kit as hot as ever I lost heart, and stormed at myself and her. This was a cruel thing to do. But Kit didn't hold it against me. Why did we leave Manchester? I said. In my heart, though, I'm more delighted than I can say to have left Manchester, partly because I have become a somebody here, a little creature amongst creatures not quite so little.

October 19, 1932

This is the seventh day of Kit's temperature. I've sent for the doctor again. I must get off the article to the *Week-End Review* and start doing some more Russian. Also there's my novel. I shall make it more biting than I intended because now, to all intents and purposes, I've done with the *Manchester Guardian* and with Crozier, the editor. Therefore I can portray him to the life. I don't think he'll dare to sue for libel.

In the train yesterday I was reading the *Manchester Guardian*. A man opposite was peering at it inquisitively and spelling out words. When I had finished reading, therefore, I offered him the paper. He was about to take it when his companion began to whisper excitedly to him. Then he refused to have it. His companion was wearing a black shirt and smart riding breeches. He must, I thought, have been a member of the Party and of the new proletarian aristocracy. They are bullies – the type of men who, in a Capitalist society, would become gangsters, foremen, overseers and, therefore Trade Union officials. Here they are dominant. It is the NCO type. Like other aristocrats, they have privileges and they walk with an assured tread. If their children inherit their places, Russia will soon have an hereditary though not perhaps a

land-owning or wealth-possessing aristocracy. Here it is difficult
to resist the class struggle theory. But then, of course, here the class
struggle theory has been worked out to the very limit. Thus, if
there had been no class antagonism it would have been created
artificially. How much of my enthusiasm for revolutionary change
and contempt for tradition and orderly preservation of the past,
continuity with the past, is due to my own low social origins?
After all, the proletariat have no traditions. When it has been
created, you will find the Tovarish Russian proletariat the most
conservative in the world. More conservative even than the
peasants.

October 20, 1932

Kit has typhus. It is not apparently dangerous but she will probably
have three weeks of fever. It will not harm our child. When I first
heard I was terrified; and even now have a ghastly premonition
that there is worse to come. Still, I have had these premonitions
before and they have proved false. Going for a walk after lunch –
morbid, withdrawn into myself, I imagined her dead and the whole
scene of her deathbed. I can imagine such a thing now and see
myself as a kind of hero, to be pitied, made prominent by losing a
wife. If it really happened I believe I should go mad with grief.
Kit was exquisitely brave. 'Will it hurt the child?' she asked, and
when she knew it wouldn't smiled and lay back in the bed.

    Apart from Kit's illness, I like this life because it is impossible
for me or anyone to do anything except think and write and read.
It is lovely to be unconnected with any institution. And for walks
there are these avenues among the pine trees; wide avenues and
grasses, with the trees as straight and regular as pillars. I never
get tired of them. I feel as though now at last, for the first time in
my life, I am ready to write something really great. 2,000 words a
day. If only I could.

October 21, 1932

Looking back on yesterday it seems a bit theatrical but a diary can
(indeed must) express every mood. Kit is better. The question is

whether she has typhus or paratyphus. If the latter then she'll only have a temperature for three more days; if the former, then she'll have a temperature for about another eleven days. So we're very eager that it should be paratyphoid and pretend that we can wait philosophically to know. A lady doctor from Kliasma came in to see Kit. She's young, her manner is brusque and first of all Kit took a dislike to her. After her second visit she liked her. She made bitter remarks about there being no glycerine in Russia because it, along with fats of all kinds, was used for export. Also she made bitter remarks about our special shop. I was surprised because she seemed to be the sort of person who would have been heart and soul with the Government. I wonder how much genuine support the Government has in any section of the population.

The doctor put little glass pots on Kit's back that caught up her flesh. We laughed, and laughing made the pots hurt all the more. Even so, we couldn't stop laughing.

October 22, 1932

At last I've started on my novel. I worked at it solidly today and typed seven pages and wrote more than 1,000 words. I'm just in the mood for writing it. Kit is very much better. She's beginning to be rebellious which is a good sign. I wish I could stay quietly here in Kliasma until my novel is finished. But I'll have to journalize a bit in order to earn money. We've almost decided that Kit shall go home to have the baby. On the whole it's better, I think.

It's quite clear that anything might happen this winter. The food situation is nearly desperate. I remember reading jn Rousseau's *Confessions* how when he got down to his last 100 louis he just went on quietly spending them living an abstemious life and without any financial cares. I feel rather like that.

October 23, 1932

Today the Chamberlins brought bad news. The Government has decided to shut the special shop and make us pay for everything we buy in Valuta. This means that from being quite cheap Russia becomes suddenly one of the dearest countries in Europe. To cap everything else none of the stuff I've sent to the *Manchester Guardian* has appeared, not even on the back pages. So it looks as though Crozier is set on having his own back on me. However, Chamberlin has changed his mind and will be going on short leave, so while he is away and I cover for him on the *Manchester Guardian*, I ought to be able to earn enough to keep myself here and Kit in England. Otherwise God knows.

October 24, 1932

My fellow journalists are beside themselves with fury about the closing up of the special shop. The diplomats even more so. Actually the whole position in regard to currency is indescribably complicated and fantastic. We all get on the 'Black' Bourse an exchange fifteen times the official one – i.e. about 25–30 roubles to the dollar. This means that, if prices are normal, we can live very cheaply. Some weeks ago the Government announced that diplomats and journalists were to be rationed. There was a fearful hullabaloo and the rationing regulations were withdrawn. Now it has shut their special shop.

It is queer to reflect that in Russia Capitalist currencies are the most sought after and the most stable exchange medium. No one wants roubles. A five rouble tip, for instance, is virtually valueless. You can't buy anything with it. Rents and rail fares being still in roubles, are cheap for the foreigner. In regard to the latter, it has already been arranged that journeys over the frontier must be paid in Valuta. All this is play. But what of the Russian workers with 100 roubles and purchasing power of about 10 gold roubles?

October 25, 1932

I went into Moscow to see a school. The educational activities of the Soviet Government are the most satisfactory of all and the type of Russian produced by post-revolution education, as far as I have seen, far the most intelligent and attractive. The children all seemed bright and happy. But what I really wanted to know was – how, for instance, history is taught with what Cholerton would call a 'Marxist slant' – I wasn't able to find out through lack of Russian.

One fact of public interest for pacifist sympathizers with the Soviet regime is the position of the military here. They are far the most favoured sector of the population: numerous, full of swagger, very much in evidence everywhere. Their boots, their overcoats, their bellies, their complexion – all mark them out in the streets as a privileged class. Russia today it seems to me consists of three elements:

1. The old revolutionary intelligentsia; efficient, idealistic in regard, for instance, to education, marriage and so on.

2. The new proletarian aristocracy, i.e. the victors in the class war, corresponding up to a point to the Trade Union bosses in England.

3. An essentially Asiatic autocracy backed up by the Army.

(1) is almost extinct; (2) is developing, and (3) is the dominant factor and in a way the guts of the whole thing. This is worth developing and would make an interesting article.

October 26, 1932

I did a splendid day's work on the novel – more than 2,000 words typed – and had two things in the *Manchester Guardian* that came today. It ought to mean five guineas. I apologize to Crozier. Even so, he hasn't answered my letters.

In the afternoon I went for a longish walk to a nearby village. I thought as I walked through it – what have these peasants lost? Church, religion, every kind of gaiety in their lives; no shops; little food. And what gains? Who shall measure? On the whole they are free now, and permanently free. It will never be possible to reconstruct the old fabric of superstition and bestiality. Maybe now is a vacuum, but whatever the vacuum is filled with it will not be with what existed there before.

October 27, 1932

Kit seems better. Her temperature went up quite suddenly and then down again. We came to the conclusion it was nervousness. I noticed when making her bed today that her limbs were quite wasted, but as soon as she's had five days without any temperature she'll be able to get up.

I read aloud two of Donne's sermons in the evening. They were almost like leading articles, so balanced and studied in their effects. But very, very good. Somehow reading them reminded me of the continuity of things. In Russia they're trying to begin all over again. Of course they won't succeed in this and of course the break they'll have with the past will prove to have been of the greatest value. All the same, the present position is in a way pathetic. Only one or two heroes. Only one or two festivals. Only a year or two of history. All the rest a blank. The past, they assume, was bad and ignorant and hopelessly inefficient. After all, the fact that Donne believed the human race to have been in existence for only 6,000 years did not seriously detract from the value of his thought, or, indeed, prevent it from being penetrating.

October 28, 1932

The deplorable plight that Kit and I are in here does, I must admit, occasionally get on my nerves. If Kit should get better it would get rid of a great part of my worries; for with us both well and strong we'd have little to fear anywhere. But with her helpless in bed, we are prisoners.

The thesis of my book becomes more and more the unhappiness and ineffectualness of the intellectual in contact with passionate realities; his inability to manage his affections, his helplessness politically and economically; and yet at the same time the power that he has in a Capitalist, or, for that matter, in a Communist country.

The point is that a bourgeoisie is in process of creation in Russia. Journalists and clerks in Government offices, all the characteristic 'black coated' types are emerging. Here the Jew has had his great chance. The liquidation of the old bourgeoisie left him with a clear field in which, even when he has large disabilities and intensive competition, he tends to excel. The officials at the Foreign Office with whom I come sometimes into contact are absolute bourgeois in their habits and in their isolation. Podolski, the best of them, has to an extreme degree the bourgeois attitude towards the family. 'I suppose,' he said, playfully shaking his head over his little boy, 'he'll be a Soviet official one day.' The Revolution has not, after all, interfered so very much with the normal development of Russia. It has served more than anything to concentrate change in a short space of time.

October 29, 1932

Kit is getting better. Each day I have seen to her, worked, taken a stroll, worked again and gone to bed. No articles written, no money earned, but 50 pages of the novel are done. This is the first time that I have been really sure that something I was writing was first-rate. I do a piece of the book and it seems to me so good that I'm half delirious with happiness. And then after a while looking back, I'm more doubtful. Is it so good? I ask myself. However, the characters have come to life. I start off with them in the morning and wonder where they will take me. Old Savory with his moods is a fascinating creature. His death – writing a New Year leader – will be magnificent. To me at least a novel is essentially a means of expressing an attitude to life, a philosophy of life. I begin with that. And then the characters I intend to symbolize a point of view come to life, like a flash; a moral comes into the book. As usual with my work, there is a tendency towards the grotesque. I like this. But it is sure to be critized. Even when I am not writing I find myself more often than not thinking about Pettigrew and old Savory and wondering what will happen to them. The work is astonishingly exhausting; and I shall have to go back of course; improve and in some cases re-write. But not much. Most of what I have done will stand. The parallel between Savory and C. P. Scott is very close. I fear it may be unsafe. But it can't be helped. No living person comes in the book.

October 30, 1932

A letter was published the other day in the newspapers from a man who, for love of country, sacrificed his gold stoppings. I asked a Russian what would be the normal reaction to such a fantastic story. Would people laugh? Or just say to themselves – more propaganda? Or would any considerable number believe the story? She said that most Russians would wonder what particular torture was used to make the man give up his stoppings, and then what particular bribe or immunity to make him write the letter offering his stoppings to the Government.

October 31, 1932

Chamberlin's secretary was saying how the packing together of people, the intensive communication of their lives, has given them a quite exceptional hunger for solitude. Even for Siberia. I can well understand this. Even having been here for some two months I feel a kind of horror at the crowded trains and trams; at the thought that, wherever I go I shall find queues, people pressing against one another, struggling to make their way here or there. A visit to Moscow from Kliasma – only thirty miles away – involves at least three hours of travelling; one hour of waiting in queues and a century of nervous irritation.

November 1, 1932

I went into Moscow to get Kit some books and generally to see how things were.

The Chamberlins were out and so I thought I'd look in on Strang at the Embassy. He was out too and so I asked to see a member of the staff named Vyvyan to whom I had a letter of introduction. He had a sprouting moustache and curly hair. We talked about Russia. I said I didn't see how there could be a peasant uprising, however bad conditions might get. He said that Voroshilov, head of the Army, might arrest Stalin. Then he suddenly got up and asked me to excuse him as he had important business. The way he did this seemed ill-mannered and I felt it was because he considered me an inferior person. When class hatred flares up in you then only is Marxism intelligible. Not necessarily admirable, but intelligible. Soviet society is based on the lust of class hatred. Theoretically it is also based on the public school of classlessness. So now I see more clearly than ever before the meaning of class conflicts. I am therefore in a way grateful to Vyvyan.

November 2–3, 1932

The Kliasma doctor is badgering me for her money and so, to my great annoyance, I must go tomorrow to the Bank. When she came this morning she looked, I thought, pale. No doubt she wants the Valutas to buy food for herself and her child.

I went into Moscow to get money and had lunch with the unfortunate Wicksteed. I said I found Russia gloomy. He said he didn't. He also said that the ordinary Russian ate more meat in a week now than in a year before the Revolution, that food conditions now were better than in 1928. He is the only person, Russian or other, who has said this to me.

Everywhere preparations are being made for the November celebrations. Huge pictures of Stalin everywhere. And ecstatic inscriptions about the Five Year Plan. Although there is absolutely no reason why the present regime shouldn't last indefinitely, I still feel that it is quite unstable. It seems to have no roots, only power. It seems to have no contact with the people. But I suppose the Tsarist Government was like that.

November 4, 1932

The chief thing I have learnt from coming to Russia is the reality and the strength of class hate. It is not nice. It has produced appalling and often unnecessary suffering and cruelty. But it is real in a way that, for instance, the temperament of even the extremist in the Labour Party is not real, and it may well be the case that a man, say like my father, would be more effective if he knowingly and openly abandoned himself to class hate, which is, in any case, the chief motive force in his life, than if he pretended, as he does, that his zeal for change is due to his having greater intelligence or more sensitive feelings than most of his fellows. He betrays the intensity of his class hatred in endless anecdotes. Once when he was delivering furniture from his mother's shop he had to sign a receipt. 'Can you write?' the person who had bought the furniture asked in astonishment. He never forgot this. The invariable retort to this kind of reasoning is that you may hate a class without hating the individuals who make it up. That of course is bosh, since hate means hating individuals and, in the last resort, killing individuals. A classless society, if it is desirable, can only be achieved by one class killing off all the members of all the others, or at least starving them into helpless submission. This has been, and is being done, in Russia. I am appalled at the cruelty it has involved; would have little stomach myself for participating in such a process. This, apart from the fact that thirty years of more or less bourgeois beliefs means that I should be liquidated and not a liquidator, and that amidst all the fantastic nonsense about the Five Year Plan and the deification of mediocrity, the class hate motif stands out as noticeable or, at least, real.

November 6, 1932

I went into Moscow to see the celebrations connected with the fifteenth anniversary of the Bolshevik Revolution, staying with the Chamberlins.

In the evening we went to a meeting in the Opera House. The Kremlin bosses were all on the platform. I thought them a rather dingy crew – Stalin himself sombre, unintelligent-looking, and full of self-conceit; not unlike a Moslem Maharajah of the less enlightened but more virile sort. A number of the usual kind of speeches were delivered and there was an ovation for Stalin, obviously worked up artificially, which he acknowledged with a great show of modesty.

Suddenly bugles sounded and small contingents representing the various fighting forces marched in. Perhaps it was the effect of the limelight that was made to play on them, but they seemed very much stage soldiers, sailors and airmen. It even looked from where I sat as though they were made up. After the speeches a concert. The orchestra played and then an opera *Lenin* was presented. Four rows of singers – two male and two female – assembled on the stage in the centre; also four violinists, the two ladies dressed like pre-war prima donnas, and the two men like Nonconformist choristers. The whole thing suggested a Handel festival at the Crystal Palace. Instinctively I began to feel in my pocket to see if I had sixpence for a silver collection. The music was heavy and dull and was interpreted by occasional recitatives breathlessly given by a blond young man in spectacles and wearing a blue serge suit. A ballet followed. Just when it was about to begin all the lights went out and stayed out for something like half an hour. In the darkness, and to while away the time, the audience started singing. This unrehearsed episode was by far the most delightful in the whole affair. The loge next to mine was full of young Communists. They sang vigorously and gaily. Their virility was aggressively sexual. I felt it, standing beside them in the Dark Opera House – a general atmosphere of informal vigorous sexuality that must be rather like the general atmosphere in an American High School, only cleaner and less sophisticated.

November 7, 1932

As a display of military power, the ceremony today in the Red Square was impressive. The troops looked excellently fed and the equipment was smart. The horses of the cavalry were magnificent. Marshal Voroshilov delivered a speech, but no one could understand it because the loud speakers below echoed against one another. Stalin, Kalinin and the others stood on a ledge of Lenin's tomb. After the troops came a small detachment of civil police; then of armed 'Shock Brigade Workers'. ('How,' I asked Andreychin, 'will they count if, by some possible chance, there is an agreement at the Disarmament Conference?' He answered cynically, 'Physical Culture!') – then an immense procession of civilians from factories and other organizations. We only waited for the military part of the ceremony. Aeroplanes flew in close formation overhead; and tanks and armoured cars crawled over the square like deadly insects. One tank broke down and had to be towed away by a tractor.

I walked about amongst the processions waiting to file through the square trying to see in people's faces what the mood about it all was, and looking at the various propagandist placards and insignia that they carried. As usual the faces expressed neither pleasure nor resentment, but were just blank. The hundreds of thousands of people might have been waiting for a train to take them to work instead of to celebrate the fifteenth anniversary of the Revolution.

Before leaving Moscow I looked over a Russian novel that Sonia Chamberlin had herself translated. The book purports to be a diary kept by two young Communist girls. According to Sonia, it is mostly an authentic document. There was much lechery, not romanticized but 'priggishcized'. Like a dirty-minded medical student, the girls made social curiosity an excuse for satisfying their appetites. I should like to find out about the usual lives of young men and women in Soviet Russia.

November 13–14, 1932

We have left Kliasma and are now safely established in the Chamberlins' flat. It is very agreeable to be in Moscow. Kit is better and I have forgotten that our money is melting away and little or none is coming in.

The walk by the river is, without exaggeration, quite the most lovely town walk I have ever known. I love it just between day and evening when the lights are coming out one by one and the little golden domes of the Kremlin make part of the sky.

We have established contact again with Klavdia Lvovna. She comes to read the papers to us and to give us Russian lessons. Reading the paper is interesting. I sent a first cable to the *Manchester Guardian* quite expecting to get one back from Crozier telling me to send no more. This has not so far happened. With my novel and journalism, I live a sort of dual existence. This diary connects the two. When I begin to write the novel I forget about Russia. The very turn of sentences seems different; the very significance of the language. I hate any sentence that doesn't say anything. I hate a word that's inexact or out of place. Journalism is all the other way. I go for a kind of rhythm and spin out words to fill the rhythm. This is inferior writing. In the diary I just write carelessly as it comes. It is easy and just notes for future writing. Sometimes I say to myself all I need now is the habit of work. I feel as though I have acquired this habit and I doubt if I shall ever lose it except when I'm ill. Having learnt to work I feel myself suddenly a man.

November 15–16, 1932

This afternoon we went to see Cholerton. He had a temperature and was walking restlessly about his room. Like a certain type of consumptive he has married an extremely robust, healthy woman with whom he can have little in common. He told us by the way that Stalin's wife, who died recently, almost certainly committed suicide.

As far as I can see at present all the stuff about a great artistic revival in Russia is, like much else, purely bogus. Art seems to be about as mediocre as it could possibly be. For instance, the ballet. We went one evening: piece called *Ballet Egyptienne*. Of all the performances I have ever seen in my life it was the most characteristically petit bourgeois in atmosphere and in content. There was an oriental prince who, while hunting, met a girl. They loved and then he married a Princess. At his wedding feast she appears and dances before him. Later the Princess killed her rival. A Holy Man brought her to life, and there was a dawn scene at the end. The general effect was of a pretentious, ornate but not good quality illustrated copy of Omar Khayyam. It was about as unrevolutionary as it could possibly be.

November 17, 1932

Reading the papers is interesting. They are, of course, wholly propagandist – either positive propaganda or critical propaganda – either saying that the workers in the North Caucasus have fetched in twice the quota of grain, or that, owing to slackness, the influence

of Kulaks (peasant proprietors of their farms who opposed collectivization of the land), bureaucratic methods, corrupt officials,
etc., etc., the North Caucasus has left potatoes rotting and fields
run down and that therefore intensification of effort is necessary
on the part of the Party. New decrees are coming out one after the
other, all, it seems to me, pointing towards a reversal of policy in
regard to the Plan.

You get occasional interesting articles and the foreign news;
when I can check it up, I find them to be quite outrageously
inaccurate. I doubt if Russians any longer believe the newspapers
much.

November 18, 1932

A fellow-journalist named Foss got the sack. He's been representing one of the American news agencies. So he sold his car to the
GPU for 30,000 roubles – about $1,000. As soon as the deal was
put through another branch of the GPU charged him with
illegally selling a car, and fined him 30,000 roubles. Part of this
he had to pay in Valuta. They then took his fur coat from him on
the grounds that it had been bought in Russia. There is no appeal
against the GPU. Foss was an American citizen. Soviet citizens
can do absolutely nothing whatever the GPU may do to them.

November 19, 1932

Abbé, an American newspaper photographer, with a wife and
three children in Moscow, and grandchildren in America, got
himself into a fearful mess with the Soviet authorities and found
himself in the New Moscow Hotel without any money and a mass
of debts. He and his family lived together in one room. They sold
old clothes for roubles to get money to live. The children were
puny little pale creatures who spoke all sorts of unexpected
languages. Kit and I went to say goodbye to them. Mrs Abbé was
full of vodka and very happy. Various people had raised a sort of
collection to pay their debts. Abbé told me that he'd been sleeping
in his trousers for weeks for fear his wife should dispose of them.

They had $30. People kept coming in to say goodbye to them. They were popular. Everyone, too, had been helping. Altogether it was a charming scene which brought out the very nicest side of human nature – even Luciani, a Corsican who is correspondent of *Le Temps*, came bustling in with 500 roubles that he'd got from somewhere.

I went to see Walter Duranty, the best known of the journalists here, correspondent of the *New York Times*, who has one leg. He was on his way to London from Russia with a bag of jade that he intended to sell, when the train (in France) was derailed. He jumped out, forgetting his jade; then went back for it. At that point another train crashed into the derailed train, and his leg had to be amputated. He never saw the jade again, but he got compensation out of the French Government. I took a great dislike to him, he, I think, to me. A smart fellow, well dressed, with a very attractive Russian woman 'parmi ses meubles'. As a prophet of the Five Year Plan he's despicable.

November 20, 1932

A very fat American looked in. He's a dramatic critic on the *New York Times* and a writer in *The New Yorker*. He made a lot of quite good jokes and asked me to dinner. He made much of his literary friendships, and told jokes about Bernard Shaw and Mrs Patrick Campbell. It was at that point I decided, if Kit wasn't very keen, not to accept his invitation to dinner.

I've so far been a complete failure as a journalist here. My novel is my only stand-by. I wish, all the same, I was as sure of the second part as the first, that it has even a satisfactory finish.

Cholerton's secretary, a really remarkable woman, told me of the famine in the Crimea in the 1920's. She described how famine alters all your values; and how once when she was pregnant her husband (a consumptive, now dead) had managed to get hold of a piece of white bread, thinly, very thinly buttered, and had given it to her. The exquisite flavour of the bread and her delight in it made her realize intensely the suffering she had been through. She wept profusely over the bread.

November 21, 1932

Sloan came to supper with us. We talked, of course, about Russia. He makes the Marxist case. I tried to explain to him why this place seemed so evil to me. Evil is the only apt word. Evil because there is no virtue in it; and because it has utterly failed. In a Marxist state, evil and failure are the same. To say Russian Communism is evil is not to say that Capitalism is good. But evil, in the Government of a Communist state, has more immediately serious consequences because there are no safeguards. Actually, just because economic and social collectivism is so necessary to the world, its failure in application in Russia will have the more serious consequences. More than anything, however, it is the feel of the place that is rotten. The atmosphere of repression, and want, and fear, and unhappiness (joylessness) everywhere; and of arrogance and corruption in the governing classes.

November 23, 1932

The American dramatic critic, whose name appears to be Alexander Woolcott, gave us a mighty good (if pretentious) dinner today. Duranty was there, and a Russian dramatist whose play *Fear* is now running in Moscow, and his American wife and Kit and myself. For once in a while I drank quite a lot and so talked quite a lot. The Russian dramatist was on the point of leaving Russia to go abroad. 'I can't write here,' he said. Perhaps he will join Gorky in his luxurious villa on the Italian lakes. Woolcott told some good stories; but he has a tiresome way of parading his acquaintances amongst writers. Also he is extremely sentimental. But so am I. We talked about Dickens with great gusto and pleasure. The food was extravagantly good. It must have cost a vast amount of Valuta. It was strange sitting in the vulgarly gay room with vulgar quantities of food before us and gold spoons and forks – all the ostentations of wealth (paid for, of course, in Valuta) – and in the centre of Moscow the shabby streets and hungry crowds.

November 24, 1932

This evening we went to an enchanting performance of *The Cherry Orchard* at the Arts Theatre (the Stanislavsky Theatre, with Stanislavsky still in charge). It was certainly the best Chekhov performance I have ever seen (not so many) or imagined, and it was one of the best productions, and contained some of the best acting I have ever seen in my life. Chekhov's widow took the part of the impecunious prima donna who retired to her estate only to have it sold up. Her acting was magnificent. The play seemed somehow prophetic. You felt how inevitable was the sawing down of the Cherry Orchard and of the class that, while full of senti-mental attachment to the Cherry Orchard, had lost all contact with it. The old uncle who always supposed himself to be playing billiards, was beautifully played. I like the third act best – the party; the extravagant changes of mood, the petit bourgeois joviality that has such a strange grace, inexplicable, almost tragic – (perhaps this means I remember the Revolution all the time). For myself I forgive the play its sentimentality, and count it, next to Ibsen, the best since Shakespeare. After all the talk about building Socialism, knock-about, commonsense stuff, the loveliness of the play almost broke me down. Great art lays life bare to me and a play like *The Cherry Orchard* expresses the essential sadness of life itself.

The production was something of an event. Chekhov had been under a ban. *The Cherry Orchard* was allowed because in it the gentry came to grief.

Poor Kit is ill again.

November 25, 1932

This is a very low period in my life. Also insofar as I was really enthusiastic about Communism, I feel now completely dis-illusioned. It's easy, of course, to say that its failure in Russia is neither here nor there. But the type of person who's been put into a position of power in Russia is just the type who'd be put into a position of power anywhere. Besides, when all is said and done, the world, at the moment, is exceedingly melancholy. As a realiza-tion of the hopelessness of the present situation grows, so the life

of most individual people becomes hopeless. The newspapers are
a record of the decay of European civilization. We belong to the
decay. We are the decay. I can say with perfect sincerity, and there
must be millions of other human beings who could say likewise,
that death seems definitely attractive. I'd like to die. I feel, at
under thirty, already tired out with the struggle to live, and still
more, to understand. However, we are both alive; and are likely
to go on living for some time to come.

Now the snow has come. It makes the streets of Moscow
lovely, particularly at night.

November 26, 1932

I had a panic about Kit; rushed about looking for a doctor; went to
Cholerton; in the end got Trubkin here, who pronounced nothing
serious to be the matter. It was a day, to all intents and purposes,
wasted. I tramped a lot about Moscow feeling miserable and sorry
for myself. Woolcott came to tea. I lent him my play and my novel,
partly out of vanity and partly out of self-interest.

November 28, 1932

Mirsky looked in. We discussed the possibility of sharing a room
when Kitty has gone back to England to have the baby. I tried to
get at his mood, but he gave away nothing. 'It is just as I expected
to find it,' he said. Yet somehow he seemed sadder than when I saw
him before. More sombre. I know he is a little mad. He asked about
money, and said he was paid 1,700 roubles for a single article.
On the other hand, he is going to keep a little store of Valuta that
he has. Is this, I wondered, to provide the wherewithal for a
getaway if necessary? But he is the first person I have met in Russia
whose company made me consciously happy.

November 29, 1932

Woolcott gave a little farewell dinner to us. He was enthusiastic
about my play, but did not, as I had half hoped he might, offer to

try and get it produced in New York. What he had to say about it was interesting, however. Sometimes I have detected a kind of cheap genius in this fat absurd American. When he tells an anecdote – for instance, he was describing how, in memoirs, you can always tell whom the writers love, because writing about them, their memories become suddenly perfect; or again, he was telling the plot of O'Neill's *Desire under the Elms* – you realize that he is not just a buffoon, nor even just a literary plutocrat, but a genuine artist in his way.

Late in the evening, Rubinstein came in. He at once invited me to his theatre, the Karmeny. A battered, un-Russian Jew; altruistic I thought, but lonely, feeling himself cut off in Russia from the rest of the world. As he is. Not only as far as travel is concerned (though his company has made one or two tours abroad) but books and periodicals and contacts with people. To such a man the fixation of atmosphere in Russia must be very tiresome. He talked more critically than most Russians of the regime, particularly in relation to the theatre. We shall see *The Beggar's Opera* at his theatre, which should make a good article.

Though I have still earned no money, and am no nearer being settled here, I feel much happier. In the first place, Kit is better; in the second, I am getting towards the end of my novel; in the third – well, for no reason, I just feel happy and interested in things and careless as to the future.

December 1, 1932

I let the diary go, at this point, for three weeks to finish my novel. Now, thank God, it's done. Not as good as I hoped it would be; but, still, not so bad. It will be interesting to know what Constant Huntington, Putnam's representative in London, makes of it.

Mirsky is a great puzzle. As time goes on he is less and less eager to see anything of me. This may be because he finds me a bore, or because he is a bit frightened. He would never, of course, say. I don't think he is happy in Russia; but then I doubt if he has ever been particularly happy anywhere. He is difficult to talk to. All the while his eyes move here and there. It might be shiftiness; but I'm sure it's not. His face is full of fanaticism, and sombre.

He says he has been drinking a lot since he came to Russia. He might go mad. I would give a lot to know what he really thinks of things. Once he came and had a bath. I saw him naked. His body was white and curiously young-looking; rather well-proportioned and handsome. Do I like him, I sometimes wonder, because he is an aristocrat? Is there a kind of ingratiatingness in my manner when I am with him? This is possible. I remember Wicksteed saying apropos someone: 'He would have been a Count if the Revolution had not come.' There is a lot of that kind of thing, particularly amongst the sympathizers with the regime.

We have been several times to the Karmeny Theatre. We saw one pure propagandist play called *The Unknown Soldier*. The production was excellent, but the play itself, negligible. The audience was not particularly interested. They knew exactly what was going to happen. The play was about the Allied intervention in Russia at the end of the 1914–18 war (autocracies return to old battles like dogs to their vomit). A young boy and girl get caught by the interventionist army and, at last, shot. The crew of a French cruiser revolt and shoot their officers. A capitalist is shown as being behind the intervention. He has a sadistic outburst while drinking liquor in a small room wherein a picture of Napoleon is prominently displayed. Workers strike and then fight. A party of Bolsheviks are shown at work printing leaflets in an underground cellar. The Red Army march to victory. The young boy, to save the girl, reveals the whereabouts of the Bolshevik headquarters. And so on. The whole thing finished up with singing the *Internationale*. Whatever else happens in propagandist plays, it is invariably the case that one view prevails, an orator, male or female, gets up and delivers a passionate oration. There is always, too, a lot of play with the telephone.

The aspect of the audience in the way we saw *The Unknown Soldier* was very marked. Rubinstein told me that whenever they put on a real play – e.g. Ostrovsky's *Storm* – the run on the ticket office is prodigious as compared with when they put on a propagandist play. People, I am told, will even go to church just for the sake of hearing real music. They queue up for ancient American cowboy films because, however silly, they provide a relief from propaganda. Too well organized, and too lavish propaganda, in fact, defeats its own object.

The gloom of Moscow on a grey, cold day, when the streets are full of slush; gloomy crowds with anxious faces and old, shabby clothes; people leaning against the wall because too weak to stand; obscene slogans printed on buildings; queues waiting for bread; peasants wandering forlornly about the streets; only soldiers well-dressed and well fed with occasional vulgarly smart women; cruelty in the air – cruelty that had a purpose, and is now aimless; the relics of the November celebrations. This is Moscow – and outside Moscow – utter desolation. Yet this desolation is in a way hopeful. Like the desolation that, in one form or another, exists in all corners of the world, reflects the corruption of human society, and will, at last, make it necessary for human society to be uncorrupt.

One day a young man came to the door and asked to see the Correspondent for the *Manchester Guardian*. I asked Klavdia Lvovna to interpret. He said he had secret information to impart. Very sensibly she refused to interpret. He went away. Afterwards he went to see Cholerton, whose secretary also refused to interpret. Cholerton asked him to come back in the evening. We both assumed he was a spy. In the evening, however, Cholerton decided to hear his story. He was, he said, from the North Caucasus where people were starving and being shot for storing grain. He left us a pile of newspapers and a pamphlet. These we went through and made notes. They told an appalling story. The treatment of the peasants by the Soviet Government is, in its way, one of the worst crimes of history. I shall send an account of it to the *Manchester Guardian*. 'Ask them abroad not to buy our food,' he kept saying, 'Tell them to stop buying. Otherwise we are ruined.'

Kit and I went to dine at the French Embassy. It was a different world but I hated it just as much. Luciani of *Le Temps* introduced us. I asked him to change some pounds into dollars for me in France (he is going there for a few weeks) and bring them back here. His eyes began to roll in a paroxysm of fear. 'Don't talk about such things here,' he whispered.

Kit and I felt a bit awkward because our clothes were not right. I was wearing a light grey suit and she a green costume. After dinner we played roulette for small rouble stakes. Podolski and Nehman – from the Soviet Foreign Office – said they didn't play; then they hung over the table; they couldn't resist joining in.

They showed themselves unusually quick at picking up the game. In fact, they won. It was queer, in a way – sitting there and playing roulette for rouble stakes in the French Embassy – just the kind of thing I didn't expect to find myself doing in Moscow.

One thing I want to write about and shall write about, sometime, is the 'Journalistic Racket in the USSR'. The racket is based on the fact that the Soviet Government can always, by withdrawing a visa, deprive a journalist of his livelihood. Also, as journalists come to settle down here, perhaps marry a Russian wife, and form economic links with the country, it can get at them by arresting hostages. Therefore, nearly all foreign journalists in Russia are frightened of the Government, and frightened to write anything that will seriously displease the bosses. Cholerton's sister-in-law has been sent, they think, to Siberia, and his wife's relations have been persecuted, in order to bring pressure on him. A correspondent of the *Neue Freie Presse* once wrote an article in the course of which he quoted from a Soviet paper to prove that there was forced labour in Russia, and that a party of journalists in the north had seen specially rigged places. He was given forty-eight hours to leave the country. Rather than do this – his wife is Russian – he recanted; said he'd been misinformed. Podolski was the intermediary in arranging this affair. 'I thought to myself,' he said, 'how he'd got a wife and children, and how, if he didn't recant, he'd lose his job.' Even William Chamberlin, soul of caution, who, when he thought he was leaving Russia for good, grew a little bolder, and published in the *Manchester Guardian* a dialogue with a worker at, I think, Magnetogorsk, showing conclusively that there were 10,000 forced workers there, was told by Oumansky that such reports 'were not good for Russian trade'.

It is not surprising, in view of this state of affairs, that the world has been consistently misinformed about Russia, and that the Soviet Government has been able to put across a lot of bogus propaganda. It is fantastic, for instance, that there should still be any doubt about the question of forced labour and religious persecution, and Valuta extortion, and peasant shootings, and, in general, the character of corrupt dictatorship. But there is.

December 17, 1932

Kit left today. It happened that the Polish Ambassador was leaving on the same train, and the whole diplomatic corps was assembled on the station; a gathering of rather seedy men in bowler hats all shaking hands with one another indiscriminately. She had a first-class ticket because Strang was good enough to get it for me in roubles; and she was travelling with Mrs Strang. Kit is the most lovely woman in the world. After five years, she seems infinitely more lovely to me than ever before. Yet I am glad that she has gone back to England to have the baby. Things are so unsettled here, and she has been so ill, that all the time I have a sort of fear about her.

I felt very lonely in the house by myself; but I made up my mind to work hard and make it possible for us all to be together. Work hard in any case. I have reached the stage in life when work is the essential thing. And work, for me, means writing. I wish now that I felt surer about the future. And yet, I know that if we were sure we should be unhappy because we are both adventurers; and because, as I try to show in my novel, security is inept and unreal in an age like this. To be secure now is like dressing for dinner on a desert island. I want to belong to my times even if I hate their character. I want to be in things. Sometimes I think – if I write a bestseller, or even a moderate seller, we shall be able to live quietly in some lovely place. How ghastly! Here we should grow stale and wretched! At whatever price, I want to dabble in politics and journalism and love-making – but lightly, not ponderously, keeping always a sense of what is real. Only so is it possible to comprehend reality – part of the ebb and flow of time and history.

December 18, 1932

Sonia Chamberlin came back here in the morning, leaving William Henry behind for a while in America. She had an immense number of packages; and, praise God, she brought me some Gold Flake cigarettes. Russian cigarettes, as now manufactured, are revolting.

We arranged that I should stay on here and pay one and a half dollars a day. This is very reasonable, and suits me very well.

The young man who came with the North Caucasus news-papers has terrified Klavdia Lvovna! She is convinced he was a spy; that he came to the house before; that he will get her into trouble. For the last two days she has not come to read the papers. I went to her room and found it locked up. This frightened me rather, as I was afraid it meant that she had been arrested. I went round to Cholerton and told him what had happened. He took the matter very seriously; told me that I was indiscreet and that in time I would learn how to conduct myself in Russia.

December 19–20, 1932

Sonia and I went to a song recital in the Conservatory. Portraits of great composers were hung round the walls, and amongst them, in the same manner, portraits of Stalin and Lenin and Marx.

The following day I went for a walk with Sonia by the river. It is frozen now and looks very beautiful. We argued all the time. She made a case for the Soviet Government, but her case is based mainly on the fact that she and William are happy and comfortable here, and that the Jews are getting their own back. She was one of a large Jewish family that emigrated to America after the 1905 pogroms. Somehow they got on in America. Sonia got scholarships – and became a High School teacher. Then she married William, and came with him to Russia, where they became somebodies. She sees Russia still as a place where she and her family were persecuted. Now, in fact, they would belong to the governing class. The Jews have come to the top in revolutionary Russia for the very simple reason that since the old bourgeoisie have been liquidated, they alone are capable of handling administrative work. They tolerate insults meekly, but, at the same time store up resentment, which they let out when an occasion offers. I some-times think that they are letting out in Russia now the accumulated resentment of centuries of cruel persecution.

It is not only because Sonia suffered herself the consequences of Tzarist intolerance and cruelty, that on the whole she admires the present regime, but also because all the cultural side of the Soviet Government is just what she likes – mediocrely high-brow; quantitative rather than qualitative; done by artists who neither frighten nor repel her; who are like herself. Perhaps, in a way, she is right. Culture, I suppose, has to be quantitative, and then it may get quantitatively qualitative. For myself, I like more and more the rare, the exceptional thing; the masterpiece; what transcends the battle of interests going on between one individual and another; one class and another. The strange rare product of genius. For this, the Soviet regime makes no provision, and of course, it would be ruthlessly suppressed under a Marxist system.

December 21, 1932

I heard a remarkable story in connection with the grain collection business. A peasant woman with five children, from whom everything she possessed had been taken, murdered her children and put them in a sack in her empty barn. Then she went to the GPU and reported that, after all, she had lied when she had said that she had no more grain hidden; in reality she had some grain in her barn. An officer went with her to inspect it. She pointed to the sack with her dead children in it. The officer opened the sack, and drew back, full of horror, when he saw its contents. She, standing behind him, hit him over the head with an axe, killing him, and then gave herself up to the police.

December 25, 1932

We had a Christmas party with Barnes, an eager American reporter, and Andreychin and his wife. Sonia's idea of being festive is always to eat. She is lascivious about food.

Andreychin has lost his job and his wife is pregnant. Also he has doubts. They are all getting doubts now because things are in such a mess. Whenever he sees me he cross-examines me about my views, obviously to pass them on elsewhere. He and his wife look back on the time they lived in Hampstead, when he was attached to the London Embassy, as a golden period. Hampstead! A little flat! Taking the baby out in a pram in the mornings! In a way, it is queer to find so ardent, and, in the past, active a revolutionary with such essentially bourgeois conceptions of happiness.

But, as I have so often written, Russian Communism is about the most bourgeois movement that exists in the world.

'Can you explain to me?' Barnes kept saying, 'can you explain to me how it comes about that the figure given for pig iron production during 1933 is 141$^{\%}$ greater than in 1932?' There was no satisfying him. He shook his head; every now and again I heard him mumble: '141% greater. They must be mad.' He is a quite exceptionally stupid man.

December 27, 1932

Every time I sit down, or let myself think, I wonder about my novel. What will happen to it? Go over the episodes in it. Wish it was better done. Should I, after all, re-write it? But I know that hereafter, my main object in life will be to write.

December 28, 1932

Today I've done nothing much – an article for Cholerton in the afternoon and a cable about a new census purge that is to be conducted under the patronage of the GPU. I had a rather cantankerous argument about Soviet propaganda with Sonia. I said (perhaps a bit priggishly) I had seen Woolcott with his pretty girl tourist guide and had realized just his attitude of mind about her. 'Could Russians, after all,' he'd be thinking (perhaps unconsciously) to himself, 'be so bad; could there be forced labour and all the rest of it, when the Government provided so attractive a girl, so prettily dressed in so essentially bourgeois a style, to entertain him?' The Soviet Government's propaganda, in fact, is calculated to satisfy the senile and the lecherous – the typical products of decadent Capitalism – and repel all who sincerely sympathize with its ostensible objects. I sometimes think that with all the brutality, the most real product of the Russian Revolution is the GPU. At least it means somethjng. At least it stands for something definite – brute force. I don't care how soon I leave Russia.

December 29, 1932

In the evening I went to the theatre and saw a dreary musical comedy. I was able to miss the last act because I got a note at the theatre telling me that the Government had taken away food cards from wives and dependents of workers unless they were over 50 or under 12. It means another step towards starvation. I am personally convinced that the Government's supplies of food are running very low indeed. Suppose they run out? It is possible. Then Russian Communism will end in one of the most ghastly calamities the world has ever seen – 160 million people starving. At the moment the Government's chief object is to clear people out of Moscow. Incidentally, for the last two days the cook has been unable to buy anything at all in the open market.

December 31, 1932

It is after midnight and the New Year has begun. I find myself inclined to comment lacrymosely on the world's prospects of 1933 (last year I did this in the *Manchester Guardian*. It was the night old C. P. Scott died) and on my own prospects. I sent a telegram to my darling. Telegrams are so cheap in roubles that I find myself constantly tempted to send one to her.

Certainly I start out this year in quite a different mood from the last when I felt myself to be rather on top of things. Russia, thank God, is behind me. It sometimes comes to me with a pang of horror that I am earning practically nothing; and that when William Chamberlin returns to Russia in April it will be literally nothing unless Cholerton has worked something with the *Telegraph*. I must write some short stories; then begin work on a play. Perhaps, also, an article for *Reynolds' News*. God help me. It crossed my mind that after all I could always commit suicide. I wonder how many suicides there are in Russia? A lot I should think. A lot everywhere; but not nearly as many as one might expect.

January 1, 1933

We had a little dinner party today with Mirsky, the Cholertons and Barnes. It was an ill-assorted company. Barnes lives in terms of 'stories'. As Cholerton put it – 'The front page or the gutter as far as he's concerned'. Barnes said 'Have you heard that Krupskaya has written an article favouring the re-introduction into the schools of the story of Goldilocks? Very significant. I cabled 500 words about it a few days ago.' This remark I intend to treasure for my play *The Foreign Correspondent*.

Sonia treats Mirsky with exaggerated respect. Mirsky himself sat in glum silence most of the evening. 'Oh, Mr Mirsky,' Sonia said, 'We met Sir Bernard Pares in London. He talked a lot about you, and said how sorry he was to lose you from his staff.' 'The bloody liar,' Mirsky suddenly interrupted, and then relapsed into silence.

January 3, 1933

In the evening I went round to the Cholertons. Mrs Cholerton is going to teach me to skate. We begin tomorrow.

Walton, who lives in Moscow, was there and later took me into a night club. It was in a cellar, and full of smoke and heat; corrupt and stale; in some ways characteristic of the condition of Russia; pretentiously modern; genuinely proletarian; copying the form of bourgeois entertainment at its worse and copying badly.

January 4, 1933

In the evening I went to a concert. Sitting next to us was a correspondent for an Indian newspaper. His main source of income, so I believe, comes from the housing racket, and he may well be in with the Lubianka boys. Cholerton told me once that he asked him for an introduction to the British Embassy and remarked that he was ready to undertake any sort of work, however dangerous. I sometimes wonder nowadays why, in the past, I have always taken the side of the under-dog. May not the under-dog sometimes be wrong? Indeed, may he not sometimes be an under-dog because he is wrong? For instance, some years ago I would have inveighed against British Imperialism in India. British Imperialism is a nasty thing; but the people who oppose it are on the same racket – the power racket. This power racket is the essence of history, and though one form of it may be more expedient than another, there is no moral issue at stake! It may, on the whole, be more expedient for the Indian peasants to be bled white by their own kind than by Sahibs; there may come a point when it is necessary to bring them in on the racket, or even to hand it over to them; but the handing over isn't necessarily a high-minded noble gesture – just a racket adjustment.

At the concert was a Dr Rosen who is in charge of the work of Jewish settlement. Peasants, he told us, are wandering about in thousands with their bodies swollen by lack of food. What has happened is simply that the Government having, by its collect-ivization policy, ruined agriculture, is now engaged in extracting every ounce of food left in the country to feed its friends during the winter. After that it proposes to reverse policy – let the peasants pay a tax in kind, leaving them to dispose of the rest of their produce as they see fit. Meanwhile the peasants have to live through the winter as best they can. Millions of them will die.

January 5, 1933

I have been reading Cobbett's *Rural Rides* again. It is peculiarly apposite to the situation in Russia. 'How long will it be ere the ruffians, the base hirelings, the infamous traders who own and who conduct the press; how long ere one of them, or all of them together, shall cause a cottager to smile; shall add one ounce to the meal of the labouring man!' This, I think sometimes as I read *Pravda* and *Isvestia*.

January 6, 1933

In the evening I went to church. It was the Russian Christmas Eve. The churches were packed with people; so much so that I didn't get near the service itself. Even so I liked being there. The

congregation were very devout and a good number of them, to
my surprise, young.

Christianity is at its best in difficult times; and the priests'
faces at this service approximated to the faces of early saints that
I had seen in Italy, carved in wood; lean and sad and full of a kind of
wistful lovingness. They wore queer vestments – enormous gold
hats like saucepans on their heads. The interior of the church was
in good condition. I noticed a Red Soldier amongst the congregation, very devout. As I grow older I find myself suspecting
Christianity more and feeling less inclined to support any of its
organized forms. The Soviet attitude is the most unintelligent and
crass of all – they believe that *science* explodes religion. They are
so out of date and naive that they think you can make a church
ridiculous by demonstrating in it, say, the Law of Gravitation. In
any case you never are presented with a choice between clear
thought and foggy mysticism, but only between inadequate
thought trailing off into mysticism and mysticism trailing off into
thought. People who go all out for the scientific outlook end by
producing the greatest of all absurdities – mysticized science;
the worship of something idiotic like the Five Year Plan. After all,
it is more sensible and more dignified to worship God than a Five
Year Plan.

January 7, 1933

Today there was a Foreign Office party. I drifted round chatting
to people – a man from the *Chicago Daily News*; Andreychin, very
pale and anxious. Oumansky drew me aside and remonstrated
with me about an article on the Lubianka. He said I had belittled
it. I laughed. Someone called him away and we never finished the
conversation. But he was not very pleased. I felt intoxicated as I
realized that I didn't care a damn.

January 9, 1933

We were to have dined with Barnes, but Stalin's speech was
handed out at the Foreign Office and the party was off. All the

chaps were there with their secretaries – smart Valuta girls. The whole scene was rather like a gangster play. People sitting with typewriters in odd corners; coming and going; Oumansky a little pale and flurried, at the centre of it all; GPU chaps guarding all the doors, then the speech, in three batches, handed out to us; a mad, idiotic speech – megalomaniac, aggressive, like a drunk prizefighter mechanically repeating an opinion. It was all fantastic – outside, bread queues; in the Ukraine; in the North Caucasus; in Western Siberia, starvation; and here in the warm Foreign Office, a crowd of villainous-looking foreign press correspondents sending off messages about an insane speech.

I saw Cholerton with Oumansky, speaking nervous French: 'Mais Stalin a dit ça; Stalin a dit ça.' Oumansky turned over the pages of Stalin's speech. Again I felt ready to die. People waiting for trams, black against the snow. Dictatorship of the Proletariat. The only difference was that they were particularly hungry. Anyway I don't want to dictate. Never, never to dictate. Russia has set me irrevocably against a dictatorship by Muggeridge. Better to suffer than to make suffering. I lay down to sleep, tired out with nothing. Another day was over.

January 11, 1933

They say that even the Party people are very upset about Stalin's speech; but today's *Pravda* hails it as 'the greatest document of our epoch.'

In the evening I went to see Dr Rosen. He came to Russia first of all in connection with the American famine relief organization, and then decided to stay on in connection with Jewish settlement work, believing that Russia was a better proposition than Palestine. There was something exquisitely simple and ascetic about him that appealed greatly to me. He spoke about the present situation with quiet despair. 'What can they do? The Government is despised; the peasants no longer trust it; nothing can alter the fact that horses and cattle have been, to the extent of at least 50%, destroyed. He told a characteristic story. Owing to lack of fodder, an epidemic had broken out amongst such horses as still remain in the country. To deal with this situation, the GPU arrested almost the entire staff of the Moscow Veterinary College on the ground that they were saboteurs and had been sending infections out into the villages in order to frustrate the Government's efforts to build Socialism.

I was rather arrogant and opinionated, which was a pity because I wanted Dr Rosen to like me and I'm afraid he didn't. 'Can't you see,' I said, 'that the effect of the Government's policy in regard to the foreign press and to foreign opinion generally, is to alienate everyone whose support would be worth having; to get a certain amount of ostensible approval from nice tourists, and to limit their real protagonists to rogues and simpletons – Duranty and Fischer?'.

January 13, 1933

Mirsky and I went in high spirits to see some friends of his – a Polish writer and his wife. They had an apartment in a house specially reserved for writers. The Polish writer spoke French. He had a large number of Russian books and some French. He showed me various 'Editions de Luxe' published since the Soviet Regime. They were not very good though I professed unbounded admiration for them; pretentious and tawdry. I asked about the censorship and he said it was not severe. 'The old classics have all been published since the Revolution,' he said. The Polish writer's wife turned on to me a great flood of advocacy of the Soviet Government. I could just manage to understand what she said, but not, of course, to reply to her. It was a little embarrassing. 'We're rich,' she said. 'We've got Magnetogorsk, Dnieper-stroi, all the rest of it.' She had a bull-dog whom she constantly caressed, and she said she admired very much Napoleon, Austen Chamberlain and one other, whom I can't now remember. The strange fascination of Austen Chamberlain in this country is interesting, and like the popularity of Galsworthy. The Polish writer was less enthusiastic than his wife; walked nervously up and down the room while whe was talking. A Jew, though Mirsky said not. I have an idea that the Jews, with characteristic shrewdness, are beginning to feel that it is time to move on.

January 15, 1933

Today I walked into the Kremlin with Sonia. The buildings are lovely, with irrelevant domes and towers, and exquisitely painted doorways. There are, I think, three churches, now used as museums. The whole place has a fanciful dainty air, curiously unsuitable for the ponderous and ungainly speeches of the Comrades. I had a queer fancy walking about them, that, when the crash came, even if Russia had become a chaotic wilderness, men in leather coats and with a bullying manner would still meet in the Kremlin and announce triumphant statistics and pass unanimous resolutions about how the party would proceed unflinchingly with its task of building Socialism. This is how I see the thing – the logic of simple, and often debauched, minds, cut off from the population of Russia, from the peasants and even from the workers, existing, a little separate world and listening to the echoes of its own words. Whose only reality is the armed force at its disposal; the logic growing staler, shriller, more unreal; desolation in its naked, oriental form, more real. If I had ever had any doubts about the existence of evil, this place would have convinced me!

January 16, 1933

Mirsky took me off to a party. It was in the very spacious and, for Moscow, luxuriously furnished flat of Louis Aragon, the French 'Surrealist' poet. I think Mirsky is in love with his girl – Elsa. The Polish writer and his fat wife (who called me Maharajah all the evening and kept asking where my hubble-bubble was) were there. Elsa is beautiful. She wore a white stone necklace, heavy for her slender neck. When I looked closely at her I saw that she was hard and unhappy. We ate with a great air of joviality, and Mirsky drank a lot of vodka. He grew rather flushed, and more talkative than usual. I was shy and gauche. After supper the bald Russian took Elsa in his arms and began to kiss her; Aragon walked about uneasily with the familiar strained expression of someone who is jealous but who doesn't believe in jealousy; Mirsky sank into a state of utter gloom; sat on the floor; wouldn't speak or smile. They were a dingy crew; intellectuals who had moved their tents to Moscow and who now contemplate moving on somewhere else since things are running rather low for them. Meanwhile the vodka had run out.

I got back to find Sonia with a group of her pre-Revolution intellectual friends – very, very like lib-labs at home. A woman with rather a strong old-fashioned face was telling anecdotes of Chaliapin. 'We've had a lovely evening. All Chopin's music, and now this.' I wondered which was the more dreary, Chaliapin anecdotes or Aragon and his fellow parasites.

January 17, 1933

Today I went skating, and then with Cholerton and Mrs Cholerton and the daughter of the Swedish Ambassador to see an exhibition of Icons. There was one called 'The Trinity' by Rubin – three exquisite women in blue with long graceful necks sitting round a table with a bowl on it. The colouring was lovely and, as Cholerton said, the picture had a 'budding quality' as though it was capable of development. The earliest icons are entirely oriental (Byzantine) and later became Europeanized; at last Nordic. One of a Pavlova Christ – morbid, distorted – was like a portrait of the Bolshevik Revolution – the mind of a Stalin. They are a lurid form of religious art, more interesting and varied than the Italian Madonnas and Christs – in a way, literary rather than paintings – full of plot and movement; crowded with incident; lacking form, but full of vitality and, like everything Russian, colour. The priests and saints in them all have a particular kind of head – enormously developed in front but small behind, rather like C. P. Scott's; the forehead knotted and grained like a tree.

January 18, 1933

Crozier has made a great effort with an article of mine, and written a leader on it. He didn't alter a single word. The article is very critical. Sonia accused me of being too influenced by Cholerton. I denied that I was influenced by him; yet, in fact, despite all his obsessions, I feel that, of all the people here, he is most right because he alone has preserved a certain intellectual integrity in spite of having to deal with a corrupt Government.

'Isn't it a wonderful place for a correspondent!' Sonia said. 'I like to stay on for twenty years more.'

Nehman of the Soviet Foreign Office came in the other evening. 'After all,' he said, about the new regulations for clearing people out of Moscow, 'Moscow's very overcrowded, and it will be a very good thing if even half a million leave.' He said it so smugly, so complacently, knowing, of course, that there was nowhere for them to leave for, and that they would probably starve through the winter.

January 19, 1933

Chekhov said that a bottle on a raft gleamed, and so implied the whole of a moonlit night. This is the kind of thing I want to do.

At four o'clock I went to see the Sokolnikovs. She was alone when I got there. In Passfield I had flirted with her. Obviously she remembered. Shall I have to flirt with her again? She is not so very attractive, but I know she is rather in love with me; thinks of me as a clean, nice, English boy. I played up to this part. Sokolnikov himself was a bit dim. The story is that he has been arrested. Certainly he is out with the Government. In opposition. He seemed battered, but with a kind of dignity, even integrity, as though he had come through an ordeal without losing his self-respect. I think he might be quite a good fighter in his narrow way. Very cruel and crooked, except that he would not be dishonest about, say, currency questions. A man who had passionate views on currency questions.

In the evening Wadsworth came. He was a shop assistant once in Calcutta, and has recently been in the Crimea. 'When I saw the workers filing into the Red Square on November 7,' he said, 'I felt, what you could never feel, just exaltation to think that at last the miracle I'd dreamed of had happened – workers in power.' He didn't add 'myself in power.' But that was the point. If this was really so, the Revolution and the Soviet Government would be justified. But it isn't so. Wadsworth is not in power; only Stalin and his friends.

I ought to be with Kit when she's having her baby; standing by her; making her happy; helping her. Yet it's both our faults that we're vagabonds. Both our faults. How glad I am that we decided to be vagabonds. How sorry I'll be sometime. How squalid living in a flat in Manchester and writing Liberal Party articles and quarrelling.

I shall work all day tomorrow.

January 20, 1933

In the late afternoon came a new decree about grain collection that required a telegram. Cholerton arrived with his car, but I wasn't ready; got flurried and then told him to go on alone. Thus I had to go by tram; staggeringly crowded; fought my way through it, everyone laughing and grabbing my coat. I laughed too. Russians are lovely people. Then, sitting together, Nehman and Podolski – the former with a frost-bitten nose. Made me laugh and generally felt very much on top of myself. This enchanting dry-cold weather is enormously exhilarating (today 23 degrees of frost centigrade) and, walking back to supper, I longed to be able to stay in Moscow. But a mood. Everything is moods – love, hate, convictions – when you have no belief.

January 23, 1933

Today was the opening of the session of the Central Executive Committee of the Soviets. There were some hundreds of delegates sitting in a great gilded hall fitted with loud-speakers – an interesting looking lot; racially very mixed; on the whole nice. But, of course, the Committee has no function except to listen, applaud, and carry the image of Moscow to their particular part of the country. To the delegates it's mostly an outing – free trip to Moscow, sights of the town; three meat meals a day; the fun of being in the Kremlin. You see the workers about the corridors, and staring up at pictures. The Bolsheviks have a queer strain of ultra-conservatism. Thus they have kept scrupulously all the 'palace qualities' in the Kremlin, and just, as it were, interspersed an occasional hammer and sickle amongst the imperial ones.

January 24, 1933

At ten o'clock I went with Sonia to a party given by the Soviet press to foreign journalists. What a gathering was there. We all drank a good deal. Aaron, who used to be in the Foreign Office, and who is now, he proudly told me, 'on construction' in Magneto-gorsk, fluttered over a negress, amongst others. Most of the Aragon party was present. Aragon read a poem in impassioned French. Mirsky was drunk and melancholy. I rather enjoyed myself and danced with Aaron's negress.

Luciani turned up late. 'It's like the eve of Waterloo,' I said to Duranty. 'You're wrong,' he answered. 'Absolutely wrong. They're getting away with it again. I regard this new decree in the North Caucasus as victory – harnessing the pleasants to the plough because their horses are all dead – Victory!'

Luciani kissed Madame Basacus. Basacus, a little piqued, joked about it. But what a strange affair it was! An orchestra playing and a dingy company, more than half drunk, making merry in the middle of a vast country that, by a chance, had fallen into their hands! Few stranger things have ever happened in the history of the world. I am glad to have seen it.

January 25, 1933

The snow has come again and the streets are lovely, especially at night. Walking along them, late, you feel that everything is unreal. It is like India at night, only cold instead of hot. It makes death seem pleasant, but not a thing to be sought.

January 26, 1933

In the morning, feeling rather liverish, I went for a walk. Then wrote three letters to clear up the question of my novel. Huntington has refused to publish because he is afraid of libel. Kit is going to try Hart-Davis and see if he can do anything at Cape's. I wrote rather bitterly to Huntington. Suddenly I realized, or thought I realized, how good the book was; and that he hated to publish it because it was good. Perhaps this is all nonsense. Then I wrote to Arthur Ransome, who had advised Huntington not to publish, telling him what I meant by the book and why, in my opinion, it was not slanderous. All this is rather silly but since my work is to come to nothing, I am at least entitled to a little self-righteous indignation, especially as Huntington himself has found it, as liberature, very good indeed. Economically, it is one more blow – £50 that I had regarded as certain, lost; and, specially, another ladder kicked down, my publisher.

In the evening I went to the Meyerhof Theatre to see a play of Ostrovsky's. It was wretchedly done. I shall never go to the Meyerhof Theatre again. The awful mediocre pretentiousness of it is very depressing. (How, by the way, anyone reading this diary, would say: Look, he hasn't really seen anything of Russia – visited no cooperatives – not even the University. Studies nothing, not even the language. And yet I know I've seen, not Russia, but the Soviet Regime; and I hate it.)

January 27, 1933

I worked at an article for *Reynolds' News*; finished it; started another article, and then went round to Cholerton's. Katya was in alone. I sat and talked with her. She told me about the Revolution as it had affected her; about her estate in the Caucasus. 'You should go and see it,' I said. 'No,' she answered. 'Somewhere else, but not there. It was a rather nice place.'

In the evening we all went to an appalling gymnastic display in the Opera House. First a great array of lusty youths and maidens, scantily dressed. One – a giant with a brutal face – came forward and delivered a speech with the inevitable propaganda and Comrade Stalin ending. Then there was an immensely silly tableau – soldiers firing; workers heaving hammers, and all the rest of it. As an assertion of vitality it was a failure. Stupidly enough, the girls' armpits were shaved. How much of a piece everything is here! Always the same attempt to produce showmanship results. I have always found 'nakt kultur' unexciting; as I grow older, I find it offensive.

It's no good in my case my staying in Russia. Something unutterably second-rate in the whole 'interesting experiment' gets on my nerves. I know it is all unreal. I know that physical culture is just an idea in someone's mind and that these rows of half nude giants with limelight flashing on them, shouting out slogans like robots, are just fetched out for the occasion. The women were particularly ugly. One set of exercises was accompanied by *If you were the only girl in the world*. No. It is horrible. In a way, I've seen the whole thing. There's nothing more to see, except the peasants being made war on. I'm kicking down ladders. There are scarcely any ladders left now.

January 29, 1933

I skated and had lunch with Vyvyan; then went to see Nehman. He had asked to see me. 'Your article in the *Manchester Guardian*,' he said, 'was terrible.' Thus we began. It was foolish to argue with him because by doing so I to a point accepted his position. He had been to a funeral – a little child who had died of appendicitis. 'So sad,' he said. 'So very sad.' The room darkened as we sat there together. He has a dusky, slight face with a thin beard. Having hurried back and sweated he smelt rather. Not a bad sort of fellow. I think he likes me. He seemed genuinely upset that I should have turned against the 'interesting experiment'. 'Sidney Webb up in Edinburgh,' I said, 'has been indignantly denying there is any forced labour in the Soviet Union. Who put him up to that? What humbug, when we all know there's forced labour, and plenty of it!' All the time I was uneasy because I couldn't tell him what I really hated; couldn't say: 'It's you, Nehman, that is the matter. Chaps like you with a grudge. Chaps who've arrived. Chaps without any roots and any values. Chaps who'd weep over a little girl who died of appendicitis, and sit, quietly in their offices and in their quiet little houses, with terror and horror all round them. Indifferent, unaware. The mediocrity of you, Nehman, a scholarship boy.' Anyway the pose I adopted was: 'Of course, I'm not interested in journalism. I'd much rather live in Russia for a year and never write a word about it. But since I must write to earn money, then I've no alternative but to write what seems to me to be true. I'm a man of moods. An artist, not a journalist. Atmosphere is what counts with me; and I just use facts to fill in a picture because newspapers demand it; won't pay otherwise.' We parted good friends. As I left him I had a yearning to get away from Russia; to leave it all to come to its wretched end without me watching and writing about it. Poor Nehman. I have a conviction that he will be killed at last.

From the Foreign Office I went to have a drink with Richardson – simple Stan. There were a number of Americans and their wives, and Duranty. After three or four cocktails I felt excited and self-confident. Duranty set out to make me look absurd. 'These *Manchester Guardian* correspondents,' he said, 'all so chaste.' 'On the contrary,' I answered, 'great whore masters. Do I strike you as chaste, Mrs Richardson?' – a dull, exceptionally stupid, exceptionally beautiful woman. She said I did strike her as being chaste. 'It's the accent,' she said. 'A chaste accent.'

I said I must telephone, and, after leaving the Richardsons', I went, fairly drunk, to see Cholerton. He was in bed. Ill-looking. Wretched. I really like him very much.

Monday, as can well be imagined, was a grim day.

Extract from article – 'Many Winters Ago in Moscow' (1958)

I came out of the USSR by way of Latvia (then an independent state), stopping off at Leningrad. While there I went to the cemetery to look at Dostoevsky's grave; it was difficult to find, and quite untended. As I stood beside it meditating upon the greatness of the writer it commemorated, a Communist funeral was in progress nearby. The hearse was red instead of black, but otherwise it seemed like any other funeral, with the same tears, the same consigning of dust to dust, the same embarrassed expression on the faces of the less involved mourners.

There were not many passengers on the train to Riga, but when we crossed the Soviet frontier all of us with one accord went into the corridor. We looked back at the small white stakes which marked the end of Soviet territory, and at the GPU guards in their long grey greatcoats, and suddenly, ridiculously, we all began to shake our fists and shout and jeer. It was quite spontaneous, and drew us together. Up to then we had not exchanged a word.

The buffet at Riga station seemed like paradise, and all the open, well-fed and unfrightened faces were wonderful to behold. This delight soon passed. Man cannot live by buffets alone, and as things got into focus one realized that all these seemingly radiant visages were only fat, pasty, bourgeous Latvians clutching their briefcases and reckoning up their money. . . .

When I think of Russia now I remember, not the grey, cruel, set faces of its present masters, but rather how kindly and humorous the people subjected to them managed to remain despite the appalling physical and mental suffering they had to endure. I remember a little painted church standing in the moonlight like an exquisite jewel, someone having managed in inconceivably difficult circumstances to keep its bright colours fresh and triumphant. I remember, too, seeing a superb production of *The Cherry Orchard* at the Stanislavsky Theatre in company with a Russian lady who had been through the Civil War and the terrible famine which followed, and how she remarked of the play: 'I can't understand what they're all bothering about; they've got plenty to eat.' Above all, I remember going to an Easter service in Kiev – the crowded cathedral, the overwhelmingly beautiful music, the intense sense which, as they worshipped, the congregation conveyed of eternity sweeping in like great breakers on the crumbling shores of Time.

I left Moscow in the spring of 1933 to join Kitty and our two sons – the second, John, having been safely delivered – in Switzerland. Even if I had wished to stay on in Russia, it would have been impossible. My money had almost run out, and with the return of Chamberlin much sooner than was originally planned, and his resumption of the Manchester Guardian's *Moscow coverage, I had no longer any credentials, and so no possibility of functioning as a journalist in the USSR. Furthermore, after Kitty's departure, I managed to make my way by myself to the Ukraine and the Caucasus to report on the famine conditions there as a result of Stalin's enforced collectivization of agriculture. The articles I wrote describing the suffering and privations of the peasants, and the monstrous brutality of their treatment, were dispatched to the* Guardian *by diplomatic bag to avoid the censorship, and I knew that when they were published my position would be untenable. The articles duly appeared, heavily sub-edited, but even so caused some stir. In both the* Guardian *and the* New Statesman *letters were published calling me a liar. For confirmation of the truth of my report I had to wait for Khruschev's speech at the 20th Party Conference in 1956, in which he gave his account of the 1933 famine and its consequences, showing mine to have been, if anything, an under-statement. While in Switzerland I wrote my book,* Winter In Moscow, *about my time in the USSR.*

1934–1935

Indian Diary 1934-1935

Returning to London in 1934 from Switzerland – where I worked for some months in the International Labour Office, attached to the League of Nations – I found myself once more in difficult circumstances. Kitty with her usual skill had fixed up a home for us in Parliament Hill Fields, but now we had a baby daughter, Valentine, in addition to our two sons, and were soon short of money. Winter In Moscow *had appeared and been reprinted, but, if anything, it hampered my efforts to get a job in Fleet Street. As I discovered, taking a strongly critical view of the Soviet regime and its bosses was a handicap rather than a help as far as the national press was concerned; the more so in my case because my abhorrence of a Marxist dictatorship as operated from the Kremlin did not make me any better disposed towards a capitalist economy as operated from the City of London or Wall Street. Although I did not recognize it then, the liberal consensus which was to provide the orthodoxy or Party-Line of the so-called free world, was already in process of formation, and beginning to be enforced. Then I noticed an advertisement by the Calcutta* Statesman *for an assistant editor, put in an application, and to my amazement got the job. It meant another departure; this time I left with a heavy heart, and in a very different mood from the first time I went to India, ten years before, to teach at a Christian college. Now I was a Sahib, travelling first-class, part of the ruling* apparat *of an expiring empire.*

September 25, 1934—On a P and O Steamer

I didn't expect to be off again, so have to start another diary; but I am off again, and on my way to India in the *Viceroy of India*. Kit saw me off at Victoria; and I shan't see her again (unless something unexpected happens) for at least a year. However, it was a chance to be free of money troubles, to have money, to be rich, that put me on this boat. That and a kind of inertia, or fate, a gloriously inevitable unfolding of my own life.

I feel full of foreboding; as though, somehow, I'd sold my soul. I shouldn't be at all surprised, or much mind, if I died quite soon. Now that I've digested my repudiation of all dawnism, and reconciled myself to doing nothing about anything, but writing, it seems as though I'd shot my bolt. I know now that, whatever may happen to me, I shan't be happy – will go away from my family, in love or out of love, rich or poor, successful or a failure – it'll make no difference.

My novel about the *Manchester Guardian*, now vilely re-named *Picture Palace*, will be published in three days' time; I am singularly uninterested, unelated. I've barely begun on the book on Samuel Butler.

Hitherto Samuel Butler has been seen entirely through Festing Jones – that is through himself. It is, of course, largely Butler's own fault that this should be so. He was so sure of his own immortality, so determined to leave ample and orderly material for the biographies he knew were coming, careful even, to breed a biographer, Festing Jones himself, after his own heart. And, by a curious chance, though he and Jones became estranged, Jones did become more or less the sole medium whereby Butler has been presented to the British public. Thus was Butler hoist with his own petard. Jones was able to suppress all, or, so I shall show, nearly all, trace of this estrangement.

Butler, more than any other 19th-century writer, is us. The empty space he cleared has been our heritage. In him, the strange fantasy of the Victorian Age peters out, with, to follow, only the tiresome emptiness of a few such as Bernard Shaw, and ourselves. Against the background of Victorian fantasy I see him a product of it, its doom; a final clearing of the decks, a final explosion.

September 26, 1934

I don't know anything on the whole more unpleasant than sailing down the Red Sea on a P and O boat in the first class. The steamy heat, as it were, brings out people's innate coarseness. We are all sticky, indecent. And these fifth-rate people, so pleased with themselves, so absurdly arrogant. I feel sorry for them, in a queer way feel myself to be one of them. Battered, egotistic, social climbers, desperate creatures at the end of their tether, full of bounce, dressing for dinner, talking, their accents slightly clipped, as though superimposed on others.

September 28, 1934—Calcutta

It has been curious, this coming to India again. All the way I was full of dread, and then, suddenly, when I saw the country, I felt a queer sort of happiness, a queer sense of fatality, as though it had to be.

Calcutta is very hot and damp. It is nice not to have to go to a hotel. Sometimes, when I look into myself, and into others, and see the strange tangle of conflicting appetites and hopes that compose me and them, I feel suicidal, knowing that, whatever happens, there is neither contentment nor happiness available – only a hopeless struggle and the final peace of surrender, of death.

Well, I must work, and thin down my appetites.

October 3, 1934

This evening Wordsworth and I went to have our hair cut. He is deputy editor of the Calcutta *Statesman*, in whose flat, above the paper's office, I am staying. He is a funny dissatisfied man, with an inferiority complex but a kind heart. I don't like him. I don't like this place or anything about it.

Moore, the editor of the *Statesman*, took me to lunch at the Bengal Club. It was the inevitable club, with noiseless servants, and the faces I had seen in the *Viceroy of India* – some actual, and some like. We talked about politics. I showed off. The smell of success is not here in my nostrils. Has the tide turned? I don't really care.

October 4, 1934

It's strange to be back at the old game again. I've only just realized what I've let myself in for; but it doesn't matter. Perhaps, even, it's best. It struck me that the time had really come to look for the inwardness of things. For once I (so often, often, written about) looked up at the stars and thought – there alone hope. I mean to struggle on.

A tailor is making me a pair of riding breeches. They burst when I put them on. He said, dismayed, that I had a heavy ankle. (My weight, I find, is still decreasing.) His son, in golden shoes, stood by and laughed at my silly jokes, but the old man continued solemn. I thought enviously how happy they all were in their shop.

October 6, 1934

I tried to get hold of Shahid Suhrawardy, Brian Lunn's friend, who is Professor of Fine Arts at the University here. I'm very anxious to see him because I find myself so completely with the philistines. How I miss Kit and the children! I don't think I've ever really missed them before.

October 8, 1934

I went for a ride in the country. It was all damp and still, with occasional pools covered with water lilies, and groups of Indians squatting about, or arranged in indolent, curiously graceful groups. The same smell of decay (perhaps it is in me, and that's why I can never get it out of my nostrils), as though every institution, big and small alike, were mouldering away, its glories behind it and only disintegration ahead.

This British Raj, for instance, seems to me to be nearing its end; these arrogant, rather vulgar, fellow-countrymen, half aware that their day is done, and stretching out to its utmost limit the delights of being a sahib.

I met a man on the boat whom I'd known some years before in Egypt. 'You've changed,' he said. I realized with a start, a little fear, that I had. People didn't like me much now, as they used to; they think I'm conceited and opinionated, whereas I'm only unhappy.

October 9, 1934

Yesterday was a bad day with me; however, I managed to work, and, in the evening, went for a walk. It was sultry. The queer stale fragrance in the air sometimes disquiets me, and sometimes gives me a pang of excitement. I try to understand, say to myself – 'This is thus and thus, and has come to pass in such and such ways'; but it's no good. Eternity weighs on my spirit nowaways (like loneliness. I'm very lonely. Perhaps eternity is loneliness.). I can't sense, as I always have before, the conflicting interests round me.

October 10, 1934

I got a letter from Kit, and was delighted.

The India question. I'm not sensitive to it now, except in the broad sense of us, an Empire decaying, and them, the debris of a hundred decayed Empires, and the mess that'll come. Occasionally, when I see two bank clerks with their feet up, say, or a particular piece of racial arrogance, I'm disgusted – but then the older I get the more I find to disgust me everywhere.

October 11, 1934

Yesterday I worked all day, but not with much result. I had my photograph taken – for Kit's sake and not out of vanity. A servant took me up in the lift to the studio, a hot, tumble-down sort of place with scenes of arbours and sea shores and terraces spread about. There I waited, getting hotter and angrier. Altogether I

behaved arrogantly, and thereby understood exactly how it happens that Europeans get into the way of behaving arrogantly in the
East. At last an Englishman came up in the lift. He was flurried,
and he, too, let off his spleen on to the servant. I told him I was
in a hurry. He bustled elaborately, flinging aside curtains, swinging
an arc-lamp about. His breath smelt heavily of garlic. Even in this
hurried photography, his professional manner persisted; he smiled
in a simple way, and asked me to smile. I wanted the photograph
to be mournful, but dared not disobey. He, I imagine, like so
many others, bitterly regretted having come to Calcutta, but saw
no way of getting back to England. I felt guilty about the whole
affair, as though I had been insensitive. This feeling was intensified
when the photographer left me rather abruptly, as much as to say:
'I know you're in a favoured position, and can do as you like; and
I'll put up with it professionally, but not a moment after'. Probably
he had seen some advertisement in a trade paper, and jumped at it;
then a riotous 2nd Class P and O passage, and this.

I'm doing a lot of work; but my brain isn't working very well.
This is serious, because if I'm to get away from here, it'll have to
be because of something I do on my own.

October 12, 1934

I closed my eyes to see eternity, and all that flitted through my mind
was plans and hopes; amongst the former, an article – *India after
Ten Years* – in which I'd say that one of the most remarkable
things about India is that you do, when you close your eyes there,
see eternity.

When I did close my eyes to see eternity, I remember now that
I saw something – the basic paradox, on which all religion is based,
and which the lack of religion obscures, weighing down on one
side or the other – the intense egotism of a single life and the intense
informality of life as a whole; the intense importance to me of
here and now, yesterday and today and tomorrow, are, seen
against a background of time everlasting. Christianity, it seems to
me, has expressed this paradox admirably with its idea of God
having numbered the hairs of everyone's head, being privy to the
fall of a sparrow to the ground and, at the same time, of a man being

dust and ashes in his sight, like the grass which grows for a little while, and then is thrown into the oven to be consumed. Both these conceptions are right; a life lived properly must take account of both. The present tendency is for most to accentuate the numbering the hairs of their heads business, and to lose themselves in the fat of their own egotism; while the few who appreciate the dust and ashes point, smell dust and ashes everywhere, bury their heads in dust and ashes, waste away their days in barren melancholy. I am one of them.

October 15, 1934

I've got one of my stomach attacks; mind and body imprecise. I wonder whether I'll ever be able to stop them coming. If not, I don't see much chance of being happy ever. They poison my whole life. No one knows, unless he's experienced it, the horror of this perpetual clouding of one's faculties. One day I'll write a short story called *Dyspepsia* showing someone tortured by a bad stomach, agonizingly straining to excrete, and looking at a filthy tongue; with his complement of pills and bottles of all sorts; with his syringes and suppositories, and all the rest of it; the sense of being unclean that goes with the disease, the curious indecision, starting off for a walk and coming home again; beginning to work, and then petering out; the venom, resentment that it engenders.

On Sunday I went for a ride on my new horse, and didn't do very well; she had a curious trick of suddenly side-stepping when I galloped her, which nearly made me fall off several times.

October 16, 1934

On my morning walk I saw the puja procession coming up from the river. This was rather charming – families of three generations, very simple, the women with the soles of their feet stained red, and in white saris trimmed with red; drums beating and cymbals clanging, and an occasional trumpet; the men in dhotis only, sometimes carrying flags, or pausing to raise their arms in unison; here and there a decorated bundle of sugar cane, also red, held up suggesting a harvest thanksgiving.

Beggars lined the road, some of them outdoing anything I had seen before even in the East. One, for instance, had no face at all – just a shapeless, formless mass of heaving flesh – no features, no expression, a queer moaning noise coming from somewhere within it. Another's arm trailed off into a spiral, into cumbersome folds and curves of flesh. Kneeling in the road, lean as a rake, a woman was in a kind of trance – chanting, sometimes in a whisper and sometimes ecstatic. Every sort of physical monstrosity was there, every sort of filthy disease, bodies so thin or so eaten away that it seemed astonishing they were able to live sufficiently to moan for charity by the roadside.

The merry-makers crowded round these beggars, gave them a handful of rice, money. They were doing a thriving trade. What a curious impulse that makes such creatures part of festivity! – akin, I imagine, to gargoyles in churches (these living gargoyles) – mixing horror with pleasure, seeing the worst in order to appreciate the best, a black background against which white is the more ineffable.

The singing has a queer fascination – so abandoned, incoherent, despair and exhilaration mingling. And the rhythm of the drums more subtle than just a hard rhythm, reflecting, in some queer way, the beat of one's innermost being, so that the processions are not merely in step, but one entity because of the rhythm.

October 17, 1934

I've got, I think, the key to the book I shall write on India. It'll be about the decadence of the West as transplanted here, and as eagerly absorbed here. Take, for instance, the character of Bannerjee, an Indian who had been at Rugby with E. T. Scott and hated India, with his poor eye-glass, and his poor sad face; take the Anglo-Indians, topees falling over their ears and their melancholy, grey complexions; take a set of English people, so common and noisy and cheap. Yes, I see how the thing will go. But meanwhile Butler.

Yesterday afternoon I had my first lesson in Hindustani. My teacher is a Brahmin. I had thought, for some reason, that he was a Moslem; but should have known that he wasn't from his eyes.

October 18, 1934

Flat-footed time. I'm very bored and friendless. Wordsworth said of a man named Mackie last night: 'He was at Charterhouse and Trinity, but you'd never think it.' He knows everyone's school as schoolboys know the makes of cars.

October 20, 1934

There's an odd fellow here named Bowman. Every now and again he's missing for a day or so; that's when he's off on the booze. In his flat he told me to pick up a jade figure and wish, betting me a thousand rupees to one that my wish would come true. I've got a routine wish. It is to be happy. On this occasion, for some reason, I couldn't wish to be happy, but wished only to be a great writer. A reckless wish. If it came true it would mean unhappiness instead of happiness. I didn't fix a time limit. I couldn't. So it might as likely as not come true after I'm dead – which won't, I know, be so very long. All the same it's the only thing I really care about.

October 21, 1934

Yesterday evening I dined at the Saturday Club. It is one of the most horrible places I've ever been in. It reeks of exactly the quality I want to get into a book about India – pretentiousness, commonness, philistinism, sentimentality. Most English people out here romanticize themselves, live on the chap who dressed for dinner every evening in the jungle, the clean white man who trod bravely through oriental filth, the chap who, far from home, stiffened as the band played *God Save the King*, while a manly tear squeezed out of the corner of his eye, Sahib and faithful black servant who loves him dearly, humbly.

October 25, 1934

My teacher wouldn't let me say: 'I'm sad,' in Hindi. Say, 'I'm not sad,' he said, 'if you want to practise the word.'

My rides in the morning now are lovely. It's cool and fresh in the morning, and I feel much easier on my horse, and let it gallop round the race course. If only my stomach would get well!

October 28, 1934

Yesterday, I went to see Mr and Mrs King, who were on the boat. She is an Anglo-Indian, he a simple soul who speculates in jute. King told me that he ran all his jute speculation on prayer. This did not seem at all funny, only slightly pathetic, and that not in relation to him, but in relation to things in general. I found them sitting on a verandah with various of Mrs King's relations. They sat round a table as foreigners always seem to, ponderously, as though part of a set group. I joined them. Almost for the first time since I'd come to Calcutta, I felt easy about my company. (Was this, I wondered, because they treated me respectfully, whereas to to the others I was rather a poor jerk?) King had visibly wilted. He said that with business being so bad he hadn't been able to sleep, but had got up in the night and prowled about, and written letters. I saw him praying passionately against a falling market. Mrs King was playful with him; yet I felt the closeness of the bond between them, and it made me happy. There is nothing better than one person truly loving another. It was a pleasant visit; and I suppose most of my feeling ill is due just to loneliness and depression. It struck me that I should have been better advised to have wished for health when I held Bowman's little jade figure. And yet I'm glad I didn't, because I must be a writer or nothing.

October 30, 1934

I dined with Mr and Mrs King. It was an Anglo-Indian company. There was a clergyman there named Randolph; I had a great argument with him, my point being that a Church which confesses to seeking after truth, and not to having truth, is a public nuisance, and only part of the general disintegration of society. A Church, I said, ought to love God; anyone can love truth.

The Anglo-Indian is something to describe. There's nothing like him I've ever met in the world, and how he symbolizes the whole situation in this country! The two last night – one slightly Mongolian, his complexion dull grey, his forehead high, his voice quick, his dark eyes very sad, almost agonized, his ways defiant, a curious air even then, just sitting at a table, of having no moral fibre, so that you knew whatever happened he'd let you down and himself down, putting away a fair amount of whiskey, bringing in references to home, to sahibs, to natives, yet so utterly oriental in his bearing and mentality and habits, quite like an Oriental, and soft. The other less dusky, scarcely dusky at all, his face curiously pitted, all his nose swollen and punctured, not talking in the lilting way that most Anglo-Indians do and yet slightly parodying the public school accent he affected, more than a slight parody of an English gentleman, living gaily, hardly, in the East. (In many ways, however, I preferred him to what he parodied.) I pictured both of them travelling about in India being Sahibs, and never quite sure whether they'd be treated as Sahibs.

The ladies were immense. I don't know when I've seen such swollen ladies, especially the wife of the Mongolian-looking Anglo-Indian. They eased themselves into chairs; and ate. Occasionally they were coy with their husbands. I think they were happier, more reconciled, than the men. Just to have such a ménage was such a tremendous thing for them, such an achievement in itself, that they wre indifferent to any little social difficulties.

The house itself was a suitable setting for such a company, with pictures on the walls of ladies playing pianos with large dogs yapping round them; chairs upholstered in bright colours, and arranged symmetrically, not giving an impression of being often sat in, thick curtains, and so on.

King sat there, a strange simpleton of a man, his face inordinately long, amongst all those Anglo-Indians, to them a hero, if only because he had been rich, and was *sans peur et sans reproche* as far as his racial origin was concerned.

November 1, 1934.

My teacher said to me yesterday: 'You are ill; you have cough and cold.'

In India, it's difficult not to fall into all the Yeats-Brown breathing exercises. And there is this about deep breathing – it concentrates the attention; you can't do it if you're thinking; your mind has to be quite blank and therefore in the state prescribed for spiritual receptivity. This morning, doing my breathing and looking into the sky, I seemed to see a white bird, and the exquisite Biblical phrase, 'the Heavens opened', occurred to me in all its richness. From that I mounted into the sky myself, understanding that freedom was inseparable from death of the body. It seemed almost as though I did escape from my body and was free. It made me happy all through breakfast, but not now.

Yesterday Wordsworth and I dined with Alfred Watson, manager of the *Statesman*, and a fellow called Ritter, who is Law Member in the Viceroy's Cabinet.

I asked about terrorism. Ritter said that it was still spreading, but that our knowledge of what was going on, of the movements of terrorists, was much better than it used to be.

Ritter said one good thing: 'All this talk of survival, and this and that,' he said: 'What's it amount to? – race hate.'

This is true. However you resolve the India problem, the ultimate is race hate; the Anglo-Indians are, as it were, the no-man's-land, the battleground. I sense the race hate constantly. It is in the air, manifesting itself in a million incidents, in the very crease of faces, in the very love of gestures. This is why India is so melancholy a country. Yet everywhere is melancholy.

November 2–3, 1934

Kelly, Watson's assistant, thinks the *Statesman* is going downhill (if indeed it was ever up hill to go down) and that he's the man to put it right. Unquestionably, he's the only person here with any real character. I felt faintly flattered that he should have selected me to be his lieutenant, and ever since have been toying with the idea of getting control of the newspaper, and making an immense success of it. If I don't get control of the *Statesman*, I certainly shan't stay on it. It will be dead as mutton in a few years unless it's altogether changed. Kelly and I complement one another in a quite remarkable way. He's a hard bullying egotist with a core of sensitivity, complexity; I'm a sensitive complex artist, with a core of hard bullying egotism; together, we'd be irresistible.

November 4, 1934

I had another talk with Kelly, and got very excited about the *Statesman*. Then I put on shorts, and went for a sharp walk. It had suddenly got bitingly cold. I went along furiously, turning over this thing and that thing I'd do to make the paper better. Ambition surged up in me like lust. (It is the same as lust.) I was so well now. Nothing would stop me now. Suddenly, I felt cold, wretched. I hurried home, took a hot bath, and felt silly, as though I'd tried to seduce a woman and been repulsed.

November 6, 1934

I was having my customary gallop this morning on the race course, when a policeman came up to me and stopped me. 'Are you aware,' he said, 'that the Governor of Bengal is riding here today?' I said I was not aware. 'No one is allowed to gallop when the Governor's riding,' he said. How fatuous! At the same time I was shaken by the episode, and annoyed, because, such is my innate cowardice, I know I'll never enjoy a gallop there again.

November 7, 1934

It was a festival here, and we went to call on some Jains whom Wordsworth knows. (Jains are the only Buddhists left in India, and their prophet is not Buddha, but a contemporary of his who taught very much the same things as he did.) They were rich merchants. We turned from the main street, and found ourselves at once in narrow streets, gay with lights and garlands. It was another world; I looked at it a little wistfully, thinking how full of joy and movement it was compared with ours. The Jains' house was large; round the doorway a cluster of people, some beggars, some just poor dependents, lots of children, two old bearded men, their faces grey with sandalwood, their hair falling over their ears. We climbed to an upper storey, each floor on the way crowded, but the social level gradually rising. On the top floor were our hosts, features Persian rather than Indian, golden hats on their heads, wearing long silk coats and exquisite silk scarves, scented. We were shown into a room with purple furniture ranged round the walls, Victorian, expensive; a cupboard full of carved ivory. Servants brought us flowers to wear, and our hosts dabbed scent on our hands and squirted us with rose-water. The air was laden with scent. The scent they put on our hands was pungent. I smell it still after three baths.

Other visitors came and went all the time – Moslems with hard, inscrutable faces, Bengalees round and soft and intelligent, Jews, a few other Europeans. There was a general atmosphere of sensuality. All the family of our hosts were absurdly alike. Outside was a huge verandah where refreshments were being served. I peeped out, and saw a multitude of windows, each one lit and festive. People were singing, gramophone playing, trumpets blowing; a band played *Auld Lang Syne* with variations. I took away with me a sense of lovely cloth and pungent scent and an all-pervading, but impersonal, sensuality. While I was looking over the verandah, I caught a glimpse of the women peeping at what was going on, shrinking from being seen.

This morning over breakfast I thought that I'd write an article on how Bolshevism seemed seen from India; explain frankly how the British Raj is calculated to swing back one's feelings from one disgust to another; how it required a certain effort to remember the other; how, disgust apart, a rotting Empire gives one (except in venomous, irritated moments) no sympathy with Bolshevism, but does make one better able to understand its occurence, perhaps inevitability; how, at bottom, the two things – the Raj and Bolshevism – are rather alike.

November 8, 1934

When I was doing my breathing, a great longing came to me to escape from the inadequacy of flesh; I felt the existence of something living uneasily in the physical me, like a bird fluttering helplessly against bars, its feathers ruffled, its eyes bloodshot. This kind of thing is prayer. I longed for the detachment and peace of being unmixed with flesh. It is because my body does not work properly that I am impatient to have done with it; sensuality is unattainable for the diseased. We have to fall back on soul, to die in the flesh and be reborn in the spirit. Towards this I strive. Towards one death after another, a succession of deaths.

November 12, 1934

I lunched with Brian Lunn's friend Shahid Suhrawardy at Firpo's. There was also his brother and another Indian. Suhrawardy had spent two years in Moscow at the Stanislavsky Theatre, and had lived in Arbat near where I lived. He described how when he first got back to India he had a great orgy; but found the available women insipid, and therefore gave it all up. Insipid! There's a sort of tragic inevitability about the way Indians either Westernize badly and become absurd, or Westernize so well that they're pathetic and make you uneasy, like being with a 'cultured' American. I never felt this so much as with Suhrawardy. All the same, he understood things, and didn't tell funny stories, and had, I suppose (I thought of this a bit ruefully), the same sort of spiritual background as I have, and hated the Bolsheviks as much as I do.

The other Indian was a Hindu (Suhrawardy, of course, a Moslem), fat and rather charming; intelligent in quite a different way from Suhrawardy, easily, indolently, intelligent. His eyes were bright, but cloudy round the edges. He had a lovely 'streamline' car, and told us with an apologetic, cunning smile, that he'd been Acting Director of Public Instruction. The smile was so ample that it seemed at a stroke to demolish the office of Director of Public Instruction, and public instruction altogether. Moslems aren't really Oriental; Hindus are. I recognized in Suhrawardy a brother in unhappiness; but the Hindu was happy. He, I felt

sure, had not found women insipid. He was saturated with
sensuality, as a good lecher should be.

November 13, 1934

Yesterday evening I went to see Suhrawardy at his house. The
house was typical – pretentious, full of ugly furniture, not too
clean. Chanda, the plump Hindu who'd lunched with us the day
before, looked in, and then Suhrawardy's brother with a man named
Goswami, who is a great Swarajist (Nationalist) and Congressman,
and at the same time very rich. I should have known that he was
very rich from the texture of his personality, although, being a
Congressman, he wore only a flannel shirt and dhoti. I talked a
great deal, mainly to impress Goswami. He understood and
responded.

We sat out on a sort of terrace; poor old Suhrawardy trying to
be, as it were, mystical-aesthetic, and only being rather pathetic.
I knew just what he had modelled himself on – saw the drooping
pince-nez and hair, the black ribbon attached to a waistcoat
button, the detached manner – some just pre-war aesthete who
had dined once or twice at the same table as Augustine Birrell.

His uncle, Sir Hassan, who came and sat with me, was a very
different type. Western educated Indians are like novels; the
character they assume gives the key to all their hopes and values.
His model was, say, a back-bench Conservative Member of
Parliament, or an Alderman who had been Mayor. He talked about
England and the qualities of Englishmen, and I tried to show him
that the England he so admired no longer existed, and that it only
had existed as a result of certain artificial factors, mainly economic.
India is a living museum, where old customs and habits, even
clothes, still persist, but mostly as echoes. Thus Sir Hassan
Suhrawardy was a sort of shadow of what, say, the National Liberal
Club used to be.

I saw a man fall down in the road, make a mark with a little
knife he carried, get up and move to that mark, and then fall down
again. He was making his way, I understood, to Bombay so. His
expression was not in the least fanatical, but cheerful and normal.

We sat and talked till about eight o'clock. Goswami drank a

fair amount. We talked and talked about India and its future. I suppose that the reason I was so pleased with Goswami was that he corroborated entirely my view of the political situation here, and of the changed mood of Congress, at least of Congress leaders.

November 14, 1934

I find that if I'm feeling ill and simply make myself work I get better. I suppose this ought to be obvious enough, but the iller I am the greater the effort required to make myself work.

Last night I had a fit of depression. If only, I thought, I'd been able just to get ahead with Butler, working as I'm working here but only at it. It was a stuffy evening, and I realized how I was going to suffer when the hot weather came, and how it would get harder and harder to work, and how I shouldn't put the best of myself into Butler. All right, I thought, I'll put the best of myself into it notwithstanding. If I win what I've taken on here – doing three jobs in a climate that knocks most people out – I'll win anything.

November 16, 1934

I went to see a doctor yesterday; and at once felt better. Obviously it's nervous dyspepsia that I've got. If my soul were at peace so'd my stomach be at peace.

In the evening I went to the Market and bought Kit a jade ring for Rs.35 to send her as a Christmas present. The Market was gayer than the rest of Calcutta; full of lights, and buying and selling. Characteristically, the big European shops are always empty, dead. Anglo-Indian shop assistants stand dully about, and imitation managers in cutaway coats bow obsequiously to imaginary customers. Whereas the Market is rich in colour and movement. I like Moslem shopkeepers; they are at their best as merchants; and it is as merchants that in India (where everything and everyone is sorted out) they've been most successful.

I read the introduction to Butler's *The Fair Haven*. Better than anything else I've ever read, it shows how and why a Church is more important to society than the teaching of a Christ. How silly, and how characteristic of the times is the idea that truth is to be got by going back to, say, the Sermon on the Mount, and leaving out of account the historical fact of the Church, as though it was a sort of false parasitic growth, poisoning, sucking up, the truth of its founder's inspiration; whereas, in fact, the Sermon on the Mount is platitudinous and ineffectual, and has only come to be startling and effectual through being embodied in the doctrine of a living Church.

November 17, 1934

This is a bad time with me; the moment I stop working or reading, loneliness and melancholy eat at my heart. I should never have come here; and yet, if I'd stayed in England, I should never have re-adjusted myself after my Russian turn-out. Now I see that for good or ill I've quite isolated myself. I stand, and I'll have to stand, quite alone. My position here on this paper is as false as my position was in Moscow; I'll have to put up with it for a little while, and after that I'll be alone and always alone then till I die. Sometimes I get a pang of regret at having left my soul in Russia; and yet I'd have had to have left it somewhere. There's no keeping a soul for me, who am, with all my faults, incapable of sustained insincerity.

Also I'm obsessed with this feeling that I'm on the wrong side. It's silly, because what's the matter with me is that I'm on no side. Dictatorships of the Proletariat and British Raj – they're the same; it's absurd to let hating one drive you into the arms of the other. Only, when I meet people who agree with me, I nearly always find they're the enemy. And though I know what the Indian Nationalist Movement amounts to, it pricks my conscience sometimes to read Congress newspapers.

November 18, 1934

This morning I had the most lovely ride since I came here. It was out in the country. The morning was fresh, the fields gleaming with freshness; and I rode along enchanted with the world. My old sensuality came back to me for the first time for months. I was aware, as I used to be so often, of the infinite richness of everything, and didn't mind any of the things that I waste my life hating, because I was so aware of the abundance, the reckless profusion of life. This seemed its only quality. I wanted to shout. I was too happy to work; even now to force myself to formulate what I felt. Work is a product of misery, and discontent. I only work because I'm unhappy. If I was happy I should never work.

Just now a procession went by, at its head a red flag with hammer and sickle. I looked down on it with mixed feelings. The fact is I'm always sympathetic with the side that's not batting; in Moscow I hated the Red Flag in precisely the same way that here I hate the Union Jack – because each is the flag of established power.

November 19, 1934

I dined last night with Suhrawardy, Chanda, Goswami and a rather nice man named Sudhindranath Datta, who edits a literary paper here. We dined at a Chinese restaurant, in a little cubicle to ourselves, and decided that we'd meet once a week hereafter. Goswami fascinates me most. He is a heavy drinker, and most of the time says nothing; then suddenly interpolates a remark, which is always good. He has a lovely voice.

Datta has patterned himself on the first post-war intellectuals. He has (with some difficulty) kept himself slim; only his enormous teeth show how big he would have been if nature had taken its course. A bit battered, too, and bewildered, yet holding to the fact of his being a poet. 'Is there anything in this talk of a literary renaissance in modern Bengali?' I asked. 'The renaissance,' Chanda answered, 'is sitting in front of you.' Chanda is fat and easy-going; if ever aggressive, only to assert the fact that he feels no sense of inferiority through being a Government official. As he drinks his eyes mist over; their light always is a bit clouded, like street lamps through fog. He is, however, amusing, and, I should think, shrewd. They all play up to Suhrawardy as the great sensualist, the artist. He told me on the way back that he had a secret telephone at the University, and implied that he used it for

making assignations with mysterious women. All the same, I
like him.

November 20, 1934

Yesterday was a lovely day. I felt well, I worked, my spirit was
easy. In the evening I walked about the streets, delighted, as I
always am, with the little shops and the groups of people in them, at
that hour making up accounts, or rolling out dough to make cakes,
or just sitting cross-legged amongst heaps of grain, piles of old iron,
bottles and powders and ointments, rolls of cloth. The warmth of
a baker's oven would blow against my face, the fragrance of spices,
of new silk, was in the air, carriages rattled by, and rickshaws,
jingling bells. I felt what I most love to feel, delight in the luxurious-
ness, the sensuality, of everything, a sense that nothing matters
because life is so abundant, so generously forthcoming. Little
grudges and bitterness melt to nothing when I feel so, even my
restless egotism, drunk on fecundity, reels into unconsciousness.
When I am happy, I seek out crowded streets rather than the
Maidan. Solitude, nature, are the refuge of the melancholy;
happiness craves the stench and the movement of humanity.

This morning I tried out a horse that had been racing at
Tollygunge. She wanted to get away. Holding her made my arms
ache. But I held her. It was exciting, gripping at the reins, battling
with her. I think I shall buy her.

November 21–22, 1934

I got a telegram yesterday, to say that Douglas Jerrold, my
publisher, was going to settle the *Manchester Guardian* libel action
out of court for £700, and withdraw *Picture Palace* for always
unless I'd put up £2,000. So that's the end of my novel. Also, as I
say to myself untruthfully and self-pityingly, of a year's work.

The *Picture Palace* news shook me, but not consciously. I
realize that I've been in a state of excitement ever since I got
Jerrold's telegram, and yet I don't brood on the book being lost;
in a way, mentally, I'm relieved, because I didn't like the title, or

the way Eyre and Spottiswoode got it up. I think my state of mind must be like a woman's who's just had a child aborted that she got by a man she was not very much in love with.

This is a letter I've just written to Kit, but shan't send:

'My dearest Kit. I had a telegram from Jerrold yesterday to say that he would have to settle with the *Manchester Guardian* for £700, and definitely withdraw the book unless I could put up £2,000. This, of course, was impossible. I had to wire back telling him so. It's left me a bit shaken. They've won, haven't they? – the others. Whether I'm melancholy because of this, or because of loneliness, being away from you, who are the only person I love, I don't know. But I am very melancholy. The world, to me, is an inhospitable place. I don't think I really care about its present chaos; even like it, since it reflects my own state of mind. What I feel all the time is a sense of being an alien, a stranger in a strange land. I don't think I've known five minutes real happiness for years and years. Now I'm in India, I watch boats sailing down the Hoogli with deep longing; when I'm in London, I watch boats sailing down the Thames in the same way. A lot of my waking time here is just wishing I was with you and the children; when I was with you, and might, after all, have stayed with you, I chose to come away.'

November 23, 1934

I think now that I've really touched bottom. It's not even entirely physical. A sense of unutterable negation. I should like to be very very ill, to have to lie in bed for weeks and weeks without any cares or even thoughts, just letting time slip by me. The struggle is too great for me, whether because I have to struggle more than most, or because I'm feebler than most, I don't know. If I sit still a moment, melancholy and fear surge up in me. I can't manage my life. I don't know where to turn. If I was alone, I'd perhaps commit suicide, or make for some remote place. There are Kit and the children. I have to earn money. I see myself as a discarded product of a discarded civilization, believing nothing, hoping for nothing, fearing nothing except the consciousness of my own melancholy. Two nights ago, as I was getting into bed, I thought: Perhaps I'll die in my sleep tonight, and never wake again. And it was like the parched sailor in *The Ancient Mariner* crying: 'A sail! A sail!'

November 24, 1934

Calcutta is full of statues, and nearly all of Englishmen. Their faces, bewhiskered, look down on passers-by. I imagine them to have been Governors and Commanders-in-Chief and what not, who enjoyed their five years of authority in their day, and now stand, or sit on horseback, about the Maidan. Not having been able to get into Hyde Park, they are content with the Maidan. This is characteristic.

I called on Mrs Price-Hughes yesterday. She was in a room with a friend, and an American woman. The room was rather self-consciously gilt and white, and, for Calcutta, exceptional. The conversation was dreary. We were shown a book that Mrs Price-Hughes had written. It was printed privately, 150 copies, translations of Tibetan fairy stories, very expensive-looking, with indeterminate illustrations. A Mr Van Maarten, a Dutchman, came in. He asked me if there were any significant literary developments in England. I began to blather about the flight from mind. He said he thought W. J. Locke (1863–1930, the author of *The Beloved Vagabond*) the greatest modern English writer, and Mrs Price-Hughes murmured about Wilder's *The Bridge of San Luis Rey*. I said I hated Locke and *The Bridge of San Luis Rey*. It made a good impression. He then began to talk about Epstein, and about how stories moved all over the world, so that the same one would crop up now here, now there. I felt it all to be a bit bogus, a bit thin. I got up to go, and was just about to drive off with Van Maarten when the servant told me that Mrs Price-Hughes wanted to speak to me. She'd run downstairs, and was slightly breathless, and asked me if I really had to go, if I couldn't stay a little longer. I said I couldn't.

November 28, 1934

> Because I loathe my times and fellow men
> I feel myself loathly.
> Because, to me, progress moves backwards, downwards,
> I live a pariah, an outcast,
> Waiting to die.
> Oh, music in the very word, in death.
> Oh, loveliness, blessedness in dying.

Yesterday evening Suhrawardy looked in, and read me a poem of his. It was not bad, but not very good. I said it was very good. Although I realize the sort of man he is, how much he belongs to the Isadora Duncan tradition, I like him. Thank God, though, I'm cured of all interest in the *Statesman*. The less I have to do for it, the more time I've got for my own work. I shall try and hang on for the two and a half years, and then go home with, I hope, enough money saved to be able to write on my own for a couple of years.

When I feel ill and bad-tempered, I punish my poor old horse.

November 29, 1934

After dinner I went with Wordsworth to a symphony concert. The concert was held in the hall of a Roman Catholic College. Some of the priests were there, with trimmed beards, and talking French, and smoking cigars. One old priest was wearing a red skull cap and a purple cassock. The audience were Calcutta's intelligentsia, with one or two seekers after light. A dreary enough crew. I wore my velvet dinner jacket, but somehow felt rather small and inferior. The whole British connection with India has been based on mediocrity. Our Indian Empire lacks all magnificence, even of terror; it is suburban.

December 1, 1934

I have now been here two months. Last night I dined with Suhrawardy. There were Shahid, his brother, and his niece Sogra; a Moslem with a French wife; an enchanting Parsee woman and Chanda.

Shahid had planned the dinner. It was very good – caviare, and hock, and fish with salad, and delicious wheat cakes with more salad, and rice and lightly curried chicken, and cream and fruit, and sweet rice and cream.

There's something I want to get clear in my mind. It cropped up in the conversation. I mean the curious deadness, mediocrity, which the British have brought to India, not only in themselves, but have planted in Indians. A deadness which shuts out all vivacity and joy, a sort of quintessence of everything most dreary in English life, so that every life is *Punch*, every thought commonplace, every voice a faint echo of the BBC, every section Coward–Barrie–Priestley, and so on. The scene then was an illustration of it all – dreadful furniture arranged round the walls, dreadful pictures, shoddy colours of the hangings, noisy facetiousness from Shahid's brother. I tried to explain to them what I meant, but couldn't get it out properly. 'There's nothing for us,' they said, 'nothing.' I understood. 'The effect it has on me,' I said, 'is to make me sympathize with the extreme Swarajist. His attitude may be negative, but at least it constitutes a refusal to accept what is not worth accepting.'

This, too, was nonsense, as I well knew, because the extreme Swarajist no more refuses to accept the spiritual consequence of the British Raj than the Bolshevik refuses to accept the spiritual consequences of Bolshevism. In fact, if anything, he accepts them more unquestioningly, more utterly.

I told Shahid's brother that he was going to have a great political career. He agreed enthusiastically. This brought the conversation on to Communalism. It is slowly dawning on them that the only thing Indians really feel keenly about is Communalism; that all other political issues may be resolved in terms of it; that all the nomenclature in the political game – Round-Table Conference, White paper, Joint Committee Report – has been dictated by communal considerations. This has given me a key to the general situation. I see now how it is working.

They gradually got angry. Shahid's brother put the Moslem case; Chanda pretended to be reasonable, but came out as a Hindu. Shahid alone took something like an impartial line (I see now that his passion to get away from India is as reasonable as mine. There is no place for him here any more than for me.) It appears that even the question of holidays was a source of communal strife. Sogra accused Chanda of deliberately putting the exams at Ramadan. He countered by pointing out that Ramadan was a moveable feast, whereas the exams were fixed. She then accused the Hindus of deliberately trying to kill Urdu, and admitted that Moslems were doing everything in their power to introduce more Persian words into Urdu, and the Hindus more Sanskrit words into Hindi; and admitted also that, whereas formerly the two languages were sufficiently alike for anyone who knew one of them to understand the other, now they were becoming quite different.

Just before dinner, a young Indian came in who had been to Sandhurst, and who held the King's Commission. He had perfectly got the Sandhurst manner, with only the slightest caricature; got it down to the smallest details. He asked me what I was doing here, and I said I was a journalist. 'By Jove,' he said, 'I bet I couldn't do that.'

December 4, 1934

I feel very tired. I've written two leaders and two-thirds of an article. However, I've had good news. I'm to go to Simla for the hot weather. This will get me out of the office, leave me more time for my own writing, and avoid the heat. Wordsworth's engineered it to get me out of the way. He little knows how pleased I am.

December 6, 1934

I spent the evening with Shahid. First we went to see Mrs Price-Hughes. Her friend, whom we have named Miss Bed, had just come from somewhere in the hills, and was full of tedious descriptions of dances there that were 'too exciting'. A great horsey woman with prodigious legs, who finds everything indiscriminately interesting, and everyone indiscriminately charming. Mrs Price-Hughes is better looking than Miss Bed, and so more tolerable.

At about 7.20 Mrs Price-Hughes asked me to chat with them while they dined, because they were going off by the eight o'clock train. We sat at the dinner table feeling rather awkward. Later on, we felt more awkward still, because Price-Hughes himself came in. He was on the defensive, aggressive almost as though I was his wife's lover. Mrs Price-Hughes, as though the leading lady in the Calcutta Players, held out her hand to her husband as he came in. It was, also, I thought, to apologize for me. I think she has a faint *tendresse* for me.

Shahid and I got away at last. He dined with me at home, and afterwards we talked. His niece, Sogra, is very charming. She asked to see me when I went to fetch Shahid. I like her because she is innocent and sincere and full of expectation and curiosity. She mostly has to observe purdah. Her nose is big, like Shahid's, and her teeth slightly irregular: otherwise she is beautiful, made up, as Moslem women usually are, with black under her eyes, her complexion golden, and her eyes dark and glowing. Her sari, of course, added to her charm, and the little golden slippers, and the bangles. I've asked Shahid to bring her to dine next week.

Later in the evening we went to a dreary place called the Casanova Bar. It was full of Anglo-Indians and lower grade Europeans. There was a fifth-rate cabaret. I looked round at the Anglo-Indians. They are quite the unhappiest people in the world. Ghosts haunting the British Raj. It was easy to talk with Shahid about our favourite subject, the strange deadness, the unhappiness, not active, but passive, the unrelieved hideousness, that the British connection with India has engendered. I saw it all clearly in that café.

December 10, 1934

I visited Sudhin Datta in his large old-fashioned Indian house with a courtyard, and a large number of little rooms; facing the court-yard, a temple. Sudhin's study was lined with books. He showed me the Bengali magazine that he edits. There were also present a famous Indian wrestler, and a friend of Sudhin's, very handsome, and, of course, Chanda and Shahid and Goswami. The house charmed me. I suppose everything that belongs to a tradition is charming. It was somehow spacious and dignified, very different from the ugliness of Shahid's house and Goswami's house. Servants and women moved about silently; they had manners. It was like another world from the world of Anglo-India.

We went upstairs to dinner. One of the little rooms was pre-pared for us. The others took off their shoes and sat cross-legged on the ground, I at a table, though I'd often sat on the ground myself in Travancore. The dinner was on a brass tray – little dishes laid out. It was exquisite food, only perhaps a shade too highly flavoured. I ate heartily, having about starved all day. Somehow I didn't enjoy myself as much as I had at our other meetings. I shall, however, never forget the spacious house, so quiet, dignified, so made for Calcutta and all that it stands for.

December 12, 1934

I worked hard at Butler all day, and made a bit of progress. In the evening, I went with Wordsworth to dine at his club. It was incredibly gloomy. Two men sat at our table, one quite white and with an immense nose. He chewed with deliberation, never speak-ing or smiling; like a white mask. The other I imagine to have been an Army officer, ruddy and sullen. His face, too, showed no sign of animation. It, too, was a mask, but more defiant than the other. The only alteration in the set of his features came when they brought him the bill to sign. Then his mouth tightened into a sullen line. This is India. For the first time I was really hungry to get away.

The Sahibs Dine

Servants move noiselessly to and fro
    Servants in red, and numbered;
At each table four or five black and white figures
    Eating and drinking
A dim hum of conversation, like a low wind.

December 14, 1934

I went with Moore to tea with an Indian named Birla, a Parsee, a great intimate of Gandhi's. Birla had an idea that Gandhi ought to see the Viceroy, implying that if Gandhi once sat down to tea with the Viceroy things would be different. I contended that this was not so. I talked about the fallacy of compromise, which God knows I have come to see clearly enough. I thought I saw at the bottom of all Birla's ideas fear of losing his money. It seemed to me that the whole structure of his sanctity was built on that fear.

I went back with Moore to the Bengal Club, which he wants me to join. It is rather different from the United Services Club, Wordsworth's club; less dead and moribund, but more vulgar; full of business men, not as full of beans as they once were, but still full of beans enough. Moore took me into the bar to meet members of the Committee. One of the Committee members came and sat with us, a fat man, rather a good sort I should say. Very arrogant in a way, but within limits honest and sincere. Then two fearful creatures: one almost bald, an architect who told me about how he knew this and that person, how he liked the Curzon Cinema, and modernist architecture; the other like Owen Nares playing the part of an army officer. He even looked made up. When I got home a terrible fit of depression seized me. I felt somehow contaminated, and wished I'd never taken this job. Only I know it's good I took it, because this reaction too, was necessary.

December 16, 1934

I went to tea with Shahid's niece, Sogra. She is very charming in her way, and intelligent. After tea we went on to Shahid's Parsee friend, Khurshed. I found her ravishing despite her hardness; lovely eyes and a long straight nose and a golden skin. She said she had a garden. I took the opening, and strolled on to the verandah with her. Then we went for a drive with Sogra. Her delight in being out and free was charming. Only a year ago she left purdah and even now she feels strange with her face uncovered.

Sogra had to go home; so we took her back, and went on to the Chinese restaurant, where I gave a dinner. I talked and talked. And all because of Khurshed. There is such a thing as Orientalness. Its difference from the Occident lies in its exotic accentuation of contrasts – beggars and a rajah with ropes of pearls, and soft mouth, and drenched in perfume. I felt this in Khurshed; at the same time I know that what attracted her in me was my being

English, as she thought *homme-du-monde*; that she saw in me the glamour of all I most detest. (We agreed the other day that the downfall of the British India Empire began when it was possible for English women to get out here.) I expect I shall see more of her.

As I drove out into the country this morning to ride, I said to myself, and shouted: 'The morning is golden.' It was. Sunlight hovering over everything like a golden mist. For years I have not felt so happy, been so aware of the sensuality of living – as I've written so many times, to me the essence of genuine faith, happiness, love, everything that matters at all.

December 17, 1934

I lunched with a Lady Benthall. It was a large party. First I called for Mrs Price-Hughes. I felt that she wanted to fabricate an affair out of me, that she was for the moment without anyone attending on her, and that in some curious, Platonic way I had filled the gap. I could almost hear her talking to her friends about a charming young man, implying by her tone of voice that yet again someone has succumbed to her charms. I was put next to Mrs Price-Hughes and again I felt somehow self-consciously, pointedly. She was filling in the outline of a love-affair in order to show herself off more realistically.

In the evening I dined with Shahid and the others. Shahid talked about his appetites in a loud voice and I had a sort of priggish fear that people at other tables might overhear. It occurred to me, too, that the English people might wonder at my dining with five Indians. But they are certainly incomparably better company than any other people I've met here.

December 18, 1934

In the morning nowadays the race course is alive with horses like an ant heap with ants. It's one of the most beautiful sights I've ever seen. Every variety of horse, and all gently on the move, their movements deadened a little because of the mist. I'd never loved animals till I saw them altogether.

December 20, 1934

The difference between my attitude of mind now and some years ago is that before I thought what mattered was a single Gospel such as Christ's, and that organization and establishment blasphemed single Gospels, undid them; whereas now single Gospels seem to me mostly platitudinous and often nonsensical, and this organization and establishment the very structure of civilization. There have been hundreds of Christs, but only one Church. The Church is the miracle, not Christ.

December 21, 1934

I want to a Cambridge dinner. A little man named George, in the Indian Civil Service, said his great ambition was to go back to Cambridge as Registrar and that he thought he'd worked things so that in twenty years or so he would. The others at the table were Indians. I do so dislike most Indians, not because of race prejudice, but because their perpetual parodying of things embarrasses and saddens me. They were parodying the Alma Mater stuff. It seemed to me that one or two people who'd been rather cordial avoided me. Probably this was just fancy. The Viceroy, Willingdon spoke. He was like the old husband with the young wife who's cuckolded, in Restoration Comedy. Rather amusing in a vulgar, tittering sort of way but it was Twilight of Empire all right, a quite peculiar sort of degeneracy.

   This afternoon I saw Khurshed. We sat side by side on a sort of divan and talked. She told me about her lovers. She is the first woman I have met with no sense of sin where physical matters are concerned. She had always, she said, deceived her husband. Once she saw him in bed with another woman, a friend, and just turned over and went to sleep. 'I didn't really sleep,' she said. 'I think,' she said, 'I'm afraid of you hurting me because of all your people have done to us. I can't not be a little afraid.' Her husband had said that I was an ascetic except for my mouth. She kept my blood on fire, but she advised me to wait. 'We have to begin well,' she said.

   When I got home there was the airmail, with a letter from Kit, saying how she was looking forward to seeing me next month. Also new photographs of the children.

December 24, 1934

I haven't written anything here for three days. Suddenly all my life has become fabulous. I can't even sleep, let alone work. All the people here see that I've changed, and their attitude towards me is different from what it was. Even Shahid's. I've seen Khurshed every day, but only once alone. Sometimes she seems not quite sincere, as though she was acting a part. But she isn't really.

On Saturday evening I took her and her husband to the circus. First we dined in the Bristol. He is getting very jealous of me. Khurshed was excited by the circus, particularly a man fired out of a cannon. She made exclamations and hid inside her sari. I find her a queer mixture of naivete and sophistication, as there is, I think, in myself. I had been taken with the idea of going to the circus. It fitted in with the way I had dramatized this affair – the smell of horses and muscular arms and haunches. Actually it wasn't very stimulating. There was Khurshed's husband and later Shahid and Chanda. As we walked out I whispered to Khurshed. She is very practised in the art of deceiving her husband. I think she is a little disappointed in me for not having found an occasion to seduce her.

December 26, 1934

Yesterday I went for a drive with Khurshed and her husband. We went into the country, and then walked. I said to Khurshed that the taxi drivers were very good-looking (they're bearded Sikhs mostly). She sniffed and agreed. 'How I love beards!' she said. She is indescribably animal, exquisitely animal. For instance, she's got an abnormal sense of smell, and can tell people's clothes like a bloodhound. At the same time, she's terrified of cows. She said that if she could build her own house, she'd start with a high wall, then go on to a courtyard. Her great idea is to ensure privacy for herself. Even purdah is not abhorrent to her, though she admits that it's frightful for very poor people. She loves money, and hates poverty. She loves money in the Oriental way, not as money, but translated into expensive jewels and exquisite silks. Love of money is part of her sensuality. There's none of the vulgarity of bank accounts, and thumbing over stale, thumbed currency notes, and making interminable calculations. She just thinks of a handful of rupees as a lecherous man thinks of a beautiful woman. Her stratagems are interminable. She's thought out a plan whereby she goes to rest in the afternoon, shutting the doors and the windows, and I come in, not through the main door, ringing the bell, but through a side door. I asked her if this was a new stratagem or if she'd used it before. She said it was new, but I didn't believe her. When I woke up this morning, very liverish, after a frightful parlour game evening with the Wordsworths, I had a sort of revulsion against the whole business. I remembered that Khurshed's house might be cleaner, that she and I would come at last to have nothing to say to one another. Her femininity, that when I'm with her intoxicates me, suddenly sickened me. I had a premonition that I had entered upon a stairway, whose end would be disaster. Yet what disaster have I to fear when I've decided to commit suicide if necessary?

December 28–29, 1934
I can't describe my state of mind. Everything has fallen to pieces for me again; and I'm more sure than ever that the only way out for me is to die. I can't manage to live. How can I write leading articles? How do Butler? My stomach remains very bad.

> I, the father of that child, am dead.
> I died begetting it.
> The words I spoke, begetting,
> Were each an arrow slaughtering my heart.
> And now I'm dead.
> I've no more left to say;
> And so I'm dead.

Instinctively I knew that coming to India again would bust me. Even so, I had to bust. There is bustness in me. I'm just covering paper. These words have no reality. What has reality is my cowardice, my horror at what I have done, my passion to cancel it.

December 30, 1934—Bhagalpur

I came away here for the week-end with Shahid and Sudhin to
stay with a man named Singh. He's a big landowner, and lives in a
house rather like Passfield. Mrs Singh is a fat lady who was born
in Primrose Hill, and looks it. She's full of a rather self-conscious
amiability. Singh wears a long grey coat, light white trousers, white
socks and shoes with pointed ends. He smokes a hubble-bubble
and loves food. Their talk is excellent. I deride Mrs Singh for
19th-century feminism. Her breasts pulsate with fervour for
birth-control and co-education. Sudhin I love. We've spent a lot
of our time together. He's as melancholy as I am. Altogether I feel
we're very much in the same boat. It's a relief to be away from
Calcutta.

January 2, 1935

Singh is a charming character. He sits all day at his hookah; and
in the evenings puts on a flowered coat and silver shoes. When his
wife worries him, his face crumples like a child's. He's very
amorous. Once he got an anonymous letter to be at a certain place
and look out for a carriage. He carried out the instructions exactly,
followed the carriage, and found Lil, his fat wife, in it.

On New Year's Eve there was a party. All the local gentry came.
It was uncannily like a suburban New Year's party. We played
games. Shahid and Sudhin and I had some brandy to begin with.
I wore a long black coat, and light white trousers, and pointed
shoes. It suited me. Lil had taken enormous pains over everything.
We even pulled crackers. The company crossed arms and piped
something like 'Auld Lang Syne'. As the New Year began a
terrible fit of melancholy oppressed me, a feeling that the year
ahead was going to be the worst in my life, that awful things would
happen.

The next day I played a lot of chess; and Shahid kept a bridge
four going. I've never seen such a four. There was Singh with his
hookah; a terribly desperate-looking chap who carried about an
air cushion because of piles; Baker, unshaven, deaf as a post, and
Shahid. These people with their game, and afternoon tea, and
occasional slight laughter, constituted a peculiar company. I tried

to fix them in my mind. It reminded me of Gogol's *Dead Souls* and of the party in *The Cherry Orchard*, which came as near to making me cry as anything I have ever seen. At the bottom of the garden was the Ganges. Sudhin and I walked there constantly, watching boats make their way across, and the water colour in the evening. He has an exquisite character. We felt greatly in sympathy together. In the back of my mind all the while was the question of Khurshed. I know that, as usual, I want to run away; I want to cancel everything that has happened. To help me to run away, my mind wonders: Is she so beautiful? Were the afternoon hours we spent so ecstatic?

January 5, 1935

I've been seeing Khurshed regularly, but not much alone. Today I took her for a drive. Sometimes I don't like her much; but there's a sort of inevitability about my being with her. Everything real is inevitable. I hate the taste of reality.

Yesterday the Viceroy and Vicereine came to lunch at the *Statesman*. I was flattered when he said, on being introduced to me: 'I'd heard of you, of course'; and when Lady Willingdon sought me out for a chat, whose intimacy I exaggerated in talking about the episode afterwards.

They are Twilight of Empire all right. Shahid says that I evolve phrases like Twilight of Empire, and then make everything, including my own life, fit in with them.

After the lunch we took the Viceregal party round the office to see the press and so on. Moore was full of excitement. They strolled about amongst linotype machines cracking jokes and pretending to be very interested. I, too, cracked jokes, and made peace with old Bishop Westcott by raking up common acquaintances. Then it was all over.

Sudhin and Shahid came to tea. There was an elaborate business about going to Santiniketan to see Rabindranath Tagore. I wanted to get out of going, and got out of going. There's a dinner on Sunday, for Watson, who is leaving, and Moore said he didn't want me to miss it. At the same time he said he was worried about my leaders, because my point of view was so entirely negative.

I had a bit of a heart-to-heart talk. He was queerly nervous and excited, and I played my trump card – sincerity.

January 7, 1935

Now I see it all as unutterably cheap and trivial. Another mood. A sort of dislike for the whole affair, a sudden realization of the folly of stopping working for all these weeks, and of what shameful reading these pages will make. I was glad to read last evening that Florence Nightingale, at 31 (my age), wrote that she looked forward to nothing but death. Also a maxim of La Rochefoucauld to the effect that it is impossible to love a person for long without its becoming apparent, or to pretend to love a person for long without being found out. I read a chapter of *Wuthering Heights*, and it was so good that I blushed for my own work, and yet know it to be my genre of work.

January 8, 1935

I sat by the fire covered with a blanket most of the day yesterday, and read. Shahid was here; and Khurshed and her husband came to dinner. She was wearing a sort of waistcoat of gold cloth that I like very much. She told me that she had made the waistcoat herself. She pretended not to be hungry, and came away from the dinner table early to chat to me. 'You'll be better tomorrow,' she said. 'You'll be well enough to come on Wednesday.'

January 10, 1935

In the evening there was a *Statesman* party at Peleti's. I felt extravagantly gay. All the women wanted to dance with me. A man called Herries told me that I was the admiration of everyone, and I was pleased. Most of the women were Anglo-Indian, and I felt in harmony with their reckless, vapid, dissolution. I danced and danced as I've never danced before, really feeling music in me.

I sometimes think that Khurshed really only wants to have a

love affair with an Englishman. 'When you were ill,' she said,
you looked very beautiful.'

January 13, 1935

I'm not getting any work done to speak of. Yesterday I bought a
car, a huge Wolseley, old, but still massive and powerful. Driving
about in it makes me feel important. I could scarcely live through
the hour or so before it came into my possession. Then, after a
while, I thought: after all, it's a wretched old tumble-down affair.
What a fool I was to buy it!

Khurshed and her husband came to dine with me, because the
Wordsworths were dining out. When they dine with me and I'm
in charge of the paper, I have the proofs brought upstairs, because
I fancy that it makes me seem important. Khurshed knows a lot
of slang that she picked up from Anglo-Indians at the different
schools she went to. She said that she wished her two sisters were
her husband's wife as well as herself. 'How blissfully happy we'd
be!' she said. Every now and again her intuition comes out, as when
she suddenly said to me: 'Why do you go out of your way to irritate
the other people on the *Statesman*?'

January 15, 1935

Love Interred

'Do you love me still?' cross-legged, sedate.
I laughed. 'Of course.'
'You wouldn't say, dare not.'
'I'd say,' I lied.
Then the room darkened.
'It was as you'd said – the last time:
'Beauty,' I said, 'is nothing, too.'
'And do you wish,' you asked
'I have,' I said – 'that it had never been,'
And shook my head.
You sighed.

'Happiness, too,' I said, 'melts at a touch.'
'Love,' you went on, 'is quietness,
And ours so furtive, anxious.'
'We'll talk out more afternoons,' I bravely said.
Then your eyes glistened;
Nodding: 'Yes, talk out more afternoons.'
'Love's a word,' I said:
'There's some reality deeper than it.'
Then we interred dead love amongst dead words.

Kit arrives in Bombay tomorrow. I sent her a wire today: 'Longing to see you dearest. Look out for Fells. Meeting Imperial Mail here.'

January 18, 1935

Yesterday was very quiet. I'm even beginning to work again. The evening was not so quiet. Shahid came about six, and we went to Goswami, who was ill, having brought on a blood pressure attack through boozing. He was in his dressing-gown, sitting with his wife, Romola, who looked distraught. Then we went to the Nanking restaurant. And there was Khurshed sitting with her husband and his two partners (both pretty loathsome). The whole affair was rather mouldy. The partners said they wanted to go to the cinema, and we urged them for all we were worth, but they decided not to go.

January 19, 1935

Kit's train arrives at midnight, and I am sitting waiting for the time to come to go and meet it. A queer mood, foreboding. I wonder how it'll be with Kit. What a dread I have! I've forgotten my children; yet there's a sort of easiness in me that used not to be there. I suppose I'll stay years and years in India. I suppose I like the place. The last few months, looked back on, seem happy. If I read over this diary I'd see how unhappy it really was.

February 14, 1935

The end of Kit's visit. I saw her off tonight. So much meeting and seeing off. It has been a terrible three weeks, yet, at the last, I felt an inexpressible love for her. We fought and fought, neither giving way. There's never been such a fight ever between us. Then last night she said quietly: 'You'd better stick to me. No one'll love you as I do.' Chanda and Shahid and Shudin came to see her off. They had put flowers in her compartment. The bearer, to my surprise, wept. He turned passionately on Kit and said: 'India's a fine country, come back.'

February 25, 1935

Yesterday I worked at Butler in the morning for the first time for about two months, and in the afternoon went with Malikda, a great friend of Goswami's, to an astrologer. He was a Brahmin, a sleek, round bogus man. I love Malikda so much that I said I thought him very good. He sat on a couch, with his soft, supple legs folded up under him. Malikda asked him very persistently if my connection with India would be long. He said, yes. Going back in the car Malikda told me why he had asked this. 'There is something in you,' he said, 'that I've never found in anyone else; and I want India to have it.' It made me very happy, Malikda being a sort of saint.

We talked with Sudhin for a while, and then, in the evening, I went to a Christmas party at the house of a man named Hardaker, who's married to a Frenchwoman. It was rather silly. I drank vodka, and showed off. All the women made a fuss of me, which I like very much. A man recited Lancashire dialect poems, and I felt quite a home-sickening for Manchester. Curiously enough, however, the place that gives me the greatest pang when I think of it is Rossinière, where I had stayed after Moscow. I don't know why, because I wasn't particularly happy in Switzerland, although I got a lot of work done, and my own work. Whenever I hear a cow-bell, or just think of the walks I used to go there through the woods, I get a stab of pain in my heart.

Tomorrow I'm flying to Bombay and shall see Khurshed there.

I don't want to particularly. I had a letter from her that was some-how cheap, a cinema love letter; phrases and a technique she's picked up amongst European Indians and Parsees.

March 6, 1935

After all I didn't go to Bombay. The aeroplane that was coming broke down. Last night I sat listening (and to help myself along, drinking whisky) to Jim Barnes's megalomania. He is Reuter's man in Simla. He told me about his love for Italy, and how he only cared about Italy, and how, if he'd become an Italian, he'd have been one of Mussolini's close associates; how, on the other hand, his leadership capacity in England had been hopelessly reduced because of this unfortunate passion for Italy. He's cracked, but I don't mind him.

I'm so sick of Calcutta and India and politics and journalism and talk and love and hate. I'm so tired. I wrote and told Kit what is the truth, that I love her and must always love her till I die, her only. But it doesn't mean I can live with her.

March 10, 1935

These days are the unhappiest I have ever lived. They are so unhappy that I can't quite believe in them. They pass, and I scarcely notice. Yesterday I went to a huge cocktail party that Moore gave, and told and listened to stale jokes, and got rather tight and came back at eight o'clock. Goswami and Sudhin came to dine and I went on drinking, and so talking. Afterwards, I heard there was a steamer aground so we went to see her and took a native boat, and went up to her. I climbed aboard and ran into some sort of officer, and murmured that I came from the *Statesman*, and he said no one was allowed on the ship. The other three were in a tug. I looked down at them and somehow felt ashamed, and crept sheepishly off the boat. It was a horrid episode, and I cut a sorry figure, as they well recognized.

March 11, 1935

> '*Depuis le jour où je me suis donnée.*'
>
> Ever since the day I gave myself –
>   Yielding to you, my soul.
> (And who could refuse your touch
>   Resent your eyes' longing?)
> The world has been different, richer,
>   More cruel, more alien.
> More with me and more strange.
>   Ever since the day I gave myself –
> O, sure! – and nothing left;
>   And you, who took, where are you now?
> I reach to find again, and see
>   A flame still restless, and feel
> A void where once I was
>   Before I gave myself.

March 13, 1935

I had said that I would address a thing called the Poetry Society, borrowed Eliot, D. H. Lawrence and a few others from Sudhin, and thought out what I imagined would be a touching address. After the lecture a young Indian got up and said: 'I thought we were going to hear about contemporary poetry, and Mr Muggeridge has only talked about dead poets.' My heart sank. It was true. There was nothing in what I had said. An old writer's mood. It made me very unhappy.

I went on to see Mrs Price-Hughes who was, as usual, arranged on the sofa, like flowers in a vase. With her was a man with a moustache well above his lip who, she told me after he'd gone, designed furniture, and so couldn't get into debt. I understood exactly her motives in wanting me to meet him.

March 16–17, 1935

In the evening we went for a ride in Goswami's Rolls-Royce. It was a moonlit balmy night. I felt very easy. Afterwards I drove the Rolls-Royce all out, going at 70 mph. Gos was frightened.

Tonight came news of Germany's determination to have an army of 600,000. It means war sooner or later. If there is war, I shall fly home at once and learn to fly. This thought made me quite happy. I realized how completely desperate I was, had little hold on life. I want to die. Quite genuinely, I want to die. I have no appetite to live because I know what, for me, the future will be like. There must be many like me; and that is why war will come.

March 20, 1935

I had one of my worst terrible nightmares. I went to the front door of 19 Grove Terrace, and Pan (the pet-name we use for our eldest son, Leonard) and a little girl in a blue tunic were sitting on the step. 'We've been waiting and waiting,' Pan said, 'and nobody answers when we ring.' My heart sank. I knew what had happened, went into the house and found Kit dead. She'd written me a letter before she died. It began: 'It doesn't often come to a human being to want nothing; I want nothing now – not even you.' Marvelling at the beauty of this sentence, I woke up, feeling afraid. I am afraid still.

March 22, 1935

I went to a strange picnic three days ago. We were to meet at my flat. Sudhin came first, and he and I sat talking. Then much later, Shahid came. He was a bit uplifted, because his friend Ninette (as she always does) had tried to persuade him not to come with us, and, through fear of being ridiculed, he had resisted. This did him good. Next came Romola, Mrs Goswami. She had been to the races. (I was sorry she came alone, because it meant, as I had feared would happen, that Goswami would begin to count me on her side.) He and Chanda came last. Chanda had made him tight, and looked white and criminal. Goswami and Sudhin went in one car; the rest of us in the Rolls-Royce, open. It was lovely driving along in it, with the moon full, and the air warm and fragrant. When we got to Diamond Harbour Romola put on a net to prevent her hair from blowing about. I asked her to take it off, and later she did, though I think one of the others asked her to, too. We sat round and ate and drank. I'd brought three bottles of Hock and it made me a bit nervy. Then we started for a walk. Chanda and Romola went ahead, and the four of us slipped back to finish the last bottle. We drank to Goswami and he said that he'd been into the abyss. It was true that he had. I knew that he was finished, and swore to myself that before that stage – if I got near it – I'd kill myself. Chanda egged Goswami on to get involved in a row with some students who were playing about with a bicycle. Whem Romola and I rejoined Goswami, I saw an ugly look on his face. We played a few games, then came home, leaving Romola and Chanda to go off together while Sudhin and Goswami and Shahid and I walked across the Maidan. Shahid made one of his pre-war intellectual remarks. How beautiful, he said, was yellow piss in the moonlight! We laughed. As Sudhin said, it was suddenly apparent how unhappy we all were.

March 27, 1935

I'm glad to be leaving Calcutta.

Opposite my bedroom is a flat. I watch it wake up almost every day. The first thing that happens is that a green parrot is brought out on to the verandah. Then a man sleeping there stirs. He is a European, blond and ruddy, I imagine an ex-soldier. The others in the household are all Anglo-Indian. I cannot imagine what is the precise relationship, but there are a large number of them, and one baby, whose I don't know. They pass the baby from hand to hand like a plaything. One morning, when the blond man had just stirred, one of the girls, the youngest and prettiest, suddenly bent down and kissed him. Then she lent back across his legs. He looked at her, then furtively about like an animal. Somehow her gesture was very charming.

April 3, 1935—Delhi

I came here on my way to Simla. In the train I read a French translation of the *Kama Sutra* lent me by a rather attractive, salacious woman to whom Jim Barnes introduced me, who is half American and half Indian, named Mrs Chowdhry. She said I was like Shelley – anyone less like Shelley than I am never existed.

There was a terrific storm, with lightning like writing across the sky. I looked out at it and longed to be a victim of one of Nature's sudden bursts of cruelty. Sandy Inglis, of *The Times*, met me at the station. I was really very pleased to see him. In Calcutta I went native, and the company of Inglis and his wife, being in their typical Swiss hotel, is somehow a relief – even though I've written to Sudhin that I miss him like hell.

This place is dry and exhilarating after the damp of Calcutta.

In the Legislative Assembly yesterday a man with a little moustache, and light white trousers, and shoes with pointing up toes, and a Gandhi cap, but not in khaddar, told me who all the different people were. I asked him how he knew so well. He said he came each morning. I asked why. He said it was just to while away the time. I asked him what he thought of the place. He said not much – 'a waste of taxpayer's money. They all get Rs20 a day,' he whispered. I asked him where he'd sit if he was an Assembly Member. 'Behind Desai?' I asked. 'God knows where I'd sit,' he said, 'but not behind Desai. I haven't the courage to make sacrifices. My habits are my habits.' He was obviously rich, and slightly, not unpleasantly, scented, I think with sandalwood.

April 4, 1935

> Ill, in Delhi, I surveyed
>   The debris of my life
> Looked back on nothingness
>   And forward . . .
> If I might die, I thought,
>   Of some disease.
> Consume, leaving a little dust;
>   This fever magnify.
> The heavy air is death
>   My thoughts death
> If the love I crave; arms
>   Hungry for it.
> Reach out; reach out.

April 8, 1935

I drove up the mountains through sleeting rain, getting colder
and colder, ears singing and eyes aching. I sat brooding in my
room, and wondering about Kit. I do love her and want her to be
happy.

At breakfast I talked to a rather charming young cavalry
officer. I asked him if he wanted there to be a war. 'Good Lord,
no,' he said, then thought a little while and went on: 'Of course
that little show on the frontier – I'd have been glad if it had developed a bit, but not a *big* war. Good Lord, no.'

Then I went for a walk. The air seemed rich, but I didn't
appreciate it much. Nor did I, as when I went up to Ootacamund
from Alwaye, revel in the pine trees and broken horizon; but when
I heard some birds singing my heart melted. Why this should have
been so I don't know, as in the ordinary way I'm not particularly
fond of birds.

April 9, 1935

Between whiles, I read Butler's translation of the *Iliad*, and think
how nothing has changed, nothing been learnt, how the structure
of human life is just where it was. I was particularly taken with
how Alexander, after he had fought with Menelaus for Helen,
and been defeated, rushed home and called Helen to him vowing
that never before had his passion for her burst so strangely on them.

Two cavalry officers dined in the hotel last night. They both
ordered the servants about in a way that got on my nerves. Yet, I
thought, they'd probably be in real matters kinder to the servants
than I – more generous, more genuinely considerate; I treat
servants like human beings, but have no more feeling about them
than about a horse that I ride. For instance, Kurevella, my old
servant in Travancore, wrote that I owed him Rs30. I remember
that I do, but I haven't sent him the money. The cavalry officers
probably would.

Well, it's now or never for me. That's what I keep thinking.
Now or never in every way. The mountains seem very beautiful.
At last their beauty is beginning to reach me, is bringing my soul to
life, so that I see qualities in things and people that I had forgotten.

I should like to know the peace of God that passeth all understanding. I should like to feel something inside me that wasn't
just a mood. Then I'd really be ready to die. Now I'm only ready
to die out of desperation – in the same way that I was ready to
come to India last autumn.

The thing I like about the *Iliad* is its acceptance of life. It is
sometimes bitter and sometimes satirical, but it never rails against
the very nature of life, is not, that is to say, idealistic.

April 12, 1935

While I was doing my exercises, I remembered Malikda saying
to me: 'I've been good, I've worked hard, I haven't broken any
moral laws, and yet this trouble has come to me.' Personally I
don't believe in any moral laws, but I believe more and more in
Good and Evil. It is the secret of Good and Evil that I want to get
at. So that obeying moral laws as such is nothing. In fact only
rather inferior people do it – I mean, do exactly what society tells
them. On the other hand, the truest analysis of conduct and living
is into Good and Evil, and the only way to live is to abide by those
concepts. What I mean is that evil is a different thing from sin;
it is a reality whereas the other is an idea.

April 13, 1935

I love a routine like this – walking and writing and reading. If
Wordsworth continues not to use my leaders, I shall write on
Monday resigning from the *Statesman*. In any case, it is only a
matter of time before I resign. I see now that the unhappiness,
as far as jobs are concerned, is on my side. I can't fit in. I wish I
could. Anyway, this is my last attempt. When I get away from the
Statesman I'll just write, and starve, go under, anything, but
never again attempt the impossible task of cooperating in carrying
on an organization I don't belong to. How glad I am, though, that
I made this last attempt. If I hadn't made it, my mind would have
been restless; now I know that however hard the future, I shall
always feel in the bottom of my heart that I'm well out of it all.

April 15, 1935

The Inglises and I went to Wildflower Hall for lunch. It's about seven miles from Simla. They went in rickshaws and I walked both ways. It was lovely country – huge desolate valleys, after a climb through a pine forest. Wildflower Hall used to be Kitchener's house, and is now a hotel. After lunch I had my hair cut by an itinerant barber with a beard exactly like King George V's. When I pointed this out Inglis looked slightly shocked. There was a hail storm and when it was over we started back. I felt pretty footsore, but I love being out in the country just after rain. In a village we went through was a Mission Meeting House – a tiny shop – and at the reading desk an Indian thundered, open Bible in his hand, to four people, huddled together on the front bench, two of them very aged, and two children, one of the children almost a baby. It was a queer sight.

April 18–21, 1935

I love it when in the evening the hills are like grey shadows. There is a sort of peace in them that I have never known in anything else. I feel then that it doesn't matter whether or not I manage to get away with a little piece of egotism.

After lunch yesterday I had a talk with a Mohammedan named Hydari, whose father, Sir Akbar Hydari, is Finance Minister of Hyderabad. He complained that most Englishmen got on better with Hindus than Moslems, but said this was because the Hindu was a wonderful assimilator and clever at adjusting himself to the mood or outlook of the person he was talking to. I argued that the Hindu and Englishman had actually more in common than the Moslem and Englishman, that the Hindu's complexity was more *sympathique* to the Englishman than the Moslem's intellectual simplicity.

In the evening the Viceroy arrived, and Inglis and I went out to see him come, but missed him. Somehow it was all very tawdry – the entrance to his house and so on. I hated it. We went back and met P. J. Grigg and his wife. Grigg is the Finance Member of the Viceroy's Council. He's been Confidential Secretary to a number of Chancellors in England, and now, belatedly, is having an innings as Chancellor himself in India. He treasures little notes and memoranda in the handwriting of prominent politicians. Lady Grigg is very masterful. She tells long and rather amusing anecdotes. They're childless and not very happy, I should say. They're very much of the same kidney as the Inglis's. It humiliates me to think that in certain circumstances I might boast of knowing Grigg.

April 23, 1935

I lunched yesterday with Sir Akbar Hydari. Every evening at six o'clock wherever he may be, he takes off his shoes, does his ablutions and says his prayers. He eats inordinately, greedily. When anyone is mentioned, he says: 'What's his salary?' At the same time he is very well informed. We talked of course about Federation. He was pretty free. Afterwards I embodied what he said in a message and sent it off. He then, when I showed him the message, agreed that it was precisely true, but asked me not to send it. I phoned the *Statesman* and cancelled it. The whole affair was rather silly. All the same, I enjoyed talking with him. He knew all the scandal about English politicians, and still cherished a faint hope that Ramsay MacDonald might be the son of Annie Besant and Bradlaugh.

April 27, 1935

Old Hydari gave a dinner, at which there was a young and rather faded young woman who talked about being dissatisfied with her life and never having done anything. 'You suggest something for me to do,' she said. I couldn't think of anything to suggest except, 'You ought to get married.' This seemed a bit thin. One woman said she'd like to ride away in a rickshaw and vanish. I said everything was riding away, even lechery. This didn't go down well. She was one of those people with a lot of spirit and no brain who, in the upper classes, nearly always become Christian Scientists.

April 30, 1935

Yesterday I saw Sir C. P. Ramaswamy Iyer. He has great power nowadays in Travancore by virtue of being the junior Maharani's lover. Formerly he was in the Government of India. He is famous for his lechery and debts. I have always had illusions about him, have spoken of him having 'what so few Indians have got' – the sort of charm engendered by promiscuity and living beyond your income, the sort of bonhomie, etc., etc. When I actually met him I found him rather dingy and commonplace. There was certainly no sparkle. We spoke about politics. He seemed uneasy. I have a feeling that his innings is drawing to a close. Of course, it's been a pretty good one.

May 6, 1935

I've been ill, but have managed not to stop working.

I lunched at Viceregal Lodge yesterday. It was a large party. We lined up with the band playing. Then folding doors opened, and someone announced: 'Their Excellencies!' They walked along shaking hands with everyone. On the whole they do their stuff very well. The great thing is, they enjoy it, and their enjoyment is infectious. After lunch Lady Willingdon sent for me. She is really a fascinating creature in a way, so vulgar and full of vitality. She told me how stingy the Commander-in-Chief was, how he had only given Rs300 to the Jubilee Fund. She also said: 'The Viceroy's looking well, isn't he?' This she said a bit anxiously, as though she feared that at any moment he might pop off. I assured her I thought he was looking very well indeed. Then she said how she wished he could stay on for another term and be the first constitutional Viceroy. I saw how she dreaded ceasing to be Vicereine. It was so naive that it was charming. 'Our successor?' she asked. I named Linlithgow. 'He's terribly pompous,' she said. I agreed that pomposity was amongst the very worst sins.

'Look at Anderson,' she went on. She was referring to Sir John Anderson. 'How he's changed!'

'Why?' I asked.

'Not out of the top drawer.'

After a while I was passed on to a dim young man and then to the Viceroy. He looks, as I've said, like the elderly beau of Restoration Comedy, except that his eyes are pale, as though life was draining out of him from the top downwards (as Swift died). We talked about Ramaswamy Iyer and the passion of the Maharani of Travancore for him.

'While he was here,' I said, 'she sent him mangoes. Is that a bad sign?'

He said he thought it was.

He was such an old buck, almost like Lady Chatterley's father. 'Get her on her back, me boy,' with a titter.

I liked him, too, though. When I went (I'd had a sip to drink) I felt quite affectionate towards them.

May 11, 1935

Yesterday morning I had a private interview with the Viceroy. We talked together for nearly an hour and a half. I saw his obsessions. One was Irwin, the previous Viceroy (later Lord Halifax). He thinks that Irwin was a bad Viceroy, at the same time he has an uneasy feeling that he is, or is thought to be, a greater man than he. It reminded me of Birkenhead's remark about Irwin's appointment: 'How much more useful it is to be good than brilliant!' Then he kept harping on the subject: 'I wouldn't, of course, say a word,' etc., etc. I flattered him by saying that for my own part I had come to the conclusion that mankind had suffered more at the hands of good than bad men, that unfortunately a certain kind of spiritual pedantry, sea-green incorruptibility, gave men power – as Hitler and Gandhi – but that those best fitted to exercise authority were those who are most habituated to compromise. There he was though, a grey old man, full of egotism, of a sort of charm, not in the least pompous, so that I felt entirely at ease with him and prattled away. It seemed strange to think of his power and his success. I tuned myself easily to his mood. Finally he said that for his part he believed in Providence, and that but for such a belief he would never have been able to get along. 'You won't agree with that,' he said. 'On the contrary,' I said, 'It is my own opinion that if the world's troubles can be summarized they amount to the collapse of religion. But,' I went on, 'my generation belongs to that collapse, so that I don't believe in your Providences.' He was very pleased, I could see, and I walked back to the hotel glowing with pleasure.

May 12, 1935

In the afternoon I went with Hydari to the cinema to see *Chu Chin Chow*. Films reflect national characteristics. Hydari represents just about the Chu Chin Chow stage in English life – that is, the latter part of the war. His humour is of that period. Going to England for their education has the same effect on most Indians as Oxford or Cambridge on most Englishmen – it arrests their development, they are so exhilarated at finding themselves fellow citizens with the race that has conquered them that they stabilize their lives then and there. Hydari is the sort of man who says: 'I like a joke but that was going rather far,' or: 'If a man can get his greens without hurting anyone – I bar home-breakers – good luck to him. I've nothing to say against it . . .' a sort of censorious tolerance.

May 14, 1935

I got involved in a row yesterday. Grigg, the Finance Member, took great exception to two of my messages about the general trade situation, and raved and frothed to Inglis about my having fallen under the influence of Barnes and the Italian Trade Commissioner – Marconi – whom I know slightly. I wrote him one of the rudest letters I've ever written to anyone. He sent it back to me saying that possibly I might like to reconsider it, I replied saying that, far from wanting to reconsider, since I'd subsequently heard that he'd poured out the same tale about me to Rau, an Indian journalist who's supposed to be helping me here, I was confirmed in the attitude I'd taken. How the matter will end I don't know, but I feel very angry, I suppose because I'd like a good issue to clear out on. If I wanted to stay, I suppose I'd cry small.

In the evening I went to a cocktail party given by a Colonel Dickens and his wife. There was also a Colonel Fitzgerald and his wife, both of whom I like, and a number of other people. I feel with these military people that they're all a bit wistful, as though they felt that the world had gone by them, a bit envious of people like Barnes, of their own class and social background who've managed to break away, as though they felt that somehow they were going to get more out of life than they ever had. With them, I see the best of Twilight of Empire.

May 15, 1935

Yesterday was devoted almost entirely to this Grigg row. I told Barnes what had happened, and he was furious. He talked very big, but when I mentioned our consulting a lawyer, his face fell, and he almost whined that he wouldn't care to pay for this. Inglis got very nervous at the talk of legal action. In the evening Barnes saw Grigg. He said that he apologized abjectly, but I doubt if Barnes was quite as on top as his description of the meeting suggested. However, it's over. The trouble about these affairs is that they excite me so much that I can't work, and get ill.

May 22, 1935

Every now and again I like to describe a day exactly as I have lived it.

Last evening I was rather tight, and went with Sir Hassan Suhrawardy's party to the cinema to see *Royal Cavalcade*. I sat next to a young girl, the daughter of the proprietor of the Cecil Hotel. Beyond her was Duke, one of the Viceroy's secretaries. Being a bit drunk, I got worked up over the film, which was a series of episodes in the twenty-five years of the King's reign, and pretended to Duke that it was all familiar to me. 'What!' I shouted, 'you never saw Harry Tate!' I had never seen him either. I had been dining with the Inglises. Well, I woke up a bit dizzy from drink, did my exercises, read a bit of Butler, tried, but without succeeding, to write. At breakfast I was gay, sat afterwards reading the *New Yorker*, went at 10.30 to the Foreign and Political Department to a Press Conference. Metcalf, who presided as usual, gave out news in his dry way, returned me my *Winter in Moscow* which, he said, he had read with interest. I came back and typed a message to the *Statesman* about Soviet influence in Chinese Turkestan, comparing China to a great corpse with two rats, Japan and Russia, gnawing at it. At twelve o'clock I saw Grigg. It was to be our reconciliation. He sat there in coloured spectacles, nervous, upset. I talked very frankly to him. Was I sincere? God knows. I never know whether I am sincere or not. Actually, for some reason, I felt a bit shifty. His nervousness infected me. We talked for an hour, and agreed, without much conviction, to bury the hatchet. I'd put on my smart grey suit. It was strange sitting there in his dreary office, he so unhappy and unsure of himself, and I so indifferent about what had seemed so serious.

I came back to lunch and fell asleep on the sofa, a thing I hate doing. Then I had tea, talked with Rau about politics, tried to settle down to write, but still without success. I felt bilious and conscience-striken (I honestly don't see why) about Grigg and about having cut a lunch with Sir Hassan – especially when I heard that it had been attended by many notabilities. (Oh God!) All the while there was something exciting me. I'd seen a woman at Sipi Fair, half Hungarian and half Indian, beautiful in a way, wearing an exquisite sari. Warden, a Parsee, had introduced me to her, and had asked if I'd join them both at the Cecil Hotel dance. This was in my mind. I smelt emotional entanglement. Already it has affected me to the extent of not being able to write easily to Kit – the first time for many weeks. I rushed to the station to catch the post with a letter to the *Statesman*, rickshaw coolies shouting after me. Then I walked into the town, ostensibly to see about a new typewriter, actually knowing the place would be closed. On the way back, I looked in on Sellih to whom I talked about the Press in India till nearly eight o'clock, went back to the hotel, thinking: I'll not change but work on steadily till midnight; changed, took a brandy, danced with the Hungarian-Indian several times, cemented our attraction, made her promise to ring me up. She is very sensual and made-up, was wearing an exquisite silver and black sari, is rather self-consciously arty; has studied art in Paris; paints. We danced a waltz. I said I'd like to dance and dance until I swooned. She said she'd never swooned, but that she supposed I had.

May 31, 1935

This is a curious evening. (I despise myself somehow for being able to write down this evening. I wish I might die before writing it down.) I have been to the Viceroy's garden party. I have written to my wife. I have dined with Hydari, and some people. I have phoned to Amrita Sher-Gil, the Hungarian-Indian, making an appointment for tomorrow evening in the lounge of this hotel. She is dining with Warden and coming to see me on the way back. It seems wonderful now, but then will seem terrible. Everything seems terrible when it is real, and then it will be real.

There has been an earthquake in Quetta. I should have gone there, and I didn't. As Butler would say: 'Let that pass'. I did not go to Quetta because of Amrita.

At the Viceroy's garden party most people wore grey top hats and cutaway coats. I am waiting for news of the earthquake at Quetta.

Amrita's mother has red hair, a triumphantly vulgar woman. Some instinct tells me that I have met my match in her.

My soul is tired. My soul is tired.

June 1, 1935

I am sitting here waiting for Amrita to come. She will be due in about half an hour. There is a fever of nervousness in me. I wish on the whole that she wouldn't come. She is a demon. I woke up at five trembling, and unable to sleep. Stale booze throbbed my head. At seven I went for a long walk, trying to brazen it out with myself, but it was lame, lame. I sent messages. I talked, talked.

At 10.30 I begin to walk up and down the road. People will see me, and there'll be a scandal. Who cares? Jean Inglis is alone because Sandy has gone to Quetta. My wish is to have done with living. There is no place for me in the world. All I shall leave will be these diaries, out of which people will try to create a personality, a genius. It is the genius in me that tortures. I feel it like a fire, and when it burns low there's only a shell left. I've none of the things to live for that other people have. News of victims of the Quetta earthquake. I copied their names laboriously. Thirty-two years I've lived on this earth, and each day I feel it more alien.

Amrita's an old hand, that's something. She's had an abortion –
half a baby, she put it. No more.

Life's a funny thing. Amrita has been and gone and I feel gay.
She was delightful. The best thing about her is her gaiety and
sincerity.

June 6, 1935

I sat by the telephone, expecting every call to be from Amrita.
One call was curious – a woman's voice answered, and when I gave
my name, burst into daemonic laughter and rang off. On Saturday I
couldn't hold out any more, got Amrita's number from Warden
and rang up; there was no reply, though a few minutes later she
rang up to ask me to tea on Monday. Her mother was a not un-
likeable, but extremely vulgar, Hungarian Jewess, her father a
gnome-like figure with a distraught white beard and Tolstoyan
eyes. He had a friend there, much bigger than himself, whose
beard was quieter and mouth less firm. There was also a little
Frenchman called Comte Mécard. We talked about ideas. Every
now and again Sher-Gil, Amrita's father, burst in with a sort of
petulant vehemence. Once, he pointed to the tea, all chocolate
and cream cakes, and said: 'There's nothing for me to eat, nothing.'
He said it bitterly. Every night he spends on a little terrace looking
at the stars through a telescope. With another apparatus he can
study the movement of stars, and put his watch right. I've often
seen him on the terrace, beard blowing in the wind, eyes excited,
an attractive figure.

Amrita showed me her paintings. They were not commonplace,
but how good they are I can't be quite sure. At the same time she's
got a touch of genius. One of them, of a consumptive woman nude,
I praised very highly. Thinking it over now, I'm not quite sure
again whether the praise was justified, but all the same it's not an
entirely ordinary picture.

After tea I sat in Amrita's room talking. I left her there and
arranged to go for a walk on Wednesday. We went for a walk then
and sat talking together on the hillside. She told me about how
she had had an abortion, and about her lovers, and why she had
come back to India. Her friends must have been, I thought,

students in the Ecole des Beaux Arts. I knew the type very well, and yet, as I felt about the pictures, she's somehow more than an art student, expressing second-rate ideas with first-rate bitterness, and second-rate aspirations with fifth-rate sentimentality. As with all people I get to love, there's a directness and essential truthfulness about her. She was to dance at Davico's with Warden on Saturday. I suggested she should go early and look in on me on the way back. This she agreed to. I felt ill on Saturday, and in a way dreaded her coming. The night before I had been rather drunk.

From 10.30 I walked up and down outside the hotel, watching ladies bringing out their dogs, and hoping they wouldn't be there when she came to see me, wondering if each rickshaw that rattled down the hill was hers. She came at 10.45.

The next day I had tea at her house. When the others had gone we took a walk together.

The day before yesterday she came and dined with me here. It was a fancy-dress dance, a lugubrious affair but we were very happy. Yesterday I wrote resigning from the *Statesman*.

Sometimes I hate Amrita. Today, for instance, I went out to meet her. She was sitting reading tattered love letters, letters which began 'Amrita!' Another 'Maintenant je suis soldat'. She said: 'This morning I went for a walk with Warden and he asked if he might kiss the tips of my fingers'. I get a sense of someone entirely egocentric, coarse, petulantly spoilt, almost to the point of physical nausea.

We talked, both rather showing off. After every time she kissed me she re-rouged her lips, carefully shaping the colours on them to hump up in the middle. Later we climbed further up the hill and I looked with hate at her face, somehow empty of life with rings under the eyes and the mouth sagging. On the way back she said she must eat that evening, eat a lot. I laughed uproariously over one or two things and then gratefully left her.

June 10, 1935

Yesterday I went out for the day with Amrita and her mother. It was at the last moment that Madame Sher-Gil decided to come, and this irritated me, because I'd been looking forward to being alone with Amrita. They were to telephone when they set out, and didn't. I sat waiting in my room feeling liverish and wretched until one of the hotel servants came to tell me that an 'Indian lady' awaited me. This, too, was wretched. They were in their rickshaws, each with a sunshade up. We were all three bad-tempered. Amrita had stomach cramp in the night and looked ill, and sulky. I hate people to look ill, but don't particularly mind their being ill. We set out, I on horseback having planned to look impressive in jodhpurs and a polo sweater. She knew, and showed that she knew, I was showing off on the horse. I continued to show off. About half way to the Dak bungalow Vesugar met us. He had arranged everything beautifully. Amrita and I arrived first. We kissed each other rather resentfully. She rouged her lips heavily, then, after I'd kissed her, wiped mine with her handkerchief. Her stockings and shoes looked fatuous with a sari. They irritated me. We had breakfast. Amrita is just like a child when she's hungry, and shouts for food, points at what she wants. After breakfast we lay about, and I carried on a ghastly conversation about Indian politics, showing off. Vesugar photographed Amrita. She has an insatiable appetite for being photographed. I made fun of her about it, and she gradually got annoyed.

Rather pompously I went down to look at my horse, not that I had any means of knowing whether or not it was being properly looked after. Then I sat in the porch. We had lunch. I did not want any and Amrita ate voraciously, mostly, I knew, to annoy me. During lunch Madame Sher-Gil talked about a revolting French friend of hers, a most palpable charlatan. She described his meetings in Paris, the subdued lights, the great gatherings of ladies in trouble; she also told me three things about him – that he ate enormously, that he had started life as a dentist, and that he loved to astonish people by unselfconsciously unrobing in front of them. I'd seen the man, blond, preposterous, with blue eyes and a hearty manner, had even argued with him. 'He's become,' I said, 'a dentist of souls, now he stops decayed souls instead of decayed teeth.'

After lunch I pretended to go to sleep. Amrita knew I was just pretending. She was looking at scientific magazines. Then we went for a walk. To be annoying I started to climb down a steep hillside. The others followed. It was most uncomfortable and unpleasant going down. At the bottom there was a precipitous drop. The arrangement we made was that I should catch her. I caught her and jumped myself, she of course fell and we lay laughing hysterically in the dust. After that we felt a bit better.

Back in the Dak bungalow Amrita and I were together for a while, and then went into the garden and had tea. Mrs Sher-Gil talked and talked. Amrita and I made off. Now there was perfect harmony between us.

I explained to Amrita how she was really a virgin, because she'd never experienced the spiritual equivalent of copulation; she'd had many lovers but they'd left no scar. 'I'll leave a scar,' I boasted. She laughed. I was horrified when, later on, turning over the pages of old *Tatlers*, Amrita said that she thought Ramsay MacDonald and Paul Boncour had lovely faces. She has a certain genius, but no taste, no values, she belongs to that dead world of moral disintegration, disorderly hands and tangled hair, swollen, seen often as picturesqueness, in which both my feet are planted but that, with my head outside, I hate.

After supper we went into the garden and lay down together under a tree in the moonlight. Riding back, the road white and the trees black, and the mountains shadowed, I felt exhilarated. Amrita and I talked for about a mile and a half, and laughed over the day.

I sit waiting. I wonder what I'm waiting for. I believe I'm waiting for Amrita. Or perhaps I'm waiting for news. If it comes, I'll telephone, mouthing into a mouthpiece something that's happened.

June 16, 1935

I said to Amrita once, sitting in her garden very late at night, when there was a moon (even now I see that it was exquisite), that I couldn't write about her, and my love for her, because I had to feel contempt to write. Now at last I do feel contempt, so I've planned out a bitter story, one chapter, called *Arabian Afternoon's Entertainment*. Last night will do for it. She and her mother had dined with me the night before, and we'd all three sat in my room with the light out, the old red-haired mother stretched out on the floor and Amrita beside me on the sofa. All the while we kept up a desultory conversation.

The next morning, I got up at six and rode out to Wildflower Hall to have breakfast with the Inglises. I felt pretty sick. It was nice riding along, even though I had a wretched, lean, unhappy horse. I ate an enormous breakfast and sat talking with Sandy and Jean in a dry, sparkling sort of way, very tired. I'm so tired constantly.

After lunch I turned over newspapers, and slept heavily. Then I tried to work a bit, but without success, played a game of patience, walked about the room, read Boswell, gloating over this: 'When I survey my past life, I discover nothing but a barren waste of time, with some disorders of body, and disturbances of the mind very near to madness, which I hope He that made me will suffer to extenuate many faults, and excuse many deficiencies.'

At a quarter to seven I took a bath, and changed into a light grey suit and put on a blue tie and bright shirt, because this was how Amrita liked me to be dressed. She came at eight, in a green sari with a gold and red border. She talked about her lovers, her terrible obsession with herself very apparent. Then, she took off her jewels and let down her hair. It was like a third performance of a marvellous play, all the fascination, the sense of wonder at it, remains; all the same, you realize that though you might like to see it ten or twenty more times, there'll come a time when you don't want to see it any more, when it'll be wearisome. When, finally, just before she went, I tried to kiss her, she drew back. I asked why, and she said: 'Parce que je n'ai pas envie'. Furtively we crept up to the cold road; and she got into her rickshaw, three policeman looking curiously at us. My knees were trembling and my head swam. Walking back I knew that contempt had come, and that one day I'd write about this, too.

(This is dead.)

Last night, when Amrita wound on her sari, I noticed a certain loveliness in her expression that I had never noticed before. She came and sat by me, unrouged, and leant her head down and was sad. 'Pourquoi triste?' I asked. She would not say why she was sad. I knew:

'Because you're so late, and afraid of a row with your father and mother.'

'Because you're getting tired of me.'

She wouldn't say, but was sad. It gave me a feeling of great tenderness for her. I'm in one of those moods when I feel full of things to write, feel as it were fecund, but have nothing to write.

September 4, 1935

It is a long time since I wrote anything here. The same thing always happens to me when I go to a new place; the stimulus of being in a new place releases energy, then, when that is spent, I relapse into my customary inertia. So it has happened in Simla. Since I finished my book on Butler I've done absolutely nothing except be ill and abandon myself to indolence. Yet still occasionally the old magic feeling of joy in living, of richness and fragrance abounding everywhere, comes to me, and during that mood I feel recompensed for everything. I can remember such moods. They stand out, unforgettable.

Once, for instance, I was walking back on a Sunday evening with Amrita. She'd been painting a portrait of me. She went on with her painting until the light failed. In front of a radiator we drank tea and ate sandwiches voraciously. I can't say I was particularly happy, quite ready to go when the time came, even inventing a reason for having to go; only, walking back, through a heavy mist that dimmed all lights and muffled all voices, everywhere damp, slippery damp, I felt the old feeling of ecstasy in life.

Shortly afterwards I left Simla for London and Fleet Street. Amrita came to the station to see me off in the early morning – a most unusual time for her to be about. We walked up and down the platform together until it was time for me to get into the little mountain train. Through the carriage window we went on talking until, with a shrill whistle, the train began to move. Speaking in French – an affectation we practised – she said we'd had some beaux *moments together, which was true, but also some* moments noirs, *black moments. I continued to look out of the window, waving, until she was out of sight. I knew I should never see her again, and, indeed, I heard that she'd died somewhat mysteriously in 1941, when she was only 27. Later, I heard that her mother had taken her own life. Neither death surprised me.*

So many born, so many dead,
So many mated, so many delivered.
I think I know what I'm waiting for –
I'm waiting to die, for an end.
I seem to have been waiting a whole eternity to die.

Postscript

May 3–7, 1964—Simla

Very curious to be here thirty years later trying to relive my life in Simla for BBC television. Tried to read over the diaries I'd kept, but flagged, India even more depressing now than before; a ripe, withered fruit about to fall off the branch. Independence was not a beginning, but the end of an end.

Went up to Viceregal Lodge. Fantastic scene there – carpets rolled up, pictures removed leaving the blank spaces on walls, etc; throne Viceroy used to sit on with silver footstool left in place. Sat in this pretending to be Viceroy to amusement of officer and one or two others who showed me round. Felt quite fabulously exhilarated at this dismantled power; he hath put down the mighty from their seats and exalted the humble and meek. The scenery being taken away, the props sent back to store, the stage cleared for another play. I love everything which demonstrates the transcience of earthly power; never have I been served so piquant a demonstration. Upstairs, from a balcony, looking over the staggering view – range upon range of mountains, I lifted up my heart unto the hills whence cometh my help.

May 6, 1964

Drove out to Mashobra in a truck, thoughtfully provided with a divan. Otherwise packed with Viceregal Lodge furniture to be transferred to Mashobra – formerly week-end Viceregal resort, again with marvellous views; flower beds, rose-walks, orchards, etc. Accompanied by Punjab Police Officer, quite delightful chap who used flowery English phrases usually not quite correctly. Thus he would say: 'What the eye sees the heart must care for'. Occasionally he would break into old Army slang, as that 'my father was a very great boozer'. He had been in the bodyguard of successive Viceroys.

May 7, 1964

Walked to Summerhill to look for Amrita's old house, but couldn't find it. Rather distressed at my own decomposing mind, memory failure, etc.

1935—1937

Diary 1935–1937

September 28, 1935

I am back in England. The year in India already seems utterly remote. The diary I kept there is scanty, but I think contains the essence of what that year amounted to. Amrita saw me off at Simla. 'I want you to be happy,' she said. At Delhi I caught a plane and flew to Jodhpur, and thence to London. It gave me a great sense of peace and happiness to be back with Kit and the children. Nothing much else seemed to matter, does matter.

The *Evening Standard* where I work is a nightmare. There are tables scattered about a room. I write paragraphs for the *Londoner's Diary*. Most of them get taken out by the Editor, a man with a hare-lip named Percy Cudlipp. He's ferociously energetic, and yet somehow unsure of himself.

I dress immacuately, or as immaculately as I can, but inside there's the old loathing, disgust. I hurry along Fleet Street and to and from the office library with papers in my hand, but there's no reason why I should hurry, any more than if I was going to Amrita's house at Summerhill to have my portrait painted.

January 1–2, 1936

I've been back in London three months now. The *Evening Standard* is pretty grim work, revoltingly futile, and yet exhausting. Whenever I say anything to Bruce Lockhart, who edits *Londoner's Diary*, he says he's heard it fifty times.

I've decided to have one more shot at seeing a doctor and getting my stomach put right. This made me feel a bit less hypochondriacal.

I lunched with an Indian I'd met at the Sher-Gil's. Bruce Lock-hart took me there in his taxi. On the way he told me how he hated journalism, how degrading he felt it to be. I think he was sincere.

January 4-6, 1936

When Kit and I got out of the train at Hastings we were exhilarated. The air seemed suddenly fresh. The Albany hotel is an astonishing place, everyone aged, using their days sparingly. The sitting-room is draughtless and warm, and the inmates move to and from it and the dining-room like a herd of cows to and from pasture.

On Sunday morning Kit and I walked to Bexhill. Kit had lived in Bexhill with her father and mother, and described how they used to go along this road quarrelling with one another. Hugh Kingsmill, who lives in Hastings, came round. We laughed as we always do. After Hugh had gone Kit looked angry. We walked along the front arguing about living in the country, and about whether we should live together at all. It was blowing ferociously. She went back, and I on to the end. The waves poured in, and I thought how, if I'd been a Victorian novelist, I should have seen my own mood in their angry movement and thought it might be better for me to leave Kit then and there, or to kill myself. When I got back, I went to bed. Kit came up and said: 'If we part, let's not part quarrelling.'

January 7, 1936

Brian Lunn took me to lunch in the Inner Temple. It was like being back at Cambridge. I found him in a little wooden room, reading old divorce briefs. They were pencilled over with com-ment. The language was not at all bowdlerized. One contained a verbatim report of a telephone conversation a husband had over-heard between his wife and her lover. He claimed that it proved adultery because, in this conversation, she used the same pet name for penis as with him.

January 11, 1936

Hugh Kingsmill and I put an advertisement in *The Times* to the effect that we believed there was a place for a weekly, *Porcupine*, that would comment wittily and honestly on the modern world, and were anxious to meet anyone prepared to finance such a venture. The first answer came from a man named Berlin, and addressed from an LCC Hostel. He was obviously a pauper, and a bit cracked. Then we had two replies, one from a man in Woking named Bond.

On the Wednesday, we sat waiting at the Authors' Club for Bond for two hours. He didn't come. Hugh told me about how he had been left alone in the house with a young and extravagantly lustful nursemaid for five days, and how he'd managed to control himself. He also told me about how he separated from his first wife, and then, coming back to his hotel in Lucerne, saw a light in his room, and the door ajar, and there she was. He said he could never see a light in his window to this day without a pang. Hugh's company delights me, so that however depressed and ill I'm feeling, I never notice time with him.

In the evening we sat rather gloomily, until the post brought us some more answers, one from a printing firm. We decided that the thing to do was to get out a prospectus, and we began to attempt to formulate our intentions. This landed us in a morass of generalities and empty phrases, just the sort of thing, we decided afterwards, that *Porcupine* was against.

Hugh and I lunched the next day at the Horseshoe. He had telephoned the press that answered our advertisement, and they'd wanted to know if the paper we were proposing to bring out fitted in with their other publications. As their other publications are specialized engineering ones, we couldn't say that it did.

January 17, 1936

I read Kipling's verses all the afternoon (he died yesterday). It struck me how good the verses were, how full of genuine vitality, how full of contempt for what I despised – 'brittle intellectuals' – and of poetic genius; how, if he praised Empire, it was not at all because he had not counted the cost (who has expressed better the wrongs of the common soldier?) but because, men being what they are, he saw it as one of the less despicable manifestations of their urge to over-run and dominate their environment.

April 16, 1936

Kit is in hospital. I went to see her this afternoon. After I'd left the hospital, I walked along the Embankment worrying about her, imagining how I'd react if she died, then realizing that I was turning even the possibility of her death into a kind of sensuality.

April 17, 1936

Kit was better, the operation finished. When I saw her she was a bit dazed, because the chloroform hadn't quite worked off. 'Have they really done it?' she kept saying. She also told me that when she first came to she could only remember my name and the children's, and kept saying them over and over.

May 16, 1936

The proof sheets of *The Earnest Atheist*, my book on Butler, came. I read them through, dissatisfied and frightened; frightened, I suppose, because of *Picture Palace*. But at last I'm getting on with the revision of the book's introduction.

Next Friday we move to Whatlington, near Battle.

June 2, 1936

We're living in Battle now, and I've left the *Evening Standard*. It's a delightful house with a large garden. Len Dobbs, my brother-in-law, and I – especially Len – have been working away at it. This is my chance to write. If I take it – well. If I don't – then I've finished with serious writing. Of course I shall take it, but feel in my bones that things are not going to be easy. I'm all the while reaching after a particular mood. The country is lovely, but I'm not quite in tune with it. I don't feel quite easy – I suppose because of anxiety at having no regular income.

July 23, 1936

Now I shall write an account of our arrival and settling in at Whatlington.

We left London on May 22, Kit coming down the night before. Len and I packed things up. The next morning early the men came. Len travelled down with the van and I met Len at Battle.

Kit was looking tired, but showed me round the house excitedly. The next day we all worked hard, pumping water, cycling in and out of Battle and so on. My room was lovely, the best in the house, with bookshelves all round the walls.

On Monday morning I got up at six and walked into Battle to get a train. It was a beautiful spring morning. First of all I felt exhilarated, then tired. My bag, with a lot of books in it, broke, and a bird fouled my black hat. By the time I got to the station I felt tired and ill. I had to wait there half an hour, and the train, when at last it came, was a slow one stopping at nearly every station, my carriage stale and dusty.

At Tunbridge Wells the train pulled itself together, became important. By the time it reached Cannon Street it was an express. I went to the office for my last week. It was the last lap of that fantastic episode, sitting in the twilit room with twelve others, typewriters tapping, Bruce Lockhart modulating his voice according to whom he was telephoning, and Cudlipp coming and going, etc. I used to feel dazed there all the time. The memory of it is like a nightmare – grubby and unhappy and hysterical, looking up things in encyclopaedias, poring over newspapers, scribbling. 'Let's have a look at the stiffs,' Leslie Marsh used to say, meaning the obituaries. Bruce Lockhart the great lackey. He used to tell me often how he longed to get out of it all. Not happy with money and wireless talks and best-selling books. Either I find goodness and truth, or die, because I've cut away everything. I shall find it, but only when I've hunted myself and conquered myself and shed fear.

August 10, 1936

I repeated 'Oh, purity my heart. Oh, purity my heart.' If, I thought, my heart is pure I shall know God, and if I know God I shall have no more fear. Even as I thought this I began to wonder if passers-by along the road might have seen a lean ecstatic face through the bars of the kitchen window, if great austerities would bring me fame, and remembered the character in one of Tolstoy's stories whose eyes brimmed with tears as he thought of his own goodness.

Knowledge comes through experience alone. I may know that, for instance, love is preferable to hate, but I love and hate indiscriminately until I experience love and hate in such a way that my own heart is torn by the conflict between them, and left broken but understanding.

I cannot see any other way now of approaching the problem of living. Action is exhilarating, but in the end nothing. Even action for others as an end in itself is nothing. It is only becoming pure of heart and so knowing God that provides a purpose.

August 13, 1936

Brian Lunn said he liked the bit of *The Bewildered Soul* that I showed him, but somehow I was not much cheered until he said: 'It must be a terrific effort doing real writing like that'. He's been working on his Autobiography. Walking up the road with him fairly late, he wheeling his bicycle and the lamp splaying out light in front of us, he said that the 'me' in *The Bewildered Soul* was a melancholy blighter, and that life was wonderful, and didn't I feel now how wonderful it was? I said I did.

August 15, 1936

I dreamt that I was debating with Willie Gallacher, the Communist Member of Parliament. The audience was hostile. 'If you tell me,' I said, 'that the only significance history, and your and my life have lies in the proportion in which what man's labour produces is distributed, I say that I know it is a fake. You may go on believing it, others may react to the opinion, but at last its falsity must be

revealed, as the falsity and barrenness of similar brands of Materialism have been revealed in the past.

'If you say that religion, and all those concerned to spread it,
have been motivated by a desire to keep the rich rich and the poor
poor, I say it is absurd. If you say that the asceticism of Saints,
the fantastic enthusiasm of mystics, was all assumed to enable
landlords to continue to oppress their tenants, I say you are arguing
more fantastically than the most preposterous theologian, and if
you say that these saints and mystics were not Machiavellian
conspirators, but poor deluded would-be gods, then I say that
what they wrote, everything we know about their lives, proves the
contrary.'

Someone shouts: 'Do they help us to get enough to eat?'

I reply: 'No, they leave you at the mercy of the wicked. Only
they reveal, for all who care to heed them, how it is possible to see
into the significance of life, and feel the principle of love at the
heart of it. In this way alone does life become tolerable and
satisfying.'

August 18, 1936

I went to London yesterday, took part of the MS of *The Bewildered
Soul* to Rupert Hart-Davis, finding him favourably disposed
towards the way it's done, and went to see the *Fortnightly* and
Time and Tide about work, also to Eyre and Spottiswoode for a
copy of my Butler book. It was nicely got up, and I turned over its
pages with great pleasure.

At night I lay miserably in bed, and Kit, in hers, suddenly said:
'We don't love each other. We only stay together because of the
children.'

August 22, 1936

I've just been for a walk. It's a perfect morning. Dawn was an
autumnal glow and the grass heavy with dew. As I walked along I
tried to concentrate my thoughts on the necessity to escape from
self and from the flesh if I was to know God. There was so much

testimony that this was the way, and the only way. Self and the flesh, I thought, have only justified themselves in an occasional frolic, and then only partially, whereas their denial has led to all that is great in men's history. Even good became bad without this denial, as in egotistical humanitarians like C. P. Scott. Protracted sensuality always becomes despicable. At adolescence it seems a way to the absolute but this illusion can only be sustained by keeping adolescent. (Cf. Bertrand Russell.)

August 23, 1936

I keep on coming upstairs to work, and instead of writing, read *A Philosophical Study of Mysticism* by Charles A. Bennett. It has convinced me that there is really nothing for me to undertake but the mystic's long and arduous journey. This involves (1) subjection of the self, (2) mastery of the flesh, both of its ills and rapture, (3) absorption in the principle of love, which governs the universe. To think of starting forth is delightful, like starting forth on a long walk or climb. The beginning is gay and hopeful, but how many weary, fearful hours will there not be? I have already wrestled long enough with myself to know that the will cannot be willed away. It goes only as a result of loving – to a small extent other persons, to a great extent God.

I know that love governs the universe. Then what can there be to fear? I know that whatever success or ecstasy might be mine it would be dust and ashes unless I felt myself at one with God. Thus I shall seek this success, and if I fail to find it my life will have been failure, and if I find it, my life will satisfy. No other measure is applicable. It does not even matter to me whether I manage to express this sense of oneness. Yet, too, it is its nature to crave expression, and if I get it I shall express it.

August 24, 1936

Kit and I went to church yesterday. There were about twelve people in the little church, and the clergyman was a quavering old fellow much bullied by his wife. I felt greatly moved by the service.

After all, I thought, we twelve people assemble here and thereby signify our acceptance of the fact that life is based on a Mystery. It is our tribute to the Incomprehensible – worship. It binds us together. Thinking of what I knew of the Church's history, I thought: 'It's values must be true or they would never have survived it'. Kit feels very much as I do about all this, and said so just before we went to sleep. We thought we might have the children baptised.

August 25, 1936

This morning I read the first chapter of St John's Gospel aloud, and when I got to: 'Hereafter ye shall see heaven open, and the angels of God ascending and descending upon the Son of Man', I was shaken with emotion.

August 26, 1936

It is impossible for me to describe the happiness I have felt the last day or so. This happiness is a consequence of feeling myself in contact with God. Suddenly, and for the first time, life has a significance for me other than just its horror, or bizarreness, or the sensations it offers. I see into the heat of it. I sense a purpose, and know that I am part of that purpose. I can measure what troubled or tormented me against this purpose, and it is nothing. The mystery of my own being is no longer oppressive or fantastic, but glorified, because belonging to the universal Mystery. These are words. They have not said at all what I felt as last night I walked up and down beside the church, with a red crescent moon and all the story in the sky, and murmured: 'I too am to know happiness.' It was like a child who had despaired of ever receiving presents suddenly being shown a Christmas tree loaded with gifts.

August 27–29, 1936

I've just read the sixth chapter of St John's Gospel, and did not care for it. I loathe the unmistakeable traces of megalomania in

Christ's character. These are only tolerable if his pretension to be
God's son in a special sense is accepted as valid. I cannot conceive
God having a son in a special sense.

Yesterday evening I again climbed up to the church. It was like
keeping a tryst. Again there was the red crescent moon, and the
warm fragrance of hay, and again I felt (but not as clearly as the
evening before) that my soul was with God in everlasting oneness.
'Everyone must live according to his own light,' I said to myself,
'and this is, and must for ever be, my light.'

I thought how the revelation that had come to me about life
was like falling in love. The sensations it engenders are love sensations – a melting within, a feeling of joy so intense that it can
scarcely be contained, a physical exhilaration even.

When I believed that I should do what I liked I was miserable;
now I believe I must do and not do whatever will keep my heart
pure enough to know God, I am happy.

I thought, walking along, that if I died now I should do so
convinced that I had experienced the best that life held for Man.

I woke up this morning at five o'clock. It was dark. Fears
crowded my mind. I was afraid about money, I was afraid about
work, I was afraid about health, I was afraid about sex. I wished
the ceiling would fall down and flatten me out. Suddenly my mind
switched from Time and the Will. The grey light just beginning to
touch the sky had broken for aeons thus, and would break thus for
aeons more. I, lying tormented in my bed, belonged to what had
pre-existed me, and would go on existing long after I was forgotten.
My fears were nothing. If every one of them proved justified, they
were nothing. What alone mattered was finding some contact
with what was outside Time. I reached out again for this. Unless
I have this I might not have lived. Merely realizing what I was after
brought peace. The fears dissolved.

September 29, 1936

I'm having one of my blackest of black patches, with the queer
pain at the back of my head I always have with them, and uncontrollable longing to die. Kitty is like an angel. I can't work.
Everything worries me. I'm indecisive, sitting down, getting up

again, starting for a walk. It's a wonderful bright clear autumn day, with the leaves just beginning to turn. As I walked along this morning I wrestled with myself, but all my efforts were drowned in a conviction that as I am now so I shall remain, that it will always be the same. The world is lovely and life is lovely, but I seem to have no part in their loveliness, except for occasional fleeting moments. Perhaps I'm diseased. Whom the Lord loveth he chasteneth. He chasteneth me.

October 5, 1936

On Sunday I went to London to see a Fascist demonstration. A young man drove me round in his car. He was a farmer at Rye, and, I found in the end, a blackshirt himself. There must, I thought, be some way of escaping the necessity of hate. I even dared to wonder if I might not find a way, but knew if I was to, or to do anything at all, first I must subdue myself.

November 3, 1936

I've spent some weeks in great misery, but now, as always happens, and must always happen, return to the pursuit that alone means anything to me – God. Many days I've spent pottering about this room, turning over books, finding a pretext for going up and down stairs, taking little walks.

I've been feeling ill. Kit and I have been getting on badly. I haven't been working. All this is symptoms.

I've reached my crisis. Now at last I shall either know what I must do, or do nothing – that is, die. For the world is dead to me. It is nothing, and I must be reborn in the spirit or not be reborn at all.

November 4, 1936

Take today, and a day is only a year or a life in little. I woke up fearful, as I sometimes do, with my heart beating fast. I got breakfast ready, looking askance at Kit when she came downstairs, dressing the children by the dining-room fire. After breakfast, Kit and I smiled at one another, and planned to drive up to London to go to a party at which all the guests are to wear Austrian peasant costume.

I came up to my room, lit a cigarette, and, watching the grey cold day, felt stirred, aware of what life was. This inadequately described the feeling I mean. It is a feeling that comes to me when I pause, a slight excitement, expectation, forgetfulness of Time and worries of Eternity. This description is also inadequate. I wrote for about an hour and a half, describing a visit to a psychoanalyst. Then I read the paper.

Before lunch I took a walk up to the village. I felt peaceful, bought a packet of cigarettes, thought how lovely autumn was. After lunch I came upstairs, sat and read a little, started to write a letter to Joseph Hone who has written nicely to me about my review of his *Life of George Moore*. Kit came and lay down on the settee. I resented her presence. My head began to ache. I must go away, I thought. I'll go to Germany. I'll borrow money. When Kit, feeling my resentment, went and sat downstairs, I asked her to come back. I insisted she should rest while I took the children out. They came with me, and I sawed logs, and cut some with an axe. As I wielded the axe I thought I might murder the two children. Then I'd be mad, I thought. Shall I, perhaps, go mad? I took the two children with me to fetch drinking water. Kit came out with her coat on. I told her to go back, and took the children up to the little church. Val cried, and I let her cry, and then harshly wiped her face. When I came in I went up to my room and lay down on the sofa, planning to get away, to borrow money and go to Germany.

November 16, 1936

I had a happy day. In the morning there were newspaper cuttings about *The Earnest Atheist*, which I read twice. I read *Lear*, and worked in the morning, in the afternoon looked in to see Hughie and went to the dentist, and in the evening worked again. What makes me so happy is that there is harmony between Kit and me.

I renew all my prayers.

November 17, 1936

A man in a nearby house used in the summer to sunbathe almost nude in his garden. Sometimes, he'd stand at his gate, and make overtures to passing females. Nurse said he'd worried her, and once Pan came in with a story that he'd been exposing himself to the village boys. A policeman came to see me about it. He told me there had been many complaints. Today, this man came to see me, said he was moving from the neighbourhood and had to have an operation, and would I like two goats that he'd got. He seemed a jovial sort of chap, and I joked with him. While I was joking with him, the same policeman who'd come to see me passed by, and I felt ashamed and wished I hadn't complained. Once before, when I saw the man leering at a woman on a bicycle, I thought: 'That's only what most of us do, only inwardly,' and felt horrified at his objectification of lust.

November 23, 1936

Instead of getting on with my book, I started typing out a political speech that I'm to give at Chester on Thursday for the Conservatives. As I did it, I felt it was very good; when I thought about it, I blushed. Kit was gloomy, and came up and began the old business about whether we should live together. I said our quarrels were just both our evil natures coming out, that if we left each other the evil would remain, that it had to be subdued, and that since we loved each other we should remain together.

November 26, 1936

At Chester a young woman met me. I felt ill-at-ease and unhappy. The Member for Chester presided, and introduced me as the son of a Labour MP and as one who had visited Russia. The audience was a few scattered elderly ladies. They did not understand what I was getting at, which is not surprising, because nor did I. Lady Hall, who had persuaded me to come, was a sad, distraught-looking old lady, who was disappointed because I wouldn't stay the night. The Chairman and his wife took me off to tea afterwards in a swell hotel, with the wireless softly playing. I had a feeling of deadness, of the usual moribundity. He seemed to agree with what I said and believed that a Centre Party would soon come into existence, and obviously he intended to belong to it. We talked in a political-gossipy sort of way, and I felt more and more wretched. Then the young woman took me to the station, and I caught a train to Crewe, where I'm now sitting in the waiting-room writing this.

On Crewe station I saw Winston Churchill, pale-looking, I thought, and unsure of himself. He bought a copy of *Truth*. In the carriage going to Stockport were three middle-aged men, one of whom said he knew I'd been on the *Manchester Guardian*, because he'd often seen me in the Thatched House, where he used to go for drinks. Being reminded of the *Guardian*, coming back into this smoky, misty, North, stirred me. I remembered the years 1930–32 as though they had been very happy. I had, I thought romanticizing, been so eager then, and become so tired, and unhopeful, and unappreciative of life.

Alan Taylor met me at Stockport. He drove me to his house at Disley, on a black hill-side, and we talked about all the people we had known. Margaret is pregnant, and looked nicer than I have ever seen her look. Their established nice house, and Alan's safe job at Manchester University, made me envious. I made up my mind that henceforth I must give up all idea of having any finger in the pie, and concentrate all my efforts and energy on literature. That is, write a novel.

December 1, 1936

Kit and I talked, and I realized how we were at one. We agreed that all that mattered was turning away from light. One does so turn away, one will so turn away, but never so as to lose sight of the light. As long as that doesn't happen, nothing matters, so there is no ground for fear.

December 2, 1936

When I saw Alan Taylor, he told me about Mrs Anson's death, and said what a wonderful story her life would make. She was a ferocious woman, the estranged wife of a clergyman, who shot off her own arm when the man she was living with threatened to leave her. I thought I'd jot it down while it was freshly in my mind, and found I'd begun on just the novel I wanted. Without any effort at all I've written 5,000 words, and scarcely started. They came easily, because, for the first time in my writing, I kept myself out.

Hughie rang up in the morning to say that the lawyers conducting a libel action for him had written for £25, and he asked if I could let him have £15. It embarrassed me because I'm terribly in debt, and only have about £50. However, I agreed to let him have it. Kit and I went round in the evening. I said I often worried about money, and Kit cried, because she felt I was not entirely sincere. I loved her so much this day, and realized how wonderful it was to get to admire someone you love more and more. People think that sensual allurements make love, but that only makes appetite. Goodness alone makes love, and Kit is good.

We gave a cocktail party and a lot of people came. Everyone was talking about the King's proposal to marry Mrs Simpson. After the party was over I drove Hughie back, and we walked up and down empty streets, imagining Mrs Baldwin getting what had happened that day out of Baldwin in their bedroom.

December 10, 1936

In the evening we sat listening to the wireless broadcasting the news of the King's abdication. I had the feeling that the affair somehow symbolized the whole horror of life, the struggle between Man's noblest, richest impulses, and the shoddy fabric of Time. Hughie described how he had once visited in Brittany the ruins of an ancient sacrificial Temple, and how there he had first realized what sacrifice meant – the offering up of Youth by Age, a spilling of young blood by withered arms, paying Life as a tribute of Death. I felt that this was true, and an outward manifestation of what goes on in each individual soul.

We drove Hughie back. Blackshirts were selling their papers in the streets surrounded by a circle of admiring girls. Kit keeps saying to me: 'Everything's going to be all right, isn't it?' and I nod without conviction. We went for a walk this morning. It was a perfect winter's morning. I said that most people managed to evolve either a sense of grievance, or illusions; but that I had neither.

December 11, 1936

I've written to H. A. Gwynne asking if he'll let me go to Germany for the *Morning Post*, and Leslie Marsh rang up today asking if I'd go on the *Evening Standard* for three weeks at the end of January. I gladly agreed to. Also, I've had a letter from Rupert Hart-Davis asking when *The Bewildered Soul* will be ready and I've promised it for January 15. Somehow I'll finish it if I sit up all night, night after night.

On Saturday I drove with the children to Croydon. Dad was out when we got there. When he came back, he looked unhappy and restless, and began to shout, as he always does when he's unhappy, about how he hated the Monarchy, but how there had to be humbug. I could see that his conscience was troubled. He told me how, on one occasion when Baldwin went to see the King, he had found him quite drunk, and how he picked up a glass to throw, and greeted him with: 'Well, you fornicating old son of a bitch, what do you want now?' I said my only regret was that he didn't throw the glass.

My father is one of the most tragic human beings I know, and in his way, one of the most loveable. He's obsessed with the idea that he lacks dignity, but his lack of dignity is due to a kind of raw sincerity, which has kept him from ever throwing in his lot with the Establishment. He finds life bitter just now, because he's out of things, and haunted by the idea that, being 73, he may soon find his faculties decaying, and become an object of pity. My mother worries him, too. Age makes her comatose. After his outburst, he put his arms round Val, and said something like: 'Well she's all right, anyway.'

We drove back in the dark. Kit said she didn't want me to stay with her if I didn't love her. I tried to explain how I felt –

no rancour in me, but coldness and despair – and then became hysterical.

December 18, 1936

These have been monotonous days, in which I've tried to work but got little done. I put by my Anson novel, *Ripeness is All*, which I could write so easily, to concentrate on *The Bewildered Soul* for Cape. I planned to re-write the whole, ten pages a day; in over a week I've got to page 17. The whole thing has fallen through. It's not the kind of book for me, and if it weren't for the £300 advance I'd abandon the whole project, and get on with the novel. However, *I must write it*.

I read a History of the Early Church, most interesting. When I described to Hughie how the Jews got frozen out of the early Church, and how convenient it was for the Gentiles that Nero threw mostly Jews to the lions, Hughie said the lions must have come to think of Jews rather as soldiers in the war did of bully beef.

December 25, 1936

I looked back on what seemed the most unsatisfactory year of my life, and forward to a most uncertain future. In the evening I cheered up, and suddenly felt myself near to Kit again. We talked about the children, particularly about Johnny and the nobility of his character. It is a curious fact that it is still, and always has been, tacitly recognized that nobility of character alone matters.

If I can make myself work steadily, there's nothing to worry about; if I don't work I shall founder anyway.

December 28, 1936

If ever I think to myself: That is truth, or: That is how things should be, or: That is how my life should be, I shall be wrong, and lost. At the same time, what I know now to be true, which is what men have always known to be true – viz: that love is better than hate, generosity than meanness, courage than fear, and so on – will always be true. Explicit values are always false. The only truth to live by is general. Christ denounced the Pharisees because they went in for explicit values, as: It is wrong to eat before washing beforehand. Christ taught general values, and refused to pronounce himself on specific issues, as Roman Imperialism, slavery, punishing an adultress. The reason was that a man might have slaves or be a slave or not have slaves quite apart from whether his heart was full of love or hate; and having a heart full of love rather than hate was, as Jesus saw the world, what alone mattered. He was right. In the same way, a woman might be an adultress and have a heart full of love, and not be an adultress and have a heart not full of love; or, of course, vice versa, therefore, it was absurd to allot punishment to an adultress as such. At the same time men seem to need moral codes, as they need money, and prisons and kings and judges. That is their doom – to need what must betray them into falsity.

December 29, 1936

I sawed wood in the afternoon. The sky was grey and lovely. A light rain fell. Sadness filled my heart. I shall never be happy, I thought; I shall never be other than I am; I envy no man; I am what I am.

January 1, 1937

The New Year begins ill for me. I'm in debt, I've had £300 advance on a book that should have been written three months ago, and still is not nearly done, and that I'm not getting on with. I feel as restless and unhappy as ever, and more settled in melancholy than I've ever been. At the same time I think my writing has improved, and that *Ripeness is All* will make a fine novel once I can get to it. Also, I'm still learning, and I begin to see the possibility of having, not settled convictions, but settled values. The worst thing is my health, which troubles me more and more. I so seldom feel well.

Kitty and I read the Book of Job aloud this evening. I love it.

I cannot see anything substantial that has been learnt about life since it was written.

January 3, 1937

This terrible melancholy that overhangs my days. What is it? People might say, 'liver,' or 'bowels', or attribute it to frustrated egotism, or loneliness and idleness. I know that these causes are partly responsible for it, but also that it arises out of something deeper. The basis of it is a deepening sense of the illusoriness of life in Time, I mean what is going on in the world, and the necessity to play a part in this more and more illusory activity. My appetites, my egotism, a need for money, drag me into it; other impulses hold me aloof, and melancholy results from the conflict.

Today I read, in James's *Varieties of Religious Experience*, experience after experience, particularly from Geothe, Tolstoy and Bunyan and Luther. Life lost its savour, they all said. It was not that they were failures, nor that their vitality went. They had no grievance, had not entertained hopes which had been bitterly disappointed. I, too, have no grievance. The world has treated me kindly. I have done those things I wanted to do. I have children, a home, interesting work, people who love me and whom I love, marketable abilities; yet I here record at the age of 33 that I have no wish to go on living, that I cannot conceive any circumstances in which living would be to me worth while.

January 4, 1937

We talked about the fear of Hell, and Hugh Kingsmill read out a remarkable essay by a Roman Catholic in the late nineteenth century arguing that Hell had been made fearful to differentiate it from Heaven, but that as compared with life on earth it was velvet. The reconciliation of the idea of a loving God with the idea of eternal torment was one of the most remarkable feats the human mind had ever performed. Hell up to Calvin was mitigated by purgatory and indulgences. After Calvin, it really was presented as the only alternative to salvation, and began to haunt human beings, for instance Bunyan, who was almost driven mad by the fear of Hell buzzing in his ears. It was a symptom of virtue becoming unhappy. Since virtue was unhappy there had to be terrific compensation for those who practised it. The unhappily virtuous would only be satisfied by a guarantee that the happily sinful were really for it.

January 5, 1937

This morning I got a letter from the BBC suggesting I should write a short story and broadcast it. This prospect of broadcasting appealed to my egotism. My father would listen, and the people in Whatlington. Then I started writing a story about Simla, but made no progress with it, and again all the day was wasted. Shall I ever work steadily?

January 7, 1937

I managed to do about 2,000 words of the Simla story and as I went along began to think it fairly good. Whenever I make myself work, I begin to feel better, and to work better. It seems strange, since I know this is so, that I don't always make myself work.

January 8, 1937

It is curious how illumination comes suddenly, when you have given in, and concluded there's no hope except in death. I woke up this morning anxious and nervous, as I so often do. It was an exquisite frosty morning with a clear hard sky and golden sunrise. Suddenly I was aware of Eternity. I felt it beyond time as I've felt love beyond passion. I saw it as I've seen the sea, a distant gleam, beyond a wide view. Fear went and peace came. There was nothing to be afraid of except forgetting what I then knew. There was nothing to be done except hold on to what I then felt. If I did that my life would achieve its purpose, if not it would be nothing. Success and failure were in any other sense irrelevant.

After all, this day finished in irritation and misery, with nothing done that was worth doing.

January 10–11, 1937

Hesketh and Gladys Pearson and I went for a long walk in the morning. Hesketh told a story about Brian Lunn. He was in Town once, broke, and longing to drink some beer. He looked into a pub and saw three men in the public bar with glasses in front of them. Without any definite plan he went in, picked up one of the glasses of beer and drank it slowly. When the man it belonged to began to remonstrate, he fixed him with his eye and said: 'You're dreaming!' very slowly and deliberately. The man fell back, and Brian beat a retreat.

Gladys said she had heard of a man who'd only sleep with his wife out of doors, preferably on commons on Bank Holidays. We imagined the scene when he got up and said he felt like a stroll.

January 12, 1937

The difference between Materialism and Religion is that Materialism deduces the individual consciousness from the material environment, whereas Religion sees the material environment as a body built round and connecting with the individual consciousness. Materialism is like saying that music depends on extant musiical instruments. Its range is governed by extant musical instruments, but it exists because the soul exists. The soul is the essential element. Music would exist if there were no musical instruments at all; if there were musical instruments but no soul, music would not exist. If at a particular moment a new kind of instrument is discovered, it may have the effect of extending the range of musical compositions, not their content. As far as content is concerned – a folk song or a symphony may contain as much or as little. Thus, though it is true that society is constantly changing, and that these changes affect the individual consciousness and all its manifests, it is also true that life remains the same, and that, as far as art is concerned, life is what matters. The author of the

Book of Job, and Shakespeare and Wordsworth, lived in quite different societies, and the imprint of the societies in which they lived is upon them; yet their common ground is more marked than their difference. This is because the artist must go beneath even History – that is, beneath Time. Materialism belongs to Time, and so, as such, offers no scope for art.

After a day like this when I worked well, knew no fear, was not frantic, went for a walk, dug in the garden, talked with Kitty, read for an hour or so, delighted in the grey sky and winter scene and remembered that spring was coming, kissed my children goodnight, and sit just now before going to sleep with a sense of being in harmony with life instead of finding it discordant: after such a day I feel an inexpressible thankfulness at being alive, and know that I've been as near perfect happiness as it is possible to be.

January 14–15, 1937

Kitty is going away to Switzerland for a fortnight's holiday. I drove her to Newhaven and saw her on to the boat. Whenever I part from her I have a premonition that I shall never see her again. This premonition reminds me of what a wonderful human being she is, so sincere and quick-witted and unworldly. We often quarrel but, knowing her as intimately and thoroughly as I do, I have a greater regard for her than for anyone I've ever known or shall know, and feel now, sitting alone, very incomplete, as though I was without something essential to my being.

January 18, 1937

Today passed pleasantly by, seeing to the children and the fires, writing a review and some letters, planting some rhubarb roots, reading three of James's lectures, and reading aloud from *Gulliver's Travels* to Pan. Also the BBC story has been accepted. I am seldom afraid now as I used to be. This is because I know that no evil can happen to me except by standing away from life. As long as I belong to life, since its purpose is good, so must mine be.

January 21–22, 1937

The Webbs came along on Sunday morning. I hadn't seen them since 1932, before I went to Russia. They were just the same, and rather self-consciously affable, as though insisting: 'Of course, we know you'll attack us and the Soviet regime, but we're people who don't mind in the least being disagreed with. That's your point of view, and this is ours.' We only showed our fangs once or twice, and that only momentarily, as when Beatrice said if Russia and Germany went to war Germany would be 'soundly whipped'. The children came up to see them, and shook hands with Webb as though he'd been some strange sea monster.

After they'd gone, I felt miserable. People like that implant doubts because they look at life so differently, and yet seem so sure of themselves. It's like a man who has with great difficulty given up smoking, meeting a robust, happy looking fellow puffing at a cigar who says he's been told and found out himself that tobacco is good for the system.

We went for a walk by the sea and on to Brian's house. Everything seemed delightful after the Webbs and we had an interesting talk. Brian said that the trouble with mystics was that they reached certain conclusions from direct experience, and then began to play about with the formulas of these conclusions, which is boring and unprofitable. I also discussed with him the point James makes that autobiography only occurs in Christian literature. Brian had found this independently in writing his book on Luther. The reason was, he said, that Christianity was the first religion to interest people in motives.

April 11, 1937

I have been reading *Don Quixote* which is one of the finest books I ever opened. It is much better than Swift, because much truer. Cervantes' yahoos are men, and Swift's not. The attitude of Sancho towards Don Quixote is like the attitude of the disciples towards Christ. The part where the galley slaves, having been freed by Don Quixote, turn on him, and rob him, is so poignant that I almost cried over it. Also, where Sancho calls Don Quixote the Knight of the Woeful Countenance, and he likes it, and says

he'll have a woeful countenance painted on his shield, and Sancho
says it isn't necessary.

> Waking, anxious and afraid, I saw
> Eternity in a clear winter sky.
> The sentiments were traced on frosted earth,
> Its golden radiance overflowed the sun.
> Why should I fear? I thought, and was at peace,
> And begged remembrance of that happy day
> When once again my soul in darkness sank,
> As sink it must, until its last release.

1942

Lisbon–Lourenço
Marques, 1942

In the years prior to 1939, ever since 1935 in fact, I had been certain beyond any shadow of doubt that another war was inescapable. Waiting for it to begin was inevitably an anxious time but by no means an unhappy one, as we continued to live in Whatlington. I remember particularly the beautiful summer weather in 1938, when each day seemed so precious because of the thought that such days might never return. Hugh Kingsmill and I met constantly; I still earned a modest living as a free-lance writer, and wrote two books – In A Valley of this Restless Mind *and* The Thirties. *The latter was a Book Society choice, and might well have established me as a writer, but as things turned out I wrote the last pages in a barrack hut as a private in the army, and by the time it was finished the war was in full swing.*

During the war years I wrote practically nothing. After being posted as an Intelligence Officer to GHQ Home Forces and 5 Corps, I found myself in MI6, the wartime equivalent of the Secret Service, which took me to Lourenço Marques in Mozambique, then to North Africa, and finally to Paris, where I ended the war as liaison officer with the French Securité Militaire.

March 19, 1942—Lisbon

I arrived here yesterday, leaving from Poole; a sad ruin. Kitty saw
me off in London. We have so often seen each other off, clinging
together on quays and on railway platforms. Love grows as passion
dwindles. Kitty woke up some mornings ago, there beside me, and
said: 'Only death can part us,' as indeed is the case. An American
I was talking to yesterday, a Consul in various places now returning
to the United States to retire, describing how necessary it was to him
to get the next plane because his wife was ill and in need of him,
as he of her – said: 'We've no life apart. All strong emotion died
long ago, but we're like oxen which have pulled together for forty
years.'

Here in Lisbon is the last vestige in Europe of our old way of
life now precariously existing. It is like the owner of some ancestral
mansion moving when ruined into the lodge with one or two of his
pictures, a piece of plate or so, one aged servant in threadbare
livery. Here are cafés, neon signs, money haggling, *petit déjeuner*
with fat pats of butter brought in on a tray, jangling trams and taxi
cabs and newspapers of all the nations. One deep and significant
change may, however, be noted – the pound sterling has lost its
magical properties; rub, rub at the lamp, and no all-powerful,
obsequious djinn appears, at best only a reluctant slut who must be
coaxed for any service at all.

With this important exception, an entirely familiar scene.
There are even some remnants of the enormous regiment of
dwellers abroad, income tax avoiders, makers of afternoon tea in
pension bedrooms, readers of the Continental *Daily Mail*, enjoyers
of the Mediterranean or other sun, driven at last, like rabbits when
the hay is being cut, to this one remaining, dwindling, sanctuary.
Alas, alas, poor souls; poor parasites, soon to be quite crushed out
of existence.

March 20, 1942

I looked in at a church service and felt respectfully disposed;
very envious of the devout. As one grows older, I reflected, one's
hopes for mankind become ever more circumscribed; what will
make them, perhaps, a little better, give them, perhaps, a momentary

awareness of what lies beyond the range of their senses, becomes greatly to be respected. Thus of Christianity one is inclined to be increasingly tolerant. It produces *some* reverence, *some* moral order, *some* dignity *in behaviour, *some* relief from the ego's maniacal raging, and from passion's maniacal insistence. Mysticism not based on love produces, in the end, only violence. Violence is the dark side of Mysticism and love the light side.

Later, I found my way by tram to the British Embassy. At the British Institute I arranged with a bearded Englishman to get lessons in Portuguese. Here at five o'clock each day a small company assembles to hear the news in English and to drink tea.

March 21, 1942

Again I went to church. As I knelt there I had an intense sense of having exhausted all earthly hope – 'Because there is none other that fightest for us, but only thou, O God!' I had no hope whatsoever of any satisfaction through the things of this world; I knew beyond any shadow of doubt that none of my fleshly pursuits, however successful, would satisfy my inward hunger, or ease my inward restlessness. Yet there was hope. Whence came it? From whom was it derived? Hopeless, I hoped; irretrievably lost, I saw a way. 'Put me upon this way,' I prayed, 'and strengthen me and sustain me to follow where it leads.'

Also I thought, here alone, in a church, is equality between man and man; no equality in intelligence, in beauty, in charm, in capacity, in physical or moral force, in any attribute, but only in a common sense of the mystery of all our beings.

March 23, 1942

I have now taken a room with a Portuguese family. It is very pretty by the open window looking on to a little courtyard-garden, at this season with many fragrant blossoms in it. Here I can compose my thoughts.

In the afternoon I took the electric train to Estoril, and had tea in the Casino. Innumerable waiters with polished buttons and white gloves stood about, and later came many people, and a band played, and there was dancing.

March 24, 1942 (my birthday – 39 years old.)

On the way back from Estoril I ran into Madame Antoine and her son. They had been on the plane coming over. They are returning to France, where she has a father and another son and a brother. It may be dangerous as her husband is serving with de Gaulle, and it will certainly be hard because of the food shortage. However, I quite understood her determination to return. It is what Kitty would have done – somehow assemble the family at home.

I have settled into my new room; at meals I stutter Portuguese a little, and go to the British Embassy each afternoon. The black servant waits at table. She is a curious looking creature from Cap Verde, hideous, and immensely amiable. On her black round cheeks she streaks a little rouge. Walking along the road I thought of her and of how like she was to old Lady Strabolgi – who was living as an exile in Monte Carlo but is now having to return home to Scotland – and of how like are all, all of us one to another, how essentially is the whole of life a oneness, and I had one of those moments of ecstasy which come occasionally. This was, I think, the most intense I have ever had. I had to pause in the road to collect myself. The ends of my fingers were tingling strangely. Ecstasy comes from a sense of identification, whether with another individual, or with a community, or with the whole of life. It is an escape from separate existence; from the savage misery of the imprisoned ego.

March 25, 1942

When I think of Kitty, it is not of when we were young; of moments of great happiness we may have had in one another, or of great misery. When I think of Kitty, I think of her as the pivot of a household, as my companion for fifteen years, to be my companion till the end; on whom my thoughts and plans for the future will ever centre, to whom, when I am away, I shall ever long to return.

I think, particularly, of how one day, the village boys went fishing, and how clumsy old John came back very disconsolate because he had been unable to catch anything, and how Kitty to cheer him up promised to go to the stream with him at daybreak the next day, and how they went. I saw them returning, side by side, along the road when the summer sun was still low in the sky; two figures very dear to me.

In the evening I went with my teacher and his wife to a kind of Lunar Park or Fun Fair here. The little teacher in his black suit, enthusiast for Esperanto, with his little wife, also a teacher, remarked on the absence of gaiety. It would be difficult to find gaiety anywhere just now, I suggested. Was it because of the war? he asked. No, I did not think it was because of the war, but because we happened to have lived, he and I, at a time when the particular civilization to which we belonged was expiring; now it seemed almost at its last gasp.

March 27, 1942

I have settled into a kind of routine, and days begin to pass by unnoticed. The Negress brings me my coffee at eight o'clock, and I drink it, and remember Portuguese words, and look at my Portuguese grammar, till nine o'clock, when I get up. Then for an hour or so I sit in the little sitting room, writing; then go to get the morning paper and read it in a café until lunch. I dread meals a little because they often give me indigestion. After lunch I do Portuguese; then at three o'clock go to the British Embassy, where I potter around until six doing odd jobs, or writing letters. At seven o'clock my teacher comes, and is with me till supper, which he generally has here. After supper I again go to a café; read a French newspaper, scribble, or just listen and watch. In the day I walk through the streets, perhaps, six miles altogether; walking along, sometimes wretched, sometimes dazed, a continuance with that queer ecstasy which lately has come to me more than ever before.

March 28, 1942

I feel quite at home in this household now, and enjoy meals more. The husband is a retired shopkeeper, eighty years old, and diabetic; his wife, also old, is a little plump woman, who serves him with his food, watches him closely while he is eating it, as though to see his reaction to each mouthful. Various people come into meals; my teacher and his wife, a seamstress who lives alone, a woman from upstairs about whom I know nothing. All day long the household is busy, moving cheerfully about, cooking, cleaning, washing, sewing. I love the noise of a household, especially the patter of children's feet.

Gringoire has a cartoon of Daladier, the French Prime Minister at the outbreak of the war, and underneath it: 'Enfin, messieurs, vous reconnâitrez que si j'ai été vaincu dans la bataille de France, j'ai été victorieux place de la Concorde!' It also quotes Daladier's past statements that France was armed and in every way prepared for war; that the Maginot Line had been extended to the sea.

March 29, 1942

Oh to hear the church bells ring out on a bright spring morning! It fills my heart with gladness, and reminds me of everything I care for most. Who, understanding anything of our past, can fail to find in this sound the very heartbeat of our way of life, our civilization?

I went to the cinema to see a Walt Disney production called *Fantasia*; very pretentious, mostly vulgar and superficial, with only here and there a touch of apocalyptic fervour where sheer horror of life found expression. All the same, I'm glad I saw it because it is an authentic product of the age – whimsical – scientific; sweetie-pie centaurs tap-dancing on Olympian slopes, evolution set to Stravinsky and Stravinsky set to evolution, plenty of culture, yet another Park of Culture and Rest.

Negley Farson, the American war correspondent and novelist, reports in the *Daily Mail* that Soviet Red Army Commissars 'were rather like Padres in our Army'.

March 30, 1942

Work is the only possibility now. I must work. The only work I have ever done in my life has been writing, teaching, and chores and gardening. Now I cannot teach, I cannot do chores and gardening, so I must write, and as soon as I know enough Portuguese, I'll read *Don Quixote* in that language.

I took my teacher, Mario de Caires, and his wife, to tea at the Casino at Estoril. Mario is a perfect specimen of a left-wing intellectual. I know him, and the working of his mind, as perfectly as if we had grown up together. It is, perhaps, a little sad to find in this last corner of Europe a little man in a black suit still arguing that if only people could be persuaded to learn Esperanto, if only they would be *reasonable*, abolish tradition and deal sensibly with their problems, all would be well.

I considered, with much quiet mirth, Sir Stafford Cripps, the British Government's Special Envoy to India, and Gandhi closeted together; sympathy entirely with, and money on, Gandhi. He knows the game; after Halifax as Viceroy, Cripps will be easy money. The British Raj then was still powerful enough to induce Gandhi to visit Halifax, now Cripps visits Gandhi.

April 1–2, 1942

The wife of the Director of British Studies at the University of Coimbra, a Scotswoman, former elementary school teacher, gives parties to Portuguese students, and attempts to teach them folk-dancing. A scene of ineffable imbecility; Singapore lost, but Sir Roger de Coverley danced in Coimbra.

Are people so little aware, I ask myself, of what is happening that they can suppose, when everything they stand for has proved weak in action, mistaken in direction, lacking in moral or even material purpose, that on them will fall the burden of shaping the future?

April 4, 1942

For Good Friday a procession round the Rossio Square – priests, a wax figure of Mary, a flower-covered bier, and swingers of incense, etc., most tattered, aged and unimpressive effort. Dead, I thought; alas, dead. When Mario, who was with me, piped up his little anti-clerical song, I shut him up too. Respect, or at least silence seemed called for in the presence of such a corpse.

April 6, 1942

I went yesterday to a bull fight, accompanied by a middle-aged Russian woman Madame Sazanov, emigrée twice removed, from Russia and then from France, and her son Dmitry. He came up to me and said rather apologetically: 'Je suis plein d'enthousiasme, monsieur'. It was true, the poor soul was full of enthusiasm. Later, he repeated the same remark. It appeared to be the sole content of his being – this sense of being 'plein d'enthousiasme'. The bull fight was exciting for ten minutes or so, and then rather boring. It was very like the war – all the worst features of bull fighting, deception, vanity, cruelty, etc., but no kill; same bull, it seemed, used again and again.

April 7, 1942

Besides their shops, British and German propaganda take equal space on the same page of the same newspaper, to advertise their wares, these being broadcast. I read French newspapers much, and feel great sympathy with their position – e.g. article in *Candide* – 'Où Allons Nous?' Their defeat is at least outward and visible instead of inward and invisible.

April 8, 1942

As I sat writing, I broke off to speak Portuguese with a workman; dark, vivacious, vehement man in blue overalls. Very anti-German and pro-English, as he insisted all Portuguese were;

immensely pro-Soviet, anti-clerical, fond of 'futeval', married, no children. England was, second only to Russia, the land of his heart's desire; many mansions, mansions of light and love. He associated his interests, quite fallaciously, as I think, with the two countries. In their success he might hope to participate; their failure he would share. He was a living demonstration of the Marxist theory, and also of its idiocy. It is the hopes of men which attach themselves to causes. They are the fire – hope for a larger, richer, ampler, more adequate life; and, of course, these hopes are always disappointed. Crusades, reformations, revolutions, etc. are a sudden boiling up of hope; religion, in the continuing sense, their opposite, is the acceptance of our lot here on earth, and the transference to eternity of the impulse to live. My heart is with the latter. I have hoped enough.

A half-caste woman is singing in the garden in the sun. A human being has only to sing spontaneously for hope to take possession of my heart, but not of any victory or defeat in this or any other war; hope of the outcome of life for me and all who ever have or ever will live, delight in life because of this life.

April 9, 1942

I said when we were shown round the offices of a Portuguese newspaper, and saw the great printing machine: 'Lo! the arsenal of Democracy!' 'Of demagogy!' I corrected. The journalist who conducted us said that the invention of the rotary press was the true birth of Democracy; but I insisted that there was born a technique of deception compared with which all hitherto known techniques of deception (e.g. necromancy, superstition, Divine Right of Kings, etc.), were ineffectual. Henceforth, it really was going to be possible to deceive all the people all the time.

Walking along, I saw a party of fisher girls with baskets of fresh fish on their heads; swinging their hips as they moved, their breasts firm, their complexions clear and fresh, in white blouses and with coloured shawls round their shoulders. Ah! to be a fisherman, I thought; to sail the lovely sea on bright spring mornings instead of aimlessly pacing sad city streets. Perhaps they too envied me as they hurried off anxiously to sell their fish. We envy one another's lives, imagining that what is different must be more adequate, and that others, living differently, escape our own unease. Those on the mountain top dream of the plains, and those in the plains dream of the mountain top, and none can find satisfaction.

April 10, 1942

An American journalist has written an article pointing out that Japan suffers earthquakes every thirty years, and that one is now due. Thus will the sinking of the American fleet in Pearl Harbor be easily avenged, and America's enemy easily be defeated.

In the night I woke up and thought I heard Kitty sobbing bitterly.

April 11, 1942

For the last twenty years it has been like a series of farewell parties, each one seeming veritably the last, but still departure delayed and another party arranged. In India, in Egypt, in Russia even, in Geneva, in England, in the Army, I have seen these parties. Now surely, here in Lisbon, the ship really has got steam up, and at any moment the gangway will be lifted and she will be away, for what sad destination who will dare to forecast?

April 12, 1942

I heard from Kitty that Dad had died at 6 a.m. on March 25. There were two letters.

'Your father now is dying. He is in the nursing home at Hastings. Your mother is staying with me. We go in the car to see him every day and stay about 20 minutes. He has lost his angry look and lies very still with a peaceful expression, and I don't think he any longer has any fear of death. He does not eat or open his eyes, and his hands lie on the bed very lifeless. He can with difficulty speak names – Douglas, Malcolm. Your mother is distressed because he does not look at her, and she tries to lift his eyelids and kisses his brow, but he cannot make the effort of recognizing her. I tell her that he knows she is there but is unable to say so. Sitting by his bedside, although he cannot speak, I feel closer in touch with him than before. I suppose being near to death H. Muggeridge is no more and he is just one of us giving up the ghost and therefore more familiar.'

'Your father died on March 25 at 6 in the morning. He died in his sleep. The funeral was on Friday, and his grave is in the churchyard here as you said it should be and Noble took the service. About 12 people came to the funeral . . . He was buried very quietly and the people came and had refreshments here and spoke to your mother. It was a lovely day and it did not seem a very sad occasion even for your mother who received her guests with a great air, was more like Val at one of her parties than a bereaved widow. I think his death was a relief to him and to her, and an atmosphere of great relief seemed to hang about him when in the church he was hoisted on trestles in his box, as if he was singing 'Ain't it grand to be blooming well dead!' We are going to plant his grave with flowers and have a stone with his name on it. I went up with Colonel Wilson to choose his grave and we decided to have a double grave so that your mother can be there too when she dies.'

These two letters were so exquisitely written, and so characteristic of Kitty, that I thought when I read them: what inconceivable good fortune to have such a woman for a wife. It is a benefit which I would not exchange for any other; no, not even to have written *Gulliver's Travels* or *Pilgrim's Progress* or *Don Quixote*.

Was somewhat stricken by the news of my father's death even though I expected it, and in a sense welcomed it. He has found release from a protracted agony. For him now is over the struggle to assert himself, to digest food, to provide for his daily wants and for the daily wants of those dependent on him. The scene at Whatlington was very vivid to me – the little church, the little company, the Rector and his words 'Oh death where is thy sting!' – the gathering in our sitting room where Kitty would have everything arranged as it should be, and then their departure, the ceremony over, and my father left in Whatlington churchyard, only to be occasionally remembered by those to whom he was dear. Thus proceeds the irresistible current of life, as one falls another moving up to take his place, my accumulating grey hairs promising me a like release. The ancient mystery stands. From where I am writing I see a white rose, in all its freshness, drooping over a trellis. Tomorrow its petals will fall, the day after tomorrow no trace whatsoever will remain of its ever having existed.

April 13–14, 1942—Monte Estoril

I have now moved away from Lisbon and its streets to Estoril, and sit looking at the sea. In the evenings I sit with Madame Sazanov and her son Dmitry, and she tells me about her adventures escaping from Russia after the Revolution, about literary personages in Paris, about Russian literature. It means talking in French and soon makes me tired. She is shabby, spirited, rather forlorn; her son sickly, pathetic, rather sweet-natured. They will push along together, he dreaming of being an aviator, she hoping for little, and in that praiseworthy. This evening she arranged chessmen on the table to illustrate the Russian Front, the queen Leningrad, the king Moscow, the other pieces smaller places. After lunch she came up to my room with 'des petites choses qui peuvent vous intéresser.' The petites choses turned out to be a collection of British and Free French propaganda. These two are exiles, hopeless, rather weary they cling to the idea of England; there, perhaps, clinging to nothing.

April 16, 1942

Lunched with Rita Windsor and others from the Embassy, including Press Attaché, at English Club, piece of land forever England, leather chairs, subdued light, florid men reading newspapers, etc., etc. Inevitably discussed war. Rita said we were fighting for a chance to go on living as we were accustomed to, though as a matter of fact there was no possibility of our doing so in any case. It was, I said, like fighting a duel over a woman who was in fact dead and buried. But suppose, little man called Bush said, you won and had to sleep with the corpse. I agreed that that was the most appalling prospect of all. Bush took me afterwards to see the procession in connection with installation of the President for his third term of office. Troops, cavalry, naval contingent, etc., etc., and President Carmona driving by in open carriage with coachman of English type (in 17th and 18th centuries, France copied; in 19th England; e.g. in uniform peaked caps, now Germany is beginning to be copied), with the Prime Minister, Salazar, beside him. Dense, but not particularly enthusiastic crowds.

Madame Sazanov remarked this evening that as between 3/6 and 300/600, there is no progress; no more is there progress as between one horse gig and 50 horse-power aeroplane, or between mud hut in African jungle and block of service flats. No, nor retrogression either; only another version of the same fraction.

April 21, 1942

I go along perhaps for some days, and then suddenly it comes, as this evening climbing a hill, at the top the sea spread out before me, fragrant and limpid the air – a sudden happiness possessing my heart, penetrating to each corner of my being, like an electric current, physical; all fear gone, burden of self lifted, nothing to dread, nothing to regret, complete trust in whatever has shaped my destiny and the destiny of all life:

> 'Let us with a gladsome mind
> Praise the Lord for he is kind.'

I say. This is Grace.

Correspondent of *The Times*, Douglas Brown, formerly on *Manchester Guardian*, haunted, like others here, with not being in the Army. Easy for me to reassure him on that score. Lunched and talked and walked the streets together, saying nothing notable, but pleased to talk. 'This is us,' I said in effect; 'Let us not try to be otherwise, mighty warriors, stirrers up of the multitude, etc., content to be two talking away an afternoon, while thunder roars and lightning flashes across the sky; content to try and understand; words; for us, forever words.'

April 22–23, 1942

Visa granted, soon perhaps to leave for Africa.

De Gaulle wants to change the name of his movement from 'Free French' to 'Fighting French'. 'Free' not an epithet much thought of these days; rightly, I think. Clearly, it is to the extent that de Gaulle's troops are 'fighting' rather than to the extent that they are 'free' that they will survive.

Fascinating episode to describe in 'Decline and Fall of British Empire' will be Cripps' visit to India; long discussions there between this desiccated high-minded lawyer and other lawyers, Brahmins, with soft bellies and faces, and sacred thread under shirts and sometimes waistcoats – discussions about the disposal of Authority almost spent, about the delegation of powers which scarcely exist, about constitutional changes when shortly there will be no constitution to change or not to change.

The people sunbathing all day by the sea exude sexuality because they are so indolent. Lust is a product of idleness, and is most base. Nazi propaganda – toutes comforts modernes, tous les sports, etc, soldiers, athletes, factory workers, female as well as male, all with their mouths wide open in identical exaltation. These two – sunbathers indolently erotic and the identically exalted, represent, respectively, the civilization which is being degraded and the new order which is being created. Feel no urge to defend the one or prepare the way for the other, though perhaps any activity is better than passivity, any purpose better than no purpose at all.

April 24–26, 1942

Unquiet, apprehensions coming in crowds, sense of the war, its unreality, unreality of my situation here and of the journey soon to be undertaken, empty words sounding in my ears, echoing emptiness in my heart. What is to happen? What can happen? How can any happening be of significance? Why? No interest in 'Why?'; no real interest. Drifting onwards, drifting onwards. Life's a poor *pension* . . . Confused, unhappy, futile thoughts passing through my mind, and always the clear, permanent thought – it will always be the same. Go here, go there; be this, be that, it will always be the same.

Spoke with Mrs K about the war and why it should seem so dreamlike – because we had been so fed on lies. I looked back with disgust on the teeming lies of recent years – lies about wealth, lies about poverty, lies about strength, lies about weakness, hopeful lies and despairing lies, all lying, in spoken as well as in written words, in thoughts even, as many and as varied lies as there were slimy things with legs crawling about the Ancient Mariner's slimy sea. And now there is no longer the possibility of lying because there is no truth left, no means of detecting or estimating lies. When currency inflation goes beyond a certain point there ceases to be any currency; only soaring figures. So with lying. Perhaps the war has never taken place, perhaps it will never end; its beginning was announced without it being begun; its end may be announced without it being ended. There is no possibility of knowing anything about it; begotten and conducted on lies, it will end in lies.

April 27, 1942

In the train into Lisbon I read Hitler's speech – everyone reading it, discussing it, conscious of it – which had been furiously delivered to rows of identical Germans mechanically cheering whenever a cheer seemed required, in Kroll Opera House. Through the Portuguese translation, read by me with difficulty, felt the strange power, the *interest*. Though nonsensical, strangely enthralling; though nonsensical, perhaps in some strange way true, though not for me. Where there is life, however strange its manifestations, however tortuous the form it takes, there is the gleam, the glisten, the glow. Only death is dull.

In the evening dined with Shell Manager, a minor princeling, or satrap, in the great Kingdom of Oil – large, unhappy, at heart doubtful even of Shell Company, which, he explained ironically, made more profit the more oil wells were captured by the Japanese.

April 28–28, 1942

Madame Sazanov said that now she was going to America she looked with different eyes at the furniture and walls of this *pension* where she has lived for two years. In the same way one looked at all creation just before dying – with tenderness and inexpressible relief. La lutte, the struggle, is over and the scene of the struggle, the companions in it, all its circumstances, become touched with light like the trunks of trees when the sun is setting.

May 1, 1942

Went again to Cintra and climbed up to ancient monastery, now deserted. We saw the tiny cells, the slab of stone which served for dining table; chapel, chapter, walks and stone seats for meditation; all arranged among rocks, high up, remote, a true Hermitage, now abandoned, object only of curiosity, not of use. Felt in my heart the thirst, the overpowering longing, surely experienced by some at least who lived there, to know the peace passing understanding which comes of having truly left the world behind and truly escaped from the unquiet of desire. Like as the hart panteth after the water-brook.

Had a batch of letters from Kitty and the children. Read from Kitty: 'Things seem to have little ending, and I often wake early in the morning before it's light and think of you, and wonder when you will be home again.' I, too, often wake at that sad time and wish I had with them a settled life, and watch the morning come across the sea, exquisite rose, with no desire to live the coming day. Thought: 'How blessed is one who has a loving wife. Not all the treasure in the world can command this blessing, available to slaves, and mine.'

May 4, 1942

We spoke of our fellow *pensionaires* – what did they do with themselves? How did the hours pass with them? – 'En arrangeant nos vies qui n'existent pas,' Madame Sazanov said.

May 17, 1942—At sea between Lisbon and Madeira

Left Lisbon without many regrets; memorable, all the same. Memorable the lights of Lisbon because in the whole Continent of Europe scarcely anywhere else lights, yet there even Lisbon lights now in process of being diminished. Everywhere lights must be put out, in accordance with immutable law whereby outward and visible must conform with inward and invisible.

Required to take with me diplomatic bag, provided with special passport for this purpose; not, however, treated with much deference, stench of deceasing empires fairly strong, and soon discerned. Men bow their heads before the setting sun.

Scene of boat's departure somewhat touching; immense crowd packed into an open space in front of the quay, all chattering, reaching towards the ship for one last contact with a body, strong relationship or friendship or love become dear; then the last frail link with dry land – the gangway broken; gently, but immutably, the boat drifting away. I with no one to wave to or to be waved to by, participated in the general emotion, thinking sadly of Kitty and the children.

May 22, 1942

Fellow passengers on *Colonial* mostly Portuguese; spend my time with Swiss and Frenchman, both in Diplomatic Service. Frenchman formerly commanded destroyer, young-looking, most honourable and courageous; a truly loveable, rather sad man used to being alone. Speak much with him about the collapse of France, and perfectly understand his situation. Find such a one infinitely more congenial than all emigrés, romantic or squalid or both. To accentuate the contrast, and my preference, party of Belgians full of stories, perhaps true, of amazing shifts and adventures which brought them out of Belgium. For myself, now and for ever, prefer order to disorder, discipline to indiscipline, standards of behaviour to lack of standards. Of the Frenchman I know how he would behave in this or that contingency, what he would do, what not do; of the Belgians know nothing at all, cannot predict their behaviour.

Between Bissau and San Tomé

At San Vincenti, there got on boat a fantastic Englishman, residing normally in Bournemouth, now Diplomatic Courier passing from place to place on sweltering African coast. Eye-glass in eye, he wandered watchfully about boat looking for girls; spoke of war, his confidence in victory; wife in Bournemouth still, where he had with difficulty persuaded her to wear trousers for purpose of fire watching, with whom, when victory was won, Empire all regained, enemies all defeated, he would perhaps settle in Portugal procuring servants easily, reading *Thr Times* quietly in the sun, and after lunch taking a nap. Ancient playboy, very lecherous, another Knight with Woeful Countenance, strangely campaigning for justice, freedom and truth.

June 6, 1942—Lobito

Arrived here after three weeks voyage, latterly most tedious. Staying in British Consulate by the sea, in little room, quiet. Boat ploughing along African coast, stopping occasionally (once at little island, San Tomé, quite tropical), boring little world, me included. As always, often melancholy; often looking down into the sea, dark or light, glistening or sombre, with deep longing – longing which would crystallize for Kitty and the children, for death, for nothingness, for achievement, for peace and seclusion, but only for a moment, soon just longing again, just a soul unsatisfied, just a conviction that nothing which could happen to me, nothing which I might do or not do, would satisfy a hunger unsatisfied.

Much interested in the French Naval Attaché on his way to Tokyo. A solitary; like Swift, morbidly sensitive about his body, after having his hair cut changing all his clothes, bathing; enormously industrious, hours and hours studying Japanese, writing long letters; breaking off suddenly, a walk or conversation, to go away to work or to be alone; somewhat slow-witted, but strong, resolute, vain perhaps; unable to hide his annoyance if he lost at dice, surprisingly ready to tell dirty stories, but telling them well; on politics not well informed, on the whole uninterested, sulky for a day after hearing that a friend had been killed when the English attacked Madagascar, loyal to Vichy but rejoicing in every German reverse, at heart anti-English; but I was always glad to pass time with him.

At Lobito I saw off the *Colonial* and waved on the quay as the boat was unloosed, and gently moved away, in the evening light; a pang in my heart, something familiar gone, and I left standing as darkness suddenly came; turned back to the Consulate, treading the dusty road.

In the evening my train. Thenceforth, for two days, till the Angola frontier, the same – puffing along, over land now instead of sea; stopping occasionally at little stations, instead of at little ports. Arrival of weekly train an event in these places, all Europeans, all with any white blood, coming to see it steam in and steam out, making contact with the only thing which joined them to cinemas, lighted streets, cafés – like a beggar peering in through a window at remote festivity and warmth. In the restaurant car I chatted away to a farmer, to a doctor, to a veterinary surgeon. Chattering, chattering, the miles passed by, and the hours. As each got off the train, he said goodbye warmly to those continuing. Company melted away until at the Angolan frontier I alone remained. At the frontier long wait, there taken for a cup of tea by missionaries; Plymouth Brethren, elderly man, his two daughters, some ladies. Round a table we sat drinking tea and talking about God and the Bible; kindly, cheerful. I even thought – suppose I stay with them here, going no further. 'If the Bible is lies,' the elderly man said, 'then we'd lived on lies for 2,000 years.' 'Not lies,' I assured him, 'certainly not lies.'

June 14, 1942—Elizabethville, Belgian Congo

Arrived here after long journey, dust, immense distances of desolate land, chilly mornings, tepid afternoons, still evenings and nights when, like a swimmer, my soul dipped under the surface of things, treading profundity, treading, and finding no bottom, emerging again to the surface, half suffocated, to spit water and gasp for breath.

Nairobi

Three days in bed with stomach upset; days which passed peace-
fully, rather happily, sleeping, waking, reading Flaubert's *L'Education Sentimentale* and greatly admiring it, therefore longing to
write again myself, planning, greatly stimulated by the other's
spirit, entirely understanding – e.g. 'En plongeant dans la perso-
nalité des autres, il oublie la science, ce qui est la seule manière
peutêtre de ne pas souffrir.'

June 24, 1942—Nairobi

'Au fond, je sens que ma vie est toujours gouvernée par une foi
que je n'ai plus.'
                    Renan *Souvenirs d'enfance et de jeunesse*

Staying now at Government House, servants, car with flag,
black soldiers who present arms, etc. Governor, small Pickwickian
figure, kindly, shrewd, remarked that indication of our lack of
belief in ourselves and our civilization was that we no longer
attempted to make blacks like us but insisted they were better as
they were. Sad place Nairobi, like India, Twilight of Empire, all
over and done with. Young secretary attempts to suggest that, on
the contrary, wonderful new possibilities opening up, Empire
based not on fear but on genuine collaboration, etc. Governor,
wife and I listen politely. Youthful secretary's words come from
afar, no meaning in them at all.

July 4, 1942—Lourenço Marques

More or less continuously ill now since Elizabethville; journey
from Nairobi therefore very exhausting – train to Mombasa, then
flying boat over the same Africa as before, illimitable expanses
mostly of desolation. Night in Mozambique, then over the Zambesi
to Beira.

Here now for one week, installed in office at British Consulate,
finding much to do arranging papers, sending telegrams, etc.
Live in large expensive hotel overlooking the sea; wonderful

scene, to me quite savourless. In hotel German and Italian Consuls also resident, some complications in occasional meetings. German, a Bavarian, rather pleasant looking, plays piano, heard him playing German sentimental music to celebrate fall of Sebastopol. Has his small circle of Portuguese hangers-on; comes and goes, on Saturdays appearing in shorts with small Bavarian green coat.

July 16, 1942

In the Polana Hotel, Camille, a Pole with whom I have to deal, said to me: 'C'est une question de l'argent, je suis comme un nouveau né.' Then we settled down to haggle.

I continue with my Portuguese lessons, my teacher now an elderly, well-preserved Portuguese lady, well born (so she says) and a devout Catholic. She told me of someone she knew who died in Rome and who as he died said: 'The trees speak to me.' This I thought very beautiful.

All day long I am occupied with telegrams, seeing people, etc. It fills the days as they pass.

1945–1946

Diary 1945–1946

April 29–30, 1945—Whatlington

I have decided this evening to keep a journal again. Probably the decision was the effect of reading Fabre Luce's prison journal *Ecrits En Prison*.

The war has virtually ended, and I'm back at Whatlington, just as I was five and a half years ago, in my same room, looking out of the same window, turning over the same books; only five and a half years have gone by. During these five and a half years I've been here and there, and committed many follies, and sometime I suppose I shall write an account of them. The last six months I've been in Paris. Now I have to begin another life, the Nazis having been defeated. The Nazis were supposed to destroy my life, along with much else, but they've failed, and I'm left now with it on my hands – a rather battered, shabby affair now. There's supposed to be something wrong with my lungs, but whether there really is, or whether it's just pretence I'm not sure. Certainly I don't feel well – inert, without much will – but that may have another explanations. It's cold like winter, and I've spent the day by the fire with Kitty coming in and out. The one desire I have is to shake off my inertia, product of much idleness, and work again – that is, write.

But for the moment I have little desire to write about those five and a half years, or indeed anything; all I really want to do is to sit and look out of the window. The effort to write is too great to be made, and even when I read I go on for a while and then must pause. The war now seems like a dream, and might never have happened. I might have been sitting here in this room all the time instead of going here and there. Looked back on the war has no substance. I can recall different incidents, different places where I went, but only as one recalls a dream. Action, a product of the will, leaves no trace behind; only the imagination is permanent.

May 2, 1945

Gradually, picking up the threads of life.

I lunched with Tony and Violet Powell and T. S. Eliot. Eliot has improved enormously, largely, I understand, because his wife has been put in an asylum. We were gloomy together in a good-humoured way. I say to myself all day long: 'I must work, I must work' and don't work.

Saw Hughie Kingsmill after lunch and talked about Mussolini's end and Hitler's; laughed about all the strange events now happening. I felt a great desire to describe it all, to write contemporary history. Of all my friends I most enjoy Hughie's company.

May 5, 1945

Back in my room, not very tranquil. I awoke in the night, and poured out despair to Kitty, which in the morning I scarcely remembered. Hugh Trevor-Roper is staying here, nice but argumentative. He said that I looked like the devil – appearance rather Satan-like, and sometimes truly evil; sometimes on the other hand goodness uppermost, mystery of things taken upon me – Jekyll and Hyde true of all existence, collective and individual; love, for instance, monstrous lust on the one hand, and on the other ecstasy in the ego's momentary disappearance. Actually Jekyll and Hyde represent rather order and disorder than good and evil. Love after all combines the infinite tenderness of ego for ego, of flesh for flesh, with benignity for all life. It is therefore peaceful.

May 8, 1945—(The Diary of a Sad Man)

Today is the official celebration of the end of the war. I walked up the hill to get some cigarettes, and saw each cottage decorated with little flags. It is just what I did on the first day of the war.

I am supposed to be ill; sometimes I think it is really bad and will be the end of me, and sometimes I think it is just an outward and visible manifestation of my inward and invisible desire to escape from the bondage of human life. All my desire is to turn my eyes away from time and towards eternity. Like a prisoner I long to escape, and think hopefully of the completion of my sentence. Meanwhile there is the prison routine, and this too has its moments. In the end, however, returning always to peering through the bars with incoherent longing. As I write it has begun to rain – rain falling gently on the still green countryside, and the birds still singing.

May 9, 1945

We went to church yesterday. The parson said: 'Let us pray for a new world.' What a foolish prayer! Better the old prayer for that peace which the world cannot give, for the granting of petitions as may be most expedient. 'Lead kindly light amid the encircling gloom,' we sang after we had prayed for a new world; an exquisite line which made me again think of Newman.

May 18, 1945

At noon I went along to the *Daily Telegraph* to see George Bishop, the Literary Editor. He was sitting in an office surrounded with new books; pleased with himself, I thought. Bishop took me down to see the Editor, Arthur Watson, brother of Alfred Watson of the Calcutta *Statesman*. Watson asked me if I wanted a job, and I said that in principle I did. He asked me if I could write leaders, and I said that I could. (Can I still?) Perhaps I shall take a job there. Something told me I should get to know this office well. He asked me if I believed in private enterprise, and I hedged, genuinely unable to say whether I believed in it or not. He set his little wry mouth and said that he believed in private enterprise. It seemed to me that he clung to this belief savagely, it being the only belief he had; if so, a poorish one, I thought. We parted amicably.

May 19, 1945

I am sitting in the garden in the sun, and once more feel at peace. This morning I worked for two hours. I found myself writing easily again. I shall go on and on now.

May 28, 1945

'If I search my heart,' I said to Hesketh Pearson, 'I cannot discover that I wish ill to any living creature.' As I said this my eyes filled with tears and the curious ecstasy of love, general not particular, spread like warmth through my whole being. It is this sensation that the mystic pursues. I think in the end he falsifies the emotion in pursuing it, vide J.-J. Rousseau. In basing everything on a perfectly authentic mystical love of nature and of his fellows in the abstract he lost contact with earthly reality, and in losing that contact failed any longer to attempt to relate his own actions with his own convictions. For instance, he loved mankind, but engaged in squalid morbid quarrels with the individual men and women with whom he had come into contact. Thus everything was falsified. He lied about others and about himself. At last he was mad. A man who is wholly mystical is as misguided, though not as objectionable, as a man who is wholly materialistic – not as objectionable because mysticism is at any rate imaginative. Rousseau is surely to be preferred to Karl Marx.

June 1, 1945

Today I began on the *Daily Telegraph*. It was somewhat drear – old Watson seated at his desk; Bailey, another old veteran, and I discussing the day's news, Watson then disappearing to see Lord Camrose, the proprietor, and returning to say he required one leader on Syria and one from me on Burma. On Burma I duly tapped, writing almost automatic, after so many years easily coming, complete rot. Sharing my office is J. C. Johnstone, rather charming, formal, previously on the *Morning Post*. He asked me if I minded him walking up and down as he 'composed with difficulty' – whole effect very twilit, making me feel that this little calm at the end of the war presaged more and worse storms, a stillness with much to follow.

I am determined now to work and the essential thing is to plan my day. What I propose is to write in the mornings; then after lunch to read the papers and prepare for work at the *Daily Telegraph*, then in the evenings to do other writing and reading.

July 9, 1945

Lunched with Tony Powell and George Orwell, the latter exactly like Don Quixote, very lean and egotistic and honest and foolish; a veritable Knight of the Woeful Countenance. We had met before in Paris. A kind of dry egotism has burnt him out. Hughie Kingsmill and Hugh Trevor-Roper joined us afterwards, and Hugh Trevor-Roper said that Orwell wrote like Johnson. Hughie would not have this at all, and shouted out 'Cobbett, Cobbett!'

I am editing the Diary of Count Ciano, Mussolini's Foreign Minister and son-in-law.

Hughie came to supper and we strolled along afterwards to where I'm now living in Buckingham Street, a room overlooking the river and Temple Gardens. When we arrived a band was playing and people were sitting about listening. Hughie said it reminded one of love (which was true); people liked it because it was love without any of the anguish. We looked out of the window rather sentimentally, agreeing that it was pleasant to feel so detached. Younger, one would have been looking round hungrily for girls. We remarked how difficult it was, once action was over, to recover any sense of its reality. It was just like a dream. Hughie quoted Wordsworth:

> 'Action is momentary . . .
> 'Tis done, and in the after vacancy,
> We wonder at ourselves like men betrayed.'

October 31, 1945

In the morning Cholerton came in. I was trying to work. 'I know I'm being a nuisance,' he says when he is being a nuisance, in such a way as to make it impossible to stop him going on being a nuisance. He saw us together once, and had very strongly the feeling that he was a shadow of me, a sort of emanation. I said he was the ghost of Real-Politik, an embodiment of my own unreal involvement in affairs. It was like Poe's story of William Wilson, who went mad because he was constantly confronted with his own image in terms of his baser nature. To get my own back on him, the next day when he was speaking about some Swami who had bored him the evening before, I said he deserved it, and that the Swami was the ghost of Real-Mystique.

Kitty and I dined with Colin Coote, Deputy Editor of the *Daily Telegraph*. He spoke of his wife dying of cancer, and said the most terrible thing about it was the smell. She, I had heard, turned against him towards the end – her loathing, his repugnance.

November 1, 1945

In the morning I went to Heinemann to arrange editing the Ciano Diary, and foolishly failed to fix the terms. This irritated me afterwards, especially as it was Frere himself who got the better of me.

Afterwards I saw Hughie Kingsmill. He is moving out of the *Punch* office, and even that change seems abhorrent. Life is like a cold bath, which can only be endured by keeping quite still in it.

November 2, 1945

Kitty went off to Battle (where we have taken a little house), and all day I felt sad, indeed do still. After lunch George Orwell and I walked together along the Embankment. His *Animal Farm* is really very fine.

Brian Lunn is just back from Austria, where he has been working in the Interpreters' Pool of the Control Commission. His extraordinary life goes on. Now he is going to marry Belinda, the sister-in-law of his divorced wife. On his return to London he arranged to meet her in the London Library, and had one of his fits, so that she arrived to find him stretched out under a sheet.

He said that at any rate he'd never be asked for his subscription again. We talked about his Autobiography, which Graham Greene is going to publish at Eyre and Spottiswoode. As usual, he was well on the way to getting tight.

November 3, 1945

Cholerton had more tales of the behaviour of the Russians in Germany, and I boiled over with rage, not at the Russians, but at the corruption of those in Western Europe who insist that this canaille represents progress, freedom, etc. Cholerton calls the Slav Russians at the top 'performing seals'.

Hesketh Pearson came to dinner and we talked till midnight. I walked with him to the station – the streets were dreamlike and rather sad. Everything, I said, was an image of everything else. To illustrate the point, I pointed to a woman walking between two men, one tall with his arm round her shoulder, and the other minute, and reaching up to put his arm through hers, and said it was exactly like England, America and the Atomic Bomb.

November 6, 1945

Kitty's brother, Bill, staying with us, described his experiences as a prisoner-of-war in the Far East. Not being egotistic, he gave the impression that things weren't too bad – Japs mostly not unreasonable, Chinese kindly and helpful. He had to march from Singapore to Siam and all along the road local villagers arranged heaps of bananas and limes for them to take as they went past. Innumerable such acts of kindness took place – e.g. rickshaw coolie who carried his stuff and would not take money – all of which show that the over-simplifications of revolutionaries and patriots – natives hating white oppressors, or European rule depending on maintaining prestige of white races – are as ever rubbish. Hughie and I agreed afterwards that egotism is what makes for extremes, whether of delight or anguish, in describing experiences. Egotism is a kind of mental spotlight.

'So little trouble do men take in the search after truth; so readily do they accept whatever comes first to hand.' – Thucydides.

November 8, 1945

Very good speech from Ernest Bevin, the Foreign Secretary. In the course of it he said that he often watched children in parks drinking at the public fountain, and some of them took two cups of water and some only one, but there were no disputes because the water was abundant.

November 10, 1945

Spent a miserably jovial evening with Kitty and Kim Philby and his wife Eileen. Drank too much, and mixed drinks badly. Wondered afterwards why it was so miserable, and reached the conclusion that it was due to the falsity of my relations with Kim, the disproportion between form and substance. (Misery is always thus, and so, curiously enough, is humour. Poetry is *conscious* disproportion, humour disproportion which is implicit made explicit.)

November 12–13, 1945

Wrote a leader on Egypt, very foolish. Tormented with the feeling that I ought to leave the *Daily Telegraph* and settle down to write.

A man at Newnes Press asked me to contribute regular book article for a new monthly. Agreed and was afterwards overwhelmed with the idea of all I was taking on one way and another, and the fatuousness of merely earning money.

November 14, 1945

I lunched with Bernard Causton who is now in Austria where things, he said, were not too bad. He is a large, incoherent character who is occasionally amusing – for instance, quoting a *Sunday Times* correspondent in Czechoslovakia who once remarked that 'he sometimes wondered if he was licking the right boots'.

November 16–19, 1945

Saw George Orwell, Julian Symons, brother of A. J. A. Symons, and a funny little man George produced who is responsible for the Commonwealth Party. We were all anti-Communist, but for different reasons, and it was interesting how we disagreed about our agreement. I wrote a leader on de Gaulle's resignation, very anti Thorez, the French Communist leader. Cholerton told me that Thorez had broadcast from Moscow after the breakthrough at Sedan in 1940 urging the French to stop fighting.

Sleeplessness – you wake up, or half wake up, and your mind begins to turn over and over like motor car wheels in the mud which don't stop; words you've spoken, words you've written, repeat like stale garlic. The day is just beginning. Out of my window I see the grey river and November fog. The trains are always running. Kitty wakes and smiles across at me, and I am comforted. Before, I thought with a pang of longing – How wonderful to die! Another day to be lived through. I feel like St Jerome's lion, wondering why he was beating himself. For some reason my thoughts keep turning to Paris, to de Gaulle, as though whatever happens there were of great moment – as indeed, it is. I finished up my leader yesterday with: 'At the lowest point in her fortune, France found an inspired leader. Surely she needs him still.'

Hughie mentioned a splendid Air Force saying – that out of the ashes of the balls-up of today rises the Phoenix of tomorrow's fuck-up.

November 20, 1945

Kitty's mother, Mrs Dobbs, arrived. Her strangeness strikes me anew each time – something queerly animal about her, senile. Kitty said she did not believe in her existence and often wanted to go to look when she's gone to bed to see whether she was still there. Kitty also said she was like a vampire living on others' blood: she comes ruddy from new company, and alone seems to fade. Everyone, Kitty said, gets out of life what they put in, and there's no possibility of cheating.

November 21, 1945

Walking along the Strand in the rain and fog, I said to Hughie that trying the Nazi war criminals at Nuremberg was like trying a man's finger for having pulled the trigger of a gun which murdered someone.

November 25, 1945

Owing to a gas strike, in Fleet Street the blackout is on again and the office is unwarmed. Shivering, I wrote an indignant leader on the gas strike. Coote, who was acting as Editor, was ill, with a heavy scarf round his neck. I thought longingly of the cottage at Battle, with Kitty and the children and a fire blazing.

November 26, 1945

Hughie is reviewing a life of Watts, the painter, over which we laughed a lot. There was a picture of Watts' reproduced in the book showing, presumably, Adam and Eve playing together, with a lot of foliage floating about between them. It was called *Mischief*. Adam was looking down eagerly at his own genitals. Hughie said the picture should have been called *Captain, art thou sleeping there below?*

November 29, 1945

Brian Lunn's wedding at Chelsea Registry Office. Brian gave his responses with much unction, looking very Nonconformist. Afterwards we adjourned to the pub opposite. Brian's wife is an Irish woman who kept on saying that the English had 'planted' Ireland. Brian announced immediately after the ceremony that at his first wedding he had cried, but on this occasion was dry-eyed. He continued to reminisce in a gently resigned, but occasionally nostalgic voice about the days he had spent with Betty, his first wife.

November 30, 1945

Two acts of my play *Liberation* done and the third taking shape. As always, sometimes quite pleased and sometimes doubtful about the whole thing.

Lunched with George Orwell and Bernard Causton. The evening before Kitty and Cholerton and I had looked at the hoarding covered with bills announcing meetings. All the folly of the world seemed to have been emptied there, and the names of most contemporary gurus occurred – Gollancz, Sloan, Brockway, Mrs Cecil Chesterton, etc. We laughed and laughed, Cholerton being a little tight. I told George and found, of course, that he belonged to most of the organizations mentioned, had signed most of the petitions and proposed to go to most of the meetings advertised.

December 1, 1945

We went to see *Uncle Vanya*, a wonderful performance. Very good where the doctor says: 'What an absurd moustache I've grown'. For us, however, the magic of Chekhov is departed. He's really second-rate and sentimental, with some authentic humour. All his characters are bored, dissatisfied. But only with themselves. They just give way to what everyone feels. Feebleness is the only characteristic they have to an unusual degree. And how Russian it all is! – the mixture of fatuous utopianism and conceit and essential callousness which produced the Revolution and the Soviet regime.

December 5, 1945

Play almost finished but now I wonder if, after all, it's any good. I spoke about it to a theatrical manager called Solomon and he said: 'Nothing about the war. I won't touch anything about the war'.

I went to the House of Commons for a censure debate, the first motion of censure since the General Election. Somewhat strange to be wandering about there. Saw various faces I knew

among members and spoke to one or two. The debate was quite
interesting. The Labour benches were full of prigs, all trying to
say their pieces. Winston was sitting there like an old, sulky lion –
he and Cripps representing the two extremes, the one ruddy, the
other grey, the one rotund and the other sharp. How they loathe
each other! A curious moment when Cripps accused Churchill of
lack of courage. There was a slight hush before the familiar yell
was sent up.

> Sad to be old to wield no more
> The passionate spear
> To turn away, with peaceful heart,
> And thankful tear.
> Peace is most sweet, but sweeter far
> The untranquil leer
> Of the eager blood.

December 7, 1945

I lunched with Bonamy Dobrée, Hughie and Arthur Dawe, who
was, as ever, sad and somnolent, the best of Whitehall. Afterwards
we were joined by Graham Greene and Bishop David Mathew, an
enormous Roman Catholic, with huge cheeks, and bright eyes, and
a high repetitive laugh. He asked Hughie which he liked most of his
brother, Arnold Lunn's books and Hughie said he regretted to say
Roman Converts. The Bishop agreed hastily, and said that in that
work there was a glow in Arnold's attitude towards the Catholic
Church not apparent in his subsequent writings. He also said that
he had not minded being an Aunt Sally as long as they were not
forced to know about each coconut. We agreed that we only
wanted people to talk about us behind our backs.

At 7.30 Alec Vidler came for me. Just the same, only greyer.
We worked out that our friendship had lasted for a quarter of a
century, since we were at Cambridge together.

December 9, 1945

At the *Daily Telegraph*, Lord Camrose, the proprietor, suddenly
walked into the editorial conference. He had been walking about

the City – strange, on a Sunday afternoon, this millionaire news-paper proprietor wandering about the ruined City. He was really a touching figure, asking about the American Loan, and whether the terms might have been easier, and then going off again.

After working some months on the Daily Telegraph, *the notion seized me that I ought to go to Washington DC. Superficially, this corresponded to the notion of going to Moscow that I had entertained so ardently fourteen years before when I was in Manchester working on the* Guardian, *but actually it was quite different. There was absolutely no feeling, such as I had about the USSR, that I wanted to settle in America and become an American and have my children brought up as Americans ; the impulse in the case of the USSR had been ideological, in the case of the USA it was purely professional, based on the calculation that, since America had become for the time being at any rate the richest and most powerful country in the world, its federal capital must necessarily be overflowing with news – as, indeed, proved to be the case. So, when Arthur Watson told me that the* Daily Telegraph *Washington correspondent, Denys Smith, wanted to come home, I eagerly asked if I might replace him.*

December 10, 1945

We dined quietly with Hughie, afterwards being joined by Douglas Jerrold, who is Chairman of Eyre and Spottiswoode and a Catholic. We talked about Catholic apologists, and Kitty said the scientific forward-looking equivalent was Immaculate Contraception. Douglas told me he had written a play in which almost everyone was a King or Lord, all great ones. When it came to be produced, the costumes were poor, and the only character who had a good turn-out was the butler, an old-fashioned professional actor, who was resplendent. This is very typical of Douglas's whole life.

December 14–16, 1945

The last two days I have spent in the House of Commons listening to the debate on the American Loan. It was extraordinarily unreal, even absurd, and shabby. Speakers took up their position, but the only reality was the fear which none of them dared to express – the fear of the consequences if cigarettes and films and spam were not available from America. I sat in the Press Gallery listening hour after hour, with a kind of fascination, thinking of my father, and of how he would have loved so to have been there in the House, every now and again making my way to the telephone to let Johnstone at the office know how things were going; once losing my way, lost in corridors mysteriously leading into each other, with in the distance the chatter of a division taking place. It was eerie. It struck me then, as so often, how in my life everything I have seen or been connected with has given me that feeling of something past its prime, running down, growing shabby and decrepit.

December 23, 1945

After all I was able to get away to Battle for Christmas. Coming down in the train, I suddenly began to be alive again. I've always noticed this – that the recovery of mental life, with me, is like suddenly recovering the use of a limb. There's a click, and lo!, it's working again. Even the landscape, which had seemed dead, recovers its life, and faces come again into my consciousness, and ideas enliven what has been a stagnant mind. I kept thinking of all the lives I might have lived – a left-wing life, or a life of devotion to writing; all that I might have done, and understood that either life was so insignificant that it didn't matter, or so significant that it didn't matter. My play, the only thing I've succeeded in finishing since I left the Army, seems to be hurried and mediocre. All right, if I go to America, I'll settle down to a book; and if I don't go to America I will, too.

Christmas Day, 1945

Pan is playing Schubert's 'Unfinished Symphony' on his gramophone. Kitty gave him the records for a Christmas present. She knows that music will help him. In buying Christmas presents for the children she knows exactly what they want because her life is centred on them. I have no such knowledge. To me, they are interesting. I watch their development critically but affectionately. It's the difference between the imaginative and intellectual process. Pan is delicate and sensitive. He scratches his leg exactly where my brother-in-law Leonard used to, and he is very religious, reads the Bible every day and goes to Communion every Sunday. I went to evening service with Pan, John and Val on Sunday. Val loves going to church because there are people there. The social side excites her. John loves information. He is enthusiastic, and turns over the pages of books eagerly. At school he does badly, whereas Charles is consumed with ambition and must be first in everything. Of his football, his report said that if his skill equalled his courage he would be unbeatable. 'Courage' was the wrong word; they meant determination or will. In the charade they did yesterday, he was radiant when he had the part of King Canute and ordered the waves to recede.

As I write I can hear Kitty in the kitchen. She is tireless on these occasions, cooking, discussing the 'Unfinished' with Pan, bringing in a glass of Guinness because I slept badly. Alas, I can't seem to be happy. Each night I lie awake for several hours full of dark thoughts and foolish regrets, and my old longing to cease to be. Although I've often been happy, I've never felt at home in the world, and know now that I never shall.

December 29, 1945

Back in London on my own, with the daily routine – waking early, making tea, reading, then the newspapers and some work; lunch usually with Hughie, the *Daily Telegraph*, a leader of some sort, dinner usually with someone, and home, a bath, another read and sleep.

The Embassy Theatre rang me up at the office, and I thought excitedly that I should hear about my play, but it was only to tell me that the manuscript had been lost.

I went to see my mother. She was just as I last saw her, very white and sad and confused; with crumpled letters from my brothers; and Miss Roffey bullying her; brooding over the past, slow-moving, her mouth slightly open; the little house in Croydon just the same, still with its Morrison shelter in the hall. When I left she suddenly embraced me warmly, and said she had not long to live. I gave her a cheque for £25 for a Christmas present, which pleased her very much, not so much because she wanted the money, but because it somehow took her back to the days when my father was alive and she coaxed cheques out of him. Seeing her gave me immortal longings, and I travelled back all the way to London by bus through the dark streets, hearing other passengers talking like a faraway and incomprehensible sound.

January 4, 1946

It is now settled that I shall go to Washington, and on the whole I'm pleased.

Hughie, Hesketh and I discussed whom we'd choose if we had to be a saint, a man of action, a philosopher and a writer. Hughie, having chosen Cromwell, St Francis de Sales, Johnson and Wordsworth, suddenly realized that there was no lechery in any of them.

January 8, 1946

On Saturday the children came up, and with Johnstone's children we went to a variety performance, and afterwards to the Café Royal. I felt too ill to carry the thing off with much enthusiasm, but did my best. Even with my children I notice that my regard fluctuates with their success. Thus, if someone says that John is attractive, he's at once more attractive to me. This judgment on a basis of outward values is instructive, and can only be corrected by an inward adjustment or spiritual regeneration.

Later I dined at the Athenaeum with Bishop David Mathew – former Naval Cadet, romantically conceiving himself as sagacious prince of the church, etc., and in fact more a toady than a worldling, more crafty than cynical. There were few points of contact between us.

January 11–12, 1946

Got rather tight at a party given by Liza Dennis, Graham Greene's sister. All the old MI6 chaps there, husbands and wives, secretaries with husbands. Very amusing to notice the changed temper. Graham told me that Heinemann had rung up to know whether I'd be likely to join them. It would have enabled me to leave the *Daily Telegraph*, and now I almost regret Washington.

Sometimes great despair about the times, circumstances sweep over me. How fast we're going downhill now! What will become of us? I wonder. Is my going to America really flight? – all foolish.

January 13, 1946

On Saturday Pan arrived. I waited, absurdly anxious, for him from noon onwards, looking out of the windows at the path which leads from Villiers Street. At last he came, a minute figure, always smaller than I expect him to be. I shouted down, and he smiled at me. After lunch I walked with Pan to the place in Westminster where he's spending the week-end at some sort of retreat.

January 25, 1946

Generally apprehensive about going to America, work not done, etc. Things going on as before. *Daily Telegraph* each afternoon, constant meetings with Hughie, Tony, etc. Cholerton has now gone to Paris to be *News of the World* Correspondent there.

Hughie looked in in the morning. He has ceaseless money troubles: 'That all may change or cease,' he quoted from *Lear*, and we laughed at the foolishness of it.

February 1, 1946

Working hard, and all well except that Kitty has 'flu and a temperature. It reminds me of the other times that she has been ill – e.g.
Moscow, in that wooden house on the outskirts when we were
quite alone and I used to sleep on the floor at night and look after
her during the day and we seemed to be quite shut off from
everything else in the world.

Lunched today with Tony, Graham, George, and Arthur
Koestler. Found him interesting and piquant, picking up things so
quickly – English, slang even; so perceptive – too perceptive
perhaps; all antennae and no head. We were quite a party the
five of us.

Yesterday evening I dined with Arnold Lunn, Hughie's
brother, his wife Lady Mabel, and their daughter – Mabel almost
a midget, little old woman who lived in a shoe effect about her,
and the daughter even tinier. Arnold had made tremendous
efforts to get into the upper classes, and succeeded, only to find
them dying on his hands – like slaving away and saving up to buy
a mansion only to find that the dry-rot has set in and it's falling
down.

Very pleased at the office with Bevin's speech about Greece
at the United Nations Council. Such simplicity and honesty,
really finely put, a touch of imagination, almost of poetry about it.
A really great man, who makes someone like Eden seem infinitely
insignificant.

As I was writing I heard Big Ben strike – quiet and warm in the
room. Kitty sleeping. I had one of those moments of exquisite
calm which comes sometimes – here in the middle of London,
quiet, with Big Ben chiming.

February 4, 1946

On Sunday I walked over to Regents Park with Tony Powell.
We talked about our plans. I said: 'In all the fluctuations of my
hopes and anxieties, the only constant is an enduring desire that
my life should come to an end.' It was the same with him, Tony
said. We made our way through little streets behind Oxford
Street, and marvelled at one street of Georgian houses ending in a

hideous 19th-century block of flats. I said it was like publishing an edition of Johnson with a few chapters, say, from Compton Mackenzie added at the end to round it off.

I saw Violet Powell's new baby, whose godfather I am to be – strange, red little creature, straining and agonizing to get into the world which Tony and I are so anxious to leave.

February 14, 1946

Waking early in the morning at Battle I heard a man in heavy boots going down the High Street, started making some verses about it, saluting this other one, awake as I was – he and I, it seemed to me, alone awake in the Universe, everyone else sleeping. Yesterday, when I woke up, I found Kitty was also awake. I started grumbling, and Kitty said she was very content listening to the birds.

Hughie is very thin and ill-looking. I have scarcely seen him lately, probably because I got hold of some money for him. The passing of money either way creates a curious antagonism. Only a saint could give or receive money without bruising the flesh, and saints never have any money.

Yesterday I lunched with Tony and his brother-in-law, Lord Pakenham, who's got some sort of job for the Government (Lord-in-Waiting) in the House of Lords. He made us laugh about the House of Lords, most extraordinary institution which he obviously rather liked, especially the servants, who, he said, were numerous, and made you feel a Lord all the time. I asked him if there was any possibility of the present Conservative majority being used to defeat a Government measure. He said the only occasion on which a serious threat to divide the House had been made was during a debate on 'freezing in' nurses at mental homes because if they left they could not be replaced. Bad feeling was around, and the debate provided an opportunity for several peers to reminisce about their own personal experiences of mental homes. (Extraordinary adaptability of British institutions – House of Commons becoming place essentially for superannuated Trade Unions officials, and the House of Lords immediately and instinctively ceasing to exercise its powers when they become inadmissible.)

March 1, 1946

Last night Brian Lunn came in. His eyes are wild, he mutters and makes curious gestures, and as Kitty said he has that curious air of physical well-being and prosperity which madness brings. After he had gone, I reflected on how for me, all I care for now is gentleness and sanity and tolerance and humour; but how passion and ambition (love of power) etc., the tendency to rave, is always just under the surface.

March 8, 1946

Most things done now. Only Ciano Diaries to be finished before going to America.

Sometimes (but not very often, thank God) I think, as well as talk, about politics. Thinking is better because, in thought, it's unnecessary to take up a position. The emotions which fashion political positions show themselves. In thought I feel certain that Europe will be conquered by the Bolsheviks where the Nazis failed. Their triumph is coming, and is comprehensible, but still disagreeable for us and for England. Perhaps it is necessary. Even, however, if I admit to myself its necessity or inevitability, I will not therefore falsify my own reactions and approve of it. That is real sycophancy, the instinct to attach oneself to success, to power, quite apart from the implications, personal and social. I have always known that what I belonged to was doomed, going down hill. The smell of decay was abroad. Even so, I belong to what is decaying and I will go down hill with it, not despairing, because it doesn't matter. Everything decays, and in its decay fertilizes new life. Autumn is only absurd if it tries to be spring, and evergreens are sad and disappointing foliage.

March 19, 1946

Goering said under cross-examination at Nuremburg that he was sorry about the burning down of the Reichstag because he had to requisition the Kroll Opera House as alternative accommodation, and he regarded opera as in every respect a superior enterprise to the Reichstag.

To and fro, leading articles, work in the mornings, dissatisfied.
Leaving shortly for America. Week-end at Battle.

March 28, 1946

I am on the boat on the way to America. Kitty came with me to
Liverpool to see me off, but we are still strained together. It gave
me a great feeling of melancholy, which I tried to rationalize by
thinking it was due to the lack of relation between what we feel
and what we do – organ playing one tune and choir singing another.
Only right at the end did I feel a sudden authentic glow of tenderness, especially when Kitty was making her way up the hill from
the Liverpool waterfront and I whistled after her to turn round
and wave, which she did.

March 30, 1946

Voyage continuing quite pleasantly, smooth, nice cabin where I
can type.

I continued to think of Kitty. Have I been happy with her?
Do I look forward to being happy with her? Might I be happier
with someone else? Or alone? These and innumerable other
questions flow about in my mind like dead leaves as a boat carries
me to the American coast.

Foolish chatter with passengers, games of bridge, chess,
omnibus volume of thrillers read with reluctant intent, no work
done, only sad thoughts and occasional indulgences, not excessive,
in my old friend Scotch. Think sometimes of all the wasted time
and the last six years, then think: why wasted? Every thought
producing its own, not antidote, but cancellation, the result of a
sort of mental nothingness – an equation in which everything
cancels out leaving the result – o = o. Sometimes think how
agreeable to die – talk of an iceberg evoking a picture of the boat
going down and providing an opportunity to go down with it; or,
walking up and down the deck and vaguely considering slipping
overboard in the dark night, only to recall my abortive suicide in
Lourenço Marques, the awful struggle with the waves, the shivering resistance to death when it came to the point, the lights of

Peter's Café shining along the shore, so remote, so desirable, and floundering naked in the mud afterwards.

I've been looking back over this journal. Already it seems long, long ago. The past is soon swallowed up by time, falls into a vast abyss in which a few memories survive, remembered delight. This load of passengers being carried across the Atlantic are mostly business men. They talk of exchange rates and the price of cigarettes in Canada. Some are on their way back to the Far East – forlorn figures rather, expecting to resume a life which has already been abolished – native servants, etc., plantations, offices in Shanghai and Singapore, the Club. They have doubts themselves, I think. There is something apologetic about them compared with when I first made the acquaintance of the life in 1924. So I feel more and more inclined to record the whole of my life from the beginning in great detail.

Terrible is Earth

Tomorrow we arrive and almost I'd rather go on and on. It's a kind of solution being on a steamer, no news, no work, a routine of sorts, nothing expected of one. Every now and again all my life I'd had a sudden mood of happiness, a kind of humility, a release from all fear, an awareness of the mysteriousness of my own being in relation to the universe. In such moods I recite the Lord's Prayer to myself, finding great comfort and delight in its words. Then I see passion in all its forms as a foolish, far-off thing, and wonder at the strange noises and grimaces it has evoked. Human love seems like thin smoke rising into a vast sky, soon dissolved, and human aspiration, whatever form it takes, no more substantial. I love this mood and would live ever so, but of course cannot on this earth. Each little ego seeking in some way to record itself, to sustain itself. 'Terrible is earth' is a phrase Hughie Kingsmill quoted to me once – terrible because of passion, which means the same as suffering. The realization that it is so implies a promise of release – to be patiently awaited, like sleep, and not angrily sought. I cannot really be interested in anything except this reality, and if I had the courage I should now give myself wholly to its pursuit.

1946–1947

U.S.A. Diary 1946–1947

April 8, 1946—New York

We arrived at New Brunswick and hung around there all day while a single American immigration officer dealt with us. Then in a slow train with a bell on it, like cows in Switzerland, to a larger train. The attendant in the Pullman coach told me he had written a book for boys about the Canadian Pacific Railway, and gave me his card on which he is described as a 'Christian Railroader', and above a text from Holy Scripture: 'Holding forth the word of life'. In England he would have written a book called 'I Make the Beds' which Michael Joseph would have published.

Waking in the morning, looked out of the window upon Maine – wonderful sunshine, dry grass like South Africa, and little wooden houses with cars about as large standing outside them. Got off the train at Boston and bought 62-page Sunday paper and breakfast of bacon and egg. Then walked about Boston for some hours. Amazing to me quantities of food and enormous restaurant menus, but amazement soon passes. Went to outskirts of Boston to see Austrian Jewish refugee shortly returning to Europe for six months to report for *Christian Science Monitor* – 'find out what people are thinking, what new political parties are shaping, etc.' He said it like a set piece, but what remarkable powers of adaptation. Only three years ago arrived in America and there he is with all the patter, going back to Europe in American uniform, a conqueror.

Caught the evening train into New York. Itinerant candy seller on the train made remarks in sepulchral voice like – 'Crime doesn't pay – not as well as it did'; 'Yes, I know Boston, I spent three weeks there one Sunday'.

Lights and crowded streets of New York I didn't find particularly exciting. Remembered Chesterton's crack about the lights –
'Wonderful if he didn't know how to read!' Looked in on Alex
Faulkner, *Daily Telegraph* correspondent here, and picked up the
threads of the news.

Wandering about New York looking at skyscrapers, etc. I went
into a bank to change some cheques. Ignored for a time at the
counter, then little dark man apologized, showed me to a seat,
looked at my cheques with distaste asking: 'How many of them
do you want to sell?' Seated there while he went about the business,
I watched two villainous looking strong-arm men, with curious
chipped features, pistols on the hip, go off with bags of money,
and clients coming and going – First Church of Christ Capitalist.

Somehow I think this whole show is a fraud, in its own way as
total and grand as Moscow.

April 13, 1946

Following day went out to United Nations Meeting with other
journalists. Security Council seated at horseshoe table, minute
Chinese presiding, Frenchman, Bonnet, quite white and ghostly,
Englishman, Cadogan, gent but somewhat decayed, Gromyko,
dark, unpleasant, white-faced, large, parasitic texture – all truly
representative. They talked – answers flashing, lights going up
and down for television purposes, publicity apparatus for various
kinds surrounding them, imprisoning them; little creatures upon
whom forces played, dissected by the vicarious curiosity of
mankind.

Returned in car through Harlem, sudden black town, everything the same except that faces were black instead of white, as
though in a theatre the light had suddenly been changed.

April 18, 1946

Lunched with American Trade Union leader (Ladies Garment
Makers) very tough, likeable. 'We can't like to deal with Russia,'
he said, 'because Roosevelt and Churchill disarmed us morally

before we came to grips with them.' He was well versed in current affairs, intensely anti-Russia; a battered expressive face, Jewish, likeable.

As I write the bells are ringing for Good Friday – these bells which have rung for so long and reached the remotest corners of the world. They give me a great feeling of tenderness and peace.

Security Council has been continuing to function – parliament of the world in century of the common man. Their deliberations were tedious. We, the journalists, go in and out to transmit their words with little enthusiasm. This scene will also be remembered – girls' school theatre overheated atmosphere, the coming and going, the words so meaningless, so remote from all actuality – for instance, large, fat slug-like Soviet stooge, on Spain.

Easter Day, 1946

Easter Sunday crowds in Fifth Avenue, well dressed, well fed, sunshine, church bells ringing – common man in his Sunday best to celebrate his century. I met Anne Hindle and two children and with them drifted along. We made our way to apartment of Len Lye, photographer. Gramophone played, and even the two little girls danced. Dancing in America great form of self-expression – dancing to negro rhythms. (Slaves brought over in slave ships after all succeeded in imposing their rhythms, even the rumble of their voices, on the masters they served – imposed their rudimentary culture on a vacuum).

April 24, 1946—Washington

Arrived here last night, very warm, thus recapturing the mood of warm, soft climates such as Lourenço Marques. How much I'd lived in such climates, I thought, and in a way came back to it gratefully. Many negroes, still with that soft African walk, the same African murmuring voices. Life slows down in the heat, I like it slower.

April 27, 1946

Finding my way around in Washington. Quite like the place. Liking or not liking, I cannot shake off deep undercurrent of melancholy; seldom, if ever, had less zest for life than these days. Only occasionally I hear a bird sing or pause – something like that, and feel serene. The negroes give me much more a feeling of brotherliness than the whites. They seem less miserable, less tired – black girls in cafeterias ladling out fodder seem less worn and wasted, less disquieted.

Came along first day to *Daily Telegraph* office. Small room in huge block, and there was Denys Smith, who, now that it comes to the point, I fancy regrets leaving as I regret coming.

We went along to the Senate together. I thought I might do an essay one day on legislatures. I've seen so many. Quite a hobby. Sparse attendance, few members present hard-boiled looking. They began with prayers, nonconformist type, spoken standing rather than intoned kneeling. Then one Taft spoke about the loan to Great Britain. Some good sense in what he said, a lot of folly and ignorance. A limited little man with ignoble values and a tough acute mind. This assembly, too, was very beside the point – no very valid connection with what was going on in the world; holding on tightly to obsolete things.

Next morning we went to press conference given by French Minister, Lecour, a Communist. Noted how the functionaries buzzed obsequiously round him – tough looking individual full of references to 'la classe ouvrière' and 'le mot d'ordre'. Already he felt himself to be the master.

In the evening transferred myself to flat of pleasant American officer named Niles. He and I drank most of bottle of bad 'blended' whiskey (avoid it in the future). Tongues loosened, we discussed America – how it had happened, this remarkable releasing of energy. I said that throughout human history what released energy was the revelation of a New Horizon – as Christianity, this one spiritual. In the case of America, it was a new economic horizon.

Spent Saturday alone – read part of a book by Evelyn Waugh all about the Cavendish Hotel. Very vulgar, I thought, and second-rate; a rather interesting account by a woman of a public mental home called *The Snake Pit*, and some short stories by Maupassant.

The last gave me all my old anguish at not having written anything these last six years, and I resolved yet once more to get to work.

May 5, 1946

Becoming used to this scene. Go daily to and from Senate, office, press club, etc. In the evenings occasionally foregather with people; otherwise sit alone, eating in cafeteria opposite my flat, retiring early to bed. One really enchanting book, Turgenev's *Fathers and Sons*. I find now that when I like a book I deliberately read it slowly to make it last.

May 11, 1946

Lunched with William Bullitt, former American Ambassador. We spoke about France, which he knew well. Obviously wished he was still an important person. Imagined it would be possible through personal contacts, playing politics, to sort things out. This illusion unenviable – wave after wave of such persons – Chamberlain, Hoare in the old days, and later Bullitt in Moscow, Cripps in India, etc. Always a failure because the world's troubles are a consequence, not of circumstances and individuals, but of the collapse of a moral synthesis, and of the authority and power this synthesis generated. The chaos must go on spreading; the breakdown, economic and political and social, must get worse. There is no reason why it shouldn't.

As usual, I did a lot of walking about the town. It is a kind of nervous reaction – to seek the crowded streets with other footsteps beating the pavement; streets broken by parks, little areas of green, there pausing awhile, spelling out the names of monuments only to forget them, noticing persons seated on benches, elderly and sometimes feeding birds, youthful and sometimes mildly embracing. Oh cities of mankind, how glad I shall be to leave you for ever. 'Toujours tant de bruit', as Chateaubriand muttered, an old, old man, as he heard the fifth revolution of his lifetime beginning to break out in the streets of Paris.

Went out to Virginia to see Huntington Morris and his wife who had both been with me in Lourenço Marques. Nice green country which I breathed in eagerly. Huntington said he saw nothing left to do now in life except to play some part in describing the last phases of our disintegrating civilization. He also had a firm conviction that one day the seven million or so souls in New York would be imprisoned in their own machinery, perishing amidst lifts which would not work, streetcars which would not run, and lights which would not go on. I am sure he is right.

May 14, 1946

Yesterday I went to a lunch in honour of Manuel Roxas who, after collaborating quietly with the Japanese, has now been elected President of the Philippines. Roxas' oratory was entirely in the manner of Indian politicians. He had the same rather quick way of speaking, and the same imagery – 'through the ages', 'crystal clear', 'the rolling stream', derived, I believe, from missionary hymns which represented, as Roxas would put it, 'way, way back' the first introduction of Indians and Phillipinos to English poetic literature. My satisfaction at the idea that Americans also had a Pandit Nehru on their hands was short-lived. Roxas' speech was an enormous success. It went right home. At some of the more excessively sentimental passages I looked round to exchange a sly smile with American journalists who were sitting near me only to find that mine were almost the only dry eyes in the room. The climax was an episode described by Roxas with great feeling. He had obviously described it many times before because I noticed that though he read the rest of the speech he knew this part by heart and was able to dispense with his manuscript. When he was first captured by the Japanese, Roxas said, he was commanding a Philippino division, and he and his men were put into an internment camp. One of his men, a mere boy of twenty, escaped, but three days later was captured by the Japanese and condemned to death. He, Roxas, pleaded with the Japanese commandant to spare the boy on the ground of his youth and inexperience, and with some difficulty was able to get permission for him to be tried by a court martial of his own officers. The court martial was duly constituted, and the boy was sentenced to a term of imprisonment. They built a little hut with their own hands, and in this hut the boy was incarcerated. After a few days he asked to see Roxas and explained to him that his father and mother had both been murdered by the Japanese, that his inclination was to escape again, but that he was deterred by the thought that if he did retaliatory measures might be taken against Roxas. Greatly moved, Roxas explained to the boy the difficulties which would confront him as an escaped prisoner, but that he must consult his own conscience and abide by that. In fact, the boy did escape again, and was again caught, but only after he had single-handed held up a Japanese patrol and killed six Japanese soldiers. This time, inevitably, he was executed, though the Japanese allowed him to see a Roman Catholic priest before going to his death. Later, this priest came to Roxas and said that the boy wished to bequeath to Roxas all he possessed in the world, which was a package buried under a tree near the camp.

May 15, 1946

I spent an evening with fellow journalists – a somewhat touching company, all very insistent on their high spirits. One had a screen in his office made up of headlines from the American press, some of them really poetic – for instance: 'Paper ladies Blossom in the Blight of War'. This is the authentic literature of America, an authentic expression of what is truly remarkable and lovely about the country. The screen was an equivalent of the border ballads – an illiterate, vivid expression of life's simplest emotions; curiously innocent, poignant, the first cry of a developing consciousness.

May 16, 1946

Already hot and damp here, like Travancore, Bengal, Lourenço Marques – the same sleep which does not refresh, time poured out slowly like a thick liquid. Reading *The Education of Henry Adams*, the best American prose work I've yet come across. Remarkable how Adams foresees the collapse of Liberalism, the total inadequacy of high-mindedness, whether his own Bostonian or the European variety.

May 18, 1946

Yesterday Herbert Morrison here – jaunty, sentimental figure, very typical of the Labour Movement, and indeed of England's present temper. As always, being abroad, figure like Morrison more sympathetic than at home; here seeming very solid, English, admirable. No question but that the Labour Party serves perfectly as a prophylactic against violent change – such socially aspiring, capable, sentimentally traditionalist as Morrison produced out of much political toil and trouble. Curious contemporary phenomenon, I thought, the politician or individual in power followed around by journalists notebook in hand – as though they were a kind of Greek chorus, his heralds who, instead of blowing trumpets to announce his presence, tap words. Most characteristic, I thought – a marionette man with microphone, camera, pencil, etc. the wires which manipulate him. Take away those wires and he sags, lifeless. He no longer exists. Publicity creates its own manipulations. It is the mystique of the Century of the Common Man – with rites and mysteries of its own, and priests and devotees.

Lunched with Wilmott Lewis of *The Times*, wreck, or even burlesque, of what he meant to be, yet the wrecked or burlesqued of more worth in my eyes than more solid contemporary things. He said that according to William Morris godliness lay in working hopefully and sleeping without fear. I reflected that I for the most part idle despairingly and am troubled in sleep. He also said that Coleridge spoke for all journalists when in *Biographia Literaria* he wrote that like an ostrich he 'had laid too many eggs in the hot sand of this desert the world.'

The remarkable change in my spirits brought on by this conversation with Wilmott made me realize that the appalling melancholia induced by this country is due to the fact that the light of the spirit is quite out, making a kingdom of darkness, and my own spirit was correspondingly lightened. ('Lighten our darkness, we beseech thee, O Lord.') Man cannot live in darkness without becoming a prey to the creatures of darkness – fear, hurt, cruelty, melancholy, but when the light of the spirit shines he cannot be afraid whatever his physical circumstances may be.

'La vierge, la vivace et le bel aujourd'hui.'

May 22, 1946

Started working yesterday; sent various messages to *Daily Telegraph* about food conference, strikes, etc. Herbert Hoover spoke – aged ex-President from another time, not entirely unimpressive. He spoke with deliberation, as children and old men do. Then La Guardia, Mayor of New York – this really entertaining figure, Italian gestures, liquid voice, wit of a kind: quite a performance in its way. (Everyone conferring about famine, making speeches about it and plans about it, but meanwhile famine continuing, soon, I suspect, to be everywhere.)

May 23, 1946

In my little office, ninth floor, I sit with the ticker machine watching it spell out the news, then myself spell out news to send to London – this ticker, moving finger which writes and having writ moves on, now an integral part of my life. Thus news is spelt out from hand to hand. Today it was the strike – conferences at the White House, comings and goings, poor little Harry S. Truman, surely the most pathetically inadequate figure ever placed in position of exercising so great authority to so little effect. What does he make of it? I often ask myself, seated in the White House, finicky in his clothing, fond of exchanging a yarn, with a pinched, amiable, inadequate face. Now, being so pitiable, he is the target of every attack. The strike scarcely surprised me. This country, too, must become paralysed; victim of its own collective egotism – excellently symbolized by John L. Lewis, the bully as miners' leader, asserting his will at whatever cost, a kind of madness in him expressing the general madness, this the source of his power.

Ticker kept writing of chaotic stations, paralysed transport system, emergency measures, shortage possibilities, and I duly noted and faithfully transmitted. In my little ninth floor office it all seems very remote. I thought that the ticker might announce the world's end, I the only survivor to note and transmit the information. It reduced all happenings to a kind of abstraction.

May 24, 1946

Another day watching the ticker for news of the railway strike. Went late in the morning to the Senate, heard one Senator Ball, man with grey disorderly hair, genuinely troubled, but having little or nothing to suggest. New Senators listening, Capitol largely apathetic in its air-conditioned aloofness, columns, dome, etc. intended, I presume, to be Athenian – Roman – fascinating chain of cause and effect which led from Athenian democracy, through city states, through French Revolution, Lafayette to Robespierre attired in toga, through British parliamentary democracy to Senator Ball expounding labour legislation to five or six apathetic senatorial listeners.

May 26, 1946

Yesterday joint session of Senate and House of Representatives addressed by Truman. Railway strike has caused a stir. This regrettable fact, belatedly discovered, that manual workers perform an essential function and cannot be dispensed with, is becoming the crucial issue in American life; 200,000 engine drivers can bring the 120 m. population of the United States to a standstill, whereas 200,000, say, clerks or teachers or journalists can't bring anything to a standstill. Senators were shocked and rather frightened. Scene very impressive in its way – crowded House, senators filing in; then the members of the administration, then six or so of the most senior in both Houses summoned to attend the President; then a voice shouts: 'Mr. Speaker, the President of the United States' – and in came Truman, everyone rising. He looked unbelievably insignificant. A fascinating figure.

'From the moment that railways were introduced, life took on extravagance.' – Henry Adams.

June 6, 1946

Moving today into Denys Snith's flat, a sad sort of business; all the dusty deposit of his loneliness lying there. The outwardness of life is ever an image of its inward reality.

June 9, 1946

Garden Party at Embassy to celebrate London's 'Victory Parade', new ambassador, Lord Inverchapel (Sir Archibald Clark Kerr), somewhat unimpressive figure, moving among his guests. I saw Sir James Grigg and his lady whom I'd known in India and had a row with. We talked affably together, glad to see one another. He's out of office. How that, too, stamps a man, extending to his clothes, trousers somewhat fraying at the bottom overnight, and clothes hanging rather which only yesterday were a perfect fit. Nicer, I thought, now when he's slightly under the weather than he was before.

Today worked in the morning, lunched, as now I always do on Sundays, with Wilmott Lewis, who quoted Emerson and Mac-Donald, but sometimes repeats some things – as today when he said the Humunculus in the second part of Goethe's *Faust* who could only live in his test-tube and yet wanted to break out of it thereby destroying himself, was an image of mankind in his societies out of which he occasionally breaks, thus destroying himself. We agreed that tales are always parables.

June 10, 1946

Letter from London indicating that my messages were not very satisfactory, so that I'm wasting all my time at a job I'm unsuccessful at, so far anyway.

June 13, 1946

Woke early and wrote for an hour which made me happy all the rest of the day. Hoped I might do the same, at any rate just for this one hour, every morning. Awful feeling of guilt I've been having at not having done Ciano Diaries. Every reference to his Diaries – or even to Italy – makes me start like Macbeth.

Worked all day, and in the evening went up to the Embassy alone. Inverchapel talked to me for two hours. Strange, shallow, somehow affected man – he, too, seemed to symbolize England's present plight. ('Stalin and I had the same sort of dirty minds.

That was the greatest possible help.') A burlesque of a burlesque, in his Lutyens Embassy, itself, I fancy, rather the same genre as a building as he as a man.

Dined afterwards with Lewis and Frank Oliver, *Times* Correspondent. He suddenly blurted out that he's been married to a Russian, that when he said he'd decided to come to Washington his wife said: 'Good, now I can tell you that I'm not going with you!', and that he'd never again seen her. Russians, he said, can't bear to be happy. That's their trouble.

June 16, 1946

Everything has become more bearable because I've now got a sort of routine – up early, make coffee, potter around, go to the office, newspapers, etc. After a certain age a routine is essential, a framework, a scaffolding for one's tottering life.

Lunched with Stanley Morison, Jesuitical Editor of *The Times Literary Supplement*, rather attractive man, with that curiously characteristic Roman Catholic face, steady without quite being serene, intelligent without being lively – a goodly sum of blocked understanding which, like blocked sterling, cannot be liquified. Enjoyed seeing him in his black clerical suit.

Have promised Frere to deliver *Ciano* by end July, and will do so. See quite a lot of René McColl. Went flying with Frank Oliver – untidy airfield with wooden building, music playing, pin table, untidy women heavily made up, perhaps most characteristically American scene of all. My instructor a woman with blond hair and slightly animal face, little bird-woman, sub-species, shrill tinny voice; normally High School teacher of physical culture and 'adolescent psychology'. 'Is that what we'd call in our old-fashioned way "the facts of life"?' I asked her, and she said it was more or less, not quite liking this undue simplification.

Found myself yesterday morning once more singing 'Let us with a gladsome mind', first time for some while; to me most moving and satisfying of all expressions of thankfulness. Also thinking: Fear can be cast out, and without fear life is bearable and even at times wonderful. Only one prayer – to be delivered from fear.

June 18, 1946

Dined yesterday with Walter Bell, formerly at Broadway and
now the British Ambassador's secretary. He told me that Inverchapel had no notion regarding what he was supposed to be at, or
what he should say or how he should conduct himself, and that he,
Bell, who was supposed to advise him, had in fact no advice to give.

At night the black people seem to dominate this southern
town. The heat and the darkness obliterate the whites and the
blacks take over. At nightfall the place becomes theirs. A sense of
how strange a place America is, how peculiar its origins, how
unknown its future dawns on me suddenly from time to time, and I
marvel at it – this astonishing collection of restless, mixed,
energetic human beings thrown together by chance and generating
vast power and wealth. Their machinery of government, as I see it
from day to day here in Washington, alike seems remarkable – the
White House with little Harry Truman within, the State Department, Congress up on Capitol Hill, Senators, Representatives – a
very remarkable phenomenon also. Remarkable, but not solid, no
solidity anywhere. It might all disappear as suddenly as it came to
pass leaving practically no trace behind. The Capitol, etc., easily
relapsing into a swampy ruin with the blacks dominant by day as
well as by night.

June 21, 1946

One sees even in the worst books something good. I was turning
over the pages of *Love in America* and came upon this – that
human beings are imprisoned in their loneliness, and their
communication, their intimacy, is no more than the taps on the
walls of their cells whereby prisoners manage to convey messages
to one another.

June 1946–November 1947

*After the entry for June 21, 1946, there is a gap in my diaries
of more than a year, during which period I was busily producing*

a day-by-day Washington coverage as culled from the two agency tickertapes in my office disgorging news on yellow paper round the clock; as well as from visits to the White House, the State Department, the Pentagon and other government departments, forays up Capitol Hill to keep an eye on the Senate and the House of Representatives, and up Massachusetts Avenue in case the British Embassy had anything to declare. One way and another, there was a lot going on – as, the resignation of Henry Wallace, Agriculture Secretary in the Truman administration and former Vice-President under Roosevelt; the launching of the Marshall Plan for European Recovery; the Alger Hiss–Whittaker Chambers confrontation.

Journalists, when they are absorbed in their work, seldom make good diarists; what they would write in their diaries finds its way into their news stories, feature articles and other professional output. For the same reason they make poor letter-writers, having frequent occasion to follow Dr Johnson and plead with their frustrated correspondents: 'Never impute the negligence of my hand to the coldness of my heart.' Thus, I only resumed writing my diary when I was driving across America to California, taking a plane from there to Alaska and Tokyo on my way home.

November 2, 1947—Tennessee

Left Washington two days ago, very tired, rather sick from five inoculations. Drove to Charlottesville, Virginia, in the evening light, last glimpse White House, Capitol, etc. On from Charlottesville into North Carolina, wild country, stayed night at place called Roaring Rock. All these places in US, wherever they may be, essentially the same – street with electric signs, one among them DRUGS, cinema, gasoline. From North Carolina into Tennessee really magnificent, rolling mist in huge mountain gorges, mixture colours. Passed by rather pathetic Red Indian reservation with usual shop containing wickerwork, kept by Indian chieftain in feather head-dress. (How completely Indians ground out of existence by Americanism.)

Passing through Lexington, looked at Virginian Military Institute and Robert E. Lee's tomb nearby. Saw his deathmask, rather pedantic, screwed-up looking face. Extraordinary that after so savage a civil war he should have been allowed to finish up his days as head of a college in Virginia. VMI students filed past in their grey uniforms, very German looking, I thought.

Driving along on Sunday I heard on wireless a series of religious services ranging between Roman Catholic and Christian Science. Latter's preachers referred to fact that Christ, though of humble station, was 'highly successful and influential'. RC gave clever pessimistic analysis of present situation, and Methodist made vehement plea for votes against licensing liquor shops in Knoxville with much salty abuse of those who favoured sale of liquor. Nonconformists still powerful in these parts. Two great permitted indulgences eating and domestic fornication.

November 4, 1947—Alabama

In the early morning mists among the autumnal mountain slopes, most beautiful. Majestic country with frailest imaginable human habitations. If abandoned, in fifty years no trace whatsoever of them would remain.

Into Knoxville, Tennessee, and there the everlasting pattern – cafeteria, shoeshine, etc. Newspapers numerous but largely filled with agency material. Bookshops, scarcely one to be seen. Heard negro evangelist ranting the ancient doctrine of justification by faith – 'Ah shall have everlasting life not because Ah'm good; Ah shall have everlasting life not because of anything Ah'd done or not done. Ah shall have everlasting life because Ah believe in Jesus Christ. Ah'm so happy this morning because Ah shall have everlasting life.'

On the whole this part of Tennessee gives sad, desolate impression, shabby, broken-down, faces rather wretched with that curious unpleasing indefinable expression I remember in South

Africa, India, among poor whites. At Chattanooga I walked through Negro quarter – several drunks, liquor shops every other one, whores at upper windows; night scene in the light of day. As Gordon Huson, my companion, said, it was rather as though deliberately the blacks were being given every opportunity to become extinct, and only in fact multiplying the more.

November 5, 1947—Memphis

Beautiful misty morning. I went to Wheeler Dam part of Tennessee Valley Authority project. Dam itself really remarkable, even beautiful in the sunshine stretching mile and a quarter, trim. Twenty score such dams with huge turbines generating one-third of the total electricity generated in Great Britain. If everything in this country crumbled away, such dams would be the only and faithful relics of the present feverish activity. On into State of Mississippi – wretched little towns with men in dungarees sitting interminably together reminding me of Huckleberry Finn – great squalor, great misery, and an undercurrent of terror due, I imagine, to the Negro question here, very pressing because in this State alone in Union blacks in admitted majority over whites.

November 6, 1947—Arkansas

Left Memphis with relief; flat, rich, agricultural country reassuring. At Little Rock looked in on editor of local paper and discussed with him difference between British and American newspapers. (The thing to do with American bores, greatest in the world, is to let them talk about whatever interests them.)

Then went to hear General Eisenhower address Arkansas veterans – large hall quite full; trumpet blast, General arrived, all standing. Eisenhower always looks made-up as though he were putting on a slightly over-acted presentation of a General in the American Army. He gave usual address about American role in present world situation, necessity to be strong and convinced of justice of position, etc., etc. Well but not enthusiastically received. Most warmly applauded passages, as everywhere, were those with jingoistic flavour – 'America . . .' (Churchill still most popular foreigner in the country; more interest in Royal wedding than in Marshall Plan).

November 8–10, 1947—New Mexico – Arizona

D. H. Lawrence district, Faux Mexique. Drove on through miles and miles of desert into Arizona, Great Divide, top of the world. Weird natural phenomena – Painted Desert, petrified forest. Prehistoric, giving one that curious, but mystical, feeling that history only began yesterday. Indians much around these parts, rather poor souls living on selling beads, feathers, etc. ('Your picture on bucking bronco.')

Made a few enquiries re D. H. Lawrence and Frieda. Latter, it appears, living now with Italian, demon with the ladies, but Frieda rather likes it. All found, as far as Italian is concerned, and his family. Frieda's acquiescence due to fact that Italian's surplus production far exceeds Lawrence's total output. Seems fitting that royalties of *Lady Chatterley's Lover* should subsidize fornication of Lawrence's successor.

November 12, 1947—Las Vegas, Nevada

Strange scene in the grey morning night – gambling still continuing, whisky drinking, too – unshaven grey-faced men, a few women, one totally drunk, paralytic, yet still able just to fasten her attention on the game. Not surprising no taxes in Nevada. Play with authentic silver dollars, piles of them, 5,000 dollars the limit.

Other great Nevada industry is divorce at Reno, thus the two great mysteries of American life – marriage and money – celebrated in this one State. Third mystery – speed – celebrated everywhere with its immense human sacrifice of blood which all accept as righteous (unlike sacrifice of war which is deeply resented, though considerably smaller), and day when driving lience first granted to juveniles treated very much as first Communion. Driving along through the desert after Las Vegas I wondered very much whether Americans possibly could 'save Western European civilization', or whether they weren't, as I believe Clemenceau said, the only case of a people who'd become decadent without ever going through the stage of being civilized. Thought of Marshall etc. and realized that the Administration had to look to soldiers for public servants because they alone in a society like this were truly disinterested, could be relied upon to be uncorrupt.

November 13, 1947—Los Angeles

Cinema town, most frail except at night when its lights have a certain reality as though reflecting the starry sky. The American Dream here actually being given substance – Use this soap and be you fifteen, be you fifty, whatever before may have been its condition, your skin will become silky, exquisite. Take this soap and use it in remembrance of me . . .

November 17, 1947—San Francisco

Stayed with Abbé, photographer whom I knew in Moscow, now raising third family – rather wearied of it, I fancy, but still going through motions. Loved exquisite mild climate of California but knew well no good staying there. Thought of Huxley (A.), Hurd (G.), etc., finding their last haven. Not for me. Think rather of taking children to Canada or Australia or Africa.

November 18, 1947—Alaska

Pale arctic night with clear cold air, and snow mountains all round. This is my last night in America. Sitting in plane watching night come on – in West a yellow sunset, in east mountains as cold and remote as thought. Sitting in plane with no desire to go or to stay, tranquil, empty, for a while. (The eternal American pattern, with its lights, drugs signs, beauty shoppe, even in Anchorage.)

November 20, 1947—Tokyo

Drove in through industrial suburbs so squalid that it was difficult to see whether they'd been blitzed or not. From moment of arrival strangeness of set-up here experienced – short, mostly distorted, people hurrying along. No particular signs of distress though some have bad colour of under-nourishment. Emperor's palace guarded by American and Australian sentries. American troops mostly kids – only 40,000 of them. Crowds collect to see MacArthur go to lunch, just to see him. British correspondents almost despairing about situation here. Hurried straight off to cocktail party at British Embassy in honour of Princess Elizabeth's marriage.

November 21, 1947—Tokyo

Sleepless, night fallen over Tokyo, quite silent. Another party yesterday evening in honour of royal wedding, this time given by Commander-in-Chief. Aged Liberal there, Comyns Carr, now engaged in prosecuting Japanese war criminals.

This morning saw American General (Whitney) – Government Section of GHQ – who explained 'democratization' of Japan, gave me copy of constitution. (How many constitutions!) Afterwards military parade for royal wedding, march past, bands – Japs in sort of pen watching without any evident sign of feeling one way or another.

November 22, 1947—Tokyo

In afternoon went to Diet conducted by American officer. Modern building excellently equipped, unheated, icy cold – circumstance perhaps symbolic. Saw Speaker of Lower House who explained difficulties regarding coal nationalization bill now under considera-tion. (Japs exceptionally difficult to fathom. What are they at? Is all this parliamentary business an elaborate farce? Are they winking at one another with their unwinking eyes as they speak about ministerial crises? Or is it all in deadly earnest? Fact is that in-variably when they decide a course of action it turns out to conform exactly to American wishes, or what they might imagine American wishes to be.) Then saw Senate President, formerly Japanese Ambassador in London and Washington, Matsudeira. Questioned me about London, was this or that building damaged, recalled meeting Princess Elizabeth when a child. Rather a bizarre conversation in icy legislature where, by all accounts, Jap democracy in process of being born.

November 26, 1947—Tokyo

Long day in government section of GHQ, discussion, questions, etc. Indicated that the result of divorce law changes is that the fifth freedom – to commit adultery – is instituted in Japan. Simple-minded earnest attempt on part of Americans to establish democratic system in Japan highly diverting and rather touching. Despite its inherent absurdity something may come of it. (Swift or Orwell could treat it fable-wise.) What do Japs make of it?

Visited War Trial of Tojo, etc., two rows of defendants, inscrutable. Little man, quite minute, took stand, former Naval Attaché in Berlin; curious creased wizened face, and apparently ceaseless smile or grin. No self-pity as with Germans, just endurance. Whole procedure very tedious obviously to most present – trial likely to drag on till early summer.

November 30, 1947—Tokyo

Received by General MacArthur – large seeming (though actually short) rather shoddy man who talked at me for nearly an hour. His theme was that the US army had brought democracy and Christianity to Japan, and had thereby wrought a revolution unique in history. He spoke of the Sermon on the Mount, producing exceptionally large number of cliches ('Freedom is heady wine', etc.). I was bored and embarrassed. He seemed to me like broken-down actor of type one meets in railways trains or boarding houses in England who complains that his recent production of *Hamlet* at Pontypool Repertory Theatre was badly attended whereas the circus was crowded. Occasionally I made feeble efforts to check the flow of words, but with no avail. It had to run irresistibly on. China, MacArthur said, might be expected in due course to become civilized, in which case country would split up into several independent principalities. Similarly Russia. He saw no strategic dangers in US withdrawal from permanently de-militarized Japan. An inconceivable performance.

December 7, 1947—Hiroshima

Today curious experience – met Emperor at small pier, little uneasy man with moustache, standing alone on deck, nearly fell over as boat stopped. Twitching slightly, waited to come ashore; method of acknowledging cheers of crowd lifting of homberg hat and putting it back; nervous, shy, stuttering, pathetic figure, formerly god.

All along road into Hiroshima crowds cheering ('Banzai'). Watched their faces, completely baffled, except that they were obviously pleased to see Emperor, and obviously well-fed. I felt in my bones that they'd try again. In Hiroshima Emperor was taken first to enormous gathering (20,000) near where atomic bomb fell; then to roof of town hall whence could be seen all the town, and how devastated it still remained despite some repairs and much temporary building. Saw line of functionaries, black coats, white gloves, lift their arms in the air and shout 'Banzai' like all others. Travelled back to Kure in Emperor's train. Foreign correspondents had special coach at end. Penetrated into Emperor's part, here also inscrutable men in cut-away coats.

At Kure, I was shown round huge Japanese docks and arma-ment factories, mostly destroyed. Even so, impressive. Strange silence of wreckage, immense machines, some from England, where easy to imagine hum of activity only two years before. The magnitude of Japanese war effort really astonishing, in odd way touching – these little people trying so hard to be powerful, so nearly succeeding; so painstakingly and exactly copying what seemed to them to signify power, and then quite suddenly the whole thing dying on their hands like a child's house of cards falling down, and having to begin again. Brave children who won't cry, but even so tough and rather bewildered 'Where did we go wrong?', they seem to be always saying and not yet quite finding an answer.

December 10–11, 1947—Hong Kong

Met Reuters chap and wife lately come from England, tales of awful food situation there. Wife, in fact, made ill by eating since she left England. All the same glad, so glad to be on my way back. This place by economic chance little museum corner of former China, reminding me constantly of India when I first went there.

December 21, 1947—Rangoon

Entirely melancholy place, war damage unrepaired, streets filthy, quite derelict. Walked around alone for two hours or more breathing dust and hopelessness. Few days hence independence to be celebrated and British Governor to depart. Walk, for me, evoked my memories of previous times in India, country much interwoven with my life – recalled first arrival in Travancore; ten years later in North, all words I've written on subject, some genuine, some not, love affairs, drinks, etc., etc. Phrase which occurred to me long ago – Twilight of Empire. Now the night.

December 23, 1947—Calcutta

Indian Colonel from Frontier very bewildered. Says complete breakdown Pakistan and India – no coal in Pakistan so trains barely running, army equipment in India, barracks all in Pakistan, etc. Thought how different Colonel expected his life to be, how he'd have completed his service, simple character; warm send-off, affectionately respectful attitude of natives, etc.; quiet last days somewhere in England or perhaps south of France; and now, suddenly, no Indian Army at all, inconceivable chaos. Resented fatuous Singapore Governor, Jimsom, saying he'd 'heard' that British were now very popular in India. Saw my Colonel not quite such a sucker as that.

Waiting for plane to leave suddenly saw Shahid Shurawardy, stouter than before, otherwise just the same. Really delighted to see him, got news of all my Bengali friends. His amused cynical attitude to present political situation most refreshing. At moment he's sitting moderately pretty as one of few Western educated

Moslems, but he's well aware that this, for him, good time may end, and he's hoping to get job abroad. Everyone's been debunked, he said – British, Moslems, Hindus, Congress, etc. There's now only a vacuum. Calcutta slightly more depressing than it used to be. Japs set out to create East Asian co-prosperity, and have wonderfully succeeded in creating East Asian co-misery.

1948–1952

Diary 1948–1952

February 7, 1948

Dined Ralph Jarvis's. Present: character called Burgess (Foreign Office). Burgess lamentable character, very left-wing, obviously seeking to climb on the Socialist bandwagon. Long, tedious, rather acrimonious argument. As Labour Party's fortunes decline, so Conservatives, with fatuous miscalculation, move leftwards.

February 8, 1948

Looked in on Tony and Violet Powell, and laughed much over Duke of Windsor's Memoirs and Americanisms in them – for instance, 'Fatty' instead of 'Tubby'. Wondered if Royal Family had been given advance copy, or if they opened *Sunday Express* each week apprehensively.

February 9, 1948

Lunched with Gaydon (Foreign Office), leaving shortly for Washington, Herbert Ashley (*Daily Telegraph* Diplomatic Correspondent), and Johnstone. Johnstone took very pessimistic line, all up, forcing me into unusual position of strenuous optimism. All agreed Government likely to fall autumn this year, Attlee probably then replaced as Prime Minister by Sir Stafford Cripps, Chancellor of the Exchequer. Cripps typical dictator type, power maniac, vegetarian, likely to establish some form of 'Christian Fascism'.

Hugh Kingsmill joined us after lunch looking old and ill, I

thought. He walked back with me and we discussed Robert Louis Stevenson. He pointed out that Hyde was really Hitler and Jekyll Gladstone, and that Stevenson showed a great prophetic aptitude in seeing in advance that Gladstone would inevitably turn into Hitler.

Curious episode in office: H. D. Ziman, a Jew, hit Hugo Wortham (Peterborough), secret anti-Semite. Both greatly agitated afterwards. Whole incident sinister, I thought.

February 10, 1948

Statement by Cripps finally disclosing full ghastly particulars of economic situation, which should have been disclosed two years ago, now probably irremediable. Almost certain prospect of some form of collapse with Communists the inevitable beneficiary. *Daily Telegraph* now ardently supporting Cripps. When I said at Editorial Conference that he was tremendously ambitious, the editor, Watson, replied that he didn't think so at all, that Cripps was, in his view, entirely God-fearing and honest. Pathetic holding on to Cripps by Conservatives. Further indication how grave situation is. I couldn't be more pessimistic. All that stands between us and total ruin is American surplus production, on which there are many demands. When that is overstrained, as it soon must be, a break-up is inevitable.

February 11, 1948

Lunched with Tony Powell, Alan Pryce-Jones (Editor of *The Times Literary Supplement*), and Philip Jordan (Prime Minister's Adviser on Public Relations) who was very depressed and, I thought, perhaps regretful at having left Washington. His mood further indication that Attlee Government nearing end of its days.

Much disturbed by result of election of officers at Central London branch of National Union of Journalists, to which I belong. Communists elected Secretary and Treasurer, although feeling was strongly against them. They were preparing to undertake duties which others shunned and were diligent at turning up at meetings. Realised that this was going on all over the country in all Unions. Highly dangerous, since such positions in many ways more powerful and important than, for instance, being in Parliament. Reproached myself greatly for not having previously participated in Union affairs. Decided henceforth attend all meetings and, if necessary, undertake duties.

Kitty's two brothers came to supper to see their mother who is staying with us. Mrs Dobbs is in peculiarly irritating mood, can't hear what is said, but insists on joining in conversation. Kitty more patient with her than she used to be. Said 'she has quite lost her sting now'.

February 12, 1948

Lunched with Lord Birkenhead, who is writing official life of Kipling. Kipling during his last three years was frequently suicidal – ill and miserable, and hating his wife. Freddie Birkenhead physically like his father, F.E., no fool, but not enough character to be anything apart from his father. Noticed enormous watch-chain he was wearing, presumably inherited from F.E., which seemed to symbolise his condition – like a manacle. He has nothing to lose but his father's watch-chain. He had very strongly formed the impression that Roosevelt envied and disliked Churchill. This entirely fits in with my own idea of Roosevelt.

Proceeded to House of Commons where debate taking place on Government's White Paper announcing policy to freeze wages in order to bring about deflation. Government very pitiful spectacle, supporters only thinly present, listened to speeches in frigid silence. Cripps did the best he could, but even he as deflated as he hopes to make the currency. Conservatives naturally cock-a-hoop, but expressing their jubilation prudently because many of them, at least, hope to form another National Government. Thought as I watched that there appears to be no middle position between a free and a slave totalitarian economy, and that all attempts, such as the Labour Party has been making, to find and hold a middle position, are doomed to failure.

Noted that power appears to make people bloated physically, as well as morally. One or two I have known – for instance Kenneth

Younger – have become swollen in a quite extraordinary manner. Saw Hugh Dalton, Chancellor until the Budget 'leak' last year, looking very ghostly and haunted. Felt grave doubts as to whether, in any circumstances, Parliamentary procedure likely to go on for much longer. It grew out of and belonged to difference circumstances. Pitiable performance by Attlee, without any evident meaning or significance.

February 14, 1948

In the evening Colin Coote and his new Dutch wife came to dinner. Coote is expected to become editor of *Daily Telegraph* when Watson resigns. Doesn't really like me much, though always excessively friendly. He is very anti-American.

We listened to Churchill's broadcast – very jovial, irresponsible, amusing. The old tend to become irresponsible. They have nothing to lose but a few more years of life, and whatever they may say, seldom care much about posterity. Almost any of them would gladly exchange enduring fame for even one more year of decrepit life. Churchill, in my opinion, too rhetorical to be either a really great writer or orator. The greatest thing in him is his rich, abounding humour, which permeates so much of what he says. Remark of Churchill's was quoted to me about Liberal candidature Air Vice-Marshal Bennett in Croydon. 'It was the first time,' Churchill said, 'that he had heard of a rat actually swimming out to join a sinking ship.'

February 17, 1948

Visit to Heinemann. Frightened the wits out of them by suggesting that the Labour Government might not last much longer. They have a number of books on the stocks connected with it – e.g. Life of Attlee; Bevin, the Foreign Secretary's autobiography; book by Francis Williams, political journalist.

At *Daily Telegraph* Ziman told me that ever since he hit Wortham, the editor, Watson, treats him very cautiously, as though he was expecting that at any moment Ziman might slosh him one too.

Went along to Artists Rifles Depot to meet Bobby Barclay, with vague idea of joining SAS Territorial Regiment. Bobby says most people who were in Special Services in the war have joined it, and that in the event of trouble here it might be quite useful to belong to it. I suppose the mere existence of such a formation is not without a certain significance.

February 18, 1948

Kitty and I lunched with the Birkenheads. Also present, R. A. 'Rab' Butler and his wife, and Peter Quennell. Butler not very likeable, but intelligent, Chairman of Conservative Research Department. Very pessimistic about Conservative Party. Says bad candidates always chosen by local associations. Thought that Labour Government won't last very long, and obviously himself favoured coalition, in which he would be sure of getting a place. Birkenhead said that Churchill dictated all his writings, walking up and down the room and orating, but that he did terrific corrections in proof. Quennell said he thought Churchill's style was based on Gibbon, but I said much more Macaulay. Butler considers Bolingbroke to have been the true founder of Conservatism. Doubt if there is much in this.

Picked up Hugh Kingsmill at the Club and brought him home. He has just read remarkable letter by Cromwell, addressed to Mazarin, saying that thought for political reasons it would be difficult for him (Cromwell) to treat British Catholics sympathetically, Mazarin could rely on his doing everything possible behind the scenes to see that they did not suffer undue disabilities. I remarked that this was quite typical of politicians, whatever their ideology might be. It was really very like the Nazi-Bolshevik pact. The moment Cromwell was actually in power, his puritanism became of secondary importance. He dealt with a very heavy hand with the Levellers and other cranks and crackpots who enabled him to get into power, and greased up to the Catholics who were useful to him against Holland.

The Powells came in later, but the evening was somewhat marred by Mrs Dobbs' insistent, yanging voice. The will, Hughie said of her, lays everything flat.

February 19, 1948

Lunched at the Naval and Military Club with Dick Brooman-White and Ustinov, an elderly White-Russian, father of dramatist Peter Ustinov. Dick himself acute, gentle soul, in SIS during war, now a Conservative candidate up in Scotland. Ustinov short, squat, watery eyes, black coat, striped trousers, rather sympathetic. We inevitably talked about Russia. White Russians have now all become fervent admirers of Stalin, and though affecting to fear and dislike Russian policy, actually they seek to justify it. Ustinov made series of quite ridiculous claims – for instance, that Russo-German Pact was cunningly decided on by Stalin because he knew German attack was coming. I tried to show there was no evidence to justify this, but without much effect.

Ustinov said that in the war, when he was interrogating German prisoners brought over to England, German said to him that he had already seen various members of the British Secret Service. Ustinov asked him how he knew and he said: 'Oh, they were wearing the tie'. This turned out to be the Old Etonian tie.

In the evening my son Pan brought in one of his friends from Hounslow, who is going to study commercial art. Pan's friend confirmed what we knew already, that he spent a lot of his time helping the others to clean their equipment, and taking on fatigues for them. After they had gone, Mrs Dobbs said she thought Pan had the best character of anyone she had ever known. When he was staying with her in the country and she suffered from sleeplessness and went rampaging about the house, he suggested to her that perhaps it might soothe her if he read her a chapter of the Bible each evening. This he faithfully did while he was there. Like David playing music to soothe Saul.

Mrs Dobbs also said she thought the Webbs had left practically no money in their will to their devoted servants. This seemed to me highly diverting, considering Sydney's speciality was, when alive, making pronouncements on economic matters. I remember him well as a plump, greedy, rather base little man, very pleased with himself for no apparent reason. She, Mrs Webb, was a much more remarkable person, though a power maniac, especially at the end of her days.

(Webb's attitude to his servants like a dietician, starving his

staff – excuse he offered that he didn't know what people needed
to eat.)

February 20, 1948

Wrote leader on Police debate. Then met Kitty, Lady Rhondda,
Theodora Bosanquet, Richard Law and his wife at theatre –
satirical review *Tuppence Coloured*, with admirable comedienne
Joyce Grenfell. One or two of her acts really exceptionally good.
Law is son of former Prime Minister, Bonar Law, and served in
Coalition Government during war – sympathetic, not very bright,
well-meaning. He seemed very discouraged about the future of the
Conservative Party, but didn't quite agree with me that Eden
would be a disaster. He said he thought the future might work
out for his children, but he didn't feel that he would be able to
play any useful part in it because he disliked so much the kind of
world which was coming to pass.

Lady Rhondda, who owns *Time and Tide*, drives around in an
enormous hired Daimler. As far as she is concerned, the only consequence of the abolition of the basic petrol ration is that she uses
this enormous car with a chauffeur, instead of driving herself in
a little car.

February 21, 1948

At the 20th Congress of British Communist Party, Harry Pollitt,
Party Secretary, made long report, which he read from prepared
manuscript, without any alterations or improvisations. Middle-
sized hall was crowded. Usual slogans spread about the building –
'Marxism is the science of working-class power'. Those present
mostly lower middle classes, few working class. On platform sat
the Executive Committee, really deplorable faces. Unpleasant
thought that in many parts of Europe, such people already in
absolute power. Pollitt rather nicer than the others in appearance.
Struck me as very much old-fashioned type of Labour leader, who
I remember coming to my father's house when I was a child –
rubicund face, dentures, bald. Amused that only non-Communist

publications quoted with approval by Pollitt were *Times* and *Times Literary Supplement* (mentioned this in *Daily Telegraph* paragraph, but it was struck out by Coote).

When Pollitt had finished, leaders of delegations from various parts of the country came up and spoke. Mostly anxious to please platform, symbolic spokesmen of the 'toiling masses' which Communists use as pawns in working towards checkmate. On the whole the Congress most unimpressive. Only abiding impression was faces of those on the platform, so entirely the sub-humanity of Nazi caricatures. Indeed, part of the villainy of Nazism lies in the fact that through its activities what is predicted has come to pass.

February 23, 1948

Johnstone and I spent some time seeing how much we knew about the general course of history and were appalled at the gaps. We had both been reading fairly recently Arnold Toynbee's *Study of History* which, we agreed, despite its extraordinary erudition, had a flavour of charlatanry about it. For instance, Toynbee does not offer any answer to the question of how a number of civilizations all come to pass, apparently unrelated to one another, about 4,000 years ago. Again, I suspect that his conception of an 'internal and external proletariat' and of '*yin*' and '*yang*', are phoney. It is not difficult to see why the book has been more successful in America than here. With its analysis of the decline of 22 civilizations it complies with the Gallup Poll technique which Americans so much admire.

Mrs Dobbs' last evening, to Kitty's and my inexpressible relief. But what is to be done with her when her little remaining light of reason flicker's out finally?

February 24, 1948

Usual visit to Heinemann. Discussed Graham Greene's new novel, *The Heart of the Matter*, about which Bruce Marshall has written an amazingly adulatory letter. Felt slight pang of envy, which soon passed. Greene's previous novel, *The Power and the Glory* I consider to be one of the best contemporary novels, and this is in the same genre. I dislike his gangster books, like *Brighton Rock*, despite their remarkable competence. Greene, we agreed, is a Jekyll and Hyde character, who has not succeeded in fusing the two sides of himself into any kind of harmony. There is a conflict within him, and therefore he is liable to pursue conflict without. I remember him saying to me once that he had to have a row with someone or other because rows were almost a physical necessity to him. This pursuit of disharmony is wrong, just as the pursuit of harmony or love is the source of all the finest achievements of human beings, whether in perfecting their own characters, or in expressing the idea of perfection beyond the world. All the same, Greene is a very loveable character, and a very remarkable writer, who entirely deserves the success this new book will bring him.

Our lives have always run in a curiously parallel way. He succeeded me at the Ministry of Information; when he was in West Africa in SIS, I was in East Africa, and we used to communicate with each other in cipher. Then he went to Eyre and Spottiswoode and became my publisher, and I went to Heinemann's and became his. I always say to him that the great quest of his life has not been virtue but sin, and that this quest has been completely fruitless. He is a sinner manqué. In the Blitz we used to spend a good many evenings together, and I remember the longing he had for a bomb to fall on him, but of course it didn't, and I told him it wouldn't.

Lunched with Robin Cruikshank, now editor of *News Chronicle* in succession to Gerald Barry. He was highly complimentary about my messages from Washington, about which he said American Ambassador, Lewis Douglas, had told him that he always read them to get the news, knowing that two or three days later the State Department would confirm them.

Slept badly. As Kipling said: 'the night got into my head'.

February 25, 1948

Hugh Kingsmill in rather poor shape, worried about money, generally uneasy. He kept on complaining of the east wind, and we agreed that external misfortunes and discomforts are only intolerable when they are matched with some internal or subjective unease.

We looked in on Gaston, who buys review copies of books. His attitude to books is one of extreme distaste. He always refers to them as a rather disgusting commodity. For instance, of a certain publisher, 'they shift the stuff'. Hughie suggested to Gaston that he was doing very well and probably was able to evade income tax, but Gaston said 'No, they don't give you a chance to do any fiddling!'

February 27, 1948

Philip Jordan said that Attlee, in spite of appearances to the contrary, was a very downey old bird, who had dealt adroitly with a whole succession of attempts to undermine his position.

February 28, 1948

My brother Douglas and I went down to see our mother. Situation there unchanged – my mother, aged housekeeper, Miss Roffey, German daughter-in-law, wife of my brother Eric. Only dog now dead, to Miss Roffey's great desolation. I reflected on how curious it is that human beings, however small or large the social unit, always generate the same conflicts – generate them even in their own hearts. My mother, aged 84, finds considerable pleasure in carrying on a kind of political warfare with Miss Roffey. Miss Roffey similarly. And yet each is devotedly fond of the other. Presence of Ingrid, aged nineteen, going to have a baby in August, provides them with an additional subject of controversy, about which they both complain, but from which they both probably derive a certain amount of satisfaction. So in each society, in each little home, in each individual heart, there goes on ceaselessly this process of conflict, which is an essential element of life and time, but which beyond time will disappear.

March 1, 1948

Death of Barrington-Ward, Editor of *The Times*. He probably died of remorse as he went sailing round African coast. Thought of him being buried in Dar-es-Salaam – little funeral party, local officials, etc., interring pitiable figure, whose feebleness and moral cowardice had led to *The Times* becoming useful instrument in the hands of civilization's worst and most dangerous enemies.

March 2–3, 1948

Met Fitzroy Maclean, MP and formerly liaison officer with Tito. Maclean had much to do with disastrous policy of recognizing Tito. Churchill considered him the T. E. Lawrence of this war. I was prepared to dislike him, but he disarmed me, first of all by speaking very flatteringly about my *Winter in Moscow* and then by taking very realistic attitude in conversation regarding the Russians. Lately he has been dealing with Displaced Persons, of whom he said there are now $1\frac{1}{2}$ million, 20% being Jewish. He confirmed that former Nazi terrorists are accorded better treatment by Russians than Socialists or Liberals; he mentioned the case of one man, who had been head of bodyguard of Pavelic, the Croat Quisling, and who had attempted to commit suicide when the Allies decided to return him to Yugoslavia. As it turned out, he was given a job in Yugoslavia, and one of Tito's men told Maclean that he was considered to be a thoroughly sound citizen. Whole confusion of present world situation arises from fact that Communist movements in Eastern and Central Europe, like Nationalist movements in Far East, are related to Western European Liberal tradition rather than to totalitarian gangsterism, whence they are derived.

Wrote leader on international situation, again strongly expressed. Writing leaders one gets worked up, as in a quarrel, and then afterwards wonders whether after all the emotion was genuine. As far as words are concerned, everything is moving towards a second performance of 1939, except that all the actors in the intervening years have grown tired and threadbare, and the lines they have to speak unutterably wearisome.

Spent quiet evening with Hugh Kingsmill. Henry James, he

and I agreed, was very like P. G. Wodehouse's character Jeeves –
a gentleman's gentleman.

March 4, 1948

Agonizing neuralgia. Lunched with Lord Camrose, and the publisher of *New York Herald Tribune* and their London Correspondent. Slow pace of conversation reminded me of what I had already
almost forgotten – the laboriousness of social life in America.
Herald Tribune publisher, Robinson, said that General Eisenhower had refused many lucrative offers for his memoirs, but was
now doing them for the *Herald Tribune* and Doubleday, price
being $600,000, on which he had to pay Capital Gains Tax (about
25%) but not income tax, which of course would be much more.
Two men were helping him with memoirs, one being Joe Barnes,
foreign editor of the *Herald Tribune*, with fellow-travelling sympathies. They are based on diary which Eisenhower kept throughout the war up to D-Day. In Robinson's view, Eisenhower may
still stand for President, despite many statements he has made
suggesting otherwise, and if he does, will sweep in.

Robinson also gave lengthy account of new process for printing
newspapers, which eliminates composing room. It is based on
lithographic copy of typescript. *Herald Tribune*, he said, has made
all preparations to use this process in the event of a threatened
strike by compositors coming off.

Tony Powell has worked up a very interesting article on Gogol,
using a suggestion I had made that Gogol was like a Russian
Edward Lear. Oddly enough, both had obsession with large noses
and were given to melancholia – Gogol, in fact, more or less died
of it. Like all Russian writers, Gogol was given to occasional out-
bursts of Slav imperialism, which seemed to foretell present
expansionist regime. I doubt actually whether the Revolution has,
in essentials, changed Russia at all. Reading Gogol, or Dostoevsky
for that matter, one realises how completely the Soviet regime has
fallen back on to, and perhaps invigorated, the old Russia. Certainly
there is much more of Gogol and Dostoevsky in the regime than
there is of Marx.

March 6, 1948

After tea, Tony read me first part of new novel he is writing, *A Question of Upbringing*. It begins extremely well. His talent has now come to maturity. I left with him and Violet the first 100 pages of *In Collaboration* which, to my great pleasure, they found highly diverting.

Dined with character called Jack Rennie and his Swiss wife in flat next door. Rennie used to be with British Information Services in America, and is descendent of the Rennie who built Waterloo Bridge. He obviously would love to return to America. It is an extraordinarily clear division of Europeans – those who love America and those who find it repugnant, and the whole question generates very strong feelings. I tried to preserve a neutral position – i.e. I didn't want to live in America, but found much to admire there. We had a meal on plates in our laps. When I told Tony that the Rennies had adopted this American custom, he said it was typically destructive of order, anarchical, like so many American practices.

March 7, 1948

Andreas Mayor – melancholy but to me enormously sympathetic cousin of Kitty's, employed at the British Museum – is in trouble. Trouble consists of usual female entanglement, and I refused to advise, because I said in such cases advice never taken and usually in the end resented. Andreas extraordinary example of man with quite remarkable talent and intelligence, apparently with everything that makes for a happy and interesting life, but because of a kind of inward despair, has never been, nor ever will be able to make terms with life.

March 8, 1948

Walked to House of Commons for debate on Naval Estimates. Parliament exceedingly depressing, shabbier than ever. Dugdale presented Estimates in the manner of a rather clever boy speaking at a school debating society. One of his great points was that Warrant

Officers were now to be admitted to naval officers' messes. It seemed a meagre entry on the credit side to offset the decay of British sea power.

Winston got up and answered him. He, too, seemed dispirited, and went through his performance without much authentic emotion. He is an extraordinary spectacle, physically, and though now his powers are so diminished, he is still held in great awe on both sides of the House, and he occasionally recovers flashes of that rich humour which has made him so memorable an orator. I felt a great affection and veneration for him, but it seemed a pity that after his great performance in the war, he should have to, or choose to, demean himself by bickering with fifth-rate people.

March 9, 1948

Came back early and walked with Kitty in Regent's park. Wonderful evening light, blossoms beginning, Spring coming. In the Embankment Gardens crocuses. Nowhere in the world anything like so delightful as English Spring.

Went in to see David Astor, son of Lord Astor, proprietor of *The Observer* newspaper. Astor told me that he had been miserable at his prep school, and that his great friend there had been John Amery (son of Leo Amery and brother of Julian) who, even at his prep school, was always getting into trouble through his conflict with the authorities. In waging war on the authorities, he had displayed great courage and ingenuity. I said to Astor that this fitted in with the impression I had formed of Amery's character when talking with Rebecca West, who reported his trial as a traitor, and also when looking for evidence against him, which I had to do when we first went in to Paris. Amery, I said, if the cards had fallen a little differently, might well have won a tremendous reputation as a commando. There is a great element of chance in these matters.

> 'Who thinks must suffer, and who feels must mourn,
> And he alone is blessed who ne'er was born.'
>
> Matthew Prior

March 10, 1948

At NUJ meeting Ziman got through a resolution expressing sympathy, etc., with Czech journalists victimized in recent Prague coup. Several Communists present opposed it, but meeting strongly against them, I was pleased to note. Secretary and Treasurer of Branch are both Communists – one dark, rat-faced, rather clever looking; and the other absolutely typical features which have become recognizably the party Face – large mouth, soapy complexion, hair thick on top of head and shaved at the back, head backless.

Late news was suicide of Jan Masaryk, about which I differed with most others at the *Daily Telegraph*. In my view, Jan Masaryk was thoroughly corrupt, who bumped himself off because he saw at last where his moral cowardice and ideological 'Playboyery' had led him. I vividly remember visiting him in Washington, fat, self-indulgent face, slightly tight, coming into the room looking like a broken-down butler, with his master, the little Communist, Clementis, who never left his side when he was abroad, with him, and saying in a loud voice, looking sideways at Clementis – 'Has anyone seen an Iron Curtain? I haven't.' Well, he has now. I was rather heated on the subject, especially with Coote, who was inclined to sentimentalise Masaryk, but I realised afterwards that, from the point of view of the damage suffered by the Communists through his suicide, the more he was sentimentalised as an heroic democrat, the better. The only point is that he was not heroic, and not really a democrat. I thought of him in the big Foreign Office building in Prague, with his pretty secretaries and his buffoonery, and his liquor, and his cigarettes, belatedly realising that the game was up and that not even the name he bore was needed any longer, and so deciding to jump out of the window. It will be interesting now to see what President Benes does.

March 12, 1948

Wrote leader on Brussels agreement. Constantly writing that Western Europe can unite against Russian menace, but I doubt really if it is possible. Essentially a shadowy project, like attempt to revive Holy Roman Empire. Theoretically admirable, actually inconceivable, I fear. The march of events has its own moment½m, and is clearly now directed towards the final destruction of what remains of Western European civilization, to clear the way for some new essay in collective living. To recognise that this is so does not imply an acceptance of its desirability. One belongs to what is to be destroyed, and to pretend otherwise, to oneself or to others, is both foolish and contemptible.

March 13, 1948

Went down to Denham to lunch with Lord Vansittart. He resigned from being head of the Foreign Office in 1938 because he disapproved of the Munich policy, and then expected to get his reward when Churchill became Prime Minister. Of course he was disappointed.

Vansittart's wife, Bobby Barclay's mother, very charming and delightful woman. She likes gossip and witty remarks, and is still very pretty. We had rather an indifferent, draughty lunch, served by manservant. It always astonishes me how uncomfortably the rich usually live. Vansittart's contempt for Eden is unbounded, but he is, he says, disappointed in Bevin also. He takes the gloomiest possible view of the present international situation, asked me a lot of questions about America and about Inverchapel, whom he dislikes and despises as much as I do. Much of his bitterness is, one feels, derived from his disappointment in his own career. It is better, I reflected, for the ambitious to attain their ambitions, since thereby they are made happier and therefore better company. There is nothing more boring than a grievance, however well founded. He agreed with me about Masaryk having no moral backbone.

I later walked to the station with Bobby Barclay. Lovely evening. Strolled up and down railway platform, waiting for the train. Always to me rather pleasant, I don't know why, in the evening, on a small station platform, walking up and down, with the railways lines gleaming in the setting sun, awaiting a train.

March 14, 1948

At *Daily Telegraph* I wrote long leader on the Marshall Plan. Later Gerald Bullett appeared. Had not seen him for some years, but just the same – large, kindly, somehow dead. He is still going on just as he has gone on for the twenty years I have known him, homme de lettres living in the country, farm house, kindly but somehow irritable wife, thinking of love affairs he has not had, and writing books he will never write. Pleasant soul. 'I'd like to be religious, if only I could believe in something,' he said, characteristically. We exchanged news in the way one does when one sees someone not wholly sympathetic after a long interval. He has lately written a life of George Eliot; formerly novels, one quite successful, called *The Jury*. Kitty said of him that he resented getting old and that this demonstrated the unreality of the vague mysticism in which he affects to believe. She said the deadness of his face was due to the immense amount of time he had spent being bored. Boredom, she said, hung on his like fat. He is like a character in a Turgenev play, one of those men who keep asking whether it is not time for tea.

March 15, 1948

Wrote leader on Government's decision to bar communists and fellow-travellers from responsible positions in the Civil Service. Everything is preparing for showdown between communists and the rest. More and more it is becoming the sole preoccupation of newspapers, individual thoughts, etc. The next big battle in this war will be fought in Italy, and the general opinion is that the Communists will win it.

March 16, 1948

I noted a typical Beaverbrook paragraph in the *Londoner's Diary* (*Evening Standard*) in which it is pointed out that for a newspaper proprietor to attain Lord Beaverbrook's age of 68 makes him a prodigy. It reminded me of when I was on the *Evening Standard* and was instructed to do a paragraph on the death of J. M. Barrie, pointing out that the bronchial complaint of which he died provided a most agreeable death, and was, for this reason, known as 'old man's friend'. The point is that Beaverbrook, with his evangelical upbringing, is terrified of dying and going to hell, and that he is always trying to reassure himself in the columns of his own newspapers that he won't die, and that if he does dies, it will be pleasantly and easily. He is himself a sufferer from bronchial complaints. With increasing years he only grows more irresponsible and selfish in the conduct of his newspapers. Hugh Kingsmill once described him as 'Robin Badfellow'.

Kitty had lunch with my sister-in-law, Ingrid, who described her cellar life in Berlin in 1945. After 'Liberation' Russian soldiers, drunk, used to come down at night and feel in the bunks for females and finding any, rape them. Ingrid managed to avoid this by putting a lot of clothes on, etc., to hide her sex. We marvelled to think that there are, however, hundreds and thousands of human beings in this case in Europe. And yet I go on writing in the *Daily Telegraph* about keeping Western Europe civilization alive!

March 17, 1948

At the *Daily Telegraph* we listened to Truman's speech to Joint Congress Session, calling for renewal of conscription and promising military support to a Union of Western European Nations. The wireless didn't work very well, and it seemed quite a symbolic scene – Johnstone, Campbell Dixon, film critic, and myself in the office of a London newspaper, leaning over a wireless set that was out of order, trying to catch the speech of the President of the United States.

Went to dinner with Hugo Wortham. Present: Major-General Sir Edward Spears, during the war head of the British Military Mission in Syria. Spears, whom I had met before, told a number of French stories rather well. Shrewd character, I should suppose. He quoted one excellent remark: 'Time cannot preserve what Time has not fashioned,' relating this to the various Russian puppet regimes in Eastern Europe. Spears also quoted another remark in French, apropos of Jan Masaryk, which was to the effect that honour is like an island, to which, once you leave it, you can never return. For many years Spears was a leading Francophile, but since his personal bad relations with the French he has reversed this attitude, and now says that the only hope for a Western Union is to reconstruct and rearm Germany. He said that travelling about in France recently, he found that memories of the German Occupation were less bitter than memories of the American liberating troops. I took him up on this point, though there may be something in what he said.

March 18, 1948

To the Vaudeville Theatre, where we met the Griggs. Play was farce called *The Chiltern Hundreds*. Quite entertaining, in the P. G. Wodehouse genre, with some really brilliant acting by A. E. Matthews. We went on to dine at the Carlton Grill. The Griggs in tolerable form, though most odd couple, she older than he is, entirely devoted and dependent upon one another, but living together in a constant state of irritability. Grigg told me that he had seen Monty lately, and that, according to Monty, the Americans were pressing for immediate preparation of operational plans in the event of war with Russia. Grigg agrees with me that General Marshall, U.S. Secretary of State, is mistaken about the immediate prospect of war, but of course one never knows.

Grigg also says that Dalton was actually chosen as Foreign Secretary by Attlee, but that the King refused to agree. This act in itself constitutes complete justification for the monarchy.

March 19, 1948

Wrote leader on speech by Marshall. Walked back along the Embankment, which always delights me in the evening light. Then to BBC for *Friday Forum*. Discussion was on recent Government action barring Communists from responsible positions in the Civil Service. Other speakers: Percy Cudlipp, now editor of the *Daily Herald*, (who was editor of the *Evening Standard* when I was on the *Londoner's Diary*) and Dingle Foot, Liberal brother of Michael Foot. Difficulty about the broadcast was that the three of us were really in agreement about the principle of barring Communists from responsible positions in the Civil Service. Our only difference was on procedure. I'd like to roast them in a slow oven; Cudlipp would like to keep them out of the Civil Service, and Foot to submit each case to some kind of impartial tribunal. There was thus insufficient difference of opinion between us to make a lively discussion, but afterwards Tony Powell, who listened, said he thought it was pretty good. After the broadcast, we came back to the flat together. Mrs Cudlipp was with Kitty, she, like Percy, in the interval since we saw her last, having become rather heavy and dissatisfied looking. The Cudlipps provide yet another example of how little relation worldly success bears to individual satisfaction. No one could have been more successful than Percy, who arrived in London from Cardiff and had become editor of a national Daily at the age of 27, but somehow or other it hasn't turned out to be quite what he wanted.

March 23, 1948

At Paul Nash Exhibition, Tony Powell explained to me that Nash was really belated product of French Impressionism, whose development in England had been delayed by that utterly bogus thing, the Pre-Raphaelite Movement. As Tony put it, while English painters were fooling about with the 'Blessed Damozel' French painters were hard at work developing an authentic school of painting. Nash pictures seemed to me feeble, though some of the less pretentious ones, like a glimpse of a path through Savernake Forest, I rather liked. There is a complete absence of human beings in his paintings. It was interesting to contrast his best known picture *The Menin Road* painted in the 1914/18 war with his picture of the *Battle of Britain* painted in the 1939/45 war. The former is in its way remarkable; the latter a complete muddle. Nash, I thought, must have been very typically a product of the 1914/18 war, even down to painting coloured toadstools.

Interested to note two prostitutes in Sackville Street, nowadays quite a rarity. They had a pleasantly old-fashioned, rather touching air in this troubled time.

Very worried and alarmed about Hugh Kingsmill who I hear continues to be very sick, with constant vomiting.

March 24, 1948

Went along to Artists Rifles Depot and filled in necessary forms to join 21st SAS Regiment. Some old familiar Orderly Room scene – sergeant-major, forms in triplicate, etc. Tony came with me. As his father was a professional soldier, he doesn't react to such a scene in quite as objective a way as I do. In my case, I said, the equivalent would be a Fabian Summer School where a discussion was in progress on the need for a world authority.

Dined with Douglas Jerrold and his wife at Whitehall Court. Douglas as ever, completely unreal. Tony said of him once: 'How did he ever get out of the Forsyte Saga?'

March 25, 1948

Went to BBC to lunch, for Critics Programme. Chairman Eric Newton, whom Kitty and I had known in Manchester, name formerly Oppenheimer. When we knew him he was an expert on making mosaics in Cathedrals, made one for instance in Liverpool Cathedral, and extremely talented at this work. Married then to large, rather domineering woman, with two children, and had notion of a wonderful world elsewhere, in pursuit of which he walked out on his wife, and being talented and quick-witted managed to establish himself in London, with some success, as an art critic. World elsewhere, however, has not particularly pleased him, and he looks more woebegone than ever. Kitty said his face was 'tear-stained'.

Others present: Anthony Bertram, who had squeezed some vicarious excitement out of secret operations into Occupied France, by lending his house as a hide-out for those taking part in them. Also Philip Hope-Wallace; and M. R. Ridley, former clergyman and Balliol don. We all had a somewhat constrained lunch together. Interesting to meet again Donald Boyd, the producer, who was on the *Manchester Guardian* with me many years ago. Boyd said he had recently been up to Manchester and visited the offices, but everyone seemed dead there, he said, and he described going up to the canteen and seeing a group of people, whom he vaguely remembered, covered with cobwebs.

March 26, 1948

At the Authors' Club Johnstone and I ran into Brian Howard, who was exceedingly annoyed because Claud Cockburn, Communist journalist, had been black-balled for the Club. I contended that this was wrong – indeed I had supported Claud's candidature – because a club was a purely social organization. I said I'd be prepared to go further than anyone in the way of depriving Communists of access to State secrets and means of sabotaging economic recovery, but that I differentiated between this and barring them from ordinary social intercourse. Johnstone didn't agree, and said that, in his view, because they belonged to a conspiracy it was right to blackball them. The argument, like all arguments, was rather futile.

March 27, 1948

Went with Pan and Val to see my mother, who was well and cheerful. Noted on bus returning from Croydon how sadly blitzed and damaged was South London, and how little has been done since to repair it.

Philip Jordan and the Powells came to dinner. Philip, as always, enigmatic and got dressing-down from Tony on the subject of Attlee and the Labour Government. In Philip's view, the Government has now gained in morale as result of coming out in the open against Communists. He seems to be enjoying his job more, but has, as Tony pointed out, that curious grey puffy look, which love of power, in any form, gives people.

March 2, 1948 (Easter Day)

Listened to The Critics programme. Always rather disconcerting to hear one's own voice, which sounds so unlike what one imagines it to sound like. Thought programme went fairly well, but wondered why people should wish to listen to such chatter. Apparently they do.

Went with Kitty and Pan and Val to pleasantly conducted Evensong in local parish church, but rather pathetic, very few

present, mostly elderly and female, in contrast with enormous
crowds outside which had been to the Zoo. Thought this contrast
somehow reflected whole spirit of the age.

Tony told me that fifteen food parcels which the Pakenhams
had mysteriously received from America had, in fact, been sent
to them by David Astor. As he said, 'It is extraordinary how good
the rich are to one another.'

March 30, 1948

Usual Heinemann meeting. Business of publishing, I have come
to the conclusion, is really rather more depressing, if anything,
than journalism. Nearly all the manuscripts I have so far been
shown exceedingly tedious. In journalism there is at least the
reality – news – on which the whole phoney business is based. In
books there is not even this reality.

Went with Ziman to meeting of *Daily Telegraph* NUJ Chapel.
Curious little gathering in upstairs room of Tudor Street pub.
Only about ten present, character presiding addressed as 'Mr
Father', he being Father of the Chapel. Meeting attended by
Chairman of Central London Branch of NUJ, dimmish, not un-
sympathetic figure from Reuters. Anti-Communist sentiment very
strong, and resolution passed that election of Branch officers
should be henceforth by ballot rather than show of hands.

Started reading Goebbels' Diary. Interested to note that he,
too, writer manqué who had begun by producing a bad novel and
a play which no theatre would put on. Most men of action seem to
be writers manqué, and correspondingly most writers, men of
action manqué. Interesting theme.

March 31, 1948

Hugh Kingsmill has now been operated on and is getting better,
thank God. I have been trying to prevail on *Punch*, through
Richard Mallett, to continue paying him for the two reviews he
normally does each week, while he is ill and unable to do them.
Mallett said that Evoe (E. V. Knox, the editor) had been unable to

arrange this. It confirmed an impression which Hughie and I have often discussed, that people like Evoe, who seem to be so shy and sensitive that they can scarcely endure human intercourse are capable of being, when it's unavoidable, hard-hearted, cold and calculating.

April 1–3, 1948

Went to BBC again for Critics Programme. Donald Boyd delivered short lecture, saying that in last week's programme some of my remarks had had to be cut out because they were too strong. There is something peculiarly oppressive and depressing about whole atmosphere of Broadcasting House. It reminded me of being in Russia.

Brian Lunn rang up for news of Hugh Kingsmill. He was in an agitated state, because he had heard of his brother's illness and was very upset to think that in recent months there had been a coldness between them. Brian came in himself later, greatly tidied up and cleaned up as a result of his latest marriage, but, on the debit side of the balance, become an appalling bore, which, in his odd way, he never was before. Talked about Hugh Kingsmill and Germany, where Brian is most anxious to go in order to see former German friends and, perhaps, write a book about their present attitude of mind. Suggested British Council to him. Like all such characters, formerly left-wing, he is now sentimentally pro-German. Again I thought of Cholerton's remark, 'the vomit returns to the dog'.

Met Dundas. SIS character, eye-glass, moustache, etc. After a certain amount of beating about the bush he asked me for some information which I was able to supply. This conversation took place in Reform Club, with somnolent reformers seated around us, mostly very aged and decrepit. Every trade has its own technique and ceremonial, even costume, and produces its own characteristic types. I'd know Dundas anywhere.

April 5, 1948

Bonamy Dobrée to lunch, quite white now, but shrill and eager as ever. We knew him first in Cairo, when he was Professor at the

University there, and I a lecturer. He was bearded in those days, a gunner officer who had taken to literature, rather than a literary gent who had taken to gunnery. He and Valentine Dobrée lived in a charming white house on the outskirts of Cairo, where we spent many pleasant times – lovely garden, sunshine, Cyprus wine. Valentine is dark, rather remarkable woman. He is very much a straw blown in the wind. When I first knew him, he took an ivory tower line; then later became mixed up with T. S. Eliot and the Douglas credit plan; later, to my amazement turned left-wing; now I was interested to note, he is rather ratting on that, but with some uneasiness, lest the Communists succeed and he not be on the band wagon. He told me that he had applied for a chair in New Zealand – also rather significant I thought.

Went to *Coriolanus* with Kitty and the children. Wonderful play, very well produced and acted on the whole. Always find merely to hear Shakespeare's lines gives me infinite satisfaction. *Coriolanus* particularly apposite just now, as the political side of it so exactly conveys what is happening in countries like Czechoslovakia, for instance; the crowd is manipulated by the Tribunes exactly as by a Committee of Action. Perhaps the most poignant line in all literature is when Coriolanus says, 'There is a world elsewhere'. Children much enjoyed the play, but Val said she thought it was a shame that Coriolanus died.

April 6, 1948

Gave John dinner at the Club and went with him to a film *The Fugitive*, based on Graham Greene's novel *The Power and the Glory*. John is surprisingly mature. It is always slightly disconcerting when one's children remind one that they are growing up. For instance, he remarked while we were watching the film, with the tone of a connoisseur, that one of the actresses had a fine pair of legs.

Graham's novel, as usual, entirely mutilated in the film presentation. The whole point missed. For instance, the central character is a little, unworthy, drunken priest, who still, because he is a priest, and belongs to the Church, is capable of a sort of sublimity. This character is contrasted with the Police Lieutenant, strong and fanatical, but incapable of sublimity because he stands alone, matching his human will against the mysteries of life. All this is entirely missed in the film, the police lieutenant presented as a mere bully, and the priest as a mere saint.

April 8, 1948

At the Club Douglas Jerrold and I talked about Hugh Kingsmill. Douglas made the typically asinine remark that he thought things would be easier for him if he got a knighthood. The idea of Hughie finding all his difficulties eased because he was knighted was, to me, irresistibly funny. However DJ has a genuine fondness for him and we are both horribly worried about his present condition.

The children were shown round the *Daily Telegraph* to see the first edition being printed. Charles, who has an almost maniacal interest in machinery, was quite different from the others, darting about asking questions, and watching with a rapt and understanding eye.

April 9–11, 1948

Lunched with Bruce Lockhart, now rather broken-down, battered looking, but otherwise just the same. Always rather liked him, though of course, he is completely phoney. He has had, on the whole, very good run for his money, but gives a rather touching impression of not somehow being quite satisfied with it all. Full of stories of Political Warfare, of which he was head, and of the rogueries of people like Dick Crossman, who were his subordinates. Spoke of what a terrible nuisance Randolph Churchill had been to him in the war, and of how Winston, none the less, dotes on Randolph and puts up with his bad behaviour.

Bruce Lockhart rather at a loose end, I thought. He is too sharp not to see that what he has got isn't, after all, worth having, but not subtle enough to understand why not, or what is the alternative – if indeed there is one.

Letter from René McColl, in which he said of Masaryk's suicide: 'The window dressing finally flung itself out of the window'.

April 12, 1948

Went to see Hugh Kingsmill's daughter, Kathleen, by his first marriage. She described rather humorously how, when Hughie was admitted to the hospital in a serious condition, the surgeon asked him whether he would wish to be operated on at once or not. Hughie asked what would happen if he was not operated on at once, and the surgeon said he'd probably die. Then Hughie asked what would happen if he was operated on at once, and the surgeon said he'd also probably die. In that case, Hughie said, he would be operated on at once, because he'd rather die immediately. It is a great relief that he is better.

Went to *Daily Telegraph* and wrote leader on Russian policy in Vienna. Already find leader writing infinitely wearisome, but it is easy money, and the great thing to do is just not to worry about it.

April 13, 1948

I picked up Alan Taylor at the Athenaeum and walked with him along the Strand and Fleet Street. Taxed him with being a fellow-traveller and asked him what he thought he was getting at. He was slightly disconcerted, I fancy, but said that he quite recognised the impracticability of the position of the Socialist who believes in working with the Communists, but that he prefers this position, even so, to working with Anti-Communists. I said it seemed to me quite insane. He is now a Fellow of Magdalen, Oxford and, altogether, very well dug into the economic system which he wants to destroy.

April 16, 1948

Tony Powell had been reading Graham Greene's new novel *The Heart of the Matter* which he said was excellent in parts but, of course, to him not really congenial. He said Greene always seemed to him like a scholarship boy who was putting up a really wonderful performance. By way of parody he suggested *The Host for Sale* or *Brighton Made Me* in which the leading character would be a toothless Roman Catholic priest named Father Stinky, whose hobby was to go around at night in back streets slashing at little girls with his rosary.

April 17, 1948

Went down to Brighton to see Hugh Kingsmill, who, to my great relief, was in quite good shape though somewhat haggard and old-looking. He was asleep when I got there, but when he woke up and saw me sitting by his bed such a smile of happiness came on his face that I was deeply moved. We talked for about two hours and he was quite up to his old form. He described all that had happened, and I feel certain myself that nothing organic has been the matter with him, but only a severe nervous strain. He had been reading Sherlock Holmes stories which, as he said, with all their inherent absurdity, never quite lose their charm, especially when one is ill or fatigued. He quoted a line from Browning's *Andres del Sarto*: 'I am often tireder than you think' and said it was one of those everlasting remarks which can be described as 'husbandly'.

I walked back to the station along the sea front, feeling very happy. Pretty Regency houses, and Brighton altogether less touched by the war and oppressive post-war austerity than any English town I have been in.

April 19, 1948

The Italian elections, being watched everywhere with breathless interest, now look like producing anti-Communist result. Odd outcome of the war that all the ostensible victors should have their eyes fixed on Italian elections.

Read short stories of Henry James. After all, with all their affectation, infinitely refreshing because they are literature rather than journalism – that is, preoccupied with the significance rather than the phenomenon of life.

April 20, 1948

At the Ivy, I discussed General MacArthur with Vernon Bartlett, who said of him that he was the only person he had ever interviewed, besides Hitler, with whom he was unable to interpose a single remark.

Much excitement over the Communist defeat in the Italian elections. Discussing this with Johnstone, we agreed that it didn't amount to much, because the de Gasperi Government would inevitably, in due course, become unpopular, and the Communists would be the alternative. Parliamentary government, we agreed, only works in communities which are essentially united. The moment you have a real conflict, whether of race, or class, or religion, democracy is unworkable. The Communists know this, and when they get into power, therefore, the first step they take is to eliminate all representative institutions.

Johnstone and I thought that we might well devote the last years of our lives to a study of the causes of our civilization's decay. We might call it, we thought, *Prometheus Bound*, because our general argument would be that Zeus was perfectly right to bind up Prometheus, and that whenever Prometheus gets free, as in this age, civilization and social order inevitably fall to pieces, and cannot be reconstructed until he is again bound.

April 21-24, 1948

Read noisy, violent novel about the Pacific War, *The Naked and the Dead*, for Heinemann. Reflected, as so often before, on how America emotionally is precisely in the situation we were in in 1918.

John telephoned to ask if he might return late as he and a friend of his wanted to go to a place they knew of. I said he couldn't, and afterwards remembered occasions when I had wanted to stay out late. Very difficult to put oneself in one's children's position. He came back quite cheerfully and we laughed over the episode. He had only wanted to go and have an ice, as it turned out.

April 26-27, 1948

Walked to the *Daily Telegraph* through Temple Gardens, beautiful sunshine, people everywhere because of King and Queen's Silver Wedding celebrations, all seemingly happy.

Lunched with Peter Fleming, who is now mainly engaged in

farming. He scarcely looks older than when I first knew him, when he was youthful prodigy, only a slight touch of sadness has come into his expression, as though he still hadn't got over the initial shock of finding his pursuit of exploration and adventure constantly disappointing. It is also probably rather annoying for him that his actress wife, Celia Johnson, is now much more famous than he is.

Ziman said that the difference between 'vain' and 'conceited' is that a vain person wants others to think well of him, whereas a conceited person thinks well of himself. He said that he was conceited and Churchill vain. Actually, he was, I fancy, taken it as a personal insult that Churchill has been altering the arrangement of articles Ziman made from Churchill's war memoirs.

April 29–30, 1948

Last Critics Programme, glad indeed to think it was the last. Very delightful newcomer from *Punch*, who asked about Hughie, Eric Keown. He told me about Emmet, who draws those extraordinary railway trains. He lives in Devonshire and has an intense and quite peculiar loathing of recent developments in machinery, probably as a result of having spent the war as an aircraft designer.

April 30, 1948

Met Tony Powell at Charing Cross, and we went down together to Tunbridge Wells, near where he is staying. House is old, oak-beamed, rather draughty, very cold. It belongs to Evelyn Waugh's first wife. Delightful to be in the country again, especially that part where the orchards are so beautiful at this season.

Read Graham Greene's *The Heart of the Matter* about which Tony has to write a 'middle' in *The Times Literary Supplement*. Novel, like all his work, is excitingly written, but in many respects absurd. It is about the period during the war when he was in Freetown on the west coast of Africa and I was in Lourenço Marques on the east coast, doing the same job. We used to communicate with each other in cipher. Thus I was able quite easily to pick holes in the narrative. I said to Tony that reading the novel was like going into a Roman Catholic church in some out of the way place in

France or Italy. The immediate impression is distasteful – the half-light, the stale smell of incense, the garish figures of the Calvary. But after one becomes acclimatized to the atmosphere, it becomes interesting and even moving. All the same, when one comes out again into the light of the sun, it is a great relief.

Tony and I were able to identify most of the characters. There is every reason for the book to have the enormous success it is set for.

May 1–2, 1948

Went off with Tony and Violet to tea with some neighbours, Colonel Horden, whom I remembered vaguely in MI5 during the war, and his wife – typical MI5 secretary, type I nick-named 'hand of officer only'.

On Sunday went to tea with the Pryce-Joneses. They are living in a rather derelict farmhouse, which is full of handsome but large pieces of Empire furniture which she brought back from France. The effect of these pieces in low-roofed farmhouse rooms distinctly bizarre. Little boy there, Alan Pryce-Jones's only child, who, as Tony said, looked exactly like a successful banker. Extraordinarily self-assured – going to Eton next term.

We stayed on to drinks, and once again Colonel Horden and his wife appeared. Country society nowadays reverting, it seemed to me, very much to the Jane Austen pattern of small numbers of people ceaselessly seeing one another and doing things together. Could imagine it becoming most wearisome.

May 3, 1948

No *Daily Telegraph* this month, to my inexpressible relief.

May 4, 1948

Heinemann. Frere described travelling by car with Ernest Bevin, when Bevin had one of his heart attacks. Frere said he went a strange blue colour, groaned, clutched convulsively at himself, wouldn't return to London or cancel speaking engagement at Chesterfield to which he was en route. Stopped at chemists and then at pub for brandy. On arrival at Chesterfield, he shook himself together, like a dog getting up from a sleep, delivered an excellent speech, and spent a convivial evening there. To a politician, the practice of demagogy operates as a kind of stimulant.

Hugh Kingsmill arrived with his wife Dorothy, whom I hadn't seen for a number of years, to convalesce here. He seemed much better, though looking very old. Lent him Churchill's novel *Savrola* which, he said, was like the very promising effort of a boy of twelve. What is interesting is that its projection of Churchill's life has all come to pass, thus bearing out the feeling I have always had that history is derived from the exercise of an immature imagination rather than from the operation of immutable laws. In other words, it is like a bad novel. N.B. Other good examples: Frederick the Great's poems: 'Que notre vie est peu de choses', with or without Voltaire's corrections; Napoleon's novel; and of course Disraeli's.

May 5, 1948

Thelma Cazalet, ex-Tory MP, talked about a biography of Lloyd George (by Sylvester) whom she had known well. She described how L.G. drove through a heavy snow storm to Wales to see his wife when she lay dying, but arrived too late. The next morning, when Thelma arrived on the scene for the funeral, he was sitting up cheerfully in bed reading Ludwig's *Life of Bismarck* and expressing the keenest interest in messages of condolence. He was specially concerned to get a message from Churchill, with whom he felt a great rivalry, though always fond of him. Thelma said that L.G. was a great physical coward, and built for himself an enormous air-raid shelter at Churt, where he expected to form a government after the destruction of London, and even insisted on his wife building one in far away Caernarvonshire. Doubtless, he would have played the same role as Pétain did in France if this country had been forced to surrender.

May 6, 1948

Unable to work. Sat in Regent's Park with Hugh Kingsmill. His mind remains as delightfully active as ever. He recalled a Morrow drawing for *Punch* which was refused, showing the animals coming out of the Ark, which was on top of a hill. The animals are tearing down the hillside, and Noah is at the bottom, looking rather lost, and saying: 'Now I should like to say a few words on post-war reconstruction'.

May 7–9, 1948

Read Lermontov's *Hero of our Time*. Very charming. Introduction was written by Mirsky, whom I remembered very vividly in Moscow, where he used to come for a bath in my flat, and who was finally bumped off because he wrote a highly critical article on Pushkin, not being aware that the Party line had moved in the direction of admiring Pushkin.

May 11–12, 1948

Heinemann. Great excitement because Eisenhower manuscript had arrived.

Hugh Kingsmill left to complete his convalescence in Folkestone. He quoted a line of Matthew Arnold's, not particularly good, but very expressive of the mood of middle age – 'Calm's not life's crown, but calm is well.'

May 17–18, 1948

It appears that Evelyn Waugh was recently seen in deep mourning. On being asked why, he said it was on account of the death of the King of Sweden. Asked if he had been particularly intimate with the late king, he said 'No,' but as an officer in a Household Regiment (the Blues) he felt bound to obey the Court regulation of a week's mourning.

Tony described a dinner party given by Cyril Connolly, present being a man with whom his (C's) wife had formerly lived and a girl with whom he (C) had formerly lived.

Tony later showed me the piece he had written for *The Times Literary Supplement* on Graham Greene's new novel – quite good, but, as I pointed out to him, it is very difficult to be deceitful in the written word, and his feeling that the novel is unsatisfactory shows through his ostensible praise of it.

Andreas Mayor came to tea, looking much better than before.

Went with Kitty to supper with Valentine Dobrée. Also present Georgina Dobrée and agreeable architectural student, named Greenwood. Greenwood told me that most of the good architects were leaving the country because there seemed no possibility of any actual building here. This seemed to be characteristic of present government and of the cultural stagnation of equalitarian ideas which prevent all exceptional achievement in any direction for fear it should be unfair to others.

Picasso has now been attacked by the Russians and at this even the worm, Louis Aragon, has apparently turned.

May 24–25, 1948

Finished reading *What Maisie Knew*, whose skill and ingenuity so fascinated me that I couldn't put it down, and, at the same time, felt furiously jealous that Henry James should have been able to write so. Really wonderful descriptions of Folkestone and Boulogne. Must, sooner or later, I can see, write something on James.

Two attacks of fever in the night, both rather exhausting. Spent next day in bed. Read Montherlant's *Pitié pour les Femmes*. Two phrases in Montherlant which struck me: 'Le froid me donne besoin de l'intelligence'; '. . . Tu verras des filets de pêcheurs soutenus à la surface de l'eau par des fragments de liège. Les nuits passées avec toi sont ces fragments de liège que me soutiennent à la surface de la vie.'

May 26, 1948

Dragged along to BBC to practise Webb broadcast, the occasion being publication of second volume of Beatrice Webb's journal

Our Partnership. Found them apparently well pleased with it, though I'd had the impression that it was not quite the note they wanted.

A fascinating passage from *Our Partnership* about free love, in which Mrs Webb says that since 'you do not, as a matter of fact, get to know any man thoroughly except as his beloved and his lover, if you could have been the beloved of the dozen ablest men you have known, it would have greatly extended your knowledge of humanity and human affairs.'

May 28, 1948

Still in bed. Called in doctor, who made expected diagnosis and gave me some different sleeping pills. Discussed with him National Health Scheme. He said he was not participating and proposed to continue operating on a black market or 'maquis' basis.

May 31–June 1, 1948

In the afternoon went back to the *Daily Telegraph* and wrote leader on Dalton's re-entry into the Cabinet. Watson seemed pleased with it, and everyone was very nice.

Hugh Kingsmill said of Churchill's War Memoirs, that the extracts latterly published in the *Daily Telegraph* had become more boring. I pointed out that they became boring precisely at the point that Churchill became Prime Minister. In other words, men of action can only write interestingly about themselves when they feel a failure. Thus Napoleon never wrote interestingly about himself, nor did Bismarck. On the other hand, Clarendon, who was not successful as a statesman, did write interestingly about his own times.

We talked about Tony Powell. I said that part of his extra-ordinary charm lay in the fact that all his tastes and opinions, even his conduct, are all defined. This makes him something of a sport in this age. For instance, when I was talking to him about James Joyce and how, at a certain point, I had been myself rather taken in by him, he said that he had never been at all attracted by that sort of stuff.

Everyone at Heinemann vastly excited over Graham Greene's *The Heart of the Matter*, now published and selling hugely. They all thought Tony's notice in *The Times Literary Supplement* excellent, except Graham himself, who, as I had foreseen, detected that it was much more critical than appearances might suggest.

Kitty spent day with her mother who, she said, had now removed all photographs of her second husband, Kitty's father, and only had pictures of her first husband and son by her first marriage. I said that this was an example of how, as people grow old and senile, they move backwards in time. Kitty recalled remarkable scene when her father was being buried and Mrs Dobbs almost hurled herself upon the undertaker, demanding to know if he considered there was an after life. The undertaker, not unnaturally, hedged and refused to commit himself.

The term 'undertaker' is a perfect example of an Englishism. No other nation would produce this extraordinarily nebulous, but somehow apt, term. Americans call them 'morticians', the French 'entrepreneurs des pompes funèbres', and the Spanish 'impresario'.

June 2, 1948

Managed to evade writing leader and spent evening with Hugh Kingsmill, Denis Brogan, Bertrand of *The Figaro*, and Cummings – brother of A.J. whom I had known in Geneva. Brogan, as ever, went on talking and talking. He is an extraordinary example of a man of outstanding intelligence whose company is completely boring. As Hughie said, he has somehow got separated from his reputation. Almost the only interesting remark he made was that when he was one of the editors of the *Dictionary of National Biography*, he noticed that after about the 19th century no one died of GPI whereas formerly quite a number had. This, he said, was because at the turn of the century it became known that General Paralysis of the Insane was a consequence of having had syphilis.

Ronald Lewin looked in to ask if I could suggest further subjects for BBC talks. He said that they were pleased with the

Webb broadcast, but that there had been criticism from without because of the line I took.

June 4–6, 1948

Doctor came again. Suggested X-ray of chest. I read a life of Smuts, late Premier of South Africa (*Grey Steel* by H. C. Armstrong) who is to become Chancellor of Cambridge University. Remarkable career. Interested to note even then the same sort of Liberal fallacy that resulted in Munich etc., e.g. Morley, the last of the Gladstonian liberals, saying that if only Milner 'had shared Kruger's tobacco pouch with him, agreement would have been reached and there would have been no Boer War'. Mentioned this to Tony, who said that liberalism (to which the Labour Party also essentially belongs) is a force unconsciously seeking anarchy. I agreed, and pointed out that Smuts after the Boer War was sure of a warm welcome among Liberals in England because he had been an enemy of England.

In a sense, though, Smuts did betray his Dutch compatriots and was won over by the English by honours and flattery, adroitly bestowed. At the same time, he did unquestionably have some sense of the future, a prophetic quality, which made him exceptional – a sort of mixture of a minor Hebrew prophet and Polonius.

Pan went off en route to Africa, his embarkation leave over. I felt great pang at separation, but he, Kitty said, went off cheerfully. What he wants, and I quite understand it, is to get off. His self-contained, self-denying character is very strange to me, but also very dear.

Found Sunday papers particularly gloomy. The sense of impending catastrophe is very strongly in the air again.

June 8, 1948

Went to lecture by Arnold Toynbee. Toynbee said that it was an open question whether our civilization was in a state of decline and was going to collapse, but it certainly had in a marked degree three of the symptoms of the decline of Greco-Roman civilization –

namely: Falling standard of life, an increase in lawlessness and a great deterioration in intellectual standards. He said that in the 5th and 6th centuries there were even Romans who welcomed falling under the barbarians, because it relieved them of the taxation and complicated administration of the Roman State. He also said that at the time of the Roman decline, there was much anti-aristocratic and equalitarian sentiment.

Toynbee is undoubtedly one of the intellectual figures of the age, though not, I think, quite in the first rank. He is married to a daughter of Gilbert Murray which, as Hugh Kingsmill said, seems slightly incestuous.

June 9, 1948

Drove out with Coote to his house for dinner, picking up Kitty and Lena Ashwell, the actress, and her sister on the way. As always with Coote, the evening curiously embarrassing. Kitty always breaks something in his house – this time his spectacles!

Got Lena Ashwell on to the subject of Shaw and Barrie. She described curious circumstance of Barrie's wife and how she came to leave him. After she had gone off with Gilbert Cannon Barrie said that he was quite ready to take her back if she would admit that she was 'contrite'. This, as Lena pointed out, was extremely unpleasant. She said that Mrs Barrie was an attractive, vivacious woman, who only married Barrie because he was desperately ill for love of her and apparently on his death bed. The moment she had married him, with typical Scots cunning, he got better. He then more or less shut her up in his house. Everyone used to ask her, according to Lena, why, as Barrie was so fond of children she didn't have some, and the answer she gave seemed to indicate that Barrie was incapable of having any.

I asked her whether she thought that Mrs Patrick Campbell was really keen on Shaw. She considered that probably there was not a love affair in the ordinary sense of the world. One of the reasons she thought this, was that once when she was walking with Shaw in Battersea Park, he pointed to a seat and said that it was where he used to sit with Mrs Pat. This scarcely suggested the lover.

June 10–12, 1948

Went to hospital to be X-rayed. (Learnt later that X-ray showed previous lung trouble had dried up.)

I took my godson, Peter Barclay to the Zoo. Rather enjoyed the aquarium. Fishes have always seemed to me the most fantastic variant of life. I remembered reading famous Portuguese sermon addressed to the fishes on the ground that they must have been particularly favoured of God since, when, at the time of the Flood, all the animals perished except those in the Ark, the fishes multiplied. It was a good time for them.

Noted that quite a number of the cages are now empty at the Zoo, but that the crowd stared as interestedly at the empty cages as at the others. In other words, the Zoo, like so much else, has only a kind of symbolic existence. It is the idea of seeing rather than actually seeing the animals which matters, and if there were no animals at all, but only a lot of empty and carefully labelled cages and pools, probably as many people would go.

June 14–15, 1948

Read long account of General Stilwell's Papers. Of Lord Mountbatten Stilwell said: 'I have been thinking of Mountbatten as a sophomore but I have demoted him to freshman.'

P. J. Grigg has been seeing a lot of Monty (this indicates that Monty, momentarily at any rate, is going down hill) and told me that Monty is coming to hold present Government increasingly in contempt except, oddly, Shinwell, Minister for War, who, he feels, as Grigg put it, 'to be a fellow pariah'. Grigg said the awful thing about this Government was not that one disliked them so much as that they drained public affairs and daily life in this country of their interest. We talked about one day writing together a history of the decline and fall of British rule in India. P.J. said that Monty had told him that the British Government had given an undertaking to the Americans that if the Russians moved into the Western Occupation Zones in Germany, they would fight.

June 18, 1948

Received letter from BBC as follows:

'Dear Mr Muggeridge,
          We have learned that your talk on Beatrice Webb's Journal has given some pain to friends and admirers of Mrs Webb's and, in the circumstances, we have decided not to repeat it on Monday. We will, of course, pay in full the fee which you were offered for the repeat, and we shall merely make a routine statement at the microphone announcing the substitution of another programme.
          I regret very much if this decision of ours causes you disappointment, and I hope that you will agree with us in regarding any pain caused to living people about a friend recently dead as over-riding other considerations.

Yours sincerely

(signed) George Barnes
Director of the Spoken Word.'

Afterwards learnt from Andreas Mayor that various relatives of Kitty's had complained and that a joint protest had been sent to Lord Simon (formerly Sir Ernest Simon), who is now Chairman of the BBC Board of Governors. Simon, I remember when we were in Manchester – red-faced, pompous. He has also got a pushing wife called Sheena, who both detested and modelled herself on Mrs Webb. Thus, it does not surprise me that he should have been only too ready to act on this protest from the Potter clan. Andreas also told me that they had been saying that I particularly asked to give the talk, and described myself as Mrs Webb's favourite nephew – very typical Potter untruth. Imagine that this is the end of my brief connection with the BBC.

In the street ran into Dick Scott, son of Ted Scott, and grandson of C. P. Scott. He was very charming and friendly, which both pleased and surprised me after my row with his family over the publication of *Picture Palace*.

June 21, 1948

Philip Jordan, very white, exhausted looking, a living symbol of the Government he serves, came to dinner. Present situation, he said, could not be worse. Talking with him, once again gave me the feeling that really there is nothing to be done, and that the last little flame of civilization will soon flicker out. As between prospective Republican presidential candidates providing free cheese and soft drinks in Philadelphia and the ruthless Slav terrorist machine operating in Europe, there is not much room left for what is represented by this country.

The same sombre thoughts were intensified by reading through long, tedious, but, to me, in a curious way rather fascinating, manuscript which Lothian, whom I met in India when he was in the political department, asked me to look at. It is a record of his long years of service in India and illustrates vividly how much we have lost there, and how quickly we surrendered a position seemingly, only a short while ago, so powerful and magnificent. Power built up slowly is dissipated quickly, leaving a vacuum behind. The courts of Indian princes in which this dour, but conscientious Scotsman passed so many years must be ghostly places now with the disappearance of British power in whose shadow they existed. Seen against eternity the rise and fall of empires is an ordinary enough occurrence, but to the individual who sees the process at work, strange and sad.

June 24, 1948

Lunched with Sir Walter Monckton at Simpsons. First met him in Simla in 1935. He seemed to have grown smaller, more wormish, I thought. He had just returned from Hyderabad, having for a number of years made a lot of money as the Nizam's legal adviser. Belongs essentially to the Duke of Windsor – personal contacts – let's try and understand the other fellow's point of view school, now totally obsolete. He seemed to be conscious of this. Although, technically as successful and prosperous as ever, he has a queer sort of apologetic manner.

The situation in Berlin is becoming steadily more critical. Coming to be realized by everyone I think now that a showdown is unavoidable, and a showdown might mean war, though I personally think it would be an entirely different sort of war (all wars are different) very much a continuance in a more acute form of the present state of affairs.

Lewin told me that the Webb row at the BBC was still going on. He was very evasive, but I gathered that I was not without defenders there.

June 25, 1948

Finished off *Ciano*. Two last Hitler–Mussolini conversations extremely interesting. Again remarked how Hitler, in some respects, saw so clearly what was happening in the world, but, nonetheless, was swept along like Macbeth to his ruin – various remarks he made, e.g. that Europe would have to defend itself against American imperialism.

June 26, 1948

Walked with Tony in the sun and sat talking with him, always a great delight. Remarked as an excellent example of coincidences, which we both tend to collect, that when Attlee was a little boy his parents got a governess for him, who turned out to have been recently sacked by the Churchills because she couldn't at all manage an unruly little boy named Winston.

June 27–28, 1948

Kitty out of sorts. In the morning I browsed over journal I had written while in India which seemed inconceivably remote, and I blushed for some of it. Not, however, without interest, and useful if I ever write an autobiography.

On the Monday morning saw Pan off to East Africa. He looked minute, with all his equipment and his huge overcoat, and obviously was upset at the thought of leaving, but, as always, plucky and master of his feelings. He went off in a troop train, the old familiar sight, troops being packed in, officers checking lists, etc., etc. I felt a moment of intense irritation at all this business going on, since one has the illusion that it belongs only to war, and with the ending of war ends totally. After a little thought I realized that such irritation was rather absurd, and that, in point of fact, a trip to East Africa at that age would be in the end a rather pleasant adventure.

At the *Daily Telegraph* considerable excitement over the state of emergency declared by Attlee and Tito's row with Moscow.

Tony and Violet came in to listen to Attlee's radio appeal to the public and to the dockers. It was a commonplace and uninspiring performance. He has that curious trait I have always noticed with social workers of adopting a different sort of voice when addressing poor people, a kind of version of their slang, a feeble attempt to be salty and emphatic. The poor little man seemed very nervous, and incapable of rising to his responsibilities. At the same time, one should be grateful that he is a decent little man and took the line he did.

June 30, 1948

Went to Heinemann, where we discussed present book slump which, according to Frere, is not really a slump at all but merely that readers, from having been ready to take anything, are now again exerting taste. He considered this a good thing and said that as far as Heinemann were concerned their sales were better than last year.

At the Junior Carlton I picked up Bill Deedes and we walked down together to the House of Commons. Bevin made statement on Germany, quite good, but he seemed in a pitiable condition of nerves, hand shaking, etc. His own benches were sparsely attended and gave him no supporting cheers. All his support came from the Opposition, though none of the Zilliacus gang ventured to pipe up against our remaining in Berlin.

Hugh Kingsmill quoted the sentence in which in *The Pilgrim's Progress* Christian looks forward to being relieved of his burden, and said that it is difficult not to feel like that about life. He told him : 'As to thy burden, be content to bear it, until thou comest to the place of deliverance; for there it will fall from thy back by itself.'

Read book on the trial of Oscar Wilde, giving verbatim account of proceedings. Whole thing very squalid, I thought, and extraordinary to reflect that it had been dished up previously as a sort of Calvary. Moral depravity could never produce anything first-rate. Other conclusions from Wilde book – Alfred Douglas even more contemptible than I'd thought, Wilde largely activated by snobbishness and vanity. Clarke, his counsel, behaved extremely well and everything possible was done to prevent his conviction. He wanted it, really. He was sick and tired of being Wilde.

July 2, 1948

At *Daily Telegraph* wrote leader on Lambeth Conference. Watson, for once, went out of his way to say he liked it very much, which pleased me. Actually feeling pretty rotten but curiously enough, as often happens, mind rather clear when body disordered.

July 5, 1948

Hugh Trevor-Roper came to supper. Hadn't seen him for some time. Youthful don, intelligent, rather full of himself as a result of the great success of his book *The Last Days of Hitler*. Very typically donnish, and when we asked him a few simple questions about Hitler: as, what sort of pictures he liked, had he slept with Eva Braun, he seemed quite unable to give a cogent reply.

July 6–7, 1948

Read *Pilgrim's Progress*, a life of Bunyan and other writings about him, for an article. Parts of *Pilgrim's Progress* I find more than ever wonderful, but doubt if Bunyan was a particularly pleasant character. He seemed to me to be very egotistic – for instance, his favourite example of Our Lord's kindness to him was that when he was serving in the army, he was ordered to go to a certain seige, and at the last minute his place was taken by another man whose head was shot off in the action. Bunyan's belief that this was an example of the Lord's loving kindness towards him, seems rather lamentably to leave out of account the position of his substitute.

Mentioned to Tony that all allegorists have something in

common – e.g. Bunyan, Swift, George Orwell, Kipling. Perhaps it is their desire to get away from human beings, to present life in terms of allegorical abstractions rather than of men and women. All the same, Bunyan one of the great writers in the English language without any question. He had that trick of all egotists, of exaggerating both his sins and his virtues. For instance, when he was describing his conversion, he spoke in the most exaggerated terms of his past delinquencies, but when, after he had become a preacher, he was accused of moral delinquency, he was furiously indignant, and insisted that his life had been impeccably virtuous. Egotists always want it both ways. Interesting to note that all through the period of Cromwell's Government, the encumbent and ritual in Bunyan's local church remained largely unchanged. Bunyan's circumstances were not as miserable as he liked to suggest.

Having series of penicillin injections – somewhat uncomfortable, but, according to the doctor, infallible cure.

July 9–11, 1948

Read long life of Bunyan by John Brown. Much interested in condition of Non-Conformity in those years. Dissenters, like Bunyan, very similar to French Resistance and, in the same way, when they were liberated, developed mystique of time when they had to go about in disguise, etc.

Discussed in detail with Tony very ominous international situation. I said I still thought most likely immediate development was a state of political warfare, growing steadily more acute, but not turning into actual declared warfare – an indefinite extension of phoney war. Tony had been to the Eton–Harrow match, said there were a surprising number of toppers, but that he noticed almost complete absence of boys from Eton and Harrow, only old Etonians and Harrovians like himself. Have very strongly the feeling that in all these affairs participants consciously or unconsciously aware that it is positively the last appearance.

Interested to note in Bunyan's Life, even at that time in a letter addressed to the Earl of Peterborough by John Eston, dated December 6, 1687 – 'It is the misery of this kingdom that so much Democracie is mixed in the Government that thereby the exercise

of the Sovereign power should be in any manner limited by the
suffrages of the common people, whose humours are allwayes
fluctuating, and the most part of them guided not by reason, but
without deliberation like mere animals.'

July 13, 1948

Went in the evening to a cocktail party given by the Powells.
Chatted there with Osbert Lancaster who does admirable pocket
cartoons in the *Daily Express*. Wore extraordinary clothes, reminding me rather of Arnold Bennett's description to Hughie of
his apparel – 'an English gentleman with modifications'.

July 14, 1948

Increasing perturbation over Berlin. Interested to note same old
line-up as before German war – namely, of appeasers. Pacificists
this time organized by the *Daily Worker* with the idea of producing
another peace ballot, etc.

July 15, 1948

Lunched with Douglas Jerrold and Evelyn Wrench, who more or
less controls *The Spectator*. Gathered that Wilson Harris, present
editor of *The Spectator*, is shortly retiring and that I am being considered as his successor. This, of course, would suit me admirably
from every point of view, and I went out of my way to be agreeable
to Wrench. The lunch seemed to be quite successful and when we
parted Wrench said that he gathered that he and I were in agreement on most questions. I enthusiastically assented. Douglas told
me afterwards that my supposition had been correct, and that he
had little doubt that Wrench would put my name forward. The
matter, however, cannot crop up for some little time. The prospect
of escaping from the *Daily Telegraph* is indeed a pleasant one.

July 17, 1948

Went off to Battle in the early morning. Val said in the train going down that my article on Bunyan, which she had read, was the only thing that I'd written which she's understood.

Went to look at cottage next to Mrs Dobbs' house, which is being very pleasantly altered and should be ready quite soon for us. Kitty, as usual, has organized it excellently. Once it is tidied up, it will make a really delightful retreat from London.

July 18, 1948

Papers all now openly writing about the possibility of war. I asked Dick Brooman-White what was happening in SIS as result of the international tension. He said the only change he could observe was that an enormous number of appreciations were being urgently requested. He said the turn-out of paper was going up by leaps and bounds, but apart from that, nothing. I asked him how things were in the way of intelligence, and he said, in his characteristically dry way, that very good intelligence was coming from places where it was easy to get and none at all from places where it was difficult to get.

July 22, 1948

Took day off. Went with Tony Powell on expedition to Eton which we had long planned. Hadn't been before to Windsor and found it interesting. Tony showed me all over the school – chapel, houses, playing fields. He said that Eton had influenced him much more than Oxford. Boys walking about in their tail coats and battered top-hats seemed to me extremely droll. Tony said, although it was over twenty years since he'd been there, it was the other people who seemed queer, and that he almost felt the flaps of his own coat as he walked along.

We had some beer in a place called The Tap, where the barman and his wife remembered Tony as a schoolboy. They complained bitterly of the changed times and spoke with nostalgia of the past. They really seemed quite astonishingly dispirited. I said to Tony that it was quite fitting that they should most resent social changes. Probably a large number of the boys and masters at Eton were Communist by this time.

Very pleasant sitting by the river and talking, also watching a rather desultory game of cricket. Tony said it was extraordinary, looking back, to recall with what passionate intensity he had longed to have the right to wear some of the coloured caps the boys we watched were wearing. I said it wasn't really extraordinary since, in the context of the school, they represented power and authority, therefore infinitely desirable to the will.

I mentioned to him that one of the Russian women who had come over to England, having married a British Embassy official in Moscow, had said that it made her angry to think, if Eton was the best school, her son wouldn't be able to go there because she hadn't enough money to pay the fees. I said that the whole point of Eton, in so far as it has a point, was that it represented something which was available only to a few people. It didn't particularly matter how these few were selected. The only essential point was, if institutions of that kind were to be preserved at all, that they should be restricted. If they weren't restricted, they ceased to be.

Went in the evening to see *King John* at the Open Air Theatre with Eric Newton and his wife. Newton said one ought to listen to Shakespeare at least once every two months just to remind oneself of what can be done with words – rather like going on a binge. Noted many indications in *King John* of what was to come in *Macbeth*, almost as though *King John* was a sort of rough draft for *Macbeth*.

July 23, 1948

Walking back to Whitehall Court with Douglas Jerrold, we tried to go under Admiralty Arch, found it closed, and turned down Downing Street. One policeman standing outside No. 10. D.J. said, in his opinion, best thing to do if one wanted to blow the house up would be to hand a bomb to the policeman and ask him to hold it for a minute. Felt that D.J., after all, was out of place in his right-wing Catholic position, and would have been happier as an anarchist. He really would have liked to blow up Downing Street, but with Attlee there, there seemed no particular point.

July 25, 1948

Interested to note that 15,000 volumes, constituting the Webbs' library at Passfield, realized only about £200. Complete set of H. G. Wells, complete works of Lenin, and signed presentation edition of the works of Herbert Spencer, only a few pounds apiece. Dawnism, Hugh Kingsmill and I agreed, was definitely in a decline. Dawnism is his word for those with a chronic tendency to see a new dawn coming along.

July 26, 1948

An extraordinary example of the complete irresponsibility of people in authority. In the draft of Churchill's *Memoirs* which was given to the *Daily Telegraph*, he put in a sentence to the effect that the Russians always observed their agreements. When it was pointed out to him that this was entirely and dangerously misleading, he struck out the sentence. What is extraordinary, is that he had been concerned in making a number of the many agreements which the Russians have broken, and therefore ought, presumably, to be in a better position than most people to know that these agreements have been broken. I've come to the conclusion that he was so power-drunk during the last part of his period in office that he scarcely knew what was going on – just maundered along. The amended text appeared in the *New York Times*, but in *Life* magazine, which also has been publishing Churchill's *Memoirs*, the sentence about the Russians observing their agreements was left in. Someone in America has noticed this, and of course has come forward to say that the *New York Times* cut out the sentence because it was favourable to Russia.

A boring article by Eden appeared in today's *Daily Telegraph*. When I asked Watson why, he said that Eden was very short of money. When I raised my eyebrows over this, and said that surely his wife was very wealthy, Watson told me that his wife had left him and was now in Bermuda trying to get into the US on the quota as an immigrant. This may prevent Eden becoming leader of the Conservatives in succession to Churchill. If so, it would be a good thing.

July 27, 1948

Excellent article in *The Economist* on the Berlin situation. After reading it, I considered the appalling prospect of an atomic war, and realized that such a war, whatever other consequences it might have, would put out once and for all and irretrievably, the remaining faint flicker of Western European civilization.

Somerset Maugham's attitude to women, I said to Tony, was completely unreal because he, as a homosexual, knew nothing whatever about it. He based the whole thing on physical appetite, leaving out of account both procreation and affection which, in fact, are the essential elements in the whole business. It is this preoccupation with physical appetite, which he doesn't feel, that makes Maugham's work so intensely vulgar – rather like Balzac's to the rich, or like Evelyn Waugh's to the highly born, or like Graham Greene's to the good.

July 31–August 1, 1948

Read the diaries of Tolstoy and his wife relating to 1910, the year in which Tolstoy died, having first run away from home at the age of 82. Have always considered this probably the most squalid episode yet. These two old creatures bellowing and shouting at each other, while Tolstoy preached the gospel of love, is singularly revolting. I shall include him, along with Rousseau and Walt Whitman, if I ever do my little work on the origins of present disintegration. There was a photograph in the book, the last one taken of Tolstoy and his wife, on their wedding anniversary. She is holding remorselessly on to his hand, and he looks puzzled and hopeless, both obviously demented, but she probably rather more so. Good title, I thought, for an essay on him would be *The Green Stick*. Spot chosen for Tolstoy's burial place was where, according to his brother Nicholas, 'the magic little green stick with the mysterious inscription telling how the welfare of mankind can be attained', had been buried.

August 3, 1948

Worked at analysis of Russian treaty violations – a formidable list. The difficulty, indeed, would be rather to find obligations which the Russians have fulfilled. Watson rather uneasy about this line of thought. Remarked that natural deduction to make from information I had tabulated was that it would be absurd to enter into any further agreements with the Russians. I agreed that was a reasonable deduction to make. He shook his head and turned away and didn't use the article, though he may later.

Extraordinary to see so exact a repetition of our dealings with the Nazis and Fascists. Each time when they broke one set of agreements and we came forward to conclude another, as we now know, it merely served to strengthen their determination to go on defaulting. Obviously, the same thing will happen with the Russians.

John came back from his JTC camp looking very well and excited about going to France. Long, amusing and happy letter from Pan, now in Nairobi.

August 10, 1968

At the Garrick Douglas Jerrold told me that the business of *The Spectator* was, in his opinion, as good as settled, but that the appointment wouldn't be made until next Spring, or the change-over take place until the Autumn of next year. Of course, I was very pleased, but at that distance things quite often don't come off.

August 11, 1948

Little anonymous man (such officials very like persons used in human guinea-pig experiments), from the Central Office of Information wants me to do some articles directed towards countering Russian political warfare. Read me from a folder he'd brought with him the rather pitiable directives issued in this matter. He said he had been in India for a number of years doing government publicity – essentially the sort of meek, broken-down character who undertakes such labours. If he represents the spearhead of defensive measures in the 'cold war', our prospects cannot be considered particularly good.

August 12, 1948

Discussed with Hugh Kingsmill the Godwin–Shelley relationship. I said that Godwin had shown the most remarkable practical ability in that, by writing a book against property and against marriage, he had managed to get his unattractive daughter married off to Shelley, a near baronet, whom he was able to touch thereafter for regular financial help. Hughie pointed out that he not only touched him, but that he refused to accept financial help in the form of a cheque drawn by Shelley because he didn't want his bank to know that he was receiving it. Altogether a very smart chap.

A man who dropped a toy bomb by way of protest on the United Nations building was suffering, according to the neurologists to whom he was handed over, from 'hallucinations of peace'.

August 15–16, 1948

At *Daily Telegraph* wrote leader on first anniversary of Indian Independence – not very congenial subject. Exceedingly bored with writing leaders for the *Daily Telegraph* and continue to hope that I may hear something about the *Spectator* business before so very long.

Finished reading *Nuremberg Diary* by American psychologist, Gilbert. Difficult to see how Nazi legend can be created with this first-hand record of the quarrelsomeness and poltroonery of the Nazi leaders while they were being tried.

Slept vilely.

August 17, 1948

Had long talk with Christopher Buckley and General Martin, *Daily Telegraph* Military Correspondent. Martin said the War Office was in a terrific flap and that the Americans only had one division in Germany. Buckley said that from the point of view of a war between America and Russia we, the British, were 'expendable' and that from the point of view of the social conflict which is going on throughout the world, people like us – I mean the journalists, intellectuals, etc., – were also 'expendable'. In the long view we were sure of victory, but on the short view our prospects seemed poor.

August 20, 1948

Went off to party out at Highgate given by Ronald Lewin of the BBC. Quite a collection of people there – Jonathan Cape, whom I hadn't seen for some years, with his young and third wife, who had the dazed look I have always noticed on young women who marry old men. Also small, slightly bottled character named Daniel George, who reviews books in the *Daily Express*. Entered upon long and rather fantastic discussion on personal immortality with elderly, pedantic-looking person with an eye-glass, who turned out to be Eddie Marsh, whose memoirs I had once very savagely reviewed. He was petulantly insistent that he did not believe in an afterlife, and when I said I did (partly, I must admit, to annoy him), he complained that there was no point in an afterlife if it did not involve a projection of the ego, and that if it did, it would be tedious. What a figure from another world!

August 21, 1948

Read with great delight, as always, Jane Austen's *Emma*. Personally consider her, next to Shakespeare, the greatest writer in the English language. Her novels are perfect, and after wading through Heinemann manuscripts, etc., etc., like a draught of water to a thirsty man. Particularly love *Emma*. Mrs Elton marvellous character, perfectly delineated. Note of gentle satire throughout, quite irresistible. Assume that it gives an entirely accurate description of life in the country in England. Amused to notice how Jane Austen uses all the tricks of modern novelists, considered to be so very original, but uses them without ostentation and with perfect effect – for instance, the conversation over the strawberry bed at Mr Knightley's house is exactly in the manner of James Joyce, only incomparably better done, and incomparably more amusing.

In the evening we went to see Sartre's *Crime Passionnel*. What an asinine production. The sentimentalized figure of the proletarian leader is rather like Alfred Doolittle in *Pygmalion*, only even more fatuous. There is a complete absence of humour. Particularly nauseating feature of it was the suggestion throughout of the neurotic, spineless intellectual trying to suck up to the noble proletariat. This very prevalent form of obsequiousness is, perhaps, the most degraded version of a degraded and degrading instinct. Even Party Line to be preferred, I thought, to this melancholy stuff. I returned to *Emma* with relief.

August 23, 1948

Tension regarding international situation again mounting as result of deadlock in Moscow talks. Once power begins to go, it goes very fast. It was extraordinary to see the representatives of France, England and America in effect sueing for peace in Moscow.

August 24–25, 1948

Worked on *Ciano* introduction. Afterwards went to SAS regimental headquarters for medical examination, which was entirely satisfactory. Ziman went with me. Before the war he used to belong to the Artists Rifles. I got him to tell me about his war career. Interesting fact emerged that his father was a Russian Jew, naturalized British. This fact dogged poor 'Z' throughout the war, and his four years of grind at the Territorials were therefore completely wasted from his point of view.

Saw chap called Thomas at the Conservative Party office about suggestion which had been made that I might oppose a fellow-traveller in the elections. Not particularly keen on doing it, but would if required. Thomas genial person, rather of the Eden type. Very depressed when he said to me, regarding Moscow talks, that he considered it an excellent thing that direct contact with Stalin has been re-established, and that he thought the only man who would be any good at dealing with Stalin would be Eden. I only mildly challenged this pitiable nonsense. Extraordinary in the light of all that has happened, that anyone should suppose it would make the slightest difference in our dealings with Russia, who approached whom.

August 26, 1948

Much amused to learn that Jonathan Cape's third wife had previously been married to the widower of Mary Webb, so that Jonathan, by marrying her, has kept the Webb royalties under his hand.

Peggy Williamson and Tony came to supper. Peggy had formerly worked in the MI6 office in Algiers and is still with the SIS. I was amused to learn that all the worst dead-beats were still firmly entrenched. Said afterwards to Tony, naming four of them, that it would be difficult to find any organization, private or public, directed by four so essentially incompetent people. In view of the nature of the organization in question, this is particularly grotesque.

August 27, 1980

Wrote leader on Conference of pacifist intellectuals being held in Poland, in which I praised Alan Taylor, partly with the idea that praise of him in the *Daily Telegraph* might ruin him in regard to his left-wing friends and associates! Also wrote a letter to him, telling him how strongly I approved of the line he had taken. Made me feel glad that I'd given him such a talking to last time we met. Decided sometime to do a general study of the Russian attitude to literature, science, and music, as that represents the most effective means of making Communist and fellow-traveller intellectuals feel uncomfortable.

August 29–30, 1948

Read part of Winston Churchill's memoirs dealing with Eden's resignation. Interested to note that he praises Chamberlain, while demonstrating that his policy was utterly ruinous.

Resumed work on *The Forties*. Mrs Dobbs arrived for two nights. Kitty's two brothers came to supper, and Mrs Dobbs tried to pick a quarrel with the elder, Pat, about religion. I imagine that she has spoken more hard words on the proposition that God is Love than on almost anything else.

September 1, 1948

Lunched with P. J. Grigg at the Carlton. He was delighted to have been offered a couple of additional directorships, but, as ever, highly contemptuous of most people. He was going on to the Bank of England where, he said, he was going to get an extension of a £10 million pound overdraft for the British Imperial Tobacco Co. We laughed much over this.

September 2, 1948

Ciano introduction now, thank heavens, finished. Reading *Ciano*, I reflected how conclusions about what is going on in the world are nearly always wrong, because one neglects to take into account the enormous force of purely personal considerations – for instance, that Ribbentrop was pro-British because he wanted to secure a great diplomatic success as Ambassador in London, and so became Foreign Minister, whereas von Neurath was anti-British because he didn't want Ribbentrop to get away with this.

Children all arrived back from France in very good form.

September 4, 1948

Went along to BBC to give Nuremberg talk, and while waiting turned on Yehudi Menuhin playing at the Edinburgh Festival. Really delightful, sitting there in a little remote studio, listening to music, very peaceful and cut off. Talk not very successful, I thought. Embarrassed to discover it should have been timed for fifteen minutes, so I had to cut five minutes as I went along.

September 5, 1948

Read *Talks with Tolstoy* by A. B. Goldenveizer. Goldenveizer obviously a complete ass, but therefore all the better for recording Tolstoy's conversation. Noted again Tolstoy's immense vitality, his whole conception of art based on this – 'when someone sees or feels something, and expresses it in such a form that he who listens, reads, or sees his work feels, sees, and hears the same thing in the same way as the artist, that is art'.

September 6, 1948

Tony is having difficulties with his father, and we discussed when it was that the whole mystique of quarrelling with parents began. I said that Samuel Butler was the literary pioneer, but that Freud came along and really put it on the map in a big way. Perhaps, I suggested, it was a natural reaction to the Victorian hearth and home mystique, which was itself a manifestation of growing scepticism about hitherto accepted institutional and religious values. Because of this, it was intensely sentimental. Sentimentality is the inevitable symptom of the continuance of belief when faith has gone. Thus, love-making is sentimental when there is no love, and religion is sentimental when there is no belief.

September 13, 1948

I ran into Graham Greene, whom I hadn't seen for a long time. We were affectionate with an undercurrent of hostility. Greene described having a haemorrhage in New York. He seemed to me in poorish shape on the whole, talked a lot about how Russian domination would be less terrible than American, etc. I mentioned the Church and he said Russians only destroy its body, whereas the Americans destroy its soul. Altogether, he's as difficult as anyone I know, but I still like him.

John said à propos offer by Frenchman to found a new Oxford college, that it should be called Dead Souls, and we'd all become fellows.

September 14, 1948

Johnstone and I again discussed Prometheus (April 20). Since
Rousseau, I said, Prometheus has been unbound and now he's
got to be bound again with much agony for all concerned. Have now
decided to include in *The Green Stick*: Rousseau, Tolstoy,
Nietzsche, Whitman, Shelley.

September 15–17, 1948

Curious lunch with Graham Greene and Tony. Started off with a
stupid row about delay in Eyre and Spottiswoode's publishing
Tony's book on John Aubrey. Hugh Kingsmill joined us and we
laughed a great deal over a letter of protest which we drew up about
the club silence room being abolished. Graham has a decided love
of conflict. Very typical figure of this time – which is why his novels
are so successful. In this connection, much taken with remark of
Herzen: 'You can work on men only by dreaming their dreams
more clearly than they can dream them themselves, not by
demonstrating their ideas to them as geometrical theorems are
demonstrated.'

Kitty very gentle to me, as to all of us. Unforgettable picture of
her making rough draft of long letter to Pan and then carefully
copying it. Actually, letter perfectly expressed. No such thing as
style I reflected, as such – only that people write well when their
thoughts are clear and loving, and write badly when they're
confused and angry.

September 22, 1948

Everything very tense in the evening, Bevin making statement on
Russian negotiations.

SIS rang up to know if I could go to Oxford to give a lecture.
They've obviously got some sort of a course on there.

September 23–26, 1948

Dined with Philip Jordan and his wife at flat they have now got in Long Acre. Also present, Donald Maclean who was in the Embassy in Washington and his American wife, rather pretty, well off. Discussed everlasting question of Russia and the possibility of war. Philip is quite certain that there was no question of appeasement. He expected that the Americans would act, but not for some months, since they wouldn't be sufficiently armed. Thus, it really does begin to seem as though the inconceivable must happen, and that an atomic war with Russia is almost a certainty.

On Friday, I spent the day preparing a talk I agreed to give to the Intelligence Course suddenly assembled in Oxford that evening. Worked out a lecture on Communism in the United States. Dick Brooman-White came to fetch me and we drove down to Oxford, talking all the way. Dick also seemed certain war now could more or less be taken for granted. The course was being held in Worcester College – quite a gathering of people from MI5 and MI6 at home and abroad, a good number of whom I knew. I talked for an hour, and then there was an hour of questioning which, on the whole, was more interesting. Very strange to be back among those people and to be discussing again matters of war.

The following morning exquisite weather. Walked with various people round the college gardens, particularly beautiful. All rather dreamlike effect.

Kitty and I disturbed by a telegram announcing that Pan was flying home from Kenya. On Sunday he duly arrived, looking very thin and troubled, but not in too bad shape. It appeared that things in Nairobi had rather badly got on his nerves and that he had been sent home suffering from a sort of nervous breakdown. We didn't like to question him too closely, but, as far as could be gathered, he had found the condition of the blacks rather painful, and had got into trouble for giving them food and even his army tunic. He came back with two other soldiers who were in a worse way than he was, one of them having tried to commit suicide, and the other having lost his memory. Hope now that Pan may be able to get his discharge from the army, since I don't really think he can be of much use as a soldier. He said that he was unable to sleep at night and used to go wandering about the hutments.

September 28, 1948

Mrs Wodehouse (whom I had met with P.G. in 1944 in Paris when investigating his wartime activities which proved to be blameless) came to supper. She seemed very weary of wandering about the world trying to find somewhere to settle, but of course, in the everlasting justness of things, that is a suitable end to the sort of life that she and P.G. have lived. The world of which he produced a romanticized picture in his books has come to an end and left them both, like so many others at this time, strangers in a strange land.

Read *Ciano* proofs. Now the same sort of thing is happening all over again with Russia, the pilgrims going this time to the Kremlin rather than to Berchtesgaden.

September 29, 1948

Strolled to the *Daily Telegraph* past St Paul's, again marvelling at the open spaces in the City and the few people in the streets compared with when I used to go and see my father there as a boy. City's decrepitude is symbolic of what is happening in the world and in England; the outward appearance of things is forced ultimately to conform with their inward reality.

Read some of Kafka's Diary. Find Kafka very unsympathetic as a character. All the same, a kind of mystical insight, a sense of things to come. Kafka was always trying to summon up his resolution to get married but never managed to. If he ever united himself with anyone he wrote down in his Diary that he would never be alone again. His father was well off and he himself worked for an insurance company, leaving at last with a pension. I had always supposed that he was the victim of extreme poverty. Kafka was also a great reader of Kierkegaard.

September 30, 1948

Managed to do some work on *The Forties* which is becoming urgent. Read Eisenhower, and once again struck by the manner in which ordinariness, carried to enormous lengths, produces something remarkable. Actually, his account of the war and the campaigns, is the clearest and most readable yet available. Interesting to contrast it with Churchill, whose propensity to rhetoric clouds, if it sometimes irradiates, the narrative.

October 1–3, 1948

France is getting into a worse and worse mess. Everyone assumes that de Gaulle will come into power, and really wants him to, though with some dread as to what the consequence may be.

Pan returned for a week's leave. He is very thin, but in surprisingly good heart. I had several long talks with him, and found him eminently sensible. In fact, whenever I discuss things with him, I have a curious feeling that really he is much saner than I am. It is merely that by virtue of his religion, or something in his makeup, instead of always wanting to assert his ego, his inclination is the other way. This makes many of his impulses the precise opposite of those of his fellows, and so make him seem odd to them. He said he didn't feel particularly attracted to becoming a clergyman, because he didn't like talking to people about religion. This I quite understand. He described one rather striking incident about which he had thought a great deal. He was in the Guard Room in Nairobi, and an evangelist came in and said he'd got wonderful news for everybody about their releases. Of course, all the soldiers thought it meant their release from the Army and jumped up excitedly, only to be bitterly disappointed when they learnt the release the evangelist had in mind was from sin and mortality.

One of the librarians at the *Telegraph* told me that he had left school when he was 9½ and had more or less earned his living ever since. He said that the thing that had struck him in the course of doing this was that all the equipment he had acquired for living related to another world than the one he had to live in. I was struck with his having arrived at the same conclusion as myself by so different a route. I told him to read *Don Quixote*.

October 4, 1948

Alec Vidler came for the night. He has just been appointed Canon at Windsor which sounds a delightful job – a house inside the castle, and completely free for his own work except for attending wonderfully sung services. He amused me very much by describing the intrigues which go on in Downing Street over clerical appointments. Actually, his to Windsor is made by the King. He is very solid and sensible and serene. In fact, I don't know anyone who has better succeeded in making terms with life through understanding and faith.

Great Joy in Fleet Street because a major financial scandal is brewing involving a junior minister. Nothing gives so much unalloyed joy to journalists as anything of this sort.

October 6–11, 1948

It is obvious that Pan is going through the phase of shaping up to this unhappy world. He has now been posted to Aldershot, so he will be near, and seems quite cheerful.

Ethel Wodehouse came to supper. Exceedingly jovial and delightful. Interesting sidelight on present arrangements, that though she has got an enormous amount of cash in this country, she can't touch any of it, but the Bank of England has agreed to pay her bills at the Ritz, and she gets spending money off the hall porter who puts it on the account.

October 13, 1948

Read part of Harry Hopkins' *White House Papers*, about which I am to have a discussion with Harold Laski on the BBC. So far find it the most interesting of all the war memoirs, though infinitely depressing because, in the manner in which negotiations were conducted, it expresses the whole fallacy of the Roosevelt policy. Thought very good show-up of Hopkins was when he said to himself when he went to the Kremlin to see Stalin for the first time – 'Here is a man with absolute power over 140,000,000 human beings, and here am I, son of a harness maker in Iowa, going in to see him'.

October 14, 1948

Mrs Wodehouse is going off to France shortly with Gertie Dudley (former famous Gaiety girl, Gertie Miller, who married the Earl of Dudley). It appears that Gertie Dudley gave Ethel a parrot some years ago, and that when the Germans came into France Ethel asked a French friend to look after this parrot. Then the French friend, wearying of it, presented it to a zoo somewhere down Bordeaux way. Ethel, when she heard of this, was grief-stricken to think of the bird being ill-treated, so she and Gertie Dudley are now going over to try and get it back, though what they are going to do with it when they do so they don't know. I'd very much like to hear their conversation – Ethel speaking in her execrable French with the director of the zoo. If it were a P.G. story, I thought, the bird would have learnt a lot of French bad language, and Jeeves would be called in to deal with the embarrassing situation which would thereby arise.

Much diverted by book on Samuel Butler by P. N. Furbank, published by the Cambridge University Press, which consists, to a great extent, of an attack on me. First time I have found myself treated as the subject of literary criticism – secretly rather gratified.

October 18, 1948

Harold Laski came with Lewin to discuss the broadcast on Hopkins, and we recalled that it was nearly twenty years since we had last met. He has become rather a pitiable, woebegone figure. His curious mania of lying has undergone colossal development, so that now he is a positive addict, and, curiously enough, has all the same physical characteristics as other sorts of addicts like drunkards and drug takers. He talks rather well, apart from the fact that nearly all that he says is imagined – his interview with Stalin, the day he spent at the Politbureau, his intimacy with Churchill, etc., etc.

October 19, 1948

Johnstone quoted a remark of von Bülow's at the end of the 19th century in which he said that Germany would be in the years to come either the hammer or the anvil. I agreed that this showed great prescience, but argued that prophecy is nearly always an expression of the desire of the prophet. Thus, the Hebrew prophets, who hated mankind, prophesied desolation, and of course it came to pass. The point is that prophecy is a factor of the will rather than the imagination, and it is the will that brings about what the will desires.

October 25, 1948

Gathered from Douglas Jerrold that a row is brewing between him and Graham Greene, about Graham's agreement to release Tony Powell from his novel contract with Eyre and Spottiswoode.

October 27–29, 1948

Read in the evening a life of Arnold Bennett by Dorothy Cheston Bennett with whom he lived and by whom he had a child – tedious, I thought, and she obviously rather a tedious woman. Then read some of Bennett's journal, which I had looked at before. Found this really quite interesting in a way – pathetic figure of Bennett unhappily living what he imagined to be cultivated luxurious life, cruising around with Beaverbrook, Diana Cooper, Venetia Montague, etc., having to play baccarat with Beaverbrook in the evenings and lose money to him, altogether bored, looking in wistfully at the lower level passengers happily celebrating with paper hats, etc. Bennett extraordinarily good example of the fallacy of dramatising a life and then trying to make his actual living correspond with the dramatisation. Reacting from his Non-Conformist Potteries childhood, he read French novels and decided to be an artist. But it was all really a frost, because there was no correspondence between all this and his actual nature. In her muddled way, Dorothy Cheston vaguely aware of this pathos. Highly characteristic of Beaverbrook that despite his friendship with Bennett, he published in the *Daily Express* extracts from book about Bennett by his French wife, Marguerite, which must have upset Bennett very considerably. Though he prided himself on having mastered the art of living, he never could bring himself to have a divorce, and therefore crippled himself financially by having to give a big proportion of his income to his wife, and when the child was born, had to go to the trouble of altering Dorothy Cheston's name to Dorothy Cheston Bennett. In the end he died by drinking tap water on the Continent – a thing that any day tourist to Ostend might well have avoided. Though he made a lot of money, he was always in need of money and, I noticed in the Journal, was another insomniac, with all the usual business of getting up and looking out of the window at night. He thought *Peter Pan* a wonderful play, but was rather ashamed of thinking so; and tried to think *The Waste Land* a good poem, but was rather ashamed of trying to think so.

Hugh Kingsmill said that Bennett's last words, addressed to Dorothy Cheston, were very sad and touching: 'Everything is going wrong, my girl'.

Worked at my novel, and managed to get it ended. Far from satisfied but at any rate it's done.

November 3, 1948

In spite of all predictions Truman has been re-elected. Really comical turn of events. Thought of the little man, as I remembered him, so utterly asinine, genial, with his wife, Bessie, and his daughter, Margaret, and how inconceivably funny it was that he should have been voluntarily chosen, against enormous odds. Now, with Democratic Congress, the most powerful man in the world.

November 4, 1948

Delivered novel (*Affairs of the Heart*) to Hamish Hamilton in the morning, feeling, on the whole, well pleased with it.

At Pratts with Douglas Jerrold I overheard two characters discussing how they'd tried to dispose of their Lord Lieutenants' uniforms and had only been offered £4 10s. 0d. by Moss Bros, where apparently any number of them are available. Imagine that Osbert Lancaster, who is nearly always in Pratts, uses it for the faces in his *Daily Express* cartoons.

Douglas told me he had now definitely parted company with Graham Greene, who has left Eyre and Spottiswoode for good.

November 6–7, 1948

Lillian Campbell Dixon, who works for Korda, showed me the script of Graham's new film, *The Third Man* – some quite good scenes in the sewers of Vienna, etc., but the theme, I thought, unconvincing – drunken little weakling proves effective, and the villain is to be preferred to the hero. Some humour about two British officers who were running a cultural re-education racket in Vienna.

November 8–9, 1948

Lunched at the Cavendish Hotel with Auberon Herbert. Curious place, once great haunt of high life debauchery, now merely faded, Victorian, and rather pleasant. Auberon extremely well-known figure there, and treated with affectionate condescension by the staff.

Read ludicrous blank verse play on the theme of Edward VIII's abdication. There was something phoney about the whole Windsor–Simpson episode. It, like the Cavendish Hotel, belongs to the decrepitude of an age, and therefore as a great love story refuses to stand up in retrospect.

Machell and Hamilton seem well pleased with the novel, except that they want me to redraft the last few pages.

November 11, 1948

I read to Hugh Kingsmill a passage from Lincoln's speech when he was elected President: 'I have been selected,' he said, 'to fill an important office for a brief period, and am now, in your eyes, invested with an influence which will soon pass away; but should my Administration prove to be a very wicked one, or what is more probable, a very foolish one, if you, the people, are true to yourselves and the Constitution, there is but little harm I can do, thank God.'

Hughie said that Lincoln's fearful melancholia was due to the fact that he really was an embodiment of all the vain hopes which people had felt in going to America. Yet he represented whatever was great in the American people. He was, as it were, their Shakespeare, only it took the form of this curious life of action instead of literature.

Lunched at the American Embassy. Strange to be back in that American atmosphere I remembered so vividly – over-heated, boring voices incessantly and laboriously talking. After my departure from Tokyo there had been a first-class departmental row because, after I had interviewed General MacArthur, I gave a somewhat humorous account of the interview to a State Department figure. There was a young officer from Supreme Headquarters also present, and he apparently felt it his duty to put in a report on this *lèse-majesté*. The State Department chap was at once sent home. Actually, he must have been relieved, but it is an interesting example of the sort of totalitarian system General MacArthur has created. Grosvenor Square nowadays really a little America.

November 12–14, 1948

To BBC for the Hopkins broadcast. Poor Harold Laski! All the time thirsting for a job in the government and not getting it. He told one rather good story about party of American journalists, John Gunther, etc., dining with him on the day after the Truman result. All admitted that they had been completely wrong, but noticed that the waiter was smiling, so they turned to him and asked what he had thought about it. He said he'd won £30 on the election. They were amazed to think that a waiter should have been right, when they, whose business it was to write about public events, had all been wrong, but the waiter added, 'They offered me 15–1, and I take 15–1 on anything.'

At BBC I noticed a clergyman come in and whisper a question, and the answer was, 'two gynaecologists have been at the Palace'.

Wrote leader on Canada, but it was mercifully scrapped after the first edition because of the royal baby, duly born. Everyone very pleased. How much more satisfactory is the institution of monarchy than, for instance, the American presidency, with all the dangers and vulgarities inherent in the process of the election.

November 16, 1948

The Belcher story is absorbing everyone's attention at the moment. He is the junior minister, the Parliamentary Secretary to the Board of Trade, who is involved in a financial scandal which is being investigated by the Lynskey Tribunal. Most striking feature of it not so much the corruption as the total asinity of the individuals concerned – being measured for suits presented to them by State-less Sidney Stanley, birthday cake for Belcher inscribed 'Dear John', etc. In theory it ought to damage the Government, but in practice highly improbable that it will.

November 17, 1948

Lewis Namier came to dinner. Mrs Namier turned out to be a rather melancholy-looking Slav. Namier talked much about the early days of the Zionist movement, Weizmann, etc. Probably, as a result of Slav wife, note in him sinister tendency to occultism. Both of them went rather obviously silent when we spoke about Henry Wallace's (he was Vice-President under Roosevelt, 1940–44) relations with a theosophist named Rurich. Curious how Namier's hatreds all relate to the past. For instance, he still hates the Austro-Hungarian Empire although it has long ceased to exist. His only present hatred, and that a ferocious one, is of Bevin.

Received curious letter from Henri de Montherlant thanking me for my article on him in *The Times Literary Supplement* which he said he liked, but that he didn't agree with me that *Les Céliba-taires* was his best work . . . 'C'est un de ceux dans lesquels j'ai mis moins de moi-même et dont il m'a toujours semblé qu'il pourrait le plus facilement être supprimé de mon oeuvre'. It is his best work precisely because he put least of himself in it, but that would be a difficult thing to explain.

November 19, 1948

Frere, in rather good form, remarked that Sussex was littered with glasses of beer which H. B. Morton, 'Beachcomber', hadn't drunk.

We discussed a book to be written on the Bloomsbury Set, i.e. Lytton Strachey, E. M. Forster, Lowes Dickinson, etc. Remarkable how their influence and panache has faded away. I recalled incident which, to me, symbolizes their asininity. It occurs in Eddie Marsh's autobiography. He and Lytton Strachey were standing at the back at Covent Garden, and Rupert Brooke, in evening dress, was in the stalls with a large party. Strachey remarked to Marsh: 'Rupert is "en beauté" this evening'. They were a poor lot, as I was particularly ready to agree in view of the fact that E. M. Forster has just written some unpleasant remarks about me in *The Spectator*.

Pan arrived, in very good form. He seems now to be happy in the Army, and altogether to have sorted things out.

November 22, 1948

In the evening read Hobbes' *Leviathan* and looked up article on Hobbes in the *Dictionary of National Biography*. He is a remarkable and sympathetic figure, lived through the whole period of upset from the Armada to the Restoration. Spent some time in exile in the entourage of Charles II. *Leviathan* wonderfully written . . . 'So easy are men to be drawn to believe anything, from such men as have gotten credit with them; and can with gentleness, and dexterity, take hold of their fear, and ignorance.'

Hobbes described laughter as 'sudden glory'.

November 23–24, 1948

With reference to the Belcher enquiry: 'We really mustn't grumble about the government since it's the best that money can buy'.

Hugh Kingsmill talked about Kingsley, and recalled how,

reading *Westward Ho !* as a child, the only thing that had seemed to him real in it was when Amyas Leigh, who was blind, hit his head against a table and cried. He said, 'there's so little in literature that's real'.

A copy of Tony's *John Aubrey and his Friends* arrived. Was touched that it should have been dedicated to me.

November 26–28, 1948

At the Garrick P. J. Grigg talked very indiscreetly as usual, said that at the end of the war Eisenhower had told Alanbrooke that he proposed to get a divorce and marry Kay Summersby, and devote the rest of his life to promoting Anglo-American relations. Also said that the trouble between Ike and Monty was almost entirely due to Tedder.

At *Daily Telegraph* wrote leader on European unity, very remote and tedious subject, and then just caught train with Kitty down to Petersfield. Gerald Bullett, his wife and daughter Rosemary, received us affectionately.

Gerald just the same. I suggested to him that he should do a book on the English mystics. He is religious without having a religion, which is really what is the matter with him. On the whole, it is better, like Graham, to have a religion without being religious than to be in Gerald's case.

Gerald quoted to me wonderful thing he'd seen on a sundial – 'Lux Umbra Dei' – Light is God's shadow.

November 30, 1948

Philip Jordan said that reading Foreign Office telegrams these days was a desolating occupation, everything everywhere going wrong. We talked about China. He gave diverting account of how Frank Owen, editor of the *Daily Mail*, and Butler, foreign editor, had engineered a revolt in Burma, about which Rothermere, proprietor of the paper, knew nothing. End of the affair was to be Owen marching on Rangoon with the victorious Karen army. After a little while, Owen characteristically lost interest in the project, and went off to Africa. Rothermere went to the South of France to recuperate, and that was the end of it.

December 2, 1948

Hugh Kingsmill ill again, which is worrying.

At BBC Critics Ivor Brown pointed out that Stanley (the chap now being cross-examined in the Belcher Inquiry) has to perfection the current money mystique. When he was asked to pay his rent, he said he'd buy the whole building, thus evading the necessity of having to pay anything at all. It worked. Stanley's cross-examination is at present enthralling everyone, and there is practically nothing else in the paper. It bears out a theory I have long held, that civilizations, like individuals, in their final decrepitude find a particular pleasure in self-abasement. When the whole money system was tottering to its ruin, historians will see war approaching with alarming inevitability, and everyone entirely absorbed in a fairy story about money. This is entirely apt.

December 3–5, 1948

Went down to cottage. Much enjoyed being in the country again, especially the part I know best. Nostalgia to live there again. Probably impossible for urban life not to produce certain hysteria, which may well have much to do with present disintegrating tendencies.

Mrs Dobbs now has dog on whom she lavishes affection. Thought of Timon of Athens – 'Timon will to the woods and there shall find / The unkindest beast more kinder than mankind.'

Went for walk with John – walk I used to do almost every day when living in Whatlington. Noted his determination, and the way he marks out clearly certain objectives and goes for them.

December 7, 1948

Douglas Hyde, former News Editor of the *Daily Worker*, now a Roman Catholic, came to lunch. Short, dark, fanatical looking character, who has transferred himself from one totalitarian philosophy to another. Difficult to get much coherent information out of him, but he gave quite an interesting account of breaking the news of his changed attitude of mind to Rust, *Daily Worker* Editor, who, he said, betrayed great signs of distress.

David Astor looked in, just back from France. We talked about de Gaulle, etc. If de Gaulle gets into power, he will join up with the Germans to form a solid Western European block, and probably try to exploit us.

December 8, 1948

Started writing article on the Lynskey Tribunal in the evening – very difficult.

Went to BBC with Kitty to look at a television performance. Very pitiable in quality, but I suppose they will improve it in time, and it will eventually become as popular as wireless.

December 10, 1948

Tribunal in the morning. Mrs Belcher in the box. She did tremendous sentimental job quite cleverly. Much amused by the appearance at the Tribunal of low-level bucket shop keeper. Delivered article to Watson, who liked it, as did Camrose.

December 13, 1948

Worked in the morning at odd things. Read life of Joseph Toole (*Our Old Man*) by Millie Toole. I remember Toole quite well from the days when I was in Manchester. Fat, preposterous figure, who sat for Salford South, and afterwards became Lord Mayor, when he distinguished himself by using up all the entertainment allowance in the first month of office in a series of gigantic binges. His life really quite a period piece, and of great interest in relation

to the Labour Party. Thought I ought to do something on my
father one of these days.

December 14, 1948

Tiresome day. At Heinemann a discussion as to the possibility of
a life of Arnold Bennett. Then a macabre lunch alone with Jonathan Cape at his flat. Cape has that horrifying quality of an old
egotist and sensualist who is trying to fight off death. His false teeth
were noisy, and every now and again he took out lumps of meat
which he was unable to masticate. Produced in me Ancient Mariner
effect, holding me with his skinny hands and glittering eye, so that
I didn't get away until about twenty to three.

He talked about Wells and his relations with him as a publisher.
One rather good point, when he described going to see Wells about
twelve days before he died, and Wells said: 'Everything going
badly,' and Cape replied: 'Yes, and it is your fault.' He imitated
Wells's high voice. Quite a good scene really.

December 15, 1948

The Griggs came to dinner, it being P.J.'s birthday. P.J. described
arriving back one night at No 10 with Winston very late, and they
decided to relieve themselves in the garden. In the course of this
operation, Winston remarked: 'I wonder if Gladstone ever did
this'.

We talked a lot about religion, after which P.J. increasingly
hankers, and about the row between Kingsley and Newman. I
think, basically, we were in agreement. John got bored with our
arguments and went to bed. The young find these intellectual
maunderings quite unreal, and they may well be right.

Went to huge party given by Christopher Buckley at the Savoy.
Most of *Daily Telegraph* staff there, including Watson. Osbert
Lancaster told me that he was doing the dust cover for my *Affairs
of the Heart*.

December 20, 1948

Lunched with Birkenhead, who gave me amusing account of Randolph Churchill's marriage. He also told me about the difficulties over his Kipling book, Kipling's daughter having turned his manuscript down flat, objecting particularly to the bit I gave him about Kipling's adventures in Vermont.

Chess with John. He now beats me every time.

December 23-31, 1948

After Critics programme on Tuesday left for Battle, and spent Christmas pleasantly there with the whole family. Wonderfully clear wintry weather, many walks.

Mrs Dobbs madder than ever. Now lives almost wholly with her dog, a curious kind of animal existence. Difficult to convey strangeness in her appearance – inconceivably old clothes, dirty, mentally senile, but physically incredibly tough for her years. Only Pan can put up with her, and he, in his saintly way, went over nightly to say goodnight to her.

Went to church on Christmas Day at Whatlington Church, Browell, clergyman, now looking very old and frail, read the service charmingly. Much struck with the first chapter of St John, which Pan read over to us again. Consider it probably the most illuminating piece of writing so far extant.

Returned on Tuesday to London, much refreshed.

Past year, from work point of view, not unsatisfactory, and hopeful that in the New Year, *Spectator* may provide escape from the *Daily Telegraph*. Major task, *The Forties*.

January 1-January 6, 1949

Didn't see New Year in, went to bed early. Reasonably satisfied from personal point of view with past year's work, and as for public affairs, they have passed the point at which one feels troubled or easy about them. Western society is obviously in a state of dissolution, and it's just a question of how long the process will continue, and whether some chance development may affect its duration and course.

On Sunday Camrose asked to see me to discuss the Kipling book. He said Birkenhead's contract was quite hopeless, and that he thought there was nothing to be done. When I said the book ought to be rewritten, or that a threat of rewriting it should be made, he said, very characteristically: 'Was it worth it?' because the book wouldn't make much money. All the same, I rather like him. As Hugh Kingsmill says, he displaces his own weight.

On Monday I finished off rewriting the last bit of the novel which I took to Roger Machell at Hamish Hamilton. Subsequently heard that they were very pleased, so now it's gone to the printers and all's well. Also saw Lancaster's drawing for the jacket; excellent. Have a hunch that the novel is going to do well.

On Tuesday morning, Frere and I drove down to Kingswood. Attended a Heinemann Directors' meeting for the first time, and found it quite interesting – discussions about how many books should be printed, prices, etc. On the way down Frere told me that he had tried to introduce a 'highbrow element' into Heinemann, and mentioned in this regard *Lady Chatterley's Lover*. Eisenhower book selling furiously, everybody very pleased.

Went on to delightful performance of *As You Like It* at the Old Vic with Kitty and the children. Children quite spellbound – more interested in watching them in some ways than the play. Thought much about the character of Jacques, who, it seems to me, must have been a first draft of Hamlet. Shakespeare always better without a star, I think, and done by young and enthusiastic, rather than experienced, actors.

Went with John to see the David pictures at the Tate – not much good as pictures, but the subjects interested me. Portrait of Napoleon very like Hitler, with that excessive puffy vulgarity that all men of action (Hitler, Churchill, etc.) seem to have.

Read some letters between Ramsay MacDonald and Princess Bibesco which Heinemann are considering. Found them infinitely diverting, but not in the way that Princess Bibesco imagines. All the snobbishness, pretentiousness, and sentimentality of MacDonald come out in them. Interested to note Bibesco used to send MacDonald supplies of Chanel scent. Decided to recommend strongly publishing the letters.

January 7–10, 1949

I wrote leader on Dean Acheson's appointment as US Secretary of State, which pleased me very much. Acheson was the person I liked best in Washington.

Went down to see my mother, who is very poorly and low-spirited. I think really that she is terrified of death, not so much because she wants to go on living, as because it is to her an incomprehensible experience.

Tony came to supper. Read several pieces from a collection of essays on *The Old School* edited by Graham Greene. Tony Powell's on Eton really very delightful. He wrote that he'd never been able to cure himself of the habit of looking out of the window and expecting something to happen. Very typical. Hughie said he'd like to see pictures of Tony doing this at different stages in his life.

January 12, 1949

NUJ meeting. Usual depressing gathering, and the usual battle between the Communist and non-Communist elements. At a certain point in the proceedings most of the staff of the *Daily Worker* walked in to vote for Hutt's nomination as Editor of *The Journalist* – most villainous looking crew.

January 13, 1949

Norman Luker came to say goodbye before going off to America. He served as Personal Assistant to Cripps for part of the war. Said that Cripps's greatest weakness was that he could never objectify himself and his activities and so there was no let-up, but that his ability was almost frightening, and his ambition – though he agreed with me that it was inordinate – was unconscious. He also agreed with me that if Cripps got power he would create a sort of evangelical Christian Fascism.

Then went on to dine with Graham Greene and his brother Raymond, who is a doctor, rather like him in appearance. Graham looks more melancholic than ever. He told me that he had now definitely separated from Vivian, which I thought was rather a pity. He spoke about *The Heart of the Matter* in a surprisingly objective manner. I said that, in my view, it certainly wasn't his best book, but that one had to consider a writer's work as a whole, and that if one part of it received a reward it mightn't deserve, other parts received less than they deserved, so that over all it was just.

Another thing Graham said was that when he heard that his house at Clapham Common had been destroyed in the blitz he experienced a sense of relief because there was a mortgage on it and it had represented a heavy financial liability. He described arriving there, and finding the part where the house had been roped off. When he told Vivian, he said, she rebuked him for mentioning what had happened in front of the children, which seemed to him unreasonable. I said I didn't think it was unreasonable, because, obviously, Vivian felt that the destruction of their house was an outward and visible manifestation of the destruction of their marriage, and that Graham's satisfaction at the destruction of the house was not really because it released him from a financial burden, but because he saw in it the promise of being relieved of a moral one. I said that everything that happened had to correspond with what was, and that's why life is at once so fascinating and so terrible.

January 19–20, 1949

Curious upset when I arrived at the *Daily Telegraph*. NUJ representative there rang me up in some agitation to say that NUJ had just been informed that I was dead. Somewhat disconcerting, but I treated it as a great joke. Presumably Communists thought it would be funny. Pointed out that from a purely administrative point of view, rather curious that the NUJ should accept an unidentified notification as sufficient ground for assuming the demise of a member. Point was taken with some embarrassment on their side. Thought about this afterwards, and decided it was a theoretical foretaste of the sort of thing that will happen if and when Communists achieve power. It reminded me of how – as I have heard, probably apocryphal – once when Lord Alfred Douglas

was very broke, in desperation he telephoned to the *Daily Mail*
an announcement that he had died. A long defamatory obituary
duly appeared, and Douglas was able to collect.

January 21–23, 1949

Read a lot of Winston's book, Volume I, on the war, which is, to
me, mostly not very interesting excepting the purely personal parts
like his description of the day he became Prime Minister. His
judgment is extremely fallible – e.g. his assumption that the Nazi–
Soviet Pact was, on both sides, intended to be a temporary arrangement, whereas I am confident that, on the Russian side, it was
believed in wholly.

January 25, 1949

Went to Foreign Press Association lunch and heard Bevin speak.
Sat next to Chaize of *Le Figaro*. Chaize amused me by giving an
account of how he had an Irish servant who was a very devout and
strict Catholic, and who regarded him as a lax Catholic because he
occasionally attended Divine Service with his wife, who is an
Anglican. The servant therefore decided to try and procure his
salvation. She discovered that if she could bring three souls into
the Catholic Church she would be entitled to be granted the salvation of a fourth. She has already got two in, and is now working on
Chaize's wife, with the idea of claiming his salvation if she managed
to make this additional convert. He said that Catholicism in
England was too strict and arid to appeal to him. In France, he
said, 'we have the idea of the "Merveilleux Chrétien".' This
rather charming phrase echoed in my mind for the rest of the day.

January 27, 1949

Dined with Lewis Namier and his wife. She gave us a fascinating
account of her life in Russia from the Revolution until her final

escape – an almost inconceivable succession of adventures and horrors. Namier listened attentively, though he must have heard the story many times before, occasionally asking her to amplify some particular point, almost like an impresario. Actually she and her first husband returned voluntarily twice to Russia. This was because the husband had an obsession that he belonged in Russia and couldn't live away from it. This, she said, was particularly absurd because he was French by origin, and she, who was wholly Russian, felt in no way drawn back to her native land. At one point in their adventures her husband, it appears, caught spotted typhus and became, temporarily, almost an idiot. As she described this part, she gave a horrifying representation herself of his idiot laughter – quite macabre in the Ladies Annexe of the Athenaeum.

Namier, inevitably, got on to the subject of Palestine, but I managed, without embarking on an argument, to indicate my disagreement with him. Usual hatred of Bevin. I said to Kitty coming back that it was a strange fate which had led this Russian woman to find shelter at last under the wing of a Polish Jew, particularly since she must have been brought up in a strongly anti-Semitic atmosphere. Kitty said, with reason, that after all she had gone through a thing like anti-Semitism would seem fabulously remote, and that when people have suffered beyond a certain point they become insensitive, like a tooth whose nerve is dead, and that you can grind without pain.

January 28, 1949

Dick White came to lunch. He is now more or less head of MI5. We talked about the *Daily Worker* and how it is financed. He said that his impression was that most of its funds came from rich men. We agreed that rich men thus paying conscience money to an organization which seeks to destroy them presents a fascinating psychological problem.

January 31, 1949

Dined with Auberon Herbert, General Anders, Julian Amery and others. Anders everything a Polish general might be expected to be, with shaved head, a black moustache, gold teeth, and speaking gutteral French. However, quite an impressive chap in his way. He was very diverted because Yellin, the Jewish terrorist, had been one of his NCO's in the Italian campaign. They are very anxious to have something written about Katyn and want me to do it, but I hedged on the ground of being too busy.

After Anders had gone, I had a long political discussion with Amery, brother of John Amery who was executed as a traitor. Anders had interested me rather by describing how when Beaverbrook went to Moscow, to the Russians' immense relief, he immediately began to give way to them on every point. He asked me how I accounted for this, and I said that I was convinced that Beaverbrook really hated this country, and that the only consistent thread in his career was that.

We also discussed Yalta and why Roosevelt should in fact have given China to the Russians. I said I thought that Stalin's great strength was that he didn't mind how many of his people were killed, whereas both Roosevelt and Churchill were ready to barter anything in exchange for lives, and that in the power game it is lives that count. Amery took a strong line on Russia but I tried to explain to him how, though this might very well be the best policy, it was not necessarily practical.

February 1, 1949

Hugh Kingsmill came to lunch, looking better. Discussed afterwards with Kitty why it is that Hugh Kingsmill's conversation is the most enlivening of anyone's, and we decided that it is because his interest in people and things is, as far as it is possible for a human being's to be, detached from his own personal interests. Obviously, it is the degree to which life is seen objectively that it is interesting.

3 February, 1949

Tony and I walked into Fleet Street to attend an NUJ meeting at which Rust, the editor of the *Daily Worker*, was to be hauled over the coals. When we got there, we learned that Rust had died shortly before the meeting was due to begin. This I found distinctly intriguing, in view of the fact that my death had been reported to the NUJ shortly before. Rust, with his high complexion and baby face, was always to me a singularly repulsive character, with the true terrorist instincts of his type. Inevitably, however, the Chairman of the Branch Meeting delivered the usual little sanctimonious address which is invariable on such occasions. Rather a curious incident altogether somehow.

February 4–6, 1949

Wrote leader on Hungary. Find trial of Mindszenty highly disturbing – especially after seeing photograph of proceedings showing the Cardinal looking dazed and frightened, and beside him typical little gangster figure of type that crops up everywhere, and which I remember so well in France when the d'Arnand police were mopped up – always the same, peaked hat, degraded expression, usually small in stature, which the terrorist underworld brought to the surface.

A good remark of Proust's: 'A little knowledge separates us from God, much knowledge brings us back. One should never be afraid to go too far, for the truth is beyond.'

February 7, 1949

Report from *The Times* Budapest correspondent about the Cardinal Mindszenty affair particularly nauseating. I exploded about this at the *Daily Telegraph* editorial conference. Afterwards reflected that regimes and civilizations come to an end always as a result of acts of suicide rather than of external attack. Thus, the fact that *The Times* could print so misleading a report of an episode of this kind is more ominous than any number of Red Army divisions or air squadrons. The divisions and air squadrons can be resisted, but internal corruption defies all treatment.

Discussed with Watson possibility of my taking over Harold Nicolson's job as chief book reviewer when he leaves, which he will soon. Watson, as always, very nice about this, and it may come off.

February 9, 1949

Failed to get to NUJ meeting for election of officers, but understood from Tony that Communists didn't do particularly well. Nonetheless, we agreed they dominate the situation. Thought much about this – enormous procession to Rust's funeral, etc. They may well win in the end, not through their strength, but through their opponents' weakness. When I think of the mental confusion, corruption, egotism, etc., of the decomposing social order which they are attacking, it seems astonishing that they haven't done better than they have.

February 12, 1949

Tony Powell made a very good point that the reason why Churchill's memoirs, like all memoirs of men of action, were so tedious, is that the convention has to be sustained that all the people concerned with him in the war were diligent, conscientious, honest, etc., etc., etc. Writing about writers – e.g. Proust, or Stendhal, this is not in the least necessary, so that their lives and adventures are always more interesting.

February 14, 1949

Daily Telegraph exceptionally wearisome, but heard from George Bishop, Literary Editor, that it had been decided I should do the books, but that Watson would tell me in due course. This should mean my being let off going to the *Daily Telegraph* at least three days a week, and is correspondingly wonderful.

February 15–17, 1949

At the *Daily Telegraph* I put forward the proposition that the only way to attract popular support is to present people with the possibility of becoming more important. Thus, in the late nineteenth century the idea of imperialism provided the Conservative Party with an effective mystique; similarly, Hitler captivated the German people on the basis of nationalistic aggrandisement; similarly with the Socialist mystique because what it amounts to is: 'He hath put down the mighty from their seat, and hath exalted the humble and meek.' But Conservatism in its political sense, has no mystique whatsoever, and therefore no demagogic future. The American mystique, I said, was to offer everyone the prospect of getting richer and richer, having faster and faster motor cars, etc., etc. It would come to grief when the American economy ceased to be capable of any further expansion.

Spent Thursday at Windsor where I went with Pan. Delighted as always, to see Alec Vidler again. He has got a large, rambling house in the Castle wall, with a delightful view, though it is rather complicated to run. So far he hasn't succeeded in getting suitable domestic help, and is looked after by the most extraordinary old character, called Albert, who specializes in housekeeping for single clergymen. Albert looks rather like a clergyman himself, doubtless from long association with them.

Had long discussion about Pan's future. Alec most helpful – said he thought the Christian message remained always the same, at different epochs it required to be presented differently – e.g. Franciscan way, Wesleyan way, Salvation Army way. It was no good thinking that there was any possibility, merely by going to a past technique, to recover a past zeal. This, he said, had been the fallacy of the Anglo-Catholic movement. What people like Pan had to discover was how to present this message in the circumstances of today. This problem not answered so far.

February 18–19, 1949

Went off in the morning with Tony Powell to Stroud. We walked nine miles to the sanatorium where George Orwell now is.

We found George in very good shape in the circumstances, and the same old trusty, lovable egotist. He looked very thin, and said that he would probably have to spend every winter henceforth in a sanatorium. He hoped, he said, to live for another ten years because of various things he wanted to do, and because by that time his adopted boy would be fifteen. I am not sure he will pull this off. We all talked eagerly, and the three hours we were with him passed very quickly. He spoke a lot about Gissing, for whom he has a particular fondness, I think because he rather sees himself in Gissing's position; also about Kipling, whom he greatly admires. Though he has TB he goes on smoking cigarettes, and was able to produce a bottle of rum from under his bed, which we consumed. I think he is fairly cheerful, but he said that the treatment he has to have is somewhat painful.

Came back quite late, feeling extremely well. Changed trains at Swindon and went into the refreshment room there, which was entirely Muscovite, only requiring a few peasants asleep on the floor and a few characters in long military overcoats to be an exact replica of any Russian railway station.

February 21–22, 1949

Started new regime of only going into *Daily Telegraph* on Fridays and Sundays, otherwise doing books. Highly satisfactory, once properly worked out.

Had a long conversation with Fredric Warburg of Secker and Warburg about George Orwell. Characteristic remark of Warburg's was, in a rather plaintive voice, that what George should do was to use his little remaining span of life and energy to write at least two more books.

February 23–27, 1949

Tolstoy: read large parts of immense *Life of Tolstoy* by an American named Ernest Simmons. Found it, as everything about Tolstoy, quite enthralling. Oddly enough Simmons calls one of his chapters *The Green Stick*, which I'd already decided to use. Interested to note that Tolstoy, as a youth, wore round his neck a medallion of Rousseau, so great was his veneration for him. Fascinating quarrel with Turgenev. Decided that real fallacy with Tolstoy was that he tried to have things both ways – in other words, he thought he could have the things of the earth and still renounce them. This is the great Kingdom of Heaven on earth fallacy, which has produced the present chaos, and which he to a high degree exemplified.

Tolstoy seems to me to be the best possible example of the fatal consequences of failing to relate ostensible beliefs to actual behaviour. In the end life exacts a fearful price for such charlatanry. Thus Tolstoy, who spent so much of his life denouncing money and sensuality as the two major evils of life, was forced in his last years in a most unedifying manner to be wholly preoccupied with them when, in the normal course of life, he might have been expected to be relieved. This illustrates perfectly the great romantic fallacy.

February 28, 1949

Harold Laski said he's had a terrific row with Bevin over Palestine and that Bevin was very downcast and broken. We went over American broadcast, and he said that he was trying to arrange for me to edit a lot of Webb papers with a biographical introduction, which I said I'd gladly do. One extraordinary proposal he made was that Mountbatten should succeed Bevin as Foreign Secretary. Laski quite dazzled by Mountbatten, and perhaps the Labour Party likewise. I didn't say so, but it seemed to me a monstrous proposal. Curious mixture in Laski, psychologically interesting, of veneration for the British upper classes and desire to destroy their power.

March 4, 1949

Again worried about Hugh Kingsmill whose health has relapsed.

Learnt from Douglas Jerrold that the *Spectator* meeting at which the question of a change of editorship will be discussed will take place about March 18. Personally very sceptical, but in view of the change at the *Daily Telegraph*, it doesn't really matter much.

At Auberon Herbert's flat met with General Kukiel, formerly Polish War Minister, and a lot of other Poles who had been interned and otherwise beaten up by the Russians – one of them had actually been taken in the train to the railway terminus before Katyn Forest, and saw all the others go off in a bus to be shot. He was moved back to Smolensk because the Russians considered that he was an important intelligence agent – reason being he was an expert on

Eastern European economics at a Polish university. All of them
rather remarkable in their way, but slightly horrifying. Having
been in the hands of terrorists leaves a sort of unmistakable mark
behind, something tight and taut about the face.

March 7, 1949

Received rather alarming letter from Hugh Kingsmill who said
that for three days he thought he was going to die, and that his
predominant feeling was like an evacuee's who knows that all
arrangements for his reception at the other end have been made,
but who would still prefer to remain where he is. Very worried
about him.

March 9–10, 1949

Went to Exeter to stay with the Dean, my former tutor, S. C.
Carpenter, arriving there in the evening. Delighted, as usual, to
sit in a railway carriage and watch the twilight.

On Thursday morning we wandered round the Cathedral –
very beautiful. Much admired the manner in which the blitzed
part is being restored. A certain local builder, named Reed, the
day after the bomb fell on the cathedral, began to collect together
the shattered pews, screens, etc. People thought he was mad at
the time, but, as it turns out, he has been able to reconstruct a large
part of the interior. Similarly, builders are perfectly restoring the
shattered part of the structure. I found it touching, and rather
inspiring to see them all at work. Interested to learn that ancient
stained glass lets through the light without colouring it, producing
only a kind of glow, but that modern stained glass colours the light.
The secret of making glass which doesn't colour light is now quite
lost. There seemed to me to be something symbolic in this.

Carpenter rather disconcerted to learn from a letter he opened
at breakfast that the *Daily Telegraph* did not want him to contribute
any more of his Saturday articles. He told me that the money from
these was what he had hoped to live on after his retirement, as his
pension as a dean would only be £200 a year.

Finished reading *English Blake* by Bernard Blackstone.

Blake believed in the Kingdom of Heaven on Earth, the Millenium. That is perhaps what was wrong with him:

> 'To see a World in a Grain of Sand
> And a Heaven in a Wild Flower,
> Hold Infinity in the palm of your hand
> And Eternity in an Hour.'

March 11, 1949

Went on reading about Blake. Also read, with great delight, volume of verses by John Betjeman – particularly liked the one about Miss J. Hunter Dunn.

March 13, 1949

Quite early there came a telephone call from Battle that the police had broken into Mrs Dobbs' house and found her unconscious on the floor. It was what we have all along expected sooner or later. After a good deal of telephoning, Kitty and her brother Pat went down to Battle. I insisted that Kitty should not go alone. Later she rang up to tell me that her mother had refused to be moved, and that she'd had some sort of mild stroke which made her fall over every time she got up. The only way to get her into a nursing home was to give her a big shot of morphine and thus put her out. This was done by Dr Davidson, and they took her to a place in Hastings. When they went into the house the dog, Spot, was sitting on her head, which I thought symbolic, and somehow rather apt. Unless she dies, it is difficult to know what can be done about her, as she will never be able to live again in her house. Extraordinary tenacity of the will. When she was first found, the doctor gave her a sleeping draught and barricaded her in, but even so she broke down the barricade. Whole affair recalled the end of Rasputin.

March 14–15, 1949

Kitty's mother remains unconscious, and is not thought likely to recover. Kitty has been sitting devotedly by her side for several hours each day in order that, if she should come to, she would see some face that she recognizes. Kitty has also been taking in the dog, Spot, for the same reason.

I looked at George Orwell's new novel about the future, *1984*, which I found rather repugnant. It is in the Aldous Huxley genre, imagining life in a totalitarian State. These horrors in futures are really as silly as their converse – the early Wells utopias. (N.B. When did Utopias – i.e. imaginary or symbolic pictures of human society change into the Futures racket? – probably with Wells.) I was made to think of this by reading a slab of Wells' autobiography, particularly his journey to Russia to try to persuade Gorky and other Russians to join the PEN Club and allow freedom of expression – surely the most Quixote-like enterprise every undertaken by man. Conversation with Stalin particularly diverting.

March 16, 1949

Kitty returned, naturally very worn out, and full of the extraordinariness of human life. The following morning her mother died without regaining consciousness. It was a great relief.

I remember so vividly the first time I saw Mrs Dobbs in 1924, actually before I'd seen Kitty. She was sitting in a café at Heyst in the sun, and her son, Leonard, took me to see her. I don't think in the subsequent twenty-five years her appearance has really changed enormously. My recollection of her then is very much as I remember her now, with a huge nose, vast energy, and a kind of ruthless sincerity, which made her remarkable. To me, personally, she was always exceedingly kind and generous, but in her character she was, by and large, the most trying human being I have ever known. This is because she was wholly imprisoned in her egotism and desires – escaping only perhaps through her love of nature, which was genuine, and comes out in her sketching occasionally. She used to set up house all over Europe, and the ménage was always essentially the same – untidy, restless, incompetent, but unforgettable.

She was utterly devoted to her children, but it is difficult to believe that she understood what affection meant, because affection presupposes forgetfulness of self, and although she longed for this, she was never able to achieve it. If ever there was an imprisoned spirit, it was she. Her final companionship with her dog was, for this reason, understandable, the dog, as it were, meeting her on her own terms. Kitty told me that she never in her deliriums cried out for any of her children, or for her husband, but only for this dog. She was always trying to persuade herself that there was another life, but she never believed it. The only person who was wholly gentle with her was Pan, because through his own goodness he could overlook what was horrifying in her total pre-occupation with this earth.

Of course, her up-bringing in a very materialistic rich Victorian family, whose god was Herbert Spencer, played a great part in shaping her character. Also there were many personal circumstances calculated to prevent her from ever achieving an harmonious life. She struggled relentlessly to remain in time and on this earth, and it is a happy thought that now, at last, she has been released. The last terrible picture of her, as Kitty described it, clamouring and shouting incoherently, even bruising herself in her efforts to get up, is a fearful symbol of the human will making its last fight to maintain its finitude.

March 17, 1949

Continued to think about Mrs Dobbs most of the day. The circumstance of death is so extraordinary, that although one grows accustomed to it, it still comes with a dramatic novelty. As P. G. Wodehouse once put it to me, one always thinks that those with whom one is connected are immortal, despite the enormous amount of evidence to the contrary.

Mar 19–20, 1949

Finished off George Orwell's *1984*, and continued to think much about this question of the future, whether romanticized into a Golden Age, or presented as something nauseatingly horrible. It seemed to me more clearly than ever that the whole idea was a fallacy, and that this fallacy became evident if you applied Orwell's or Aldous Huxley's technique to the past – imagining, for instance, in the days of the Church's dominance, a society wholly priest-ridden. It didn't happen so. The point is that human character has survived intact through enormous changes, and is likely to survive.

March 21–22, 1949

Douglas Jerrold said that the *Spectator* decision had been again postponed until the autumn, so that's that.

Started work again, after a lamentable interval, on *The Forties*.

In the evening, Auberon Herbert came round. We spoke about snobbishness, especially in relation to his brother-in-law, Evelyn Waugh. I said I agreed that snobbishness was a ludicrous thing, but that it was relatively harmless. That is to say, admittedly, Evelyn Waugh made an ass of himself, but if his personal uneasiness had found other expressions – say in being a revolutionary – its social consequences might have been far more damaging. It was like the difference between a man who wears a funny nose, and one who tries to stab you in the back; the former is a source of embarrassment to those connected with him, but the latter is a public nuisance.

March 23, 1949

Fred Warburg, George Orwell's publisher, had been in George's Home Guard platoon, which must have been a pretty comic opera affair. He said that George was very secretive and highly incompetent, though he prided himself upon being practical. I told him what I thought about George's *1984*, but said that I felt sure that it had a very good chance of having a large sale. Warburg said that a number of booksellers who had read it had been so frightened that they had been unable to sleep afterwards. When I told this to Tony Powell, he laughed long. The idea of anything keeping booksellers awake was, to him, irresistibly funny.

Talked with Tony about my lunch with Warburg and about George. He pointed out curious coincidence that George was at the same prep school and a scholar at Eton at the same time as Cyril

Connolly. George and Connolly, Tony said, were really like two sides of the same face – one lean and ugly and the other fat and ugly; one phoneyly abstemious and the other phoneyly self-indulgent.

March 24, 1949

My birthday (46). Tony brought me as a present a plate with a quotation from Carlyle on it: 'Feed Me on Facts'. Kitty and I plan to serve Hugh Kingsmill on this next time he comes to supper. Drank a bottle of German hock for the first time since the war, and somehow it gave me a pleasanter sense of things returning to normal than anything has for a long time – not that they really are, but still, it's very nice to be able to drink hock again.

March 25, 1949

Lunched with P. J. Grigg at the Athenaeum. What a place the Athenaeum is – extraordinary death's-heads moving about, high-pitched querulous voices, atrocious food. P.J. said he felt sure that Winston had only made him Secretary of State for War in 1942 because he thought he would be a faithful stooge, and that when he found he wasn't he was bitterly disappointed in him. This is probably true.

March 31, 1949

Birkenhead told me that the Kipling book was definitely not going to be published, but that Kipling's daughter was paying substantial damages to him. This seemed very unsatisfactory, and I advised him to try and get the book published in French.

April 5, 1949

Went to Heinemann to see Princess Bibesco and talk about Ramsay MacDonald's letters. Found her highly got up, obviously had been quite good looking in a rather over-ripe way. She maundered on about Ramsay and their friendship, why she had sent Ramsay flowers. She wanted, she said, to enshrine Ramsay's memory. Did I think the letters would do that?

Honesty compelled me to warn her that a certain amount of ridicule would be inevitable. I pointed out, too, that Asquith's letters to Mrs Harrison had been a flop.

She said, Yes, but then everybody was thinking about Margot (she accentuated the 'r'), whereas Ramsay was a lonely figure. I said that the thing that struck me about the letters was how unworldly Ramsay was (I meant a sucker), which I considered a grave fault in a politician, since people who exercise authority ought to be worldly.

After a brief chat with Frere, who told me that Bevin was now constantly afraid of dying, I went to a NUJ meeting which considered a resolution complaining that Hutt's editorship of *The Journalist* showed partiality. The resolution was largely based on a letter of mine to *The Journalist* protesting against an article on Czechoslovakia. The usual maundering speeches were made. Hutt delivered quite a competent, but utterly phoney, speech in defence of himself. Altogether very squalid and depressing, but glad that vote went against Hutt by a narrow majority which would not have existed had Tony and I not turned up.

April 6, 1949

Tony and Violet very insistent that I should vote in the LCC elections, but, after much consideration, I decided that my present position was neutral. In other words, I consider that in the present condition of the Cold War, and given the Government's, especially Cripps's, efforts to establish economic stability, it would be a mistake to get them turned out. If they were turned out the Communists would rejoice, and my politics, in so far as I have any, consist in promoting what the Communists would dislike. In talking it over with Tony I had to admit also that it is extremely difficult for me to vote Conservative – rather like, I said, a person brought up as a Methodist, who has ceased to be one, but who still is horrified by the idea of entering a French bordello. I tried to convince Tony that a neutral position in politics is a valid one. If, I said, the Cold War was won, or as good as won, the best thing, it seems to me, is to encourage the moderate tendencies in the Labour Party in order that they should be responsible both for holding the line in the Cold War against Russia, and for consolidation of the national economy.

In the evening Jerrold made the very sensible suggestion that we should try and get Hugh Kingsmill a Civil List pension. Hesketh Pearson and I are going down to see him next week.

Went to see Rattigan's *Playbill*. The first piece (*The Browning Version*) about an elderly schoolmaster really quite good. Interested to note that Rattigan, like Maugham, presents women as the active or aggressive element in love-making. This is characteristic of homosexuals.

April 8–9, 1949

Wrote piece on Tolstoy (The Kingdom of Heaven on Earth fallacy) for the *New English Review*. Then went along to the *Daily Telegraph* where Watson told me that my salary was now to be £2,000 a year, which pleased me very much. Read account by Margarete Buber, wife of Heinz Neumann, of how she had been in Russia and arrested by the OGPU, then at the time of the Nazi–Soviet Pact, handed over to the Gestapo. This episode, more than any other, exhibits the cynicism and callousness of the Russians, especially as most of those handed over were Jewish.

Hugh Kingsmill is to go back to hospital, apparently for another operation. Cannot see how he can survive this.

April 17–18, 1949

Arnold Lunn talked about the depressingness of English Catholics, of whom he is one. He said that certain professing Catholics pursued the Church with relentless malignancy, but could never get rid of an uneasy fear that Catholic doctrine may be true.

Letter from Hugh Kingsmill suggests that his life is ebbing away:

'Weather outside divine, and this ward (not a shortened form for Difficult cases of Syphilis) is very light and high up. I don't know what's up with me, except that I have v. bloody nights and could furnish three not v. heroic martyrs with enough stuff to qualify on. Hope, however, that I'm definitely on the mend.

'Balmy spring breezes blowing in from the sea outside, and all past springs revive, but I hope that this decaying old husk will release me at not too long a date to recover all the beauty of those old days in some other form. Am probably rambling. . . .'

24 April, 1949

Tony Powell and I discussed Shakespeare's Sonnets which Tony had been reading. We agreed that the obvious explanation of them is probably the true one – namely, that they represented Shakespeare's romantic snobbishness which, as always, went with a certain homosexual tendency. Episode about the Dark Lady also to be taken at its face value. I said that though I thought they contained some of the most wonderful lines in the English language, no single one of them was entirely satisfactory as a whole, and that this was because the mood in which they were written represented Shakespeare's nature at its worst – namely, his distaste for himself and his social position.

April 29–May 1, 1949

Quiet week-end, made pleasant by a visit from Pan. He was, he said, in the habit of going into the Anglican Church at Aldershot from time to time to pray. On one occasion after he had done this he met the verger's wife, and she asked him if he was in any sort of trouble. Obviously, it hadn't occurred to her that people prayed unless something was the matter. More and more he finds very simple Christians (for instance a community he calls 'The Brethren') congenial rather than orthodox Church people. He told me that he had been spending his nights with a soldier who was in a nervous state and had been having nightmares. Thus, he hadn't been getting much sleep.

We all went to church on Sunday with Pan. The sermon was really quite remarkable – an account of the church finances, in the course of which it was revealed that the Communion Service just about covers its expenses – i.e. collections realized about £100, and the provision of linen, Blessed Elements, etc., comes just about to this amount. It was therefore self-supporting. The rest of the church activities were heavily in arrears. It seemed a curious subject for a sermon, but the hymns were pleasing. Pan sings them with great zest and joy.

May 4, 1949

Read Bertrand Russell's Reith Lectures *Authority and the Individual* with great enjoyment. He excellently states the dilemma presented by how to strike a balance between the liberty of the individual and the authority of the State. He writes extremely well, with a vague touch of satirical humour which is pleasing.

May 7, 1949

Went down to Brighton to see Hugh Kingsmill. Walked up to the hospital, which seemed somewhat prison-like in appearance, as most public hospitals are. When I arrived at his ward the doctor was with him, but after about a quarter of an hour I went in. Very shocked to find him so haggard and white. He was delighted to see me. I tried to talk all the time to prevent him talking, but, of course, although forbidden to do so, he did talk and laugh, as we always do when we meet. All the time I was with him a blood transfusion was going on, blood dripping into him drop by drop under my sight. He said he's had twenty pints and all his arms were punctured from fitting on the instrument through which it is injected.

He said that he hadn't liked to think about Shakespeare much, but rather Johnson because Johnson was never angry. When Johnson was dying and someone arranged his pillow and asked him if it would do, 'Yes,' he said, 'it would do – all that a pillow could do.'

Rather touched to find that Hugh Kingsmill reads all my articles and talked about them. We talked about Jerrold's History, G. M. Trevelyan, whose autobiography I had been reading, and I tried to think of some books that I could send him. He asked for Scott's Journal, and I suggested Stanhope's *Conversations with Wellington*, but we agreed that there are only a very few books one wants to read just for reading's own sake – no novels, for instance, which at the moment he finds abhorrent. I quite saw the point. Wordsworth he would like to read, but, as he said, there is so much dross that it is a little wearisome looking for the really great passages. I stayed two hours, which was really too long, but he kept begging me to stay on. He had the look of someone who was not wholly on this earth, had somewhat withdrawn himself from time, but, all the same, I felt very strongly that he wanted to live, though for no particular reason. He said he didn't want Brian to come down and see him, so when I got back I hedged him off.

I had very strongly the feeling that the doctor didn't really know what was the matter with Hugh Kingsmill. The nurses, as usual, entirely charming, and obviously devoted to Hughie whom they treat with great tenderness.

May 8, 1949

Finished off Trevelyan's autobiographical essay, felt great distaste for his character – one of the pioneers in the idea of not pitying or disliking the poor, but ingratiating oneself with them. All that Garibaldi stuff rang pretty hollow, I thought. There is something curiously odious about the secure, sedentary don getting excitement at second-hand out of tumultuous events and personalities – almost like someone getting erotic satisfaction out of pornographical literature.

May 9, 1949

Read rather a bad life of Goebbels by an American, but, nonetheless, fascinated, as always, by the story of the rise of Nazi power, which provides the pattern of all power-seeking in the Century of the Common Man. Goebbels had the right idea when he saw that the only source of power ever is the mob, in the same way that the only source of wealth ever is the earth, and that to get power it is necessary to return to the mob. Civilizations grow weak because in them power becomes divorced from the mob in the form of wealth and hereditary privilege, or even constitutional authority. Its everlasting fount is the envy of the poor for the rich, the desire of the humble and meek that the mighty should be pulled down and they installed in their place. This is the essence of politics, and everything else is phoney. As Lenin succinctly put it, politics answers the question 'Who Whom?'

May 14–16, 1949

Hesketh Pearson and I were to have gone down to see Hugh Kingsmill but Dorothy rang up to say that he was very ill again.

Late on Sunday night she phoned to say that Hughie had died at nine o'clock precisely.

Spent Monday thinking about Hugh Kingsmill and writing a piece on him for the *New English Review*, also a paragraph in 'Peterborough'. Although long expecting his death, and indeed considering it to be inevitable, still very desolate. Hesketh came in in the evening to read what I had written. We sat talking, drank a lot of whiskey, remembering the many occasions we had been with H.K. and what a lot of happiness his death shut off.

May 17–18, 1949

Cleared up a few odds and ends, but not much work. Went with Kitty to see *The Lady's Not for Burning*, verse play by Christopher Fry. Found it immature and tiresome, though with some talent. Reflected that art and thought, all activities of the mind and spirit, must have a form to be anything. In this play the characters just say anything that comes into the author's head, and therefore, in effect, nothing. It is really just words – a sort of gush of words to drive off fear and horror.

Various people rang up about Hugh Kingsmill and I told all of them who were well off that the family was destitute. Particularly interesting conversation in this connection with E. V. Knox, who kept trying to keep it on an enotional plane, I as resolutely determined to keep it on a practical one, because *Punch* ought to give Dorothy something. Respectable institutions like the *Manchester Guardian*, *The Times* and *Punch* are always the meanest.

May 19, 1949

On Monday Donald Boyd arranged to play back for me that Royal Academy banquet recording with the President, Sir Alfred Munnings' outburst about modern art. A quite extraordinary show, everybody sounded very tight. I couldn't help feeling rather on Munnings' side, though his remarks were most fantastic. I particularly liked his description of walking into an art show with Churchill, and Churchill saying to him: 'Alfred, if we saw Picasso coming in here, would you join me in kicking him on his backside?' And Munnings cordially agreeing with a 'Yes Sir.' Rather gratified when Munnings went for Anthony Blunt, a spinsterish, finicky figure, with whom I had had some dealings in MI5 during the war.

May 25, 1949

Had tea at the club with Hesketh, and settled final arrangements for Hughie's memorial service. We looked at one or two passages in the Epistles, and I was once again struck with their extraordinary intellectual and artistic excellence.

Passing through Fitzroy Square Hesketh showed me the house where Shaw had lived with his mother when he first came to London. Very typical of Shaw that when he pointed this place out to Hesketh, he pointed to one of the windows as being his study, another his bedroom, but there was no reference to any accommodation for his mother. Hesketh exceedingly cut up about Hugh Kingsmill and suffering from insomnia. I think he felt it more than anyone.

May 26, 1949

Critics Programme. Walter Allen on, now working on the *New Statesman*, but not a great admirer of its political viewpoint. Told me that he had set a competition in which the competitors were to do the first paragraph of a Graham Greene novel, and that Graham went in for it under an assumed name, and was luckily awarded the third prize, Very like Graham.

June 2, 1949

Went in the morning to Downing Street to see Anthony Bevir, the Patronage Secretary, about a Civil List pension for Dorothy Kingsmill. Thought how typical the whole thing was of this country – just an ordinary-sized private house providing the office of the supreme executive. Bevir himself funny little dark Civil Servant figure, seated at his desk with, for some curious reason, two spare pairs of shoes in the hearth. He delivered himself of long rigmarole about Civil List pensions, his main purpose being, I gathered, to make sure that there would be no danger of a counter claim by Hugh's first wife. He kept on saying: 'I didn't want to put anything on paper.' Like all Civil Servants of that type, there was a vein of shrewdness and purpose in his meandering talk. Impossible to judge his age, might have been 20 or 80; just a slightly wizened youthful face, black suit, Old Etonian tie. He is also, I gather, responsible for ecclesiastical patronage, and so is heavily waited upon by the clergy. Found it necessary to confuse him a bit about the exact ages of Hugh's children and date of his marriage, since he was insistent that a certain standard of respectability was required for a Civil List pension. He was also anxious to know if there was any money about in the family. On that point, too, I was able to assure him, not. Returned home marvelling at the strange ways of authority, the odd manner in which it is exercised. In No. 10 all round the walls group photographs of previous cabinets, rather like a junior common room.

A character from MI6 came to lunch, and we discussed at length a particular assignment. I said I'd think it over for a week and would then get in touch with him again.

June 6–7, 1949

Monday: Went off early by car to Ashridge Military College. Really quite enjoyable there, exquisite day, General Paget most affable. Talked a lot to him about Eisenhower. He told me that Monty was writing a book attacking Eisenhower. I said I thought this was a great mistake, and he asked me if I'd agree to go and see Monty and tell him so. Said I would, but afterwards felt it was a bit of an undertaking. Lecture went well. Really very stimulating audience. At question time one man asked how I accounted for the fact that someone as intelligent as Samuel Johnson should have been a Conservative. Fairly let him have it, to Paget's great delight. Paget old-fashioned type of evangelical general, to me very sympathetic. Mentioned that Winston hates Johnson and likes Burke. This is quite in character.

June 8–9, 1949

Went to the BBC to record the talk on George Orwell's *1984*. Tried to explain why I considered that its horrors have little relation to life or to anything that can happen.

In the evening Dr Davidson came to supper. He talked about the National Health Service, and said that what with the constant advance of medicine requiring more personnel and material and the extension of those requiring treatment, a complete jam was approaching. I said that this fitted in with what I felt about the Welfare State, which, in its efforts to produce everything for everyone, would inevitably result in producing nothing for anyone.

In the morning took Katherine, Hughie's daughter by his first marriage, along to the memorial service. About 100 people present, and it went off really very well. Hesketh and I read the Lessons and everything seemed to be what Hughie would have liked.

June 10, 1949

Lunched at the Authors' with Brian Lunn, Hesketh, John Fletcher (solicitor who is looking after Hughie's affairs) and John Davenport. Davenport is a curious, fat, hopeless man, who was considered, when young, to have enormous promise, but who has drifted rather aimlessly along, growing ever more vain and untruthful to recompense for his increasing sense of utter futility. He slightly touched my heart by greatly praising my first novel, *Autumnal Face*. Conversation rather scattered, Brian with his harsh voice shouting everyone else down, and poor Fletcher trying to get in a number of banal remarks about American materialism, to which I listened respectfully. Hesketh and I walked away with relief. Hesketh said he was glad there was a large party as he had felt in his bones that Davenport was about to attempt a 'touch'. He said that a peculiarity of Davenport's touching technique was that instead of combining it with a hard-luck story, the prelude was always a series of fantastic good-luck stories.

June 11–12, 1949

Read the second volume of Churchill's war memoirs. Found it really most readable except for the quoted official documents. Churchill's own narrative has an odd charm. Reflected how intensely American he was, and how, unless he had been half American, it wouldn't have been possible for him to fill the role he did in 1940 – curious exaggeration of archaisms of language, behaviour, dress, etc., quite essential at that time. His pleasantest feature is that he never attempts for a moment to disguise his great love of exercising authority. No tendency whatsoever to dramatize himself as a man longing for retirement dragged unwillingly into the centre of the stage. He loves, and says he loves, the limelight. This is most refreshing. He obviously loved every moment of the war, and perhaps was happiest in the days of the blitz.

June 15, 1949

Went in the morning to see Field-Marshal Lord Montgomery. Curious encounter on the whole. Monty received me in a large office in Dover House overlooking Horse Guards Parade. Got up in his usual fancy dress – two wrist watches, battle dress, as Tony puts it, ribbons down to his knees. Funny little wizened face, which is slightly disagreeable because it is much too fat for its framework, eyes are glazed over and mad-looking. In fact, his whole attitude suggested to me that the strain of his fame might have cracked his wits a bit. At once started talking about Communism, cold war, etc., in the manner I remembered so well from the war in which he used to analyse a military exercise or operation, pointing all the while with his hands as though to a huge map. Most of what he said was obvious to the point of banality. He was supposed to want to know what I thought, but actually gave me very little opportunity of expressing any views, and spent most of the hour I was with him expounding his own. A clear case of advanced megalomania, and now, perhaps, a bit lost in this new job he has got at SHAEF. Sort of thing he said was that the French would never be any good until they got rid of proportional representation; that if a single bomb were dropped on an American town, no American troops would ever leave the country, etc. He said that A. V. Alexander, Minister of Defence, was an absolutely hopeless person, but expressed great liking for Attlee ('Perfect gentleman') and Bevin. Spoke about de Gaulle, not with great appreciation. No use for De Lattre de Tassigny, a French general with whom he has to deal. One or two flashes of understanding – said that, after all, we are now 'at war with Communism'. If this turned into a shooting war with Russia we could win it, but unless we defeated Communism, defeating Russia in a shooting war would be no use. He thought we ought to have a co-ordinated command in the cold war, someone responsible for conducting it. At present there was no plan – his usual trick of repeating points – 'No plan, no plan at all.' Spoke about Eisenhower's book, which had obviously upset him very much. Rather shifty look when he said that all the row about the book took place before he'd read it. Said he was going to write his own account of the war, for which he had copious notes, and would be able to prove that Eisenhower's orders were contradictory, and in which he'd demonstrate that the American insistence on an attack on a wide front against his conviction that the proper strategy was a concentrated attack on a short front, protracted the war for a number of months.

Spoke about P. J. Grigg with affection, but repeated to me a rather malicious remark of Churchill's about P.J. which P.J. had already told me as coming from Monty. Told me on no account to repeat this to P.J. Usual Monty entourage of youthful officers. After talking about an hour, got up abruptly and said that he was off to see General Smuts. Altogether reminded me of my interview with General MacArthur.

June 16, 1949

Went to Heinemann, and afterwards with Frere to lunch at the Garrick. He most loquacious, full of reminiscences of D. H. Lawrence, Frieda, Katherine Mansfield. Said that Middleton Murry, her husband, had told him that Katherine Mansfield died of syphilis, though she had TB as well. She got the former from following Gaudier Bzeska after he joined the French army in the 1914–18 war and sleeping with a number of his comrades in arms. Also gave a most diverting account of taking Frieda to dine in the Savoy Hotel after Lawrence's death. We agreed that the time had come when D. H. Lawrence's reputation is likely to revive, and it would be a good idea to republish some of his novels. Also agreed that he was a bad novelist, but a nearly great poet. Frere said that when Lawrence was dying he complained that his feet were cold, whereupon Frieda warmed them against her enormous German bosom. Felt that this was a very symbolic scene worth remembering.

Ellen Terry's description of Sarah Bernhardt: 'Her body was not the prison of her soul but its shadow.'

June 18–20, 1949

Andreas Mayor recalled that at the Abbey service for the Webbs someone asked which of the two urns was hers, and my mother-in-law yanged out in her well-known way: 'It's the old, dirty one'.

H. D. Ziman said of the scientist J. D. Bernal that he was 'Prospero in the service of Caliban'.

Doing article on second volume of Churchill's War Memoirs. Perhaps exagerated praises (as had to be done in *Daily Telegraph* for obvious reasons). Even so, felt once more magnificence of his stand in 1940, and delight of his rich humour. After all, a sublime buffoon who combines Falstaff and Henry V.

Have taken to wearing spectacles, and this, at one stroke, seems to have cured, or at any rate greatly reduced, my sleeplessness.

June 21, 1949

Brief meeting at Heinemann. Frere had just received MS of anthology by Masefield, Poet Laureate. He looked a little ruefully at it, but put on a brave face, as I did, too. At week-end Frere had stayed with J. B. Priestley – huge house on Isle of Wight with 2,000 acres. Priestley, Frere said, much annoyed with farm labourers because they wouldn't work hard and thought of him as chap who'd got rich easily.

Final discussion on MI6 project. Practically decided to take it on, dropping BBC and occasional journalism. Usual set-up – improvised office, gang of uniformed porters downstairs self-consciously doing nothing, pass to get in which had to be countersigned, etc. Wrote off in the evening saying I'd do it.

Much amused by Tony Powell's account of how his sister-in-law, Julia Mount, now got new lease of life because she earns 16/– a day showing people round house of Marquess of Bath, a friend. She said she usually got two bob or half-a-crown even when she was tipped 'Because she was a lady'. Tony said that her being a lady would lead him to give smaller rather than larger tip. About 400 people came daily to house – Longleat; and Bath and his friends all greatly uplifted thereby. Good commentary, I thought, on present situation that aristocracy find new purpose in life, as well as income, by showing visitors round their houses.

June 22, 1949

Dined with Isaac Deutscher whose book on Stalin I recently reviewed. Deutscher really very charming, originally from Poland where he was brought up to be a Rabbi. (Rabbis in his family back to the 16th century.) He couldn't speak English in 1940. Now British subject; read aloud, with touching delight in its rhythm and assonance, passage from Macaulay's History. I felt that this was symbolically correct – Polish Jew, near Rabbi, reviving the delight in Macaulay's prose style and ideas. To him it was all new and magical; he loved the words, and his power to speak them, the ostensible lofty detachment of it all; it pleased his anglomania.

June 26–27, 1949

Arthur Rose, who is dealing with my play *Liberation*, talked about plays. He made one or two useful observations – as, that nothing should be kept back from the audience even for the sake of achieving surprise, which is anyway a much over-rated device. Again, no dramatist can depict a character greater than he is himself – e.g. Terence Rattigan succeeding with schoolmaster in *Playbill* but failing utterly with Alexander the Great. The emotion which had to be achieved, he said was – taking the case of *Macbeth* – the audience knowing Duncan was going to be murdered but wanting somehow to warn him of the danger into which he was running.

July 2, 1949

Marvellous day at Cranbrook. We saw John in the Corps parade, and then had lunch together in the garden. John went up to get his prize, and we applauded uproariously. Prizes distributed by the Archbishop of Canterbury, Geoffrey Fisher, who made a most entertaining speech. He looks exactly like an Osbert Lancaster drawing, but very genial and sensible. He agreed that in the public mind there was now a complete confusion between the Welfare State and the Christian religion, though, in point of fact, the two had very little connection with one another.

July 7–26, 1949

On holiday with Kitty at Sainte-Maxime in the South of France, later staying at Roquebrune-Cap Martin with A. T. Cholerton and visiting Nice, Mentone, St Tropez and Monte Carlo ('like Pompeii, preserved by chance').

English now largely departed from this coast, except for a few eking out their £50 allowance and some obvious currency crooks of the Sidney Stanley type. . . . The English have become the poor relations, and only the name of the Promenade des Anglais remains as a reminder of former grandeur – like Port-of-Spain. Two American sailors were eagerly greeted in a bar where those colonels who used to flourish here are little regarded.

July 23, 1949

For me, here at Roquebrune-Cap Martin, perfect existence. Rise about 7, drink tea, bathe, walk by the sea; 9 breakfast (crusty bread, butter, fruit, coffee) and then sit at little quiet shady table looking straight on to the Mediterranean, write a bit, read, think; at noon long swim and lie in the sun until 1.30; then lunch, (cheese, salad, ham, red wine, fruit) and after lunch doze and read; at 4.30 bathe again and in the evening walk either to Monte Carlo or to Mentone, buy newspapers and sit in a café reading them and watching people; return leisurely at about 8.30 and dine either at villa or Madame Ambert's, solidish meal (chicken or omelette au jambon or Mediterranean fish) and enough red wine or rosé to feel drowsy;

game of gin rummy with Kitty, brief read and early asleep. That –
for anyone who cares to know – is how I like to live; but I dare say,
as Kitty pointed out, it wouldn't answer permanently. As a break
– wonderful.

June 28–August 1, 1949

Returned to London and soon back in the old treadmill. Question-
able whether holidays are really a good idea – like the arrangement
that was tried out in Spain before the civil war of letting prisoners
out for a walk every now and again on parole. *Daily Telegraph* on
Friday – old Watson, everything just the same. Collected load of
books, etc., etc.

Tony Powell brought to my attention an admirable quotation
from one Tom Braddock, Labour MP:

> 'The workers of this country have agreed that they want for
> themselves all they produce, all the wealth of the country,
> all the food, all the housing, all the clothing. Their legitimate
> needs can only be satisfied by all: there is no surplus for the
> cultured few, for the royal and noble few, for the wealthy few.
> All these must be stripped of their rents, of their interest,
> of their profit and of their inflated salaries and expense
> accounts.
> 'Chuck it, comrades: be workers and be proud of it, be
> rough, be unreasonable, don't worship slick efficiency. It is
> the workers who are important, not the work, that is secondary.'

August 3–5, 1949

Worked on my new play, *Comrade Caliban*. Feel in my bones that
it is going to be successful.

Kitty and the children went off to Scotland, and I dined at the
Savile with Philip Jordan. Afterwards joined by Gerald Barry who
is now organizing the Festival of Britain.

Interested to note that Jefferson, in drafting the Declaration of
Independence, altered 'property' to 'pursuit of happiness'. This is
very typical of America and everything that has happened there
since.

August 7, 1949

At the *Daily Telegraph* wrote leader on defence – very muddled,
and made more so after Coote had corrected it. Dined with the
Griggs. P.J. convinced, as I am, that the post-war economic crisis
is now about to break, and that it's really rather a relief, like the
German attack after the phoney war. We shall at least know where
we are, even if we're in the soup. No more dollars are forthcoming
and in six months or so we shall be completely destitute as far as
gold and hard currency are concerned. P.J. obviously hopes that
in another crisis he may get back into power and so, he admitted,
does Monty with whom he'd been staying in Fontainebleau.
Actually they won't get back into office because they don't belong
to the next phase.

August 15, 1949

T. R. Fyvel much amused me by his account of a recent visit to
Palestine. He said the whole show was run entirely on the British
model so that even the Israeli military policemen looked like the
British ones with pipe-clay webbing and large moustaches. This
sort of end-result, he said, obviously annoyed people like Koestler,
but is what was intended. The Arabs, he said, were joining up fast
in the Israeli army. Altogether it sounds an amusing Marx brothers
sort of set-up which I'd like to see sometime.

August 16, 1949

Spent the day with Hesketh, long walk about sixteen miles, started
at Chorleywood, Hertfordshire countryside very delightful. We
noticed a charming rectory, and planned to get ordained and share
the duties. Had lunch at a pub and a certain number of drinks.
Then went on to nearby graveyard where George Alexander, the
actor, and one of Hesketch's great admirations, is buried. Sat on
his grave talking about him. Passing by a large country house we

looked inside and found that it was a kind of country club with a bar and three or four drunks assembled there. Joined them for one drink, and then on. Curious place, wondered how it managed to operate, rather frowsty but not entirely unattractive woman appeared to be in charge. Tea at Chipperfield, then long walk back in the evening and dined at the Café Royal, most cheerful. Much amused by one of the waiters who said he was a staunch supporter of the Labour Government because his conditions of life were now so much better than before. 'Now,' he said, 'they *persuade* me to go at 10 o'clock, whereas before they didn't care what happened to me.'

August 21, 1949

Engaged in ferocious argument with Johnstone about religion, he taking his usual rather harsh agnostic line. As I argued, felt, as always, more than ever convinced that the explanation of life, if there is one, must be in mystical, rather than rational, terms.

August 23, 1949

Lunched at the Ivy with Philip Jordan and Lady Rothermere. Lady Rothermere I thought distinctly attractive – dark, Irish, and quite quick. Her first husband was Lord O'Neill. She takes an active part in the conduct of Rothermere's newspapers, and the object of the lunch was to consider whether I might not be a suitable successor to Frank Owen as editor of the *Daily Mail*. Lady Rothermere amused me very much by describing arriving at a fancy dress dance with Pamela Berry (sister of Birkenhead and married to Camrose's son, Michael). They had to walk in and there was a large crowd watching. Pamela said that she was frightened because the whole situation seemed to her very 'tumbril-making'. As Lady Rothermere said, and I agreed with her, what is 'tumbril-making' is rich people being ashamed of being rich. As everyone naturally envies them their riches, the moment they become ashamed of them they are bound to be despoiled, which is just and proper. The only excuse for being rich is to be arrogant. Lunch went well, and more is likely to be heard of this project.

August 27, 1949

First Pan arrived, and then he and I looking out from the balcony saw Kitty and the children return. Pan in good form but very thin. He wears himself out with the intensity of his faith. Talks about nothing else, and increasingly uses evangelical jargon. Described an Army scripture lecturer who has a little hut in the camp to which he and five or six other Christians are in the habit of going. The thing is, Pan explained, that they are united, and if the Church was being effective, all Christians would be similarly united. His present intention is to sign on in the army for another two years, transferring to the RAMC.

August 29–30, 1949

Finished off Life of Tennyson by his grandson, Charles. Very close resemblance with Dickens in some respects. He, too, could mesmerize and loved giving public readings of his poems. Shrewder than Dickens on the whole, and refused an American offer of £20,000 to go there and give public readings. Nonetheless, glad to receive £1,000 for a small poem. Relations with the Queen very interesting. Noted that he was disinclined to accept a peerage because he thought that England was entering upon a revolutionary period in which being a peer might be a handicap to his son. Mrs Tennyson, like most Victorian wives, spent most of her time lying on a sofa. They were nearly all ill, and I'm not surprised.

September 1, 1949

Went along to MI6 and read a lot of papers to get material for lectures. Interested to note how the style of Foreign Office despatches has become infected with a sort of Beverley Nichols informality, expressions like 'lie doggo' occur with great frequency. Nothing in the reports I saw from behind the iron curtain countries which could not have been got from the newspapers.

September 5, 1949

Went along to MI6 in the afternoon, and, to his considerable embarrassment, saw Goronwy Rees going in. Always enter the place with a certain misgiving, something so essentially foolish about it. Read a very good report on Splinter Communist Parties in Germany.

Tony and Alick Dru, who is now farming, came to dinner. Tony much intrigued by the curious information I had received that George Orwell is to marry a girl called Sonia Brownell who is concerned with bringing out the magazine *Horizon*. Alick said that he thought David Mathew had a fair chance of becoming Pope. This would be most intriguing for all of us.

September 10, 1949

In the evening went to see *The Tempest* at the Open Air Theatre. Caliban played with fatuous zest by Robert Atkins. Play itself exceedingly threadbare and tedious, I felt, with just this one character to relieve it. Refrain: 'Has a new master, Get a new man,' slogan of all revolutionaries. Caliban's servitude the everlasting servitude of man; his flashes of poetry (the only poetry in the play) the everlasting vision of man.

September 14, 1949

Went with Kitty to see Graham Greene's film, *The Third Man*, of which I'd read the script and thought little. Actually, it has made a really remarkable film.

September 16–18, 1949

On the Saturday evening Philip Jordan told me that Cripps the following day was going to announce devaluation of the £. This information was most useful in preparing things at the *Daily Telegraph*.

Sunday: Wrote long leader on devaluation in advance of Cripps' broadcast, which stood up quite well afterwards. Dined with Tony and Violet and listened to Cripps, rather to Tony's irritation. Cripps very parsonical in an evangelical sort of way. Amused when he said that during the early 1930s the shadow of unemployment was over many of our homes. I didn't feel that this shadow was very dark or menacing over Parmoor. Everything now suggests an enormous bust-up with the Trade Unions.

Kitty remarked that in the Thirties everyone had grumbled about poverty in the midst of plenty, but that now there was plenty in the midst of poverty. She didn't know which was worse.

September 21, 1949

In the evening read a Life of Swinburne by Humphrey Hare. Swinburne an extraordinary little bird, very typical Romantic Movement figure, in some ways rather like D. H. Lawrence, I thought. Hare goes to great lengths to account for Swinburne's peculiarities, but it seemed to me that they had a quite simple explanation – namely that Swinburne being about three foot high and quite ludicrous looking but with a most ardent temperament, was always trying to prove himself a man. First he tried to get into the army, then he tried to get married, and finally, to make Adah Menken his mistress, but it all ended in fantasy, as it was bound to do.

September 23, 1949

Wrote leader on Russia having the atomic bomb which has created a great sensation. Find it quite impossible to get excited about the atomic bomb as such, can't see that it really alters anything.

In the evening listened to a new BBC radio feature, a discussion between men and women called *We Beg To Differ*. Kay Hammond with her funny voice quite delightful, but the feature, like the Brains Trust, doomed, I should suppose, to become silly after five or six goes.

September 25, 1949

Read Somerset Maugham's *A Writer's Notebook*, very vulgar like everything he does, but he writes so well that the most commonplace thoughts pass muster – or seem to – as one reads. Every now and again wonderful give-away, as when he said that he was interested in the human soul, goes on to define what he means by his soul, and indicates that it might have been completely altered if he'd had a plate when young to prevent him having slightly projecting teeth. Compared with Wells and others much more sensible and therefore less pretentious, but essentially an example of the fool who does not persist in his folly.

Noticed quotation in *Sunday Times*:

'Be not deceived; God is not mocked: for whatsoever a man soweth, that shall he also reap.' (Galatians VI, 7.)

September 26, 1949

Lunched with Ivor Thomas, former Labour MP, now a Conservative. Asked him about the social consequences of his break with the Labour Party, and he said that Attlee personally continued to be genial. Also said that at Cabinet meetings which he'd sometimes attended Attlee occasionally took very strong emphatic line which he was quite unable to carry through. This fitted in with my picture of Attlee.

Strolled in the evening with Kitty, and after supper Kim Philby and Dick Brooman-White came in and we engaged in much MI6 gossip.

September 27, 1949

In the afternoon discussed with Tony Powell various points in his new novel, *A Question of Upbringing*. Extremely taken with it as a piece of writing, and some of it very funny.

In the evening went to see George Orwell who is now in the University College Hospital. He looks inconceivably wasted, and has, I should say, the appearance of someone who hasn't very long to live – a queer sort of clarity in his expression and elongation of his features. We chatted about Hughie and other things, and then Sonia Brownell, who is supposed to be going to marry him, came in – large, bouncing girl, quite pleasant, I thought. Somewhat disconcerted because before entering she looked for a long time through the glass at the top of the door. George full of reminiscences about his relations with H. G. Wells and the quarrel they had, but I couldn't really make head or tail of what it was all about. Sonia goes to see him every day, which is very nice for him. George more peaceful than he was, but his mind still grinding over the same old political questions. Always feel affectionately towards him.

Went to see *Death of a Salesman*. Hysterical, noisy, American play, extremely well produced and extremely well acted by Paul Muni, but how it evoked the American scene and all the horror of it – that superstitious dread of failure and love of success, wishful thinking, etc. Saw Duff Cooper in a box and waved to him. Sitting in front of us, Leslie Henson, the comedian, whose appearance off stage doesn't differ at all from his appearance on it. The more I thought about the play the more clear it seemed to me that it was a wholly sentimental affair – a glorified hard-luck story.

October 3, 1949

Met Dennis Ambler of MI6 at Waterloo and went with him to Gosport, where a car met us and took us out to a curious isolated fort, dating back to the Napoleonic war, jutting out into the sea, which is now MI6 training establishment. Several of the officers attending the course I'd known in the war, and we had the usual reminiscent conversations. Course includes, I gather, operational exercises and landings on the Dorset coast.

October 4, 1949

Wondered about the course, whether it was foolish or showed some obscure reaching after the realities of the present situation, decided on the whole the latter was correct. Some lectures in the morning, and then caught the 12.20 to London. On reaching home retired to bed with 'flu.

Tony looked in and I told him about the letter I'd had from Sonia Brownell saying that she and George would be married on October 12 and that, to George's great delight, as they were to be married in hospital they would have to have a clergyman. I said that, in a sense, George had developed TB in order to be married by a clergyman which otherwise he'd never have had the face to do.

Cholerton arrived from France, having characteristically lost his luggage and caught the wrong train, but all is repaired.

October 6, 1949

Stayed with George Orwell for an hour or so talking about politics. He said that he wanted to buy a bed-jacket for his marriage. I thought of something from Jaegers, but Tony took the matter up and said he was going to get him an elaborate velvet smoking jacket. I decided to let it go at that. George in quite good form, obviously pleased about getting married, told me about special licence, etc., said that there was a clergyman on the premises and that he would officiate, but that, surprisingly enough, as George put it, 'deathbed marriages' were not very common.

October 10, 1949

Lady Rothermere has asked me to lunch again suggesting that the *Daily Mail* business is still on. This rather confirmed by curious letter from James Brough, Washington Correspondent of the *Daily Mail*, who'd heard rumours about it. If journalists collected news with the same success that they collect gossip newspapers would be more interesting.

After lunch called for by car and went and sat with character whom I'm instructing. Found it quite interesting, and he quite an interesting chap. All the arrangements typically SIS – i.e. combination of fantasy and incompetence.

Tony Powell had excellent Waugh anecdote of when the Duff

Coopers were staying with him in the country. At a certain point in the evening, Waugh's wife got up and said that she was going upstairs to change. Lady Diana poured herself out another large drink and said to Waugh that she and Duff hadn't brought evening clothes with them. Waugh looked anguished, rang for the man servant and said to him: 'Tell Mrs Waugh, only tea gown.'

Looked in at a cocktail party given by Robert Kee who is starting a new publishing business. It was in the house of Cyril Connolly who was of course there but nowadays we're not on speaking terms. Party was pretty macabre – first person I saw being Pamela Hansford Johnson who looked at me with an expression of deep loathing; with her character called Kay Dick who wears an eye-glass and with whom George Orwell once took me out to dinner, also not very friendly. I grasped their hands and hurried on, falling into the arms of David Higham, my agent, whose moustache seemed bigger and face grosser than ever. We chatted a few moments. Then saw Stevie Smith who gave me a dirty look because she'd sent me a copy of her latest book and I hadn't acknowledged it, or indeed, read it. I laughed this off as best I might. Waved to the Baroness Budberg who was charging about like a huge dreadnought. Masses and masses of people, mostly very unedifying, glad to get away.

With Tony afterwards I said that the essence of living reasonably was to be where one felt one belonged, and that all forms of social malaise and discontent derived from ignoring this most important of all principles, and that I thought his novel was a brilliant exposition of it. Also that the disagreeableness of being, for instance, a social climber must be the malaise due to constantly finding oneself in an unsympathetic and unharmonious milieu.

October 12, 1949

In the evening saw an exquisite performance of *Love's Labour Lost*, one of the best I've ever seen. Most interested in the character of Berowne, who is obviously Shakespeare, especially in his strange remarks about Rosaline.

Before the theatre went to Longmans cocktail party, again enormous gathering. Chatted with Rose Macaulay, now looking immensely aged, everything about her having diminished in size except her false teeth. Also had genial exchange with Sir Edward Marsh and Christopher Hollis. Ludicrous conversation with Richard Church, the poet and novelist, whose son was at Cranbrook as a day boy. (I've seen him at the school once or twice.) He and his wife asked me how I liked the school, and I said my boys were all very happy there. They said theirs hadn't been, because previously he'd attended Dartington Hall, and had therefore looked down on the boys at Cranbrook. 'When we used to ask him,' Mrs Church said, 'to invite boys from the school to the house, he would refuse on the ground that their fathers were bank clerks, and "Have you ever known an interesting bank clerk?"' he asked his mother. I suggested T. S. Eliot as a possible answer, which irritated her rather, and then pointed out that left-wing snobbishness of this sort was really infinitely more reprehensible than the old-fashioned kind, which was at any rate based on certain rough and ready principles, as that you should show consideration for other people. Whole episode was a wonderful illustration of Tony's general position on this subject. It is obviously far less pernicious socially that people should be snobbish in a hierarchical sense than in an egotistical sense.

October 13, 1949

Cholerton continues to maunder on about his affairs, but is very sweet in his odd way. At present he is trying to get a job with UNESCO and described to me its present set-up in the Majestic Hotel in Paris which was first a German and then a SHAEF HQ. Said that on the walls of the rooms there were graphs showing the increase of literacy in Abyssinia, and that a party had gone off to prepare a report on higher education in the Yangtse Valley but that under the stress of circumstances now prevailing there they had had to return and were studying feminism in Beirut.

At the Haymarket Theatre saw *The Heiress* – excellently contrived adaptation of Henry James's novel *Washington Square*. All the subtlety of the novel comes out even better than it does in the book. Reflected that it was somewhat ironic that James had laboured so long without success to produce a successful play (which was his greatest ambition) and that now after his death one of his novels should prove so suitable for dramatization and its dramatic version prove a highly successful play.

October 14, 1949

George Orwell is now married, but we don't yet know any details of the ceremony.

October 22–23, 1949

Andreas Mayor had lunched with Stafford Cripps a few days before, and had found him, he thought, rather deflated. Cripps, it appears, was talking about how he'd love to resign, which, as I said to Andreas, in politicians is always a sign of prostate or being on the point of being thrown out. Public affairs more than ever chaotic. Everyone wondering what Attlee will have to say tomorrow.

The following evening listened to Attlee explaining the rather petty-fogging reductions in national expenditure he had announced to the House of Commons in the afternoon. Attlee, too, a singularly apt figure to preside over the ultimate disintegration of the society whose dissolution he has constantly prophesied, but which he is now vainly, shrilly, feebly, trying to hold together a little longer.

Delighted to hear that Pan has been refused for the Army and is being demobilized.

October 25, 1949

George Orwell really does seem better. He was sitting up in bed in his cerise coloured velvet jacket bought for his wedding, and seemed remarkably cheerful. George said that he thought that old people should be allowed to commit suicide, and that 'health and beauty' were essential to the good life. I fell on him pretty heavily for this, which is a silly derivative from Gissing, Samuel Butler, E. M. Forster, etc. George would not have it. He pointed to an advertisement for men's underwear in the evening paper which showed the god Mercury wearing a new brand of underpants, and said that such blasphemy hurt his feelings much more than mockery of the Christian religion. I said I registered my disagreement and would take up the point at a later date. Sonia, now his wife, came in and seemed rather tired, I thought. She has immediately developed the trait which Tony and I consider characteristic of most matrimonial relationships – i.e. envy, rather than jealousy, of her husband. When George's supper was brought in, she said that, after all, he had a wonderful life, waited on hand and foot compared with her struggles with Connolly's bad temper at the office of *Horizon*.

October 26, 1949

Finished off revising *Comrade Caliban*.

Bought two volumes of Surtees at Hatchards as a wedding present for George. Very pleasant books with coloured prints, which I would have liked to have kept for myself. Coming back in the bus Hesketh told me that he'd just had a specialist to see Gladys, and that he'd told Hesketh privately that her case was hopeless and that it was just a question of whether she had a quick or a lingering death. He'd invented some story to tell her, but I said I thought that subconsciously, at any rate, she probably knew.

October 27, 1949

Lunched with Lady Rothermere at Warwick House. Curious gathering – Stanley Morison, Tom Hopkinson and his wife, and another female whose name I never caught. Lady Rothermere somewhat hysterical and explained that 'Esmond' (Lord Rothermere) had at the last moment declined to come. We talked about religion, and Stanley Morison gave an account of how he'd transferred from being a Free Thinker to being a Roman Catholic. I took great exception to Stanley's remark that there were only two religions in the world today – Catholicism and Communism. As I said, Communism cannot possibly be regarded as a religion.

Nothing whatever was said about the *Daily Mail*, and I can

only imagine that plans had gone awry. Lady Rothermere said that Cyril Connolly came to lunch with her once a week and gave her long instalments of his love affairs. Also that *Horizon* is going to be suspended for a year in order that Connolly may 'devote himself wholly to his art'. Indicated that, in my view, this was rubbish. Lady Rothermere said that she was trying to persuade her husband to buy *Horizon* for her, and I said I was sure she would be able to get it if she offered Connolly a long-term contract at a large salary, his art notwithstanding.

November 2, 1949

Went in the evening to *A Streetcar Named Desire* – as anticipated, quite intolerably tedious and fifth-rate piece, full of American sentimentality and hysteria. In American writing there are only two strains – one derived from Walt Whitman and utterly phoney, of which this play, Hemingway, etc., are derivatives; and the other from Mark Twain, from which whatever is alive in American writing is derived. That is to say *Huckleberry Finn* and *Leaves of Grass* provide the two roots as far as American letters are concerned.

Much distressed by the hullabaloo in the papers about the *Amethyst*'s return from the Yangtze river. It is the measure of how much of our greatness is departed that so trivial an incident should create so vast a hullabaloo.

November 4–7, 1949

Finished off my MI6 character to my considerable relief.

Read Peter Quennell's *John Ruskin: The Portrait of a Prophet* with great interest. Ruskin I find more and more fascinating, and he would certainly be my English 'Green Stick' figure along with Tolstoy, Walt Whitman, etc. All the contradictions of the Victorian Age and of the Welfare State to come implicit in him. His friendship with Carlyle most interesting. Consider him now the exact equivalent of Tolstoy. His Guild of St George, road making, etc., all intimations of a future Welfare State. He himself said he was 'another Rousseau'. Much taken with his phrase 'Nebuchadnezzar's bitter grass'. Like Kitty's mother, found his only solace in a sensual love of nature, the brightness of fire-flies, etc. When he went mad he said he had 'tumbled down the stairs of his wits'.

November 9, 1949

Lunched with Camrose. Also present Harold MacMillan and P. J. Grigg. Camrose said he'd heard that Cripps was going to give up politics and take to religion. MacMillan replied that it would be much better if he gave up religion and took to politics. P.J. brought up his old point about when the Labour Party became Socialist, and we discussed that at great length. I said I thought the process was really rather a simple one, like the three-card trick; you simply replaced one card, the Kingdom of Heaven, by another, the Kingdom of Heaven on Earth, and tried to play on as before.

Pan seems to be going through some kind of spiritual crisis. Remember so vividly when I was his age often wishing I was dead, and how futile seemed the efforts of an older generation to help. Often wonder what Pan will make of life – he is so gentle that it is difficult to imagine him making any sort of terms with a society which is, and must be, essentially cruel. He clings to his religion which is the only thing he's got, but still the world seems unkind and inhospitable – because he is religious perhaps the more so. Understand his state of mind, but understanding doesn't help one to help him.

November 10, 1949

Alec Vidler now dines quite regularly with the King and Queen at Windsor en famille. He gave me a diverting account of what they are like – the King really very simple; the Queen intelligent and au fait with everything, including books; Princess Elizabeth quite charming. He gave a comical account of his awful doubts the first time about whether he should wear tails or a dinner jacket and other complications of etiquette, but now everything is in order. He has that unusual faculty of being, as a companion, restful. Alec now has in his house at Windsor five or six middle-aged, or even elderly, persons reading theology. This, it appears, is quite a trend now – retired Indian Civil Servants, etc., sensibly enough, seeking ordination. He also said that he'd been delivering lectures at Cambridge and that he was amazed to find a big audience. He also said that although attendance is now voluntary, the chapels are crowded in a way they never were in our time.

November 11, 1949

Hamilton and Roger Machell came to lunch and brought a copy of my novel, *Affairs of the Heart*, due to be published on November 25. Find it slightly nauseous from every point of view and soon put it aside. Not very hopeful about it anyway.

Pan enormously cheered up because one of the other students at the Bible college he is now studying in said that on coming out of the Army he, too, had been quite bowled over, and, as Pan said, after that they had gone for a walk together and said some prayers together, and he felt quite restored. Amazing to me how his whole bearing lights up when he sorts himself out. Talking to Pan always think of 'Let your light so shine before men. . .'

November 12–13, 1949

Read Lord Reith's autobiography. Never read anything more characteristic of a certain type of megalomania, and the complete failure, after his initial success in the BBC, to realise any of his ambitions, makes the latter part of the book quite tragic.

P. J. and Lady Grigg dined with us. P.J. described how once, when he was with Churchill in Downing Street, one of the secretaries had come in to tell the Prime Minister Lord Reith wanted to see him. At first Churchill took no notice, then when the secretary repeated Reith's request to see him, he remarked: 'That Wuthering Height!'

November 14, 1949

Went to see George Orwell in the evening. Found him, unfortunately, more poorly. He has started losing weight again, and looked altogether pretty wretched. His wife came in, and said she'd been translating an article on de Sade for the *Tribune*, which seemed to me a pretty silly occupation. Sat with him about an hour and a half. He mentioned for the first time that he found it sometimes difficult to endure his invalid life, but that he had five more books he wanted to write, and he felt he couldn't die until he'd written them.

November 30, 1949

Lunched with Fenston, in the early part of the war one of my Lance-Corporals. Really rather a remarkable chap, half Jewish, half Irish. He smashed himself up on a motor bike and had to have one of his legs amputated and the other trimmed down, so that he is built much more on the ground than he used to be. He appears to be in a most flourishing condition, has a large house in Upper Brook Street just off the park and another large house down at Guildford, car with chauffeur, etc. It's all done, he explained to me, by buying and selling property. Said he'd bought a property in Nassau because he was certain that in a year or two it would be all up here. Remarkable how this class has developed in the aftermath of the war. Questions like petrol, foreign exchange, etc., he just brushes aside, travels a lot on the Continent, drives up from Guildford every day, no difficulties of any kind. Took me to a rather smart restaurant, new to me, where he was bowed in with great deference. Most of the clientele seemed black market, I thought.

December 1, 1949

Heinemann meeting. Tremendous discussion over a book by the governess of the two Princesses, a Miss Crawford, known inevitably as 'Crawfie'. She has written an account of their childhood which has been chosen in America as the book of the month, serial rights sold for fabulous sums everywhere, etc., etc. I strongly advised against putting up a lot of money for it here, but was overruled. They said it would sell to an unlimited extent, that such books, however bad, always do. Darkly hinted that Miss Crawford had had considerable aid in preparing the manuscript from 'a distinguished man of letters'. Strongly suspect this to be Osbert Sitwell. Better suggestion, Harold Nicolson. Tony agreed, and said that Sitwell would probably take more pleasure in it than in anything else he'd written. Said I thought that if the financial possibilities of the Royal Family in America were taken full advantage of, we could close the dollar gap. Never has existed on earth snobbery as passionate, as unbridled, as the Americans'! The more egalitarian a society the more snobbish its members – e.g. Napoleon's France. The same getting going, as I understand it, in a big way in Russia.

December 8, 1949

Heinemann. Handed over Tony's novel to Frere with a very strong recommendation. Hope they'll do it.

December 9–10, 1949

After lunch went along to Carlton House Terrace to see someone in one of the many 'secret' departments about the Eastern European journalists here – spoke to dimmish figure who stressed to me the government line about it all which, I need scarcely say, amounted to nothing at all that wasn't already known or obvious.

In the morning went to Congress of Free Journalists at the Dorchester. Quite a large gathering, rather pathetic in a way like all gatherings of exiles. American named Martin, president of the American Journalists Guild, delivered long, competent, typically American address, telling his audience in great detail what they knew already as the result of bitter experience – namely, the manner in which a censorship is clamped on the Press the moment the Communists get into power. Spoke myself much more briefly. Then representatives of various countries, including Russia, got up and orated, each very typical – large, blonde Latvian, for instance, bearded Czech who spoke about the heritage of European civilization, an amazing female from Bulgaria, who went into great detail about the former occupation of that part of Europe by the

Turks. This, she said, was much less oppressive than the present occupation because 'the Turks were gentlemen'. Odd point I thought. Reflected, as I came away, on how many different gatherings of exiles, Congresses, meetings, conferences, and all sorts of associations there have been in the past decade.

December 11, 1949

At the Newtons I met Freddie Ayer, of whom I saw quite a bit in Algiers during the war. Quite pleased to renew acquaintance with him. He is now Professor of Philosophy at London University.

In the evening read a book on Oscar Wilde and Alfred Douglas by Queensberry. Pretty silly, but one or two good remarks of Wilde's – 'to be an egoist one must have an ego' and 'with those of us who are modern it is the scabbard that wears out the sword' and 'there is no such thing as changing one's life – one merely wanders round and round within the circle of one's own personality'.

December 14, 1949

At the Garrick had a long talk with Evelyn Wrench about *The Spectator*. He is very keen on my taking it over, but explained complications. Although he is Chairman of the Directors he hasn't got a controlling interest and therefore can always be outvoted. He couldn't have been more affable, though there is something very feeble about him, but he is sympathetic essentially and would be perfectly easy to work with.

Walked in with Tony to a meeting of the National Union of Journalists. The usual crowd, with the addition of Pat Sloan, whom I haven't seen practically since we were both in Moscow. He glared at me and I glared back. In appearance he has grown curiously to look like Stalin. Both Tony and I noticed that the Comrades were distinctly piano including Palme Dutt, the Party ideologue. Javitts, from the *Daily Express*, proposed a resolution that we should reaffiliate with the Institute of Journalists, but didn't even find a seconder. Very satisfactory. Also, branch officers should be elected by ballot. This most important, and of course strongly opposed by the Communists.

December 15, 1949

Worked all day except for a brief stroll with Kitty when I bought an attractive edition of *Don Quixote*, almost my favourite book.

Read Astolphe de Custine, the French historian; some very good remarks: 'In my opinion each nation has for a Government the only one which it could have'. Apropos the Tzar: 'A man who allows himself to be considered as more than a mortal, takes upon himself all the evil that Heaven may send upon earth'.

December 17, 1949

Went with Tony out to Windsor, and lunched with Alec Vidler. Tony found Alec very eccentric, which of course he is, but I am so used to it that I scarcely notice it now. Alec was wearing his leather suit. We went for a walk in the park, very beautiful, but a harsh wind blowing. Then looked round St George's Chapel. Some of the Victorian monuments very hideous and banal beyond words, but a little 16th-century chapel with wall paintings of John the Baptist preaching to Herod, etc., quite fascinating.

There are houses in the castle for 13 poor military knights. At one time provision was also made for 13 poor naval knights, but they proved such a drunken crew that the project was abandoned. I said it was rather as though they started now to accommodate 13 poor Air Force knights. Tony said that George IV had had the idea of making naval officers wear red waistcoats, but had given it up, remarking: 'Dress them how you will, you can't make them gentlemen.'

John and Charles returned from school in good form. Charles top of his class, and also in his house rugger team.

December 19, 1949

Lay in bed, feeling rather wretched. Browsed most of the day on contemporary verse by Roy Campbell, Stephen Spender, Mac-Neice, Masefield, etc., and on a curious volume of literary essays by Robert Graves (*The Common Asphodel*) whose mind I always find a little fascinating. Excellent essay on anthologies showing how Quiller-Couch in the *Oxford Book of English Verse* repeated all the textual errors in the *Golden Treasury*. Also rather an interesting analysis of some lines of T. S. Eliot's about the Countess Volupine. Thought much about T. S. Eliot's verse and wondered if in the end it might not seem completely fraudulent. Perpetual piecing together of allusions of dubious value. Like Yeats, he obviously has a tremendous sense of the beauty of words, but not much else I think.

December 20–21, 1949

Looked in to see George Orwell, who is really very poorly. He looks quite shrunken now and somehow waxen. Said ruefully that he was having penicillin injections and they found difficulty in finding any meat into which to stick the needle. Can well believe it. He still talks about going to Switzerland, doing some fishing there, and mentioned that he'd decided to get a blue serge suit because he thought he was too old now to appear in corduroy trousers, etc. More than usually touched by him. Fancy that he's got an idea he's had it, and isn't altogether sorry. Very fond of his adopted kid, and would like to write another book or two. We talked about Eliot, and he agreed with me. Also agreed that Conrad's *Under Western Eyes* is one of the best novels of recent times. Said that he'd absolutely no appetite now, and that he was having insulin to try to ginger him up.

Alan Taylor came to tea. He is now very anti-Communist. Described visit to Harry Pollitt who, he said, had long ceased to believe in his own Party Line but carried on because there was no alternative.

December 23, 1949

Went with Kitty to lunch with Lady Rhondda and Theodora Bosanquet. Huge flat on top of Arlington House with wonderful view looking over Park – nearby roof flat, as Lady Rhondda explained, Lord Beaverbrook's, and he can often be seen pacing up and down there. They spoke about the death (in 1947) of Ellen Wilkinson, the Minister of Education, whom they'd known well. Said they thought, looking back, that they might have known that she was going to die because the last time they'd seen her she'd seemed *dignified*. I said this was one of the signs of death's nearness, vulgarity consisting in a pre-occupation with the things of this world – such as power, wealth, sensuality, – and disappearing with these preoccupations. Thus, a face would grow serene in the consciousness of soon being released from the ego's small confines and desire's harsh bondage. ('The soul to feel the flesh and the flesh to feel the chain' in reverse.)

Got Theodora talking about Henry James, whose secretary she was for some years. Said he barely had an American accent (only discernible, for instance, in his pronounciation of the word 'because'), and that he and William got on well, though William had little regard for Henry's work.

December 22, 1949

Worked at leader page article on the 1940s. In the evening went with Kitty to see Hesketh and Gladys Pearson. Gladys getting steadily more crippled, but her character correspondingly sweeter and gentler. Quite remarkable; all the harshness and envy drained out of her, expression of her face transformed and beautiful in its way. Her attitude to Hesketh now wholly loving, with no rancour, and all past troubles forgotten, become irrelevant. Always urging him to go for walks, see his friends, seemingly never resentful that she must be left alone. This all very wonderful to watch.

December 25, 1949

Children pleased with their presents. Tony, Violet and their two boys came to lunch, Kitty having arranged long table. We listened to the BBC Christmas programme and the King's speech; former very revolting on the whole – a Canadian going round the Commonwealth and finding British at last truly loved now they'd cleared out of India, set up Pakistan, etc. – 'Raffles Hotel without a single blimp'; Indian woman, Gandhi disciple, to say that 'wind of many religions blowing through my house;' and finally back to England, 'typical' lower middle-class household, father, mother, grandma, etc., and honoured guest who began his little piece with: 'I am black, I come from Nigeria. . .' The decline of power, I thought, is infinitely more nauseating than the process of its attainment – this whimpering surely horrible, even as compared with the worst arrogance. The King, it must be admitted, fitted aptly enough into the general atmosphere which had been created – his laborious platitudes and deadpan voice which bore little relation to their sense.

Having heard the King's speech, Tony and I strolled together to see George Orwell, who looked very deathly and wretched, alone, with Christmas decorations all round. His face looks almost dead, and reminded me, I said afterwards to Tony, of a picture I once saw of Nietzsche on his death-bed. There was also a kind of rage in his expression, as though the approach of death made him furious – as it did Mrs Dobbs, of whom he somehow made me think. Poor George – he went on about the Home Guard, and the Spanish Civil War, and how he would go to Switzerland soon, and all the while the stench of death was in the air, like autumn in a garden.

December 26, 1949

Scribbled a bit, walked round the Park with Tony and John, and played chess, felt contented to be with these five human beings so dear to me. Tea with the Powells, and played consequences; also saw very ancient Charlie Chaplin film. Quiet evening, more chess, Pan read aloud in his quiet sincere voice, which never fails to soothe me.

December 27, 1949

Started reading Maurois's *History of France* which I found quite enthralling – full of interesting observations about the feudal system, etc., particularly interested by his point that as far as chivalry is concerned, it was a case of the knights imitating the epics rather than vice versa; also Courts of Love very much like contemporary soap opera in America. Think everyone should be forced to read history from time to time since it is the only study which corrects the contemporary complaint of an undue sense of urgency. One sees that things have always essentially been the same – e.g. the idea of equality as old as time.

December 28–29, 1949

P. J. Grigg gave me *The Wandering Scholars* by Helen Waddell. I was greatly taken with the story of the poet Paulinus who, just before the coming of the Dark Ages, made off to the religious life. This illustrates an idea I've often had that human beings, at least the more perceptive among them, prepare themselves consciously or unconsciously for the wrath which they know is to come. One comes to feel that there is nothing one can do about things, so one tends to grow increasingly indifferent about the outcome. A sentence of St Augustine's: 'And these were the dishes in which they brought to me, being hungry, the Sun and Moon, instead of Thee.'

Bought a wonderful treasure – a teapot with a special insulating arrangement which means the tea keeps hot for an hour or more. This enables one to drink tea steadily from 6 a.m. onwards.

December 31, 1949 (New Year's Eve)

Retired early, thought about past year. Pleasantest feature for me personally taking over of *Daily Telegraph* non-fiction reviewing from Harold Nicolson. Decided that in a year or so, if possible, I'd get out of leader-writing altogether and move to Dorset. Will have a root around there with Kitty in the spring. Should have done much more of *The Forties*, which now will require a great concentration of purpose in next three months. Novel published with moderate success, but it should have been better done. Many other projects – in the way of fiction, perhaps next some short stories.

Family affairs reasonably satisfactory. Pan, in his own peculiar way, working things out – immensely diligent, wholehearted. To me, sometimes, his evangelical idiom slightly jarring, but this probably my fault. Have to admit that I only understand what he's getting at up to a point. John steady, also hard-working, humorous, decidedly mature for his years – with his large head and ardent temperament. Val growing up fast, becoming distinctly attractive, not at all intellectual, quite set that she wants to look after kids, many friendships. Charles top of his class, brilliant at rugger, working away through the holidays in his little workshop, no reader but immensely sharp, quick. Kitty, as ever, infinitely dear. Hughie's death the first which hit me hard; Mrs Dobbs' macabre.

Finance – earned a lot, but spent a lot, too. As for public affairs, though I still read many newspapers, have no longer breathless interest I once had; no present inclination whatsoever to take a hand. Quite convinced that this is a twilight phase, a period of running down, which may be protracted but cannot be altered in its essential character. My favourite image – we, now living, have rehearsed one play, and find ourselves appearing in another, quite different. In this situation, neither absolute disaster nor turning point in human affairs with early paradise looming ahead, etc. Just history; what's happening has happened before and will happen again. The true significance of life lies elsewhere, though history, like everything else, is a kind of image of it – can be sensed most clearly through the imagination (the will being quite blind to it), belongs to the spirit which is eternal rather than to the flesh which perishes. This is, to me, become a clear and sane conclusion. Otherwise, I feel middle-aged, with little zest for making new friends, moving about physically or socially; almost never bored except by others' company, reading more than ever a solace, walking agreeable; know what I want to do, hope I may be able, at any rate partially, to do it, but also aware that it doesn't matter as enormously as I once used to think whether I do it or not. Thus, for me, begins 1950.

January 4, 1950

Went with Tony to NUJ meeting which seemed even more depressing than before. Heavily packed with the Comrades, who duly re-elected Hutt as the branch's choice for editor of *The Journalist*. Probably it really doesn't matter much, but it was depressing seeing them there, a lot of women among them. Hutt himself looks very ravaged, and probably it's a bit of a strain for him too. As Tony said, doubtless when he was young he saw himself as becoming another Lenin, whereas now, like the rest of us, he is imprisoned in the shape of his own life.

January 9–10, 1950

Saw Percy Cudlipp, who was very full of Low, the cartoonist, going over to the *Daily Herald*, but exaggerated his delight because, obviously, he feared he might be getting only the leavings. Said that Beaverbrook was very reluctant to let Low go from the *Evening Standard*, about which I am sceptical.

January 12, 1950

Looked in to see George Orwell, who seems more deathly than ever, very miserable, says he's losing $\frac{1}{2}$-lb a week in weight and has a high temperature every day. Typical of him that he said the doctors won't allow him to take aspirin because it upsets his temperature chart. George said he'd been reading accounts of the proceedings of the enquiry into capital punishment, and that he was quite convinced that judges like Lord Goddard, want to keep hanging because they derive erotic satisfaction from it. Tried politely to indicate that I thought this utter rubbish. Also mentioned that Monckton Milnes, whose biography I have been reading, had wanted to marry Florence Nightingale. George remarked that Milnes's tastes were derived from the Marquis de Sade, and I said that if Florence Nightingale had married him, she might have become known as the lady of the whip.

Visited in the evening by MI6 character who wants cover to go to Indo-China. At the Authors Club Neville Cardus talked about Howard Spring, the novelist. Cardus said it was wonderful how everything about Spring was all of a piece – he had a 'den' where he did his work, if he went for a walk it was a 'tramp'. He said that once he'd been walking along with Spring in Manchester when Spring had remarked: 'Cardus, when I lose interest in women I lose interest in life'. I said that he was obviously destined to become a popular novelist because he shared to an exceptional degree all the longings of his fellows for fame, beautiful women, wealth, etc.

January 14, 1950

Read Koestler's contribution to a book of essays entitled *The God that Failed*. Very well done, some of it oddly movibg. His talent for writing English really remarkable, but the Communists never trusted him and tried to make use of him. Interesting point that the Communists all had to say Balzac was a great writer because of a flattering reference to Balzac by Lenin.

Of the *declassés* of the post-1914–18 war period Koestler writes: 'They lived on pointlessly, like a great black swarm of tired winter flies crawling over the dim windows of Europe, members of a class displaced by history.'

Of the Communists: 'The incarnation of the will of history', and 'The shadow of barbed wire lies across the condemned playground of memory. Those who were caught by the great illusion of our time, and have lived through its moral and intellectual debauch, either give themselves up to a new addiction of the opposite type, or are condemned to pay with a lifelong hangover. They are the ambulant cemeteries of their murdered friends; they carry their shrouds as their banner.'

January 16, 1950

Drove down with P. J. Grigg to see Field-Marshal Montgomery. Fascinated by Monty's house, which he has built and designed himself, very neat and clean, and full of little devices and gadgets, walls covered with huge oil paintings of himself, Freedoms of the Cities, signed pictures of the King, Stalin, swords of honour, etc., etc.

He is really rather charming in his odd way, more impressive out of uniform than in it. Talked a lot about the North African campaign, and before we came had been jotting down his ideas of what good generalship consists. Brought these notes away with me, real curiosity, written in his very immature hand. Reflected afterwards that all success in action pre-supposes great simplicity of character, and Monty in this document an excellent example.

At a certain point Grigg demanded drinks which were brought in, Monty of course not participating. He went on talking all the time, and was at his best describing campaigns. Then he came to life and one saw that he had complete mastery of the game. The two significant facts in the world today, he said, were the revival of Germany and the march of Communism in Eastern Europe. Thought much about him afterwards.

One cannot say that he is intelligent, or even altogether 'nice', and yet there is something quite remarkable about him, and one can see that, in his way, he fits into the general category of 'great men', greatness being, I suspect, a kind of vitality and singleness of purpose more than anything else. References to Churchill not particularly affectionate. Said that the only way to deal with him was to be firm. Despised him very much for bursting into tears when he came down to 21st Army Group on the eve of D-Day and wanted to address the officers, and Monty forbade it. He was right of course.

January 17–18, 1950

Philip Jordan told me he'd decided to stay with Attlee for a bit if he got in in the election, and that he hoped, when Attlee retired, he'd get something, perhaps a governorship. He mentioned Cyprus, and said he'd have great pleasure in putting down the independence movement there, which I well believe.

Read first volume of Byron's *Letters and Journal*. Some of his remarks very good, despite the essential shallowness of his character. As with all such people, much of his time was spent sitting alone, bored, even eating little and drinking nothing. Typical remark: 'I am ennuyé beyond my usual tense of that yawning verb, which I am always conjugating'. It seems to me that the nearest equivalent to him is Wilde, and that his affair with his half sister, Augusta, had a curious resemblance to Wilde's with Douglas, both being deliberately designed to make havoc and to bring about a pre-ordained doom.

January 19, 1950

Looked in to say goodbye to George Orwell, who is going off to Switzerland. Doubt very much if I'll ever see him again. He looked at his last gasp. He is flying over in a specially chartered plane to a sanatorium at Montana, near where Kitty used to live.

Dined with Graham Greene. Graham talked about a certain Father Pio in Italy whom he'd seen, and who, according to Graham, has stigmata. Graham described these in his usual lurid way. Said miracles were done constantly by him, and that, in his view, the heavenly and devilish forces in creation were now exceptionally active in preparation for busting up the universe by means of the hydrogen bomb. Told him that, to my Protestant sceptical mind, no catastrophic solution or ending to human affairs seemed to me likely.

Typical of Graham that he has made a collection of small whisky bottles which are now prominently displayed in his flat.

Said that he was bored with all the réclame over *The Heart of the Matter*, especially the manner in which it had been taken up by the Catholics, a long article appearing about *La damnation de Scobie*. Graham said that Evelyn Waugh is now writing a book about some female saint, which is very good. Really prefer his conversation when he discusses means of evading stigmata.

Mentioned the business of Father Pio to Pan who, after thinking about it, said he feared it might be the work of the devil.

January 21, 1950

Heard in the morning that George Orwell had died in the early hours (about 2.30 a.m.) of a haemorrhage, which didn't really surprise me. Thought that in a way his death was sadder than Hughie's because he passionately wanted to go on living, and thus there was no sense of peace or relinquishment in him. Thought much about his curious character, the complete unreality of so much of his attitude, his combination of intense romanticism with a dry interest in some of the dreariest aspects of life – e.g. Gissing. Remembered Hughie's phrase about him – that he was like a gate swinging on rusty hinges, and that he only wrote sympathetically about human beings when he regarded them as animals – e.g.

Animal Farm. All the same, there was something very lovable and sweet about him, and, without any question, an element of authentic prophecy in his terrible vision of the future. His particular contribution to this sort of literature was his sense that a completely collectivized State would be produced not, as Wells had envisaged, in terms of scientific efficiency, not as Aldous Huxley had envisaged, in terms of a heartless but vivid eroticism, but to the accompaniment of all the dreary debris and shabbiness of the past – mystique of materialist Puritanism, the dreariest and saddest of all human attitudes which have ever existed.

Wrote two paragraphs on George for Peterborough, and declined various requests for magazine articles. Thought of him, as of Graham, that popular writers always express in an intense form some romantic longing.

January 22–23, 1950

Pan brought a friend of his from the Bible College to supper. Very excited at the idea of going on what they call a trek, which means setting out with no money or food and walking and preaching through England. This is the sort of thing that Pan really loves.

Question of George's funeral presenting complications which inevitably reflect those of his life – namely, whether he should be buried in an English village under a yew tree or cremated with his Jewish revolutionary friends in Golders Green. Probably Finchley will be settled for – a compromise.

Rather interested to find when I spoke to the undertaker and mentioned that the clergyman concerned was our vicar here, Mr Rose, that he at once said that he knew him well and had many dealings with him. 'In fact,' he said, 'I'm lunching with him today.' It appeared that they lunch regularly to talk over present and future business. Hope that all has been satisfactorily arranged and that nothing will go wrong.

N.B. George died on Lenin's birthday, and is being buried by the Astors, which seems to me to cover the full range of his life.

January 25, 1950

Tony and Violet with Sonia Orwell came in after supper. Sonia was obviously in a very poor way. We talked about *Horizon* and Connolly. Felt sorry for her but not sympathetic. She remembered Kitty's mother one day appearing at the office with a manuscript, scene easily imagined. We wondered what Sonia would now do with herself. Tony said that she was 'a painter's girl'. I saw what he meant. She said that really *Horizon* had gone on existing because of the war, it having provided Cyril Connolly with a means of evading military service, among other things.

January 26, 1950

In the morning George's funeral, a rather melancholy, chilly affair, the congregation largely Jewish and almost entirely unbelievers; Mr Rose, who conducted the service, excessively parsonical, the church unheated. In the front row, the Fred Warburgs. Then a row of shabby looking relatives of George's first wife, whose grief seemed to me practically the only real element in the whole affair. The bearers who carried in the coffin seemed to me remarkably like Molotov's bodyguard. Tony had chosen the lesson from the last chapter of the Book of Ecclesiastes, which was very wonderful, I thought, particularly the verse: 'Then shall the dust return to the earth as it was: and the spirit shall return unto God who gave it.' Also the verse ending: '. . . man goeth to his long home, and the mourners go about the streets.'

Interesting, I thought, that George should have so attracted Jews because he was at heart strongly anti-Semitic. Felt a pang as the coffin was removed, particularly because of its length, somehow this circumstance, reflecting George's tallness, was poignant.

Read through various obituary articles on George by Koestler, Pritchett, Julian Symons, etc., and saw in them how the legend of a human being is created, because although they were ostensibly correct and I might have written the same sort of stuff myself, they were yet inherently false – e.g. everyone saying George was not given to self-pity, whereas it was of course his dominant emotion.

January 27, 1950

Went to the *Daily Telegraph* and wrote a leader on Berlin. Writing these leaders is becoming increasingly depressing and unreal. More and more I have the feeling that forms of authority like Parliament, Press, etc., are becoming emptier and emptier, and that is how regimes end – not so much in institutions being overthrown, as in their perishing on their own account.

January 31–February 1, 1950

Tony and I went on talking about George. I said that I personally hadn't really felt his death much as compared with Hughie's, and that he'd had an infinitely sadder life than Hughie – sadder because less in tune with reality.

Read a book on the Social History of the Quakers. The Quakers, I thought, had to deal with exactly the same problem as the revolutionary regime in Russia – i.e. how to maintain authority without institutions. In both cases the way out of this dilemma was the same – the institution of personal surveillance amounting to a kind of terror. Institutions make freedom possible in the same way that a routine does. Destroy them and some form of totalitarian autocracy becomes inevitable.

February 2, 1950

Lunched with Camrose, who talked about the election (polling day – February 23), Winston, etc. He said how, in the war, Winston used frequently to say to him that he would never repeat the mistake of Lloyd George of clinging to power. Yet, of course, this is precisely what he has done, with the same consequences as happened in the case of Lloyd George. I said that it looked as though power was the only appetite which never abated, and mentioned the case of Napoleon on St Helena only interesting himself in a long drawn out row with the Governor. I asked Camrose if he thought the Duke of Windsor regretted having relinquished power. He considered the matter a while, and then said: 'He isn't allowed to'.

February 4, 1950

In the evening I looked in on my brother Douglas. He is now commanding an Ordnance Depot of 600 National Service men, and
spoke in terms of great bitterness of their behaviour. Said he
thought it seemed extraordinary that when all the talk was for a
community spirit, young people only got more and more egotistic.
I said this always happened, that the effect of recent social changes
had been to develop, rather than suppress, egotism, and that when
people were released from the restrictions of traditional beliefs
and behaviour, it was always necessary to enslave them anew –
witness the Soviet regime. He didn't really understand what I was
talking about.

February 9, 1950

Read rather a good little book, *Conservatism Revisited* by an American named Peter Viereck. Very much taken with the opening sentence: 'Certainly it is true that the stairway of history "is forever
echoing with the wooden shoe going up, the polished boot
descending".'

Douglas Jerrold said that the *New English Review* was expiring
into the *National Review* next June. Remembered a remark of
Hughie's, extraordinarily typical of him, that 'whenever you see
"No Exit" it means there is an exit'. This remark contained
Hughie's whole philosophy of life, and even his biography.

Delighted to get at Sotheby's the Birkbeck Hill edition of
Boswell's *Life of Johnson* which I've always wanted.

February 10, 1950

Read a book by a Mexican police officer who had investigated
Trotsky's murder (1940). On the title page there is quoted the
remark of Stalin to Dzerjinski and Kamenev in the course of a
conversation held in the spring of 1923: 'To choose the victim,
carefully prepare the blow, satisfy an implacable vengeance, then
go to bed. . . There is nothing sweeter in the world'.

February 11, 1950

Walked out with Kitty to the exhibition of French landscape painting. Quite enraptured by the Claudes and Poussins. As Tony pointed out, the charm of them is that their romanticism is somehow serene and clear rather than cloudy and phosphorescent like the 19th-century romanticism. Always fascinated by the type of person who goes to picture galleries – the elderly ladies talking in loud voices, the forlorn-looking individuals wandering helplessly about, bearded figures with a superior expression, often in pairs and duffle-coated, who make occasional knowing remarks, the parties of bored school girls, etc. etc.

February 13, 1950

Rosie Cripps, Kitty's cousin, returned to stay for a few days. She has been reading Fitzroy Maclean's *Eastern Approaches* but by mistake the dust cover of Somerset Maugham's *A Writer's Notebook* was on it, and she remarked to Kitty that she'd no idea that Maugham had parachuted into Yugoslavia in the war!

February 16, 1950

Dined with Jan and Jeanie Nasmyth. Also there youthful couple named King, he of Reuters, and she a second cousin of Kitty's, daughter of Arthur Hobhouse. King, a bit of a leftist, said, incidentally, that in Reuters the Communist influence was enormously strong. Mentioned NUJ figures, to me very familiar. Said that when he was doing a story with any sort of anti-Communist angle he had to take care that none of the Communist sub-editors were on duty or else they would alter it.

Jan getting restless at the Treasury, thinking of becoming a farmer, Jeanie now decided to leave the Foreign Office, all typical, somehow, of the times.

At the *Daily Telegraph* wrote a piece on the American coal strike. Glad to avoid the General Election, subject which to me increasingly depressing and irrelevant. It seems clear that the only thing that matters in the world now is the Cold War, and that domestic politics are just shadow boxing. All the same, I think the best thing would be for Winston to give in, and hope he may, but I still consider it doubtful.

February 20, 1950

Picked up Sonia Orwell and Tosco Fyvel to go along to Secker and Warburg's to talk about publication of George's work. Rather an absurd conference, Warburg presiding. Agreed on the publication of a book of essays by George, and I suggested that the title of one of them, 'Shooting an Elephant', would provide a very suitable title for the whole volume. Also looked at some verses written by George, one really rather touching, particularly the lines:

> 'A happy vicar I might have been
> Two hundred years ago,
> To preach upon eternal doom
> And watch my walnuts grow.

> 'I am the worm who never turned,
> The eunuch without a harem;
> Between the priest and the commissar
> I walk like Eugene Aram.

> 'I dreamed I dwelt in marble halls,
> And woke to find it true;
> I wasn't born for an age like this;
> Was Smith? Was Jones? Was you?'.

the second of which might be put on his tombstone.

February 23, 1950

Went and voted in the morning. Elections and electioneering always very much in my childhood memories as they played such an enormous part. Strange in a way to be voting Conservative, but felt quite clear that this was the best thing to do in the circumstances.

To the Savoy at 10.30 p.m. to vast Camrose election night party. Practically everyone I've ever heard of there, champagne flowing, ran into numbers of people, whole thing slightly macabre and eve of the Battle of Waterloo flavour about it – the bourgeoisie shivering before the deluge to come. Results started appearing from 11 p.m. onwards. It became clear very soon that there was no real swing against the Government. Sat with Harold Macmillan part of the time, he very delighted about his son-in-law Julian Amery getting in, and so was I. Also enchanted that Pritt, the left-wing Labour M.P., was defeated and the Communist poll uniformly microscopic, this so satisfying that it compensated for any other disappointments.

February 24, 1950

Went along to the Rothermere's party at the Dorchester, many of the people present had also been to Camrose's party the evening before, champagne again flowing freely. Stanley Morison seemed pleased about the result. I said I'd hoped for a stalemate, which, as it happened, was exactly what there was.

Went off to lunch with the Vansittarts at Claridge's, and there we watched the electoral tide turn. Roger Makins, Head of the Foreign Office, was also lunching at Claridge's, and Vansittart said, in view of the changed electoral situation, Roger would almost certainly come up and speak affably to him. This happened exactly. Later when I recounted the incident to Philip Jordan he said precisely the same thing had happened to him with Bridges, head of the Civil Service. Have always considered one of the most fascinating aspects of politics is people's adjustment to changing situations.

March 3, 1950

R. H. C. Steed, on the Foreign Staff of the *Daily Telegraph*, amused me very much by an account of going along to the Foreign Office about something connected with Trieste, being sent to see some official there who first of all wasted about half an hour trying to get coal put on the fire with a rather inadequate scuttle and shovel, then said he'd get a report from the Trieste C-in-C sent up, phoned for this, when it didn't arrive phoned again, discovered it had been sent to the wrong chap, who in due course brought it along enclosed in a sort of cylinder in which documents are now sent round to various rooms in the Foreign Office. Cylinder wouldn't open, spent another half hour trying to prize it open, finally gave up in despair.

March 5, 1950

Wrote piece on refugees, harrowing subject. Reflected that never in history so many unfortunates, completely rootless, with only the impulsion of fear making them prefer one direction to another.

March 10–11, 1950

Read Hughie Kingsmill's book on D. H. Lawrence, which contains many good things. For instance: 'Snobbishness is the assertion of the will in social relations as lust is in sexual. It is the desire for what divides men and the inability to value what unites them.'

Went over Hugh Kingsmill letters which Hesketh and I have selected. Not very satisfied, but some of them are interesting. Poor Gladys now almost immobile, and gives that curious impression of having lost interest in this world.

Much discontent at the *Daily Telegraph* because one of the reporters has been sacked after having been employed for over twenty years. He has been given a pension of £400 a year and six months' pay, but the feeling is that his dismissal should have been handled differently. Acting Father of the Chapel out to make the maximum trouble possible.

March 17–18, 1950

Meeting at Heinemann first, then went to lunch with Tony and Frere at the Savoy. Frere more than ever a Twenties period piece – as I said to Tony, a 'Little Gatsby'. Talked in a romantic strain about the South of France, and said that to enjoy bouillabaisse you needed the sun and to be tanned and in love. Pretty good.

Read *Letters of Flaubert* – rather wonderful passage about his pleasure at writing *Madame Bovary*: 'Never mind whether they are good or bad, it is grand to write, to cease to be *oneself*, and to move among the creatures one is describing. Today, for instance, I have been man and woman at the same time, lover and mistress together, riding in the forest on an autumn afternoon under the yellowing leaves; and I have been the horses too, and the leaves, and the wind, and the words they spoke and the red sun that made them blink their eyes that swam with love. It may be out of pride or out of reverence, from a foolish gush of excessive self-conceit or a vague but lofty religious sense, but when I reflect after experiencing these joys, I feel tempted to offer up a prayer of thanksgiving to God if only I knew he could hear me.'

March 21, 1950

Went to Covent Garden to see the ballet *Don Quixote* which I enjoyed enormously, Helpmann as Don Quixote and Margot Fonteyn as Dulcinea. All the exquisite pathos of the story came out, but of course none of the humour. When I got back looked up the death of Don Quixote in the novel; very good that he should see through his delusions and Sancho want to keep them going. Margot Fonteyn the best dancer I've ever seen, not excepting Moscow. Revived all my thoughts of a Don Quixote novel of our days.

March 22, 1950

Went with Kitty to the Ideal Home Exhibition, crowded with people, somewhat tawdry, I thought, and sad in a way since none of those flowing around would be able to have any of the things displayed. This seems to me singularly typical of the contemporary world, which presents felicity always in terms of graphs and statistics and displays rather than of actual well-being. The whole thing reminded me oddly of Russia.

March 25, 1950

Slightly moved to read that Harold Laski had suddenly died, but felt, as with George Orwell, the last time I saw him, that he'd come to the end of things – no more lies to tell, no more hopes to entertain. Reflected that if he hadn't been a liar he'd have been a much more atrocious person. In a way his lying was his virtue because it suggested imaginative dissatisfaction with life. Recalled first meeting him in Manchester with his father, Nathan Laski, then BBC talks etc., and how he used to give interminable accounts of conversations with Stalin, Roosevelt, Churchill etc., which never took place.

April 1, 1950

Went off with Kitty to look at a house near Sudbury. Read on the way George Orwell's novel *Burmese Days* – not very good, quite ludicrous picture of life in Burma, absurd dramatization of the position of Europeans, particularly so now in the light of what has happened subsequently. All confirms my feeling that his heart was more with Kipling than his head was with India. Curious how the same motif of self-pity (the hero, Flory, has a huge birth-mark on his face which he is always trying to hide) occurs, as in all George's novels.

April 2, 1950

At the *Daily Telegraph* wrote dreary leader on the Council of Europe, an institution which seems to have absolutely no life in it. Interesting to note how, as Europe falls into a final condition of decay, bodies for uniting it multiply, now five or six different agencies with this raison d'être and none truly functioning. How-ever, the essence of newspapers is that one never writes the truth in them.

April 3, 1950

Heard that Watson had retired from the editorship of the *Daily Telegraph* and would be replaced by Coote. Everyone very sorry about this. Wrote Watson a note. Johnstone then called me into the club to discuss the new situation, which we did. He is very reluctant to take on the job of deputy editor. I strongly advised him that he should, but he said nothing would induce him to.

April 9, 1950

Went into the *Daily Telegraph* and wrote leader on Cooperative Societies. Coote in the chair, obviously rather pleased with him-self, asked me how I felt about things, etc., and I hedged.

Reading life of Nathaniel Hawthorne. Interesting observation of his on America: 'No author, without a trial, can conceive of the difficulty of writing a romance about a country where there is no shadow, no antiquity, no mystery, no picturesque and gloomy wrong, nor anything but a commonplace prosperity, in broad and simple daylight, as is happily the case with my dear native land.'

April 13, 1950

Wonderfully refreshed by sleep as a result of new pill, but rather wretched to be so dependent on drugs. Lunched with Johnstone at the Authors, and we talked about the *Daily Telegraph* situation again, he very reluctant to assume new responsibilities. At the office first he and then I were called up to Lord Camrose, who told me that he wanted me to be Deputy Editor. I agreed to this with mixed feelings, £500 a year more income, of which he agreed to give half in expenses to avoid tax. I couldn't help being somewhat excited about the whole business, though with reservations. Hope it won't make it more difficult to write.

Johnstone, as I said to him, has less desire for power than any human being I've ever met. He refused to regard this as a compliment, and said it was purely because he was an introvert by nature, but I didn't agree. There is a kind of innocence about him in relation to life which is most charming.

April 17–19, 1950

Wrote Wordsworth article for centenary of his death on April 23. More than ever struck with the absurdity of apologias made for his political 'apostasy'. After all, the extraordinary thing is rather that he should ever have fallen for someone like Godwin than that he should have soon seen through him. Read here and there in Wordsworth's poetry which seemed to me, at his best, more wonderful than ever:

> 'Think not, my friend, from me to roam,
> Thy arms shall be my only home,
> My only bed thy breast;
> No separate path our lives shall know,
> But where thou goest I shall go,
> And there my bones have rest.'

April 23, 1950

Got up late (Sunday) and went into *Daily Telegraph*. Curious to be sitting in the Editor's chair, felt rather forlorn about it on the whole, did what had to be done.

Interested to note in Keith Feiling's *History of England* how similar was the role of the Catholic Church and Spain at the time of Elizabeth to the present role of the Cominform and Russia. Observation by Hawthorne: 'What a terrible thing it is to try to let off a little bit of truth into this miserable humbug of a world.'

April 25, 1950

Fyvel, Symons, Woodrow Wyatt and I discussed *Tribune* and its prospects. They are obviously badly on the rocks, and I said that in the interests of the Cold War they should be kept going as a counterblast to the *New Statesman*. Developed one of my favourite propositions – that the *New Statesman*'s great success as propagandists had been to establish the proposition that to be intelligent is to be Left whereas almost the exact opposite is true. They made the usual charge that I was 'left behind by history' – very silly.

April 29, 1950

Had about ten minutes of the Cup Final on Mrs Davies' television set just to see how it was put over. Commentary very languid, I thought, compared with ordinary BBC transmissions.

May 2, 1950

Read essay by Aldous Huxley on the philosopher Maine de Biran, (1766–1824). Like all of his type Biran fascinated by the text – 'Who will deliver me from the body of this death?' Rather touched by his phrase in his *Journal Intime*: 'I am not of this world, and ought to give up the attempt to live and work for it.' Huxley obviously sees himself in Biran. Another observation I rather liked: 'Except the sickly, few people ever feel themselves existing. Those who are well, even if they be philosophers, are too busy enjoying life to investigate what it is. The sentiment of their own existence does not astonish them. Health impels us towards the outside world, sickness brings us home to ourselves.'

Goya wrote on his desk: 'The dream of reason produces monsters'. A good epitaph, I thought, for all intellectuals.

May 6, 1950

Dinner to Watson at Claridge's. Huge gathering of *Daily Telegraph* staff. I was at Camrose's table, the usual speeches, Camrose's better than I'd expected, perhaps my enjoyment of it due to the fact that there were various complimentary references to myself in it. Watson's speech also good. Coote went in for some rather far-fetched undergraduate humour, however champagne flowed freely and everyone very genial.

May 10, 1950

Curious episode occurred at the *Daily Telegraph*. Character from the library, whom I'd often noticed, there came into my room and told me a long, meandering story about how he'd been a journalist and then, when he was tight, had got his newspaper involved in a libel action, been unable to get another job, finally took up work as a proof reader. Asked me if I'd ever experienced 'the rough end of journalism'. Felt very sorry for him, but slightly embarrassed.

May 12, 1950

Went off with Kitty and Val to Windsor. Alec Vidler looking extremely eccentric in an old Selwyn blazer, said he'd just been attending to his bees. Wonderful walk in the Great Park which was inconceivably lovely in the spring sunshine. Alec said that he found the King difficult to get on with because he talked in an excitable manner. Always feel very happy and peaceful in Alec's company. One of the charms of Windsor, we decided, is that it is completely a Victorian period piece, and that of course is why Alec likes it. Had tea with him. Also present the elderly theological students who live with him, nearly all of them ex-I.C.S. now reading for Orders, one or two pretty cracked, I thought.

Interested to note that they spoke about Nehru and about 'Rajaji' in the same obsequious manner that in my time in India they used to speak about the Viceroy and provincial governors. In most people veneration for power exists quite irrespective of who exercises it. When I said that I'd known Nehru in the past and thought him rather a conceited second-rate person, they were quite shocked.

Went to evening services in St George's Chapel, which I always enjoy, exquisite singing, choir really wonderful. Read some of Gerald Bullett's book on the English Mystics. Interesting that political, social, and other such categories all break down completely where mystics are concerned – e.g. some, like Bunyan, proletarians; others, like Law, fanatical Royalists, etc. N.B.: 'It were better to have no opinion of God at all,' said Bacon, 'than such an opinion as is unworthy of him: for the one is unbelief, the other is contumely.'

Wonderful proverb: 'The spirit of man is the candle of the Lord.'

May 13, 1950

At the Garrick P. J. Grigg said that Monty was on the point of throwing in his hand because the whole business of Western defence was a bubble and that he'd explained this to the Americans and British alike. Also said that Winston had lost interest in his memoirs, and that he hadn't bothered even to revise what was put in for him. For instance, a whole chapter on Syria was written by his ghosts and not revised in any way by him.

May 23, 1950

Tom Hopkinson, editor of *Picture Post*, talked about the possibility of starting another magaine like *Horizon*, about which he had some sensible ideas.

Went in the evening to a gathering of business men. After dinner a little man read a paper about distributive trades which had points of interest. Then followed a discussion in which I participated. Afterwards whisked off for drinks by two MI6 figures who

turned up, one of whom I vaguely remembered. Reflected that
whenever at a gathering anyone is outstandingly stupid, you may
be sure that he belongs to that particular service. However, they
were quite amiable, and we sat discussing dock labour, etc. Dick
Harrison, also present, knew quite a lot about this because he is
in a shipping company. Remarked that now organized labour has
more absolute power than the capitalists ever had. In the docks
particularly the Unions are all-powerful. Walking back, thought
about the dinner and the strain of sentimentality which is always
found among commerçants of any description as compared with
intellectuals who are usually, however misguided they may be,
utterly callous and calculating. Popular conception is exactly the
opposite.

May 27, 1950

On sudden impulse wend down with Kitty to Brighton on the
Brighton Belle. Sun was shining, though stiffish wind blowing.
We walked along the coast, by the amusement places (very whimsy,
I noticed; Peter Pan much in evidence), on past Roedean. Saw a
few of the Jeunes Filles en Fleurs going about in a curious kind of
cloak they wear by way of uniform. Altogether quite pleasant,
though. Looked at Regency houses in delightful Marine Square,
and even thought of how it would be to live there. Not satisfactory
on the whole, we decided. Had tea in Queen's Hotel, and noticed
once more the advancing decay of the bourgeois way of life – very
threadbare now, hardly holding together. Much public excitement
over end of petrol rationing. Decided, with a half sigh, to get a
car again, always a source of woe to the unmechanical.

Read life of Trelawny, by R. Glynn Grylls, presented as highly
romantic figure. Liked Lady Blessington's remark: 'There are few
before whom one would condescend to appear otherwise than
happy'. Byron, I decided, much to be preferred to Trelawny. Had
in him a vein of authentic cynicism – e.g. 'I write best on things I
know the least, for then I am unprejudiced' – this when, to
Trelawny's surprise, he showed he knew nothing about navigation
and cared less.

May 29–31, 1950

Started reading book about Fox and Pitt. He and Fox (and later Gladstone) returned for Rotten Boroughs. What an illusion to suppose that universal franchise results in the election of the best and ablest. If anything, the opposite true. No system could have been more corrupt and based on privilege than that under which England became great.

Talked with Neville Cardus, who didn't seem to resent my observations about C. E. Montagu in reviewing his book *Second Innings*. He seemed downcast, had given up his job with Beaverbrook, claimed (most unconvincingly) that he liked being 'free'. I said he ought to go back to the *Manchester Guardian*, but he replied: 'First love can never be revived.'

Good observation by a Frenchman that translations are like women – 'Si elles sont fidèles elles ne sont pas belles; si elles sont belles elles ne sont pas fidèles.'

From Monday, June 5 I enjoyed a walking holiday through Burgundy ('all the way along places famous on bottle labels') in the company of Andreas Mayor until June 16 when we parted at Avignon from where I took the train to Nice.

June 17, 1950 – Roquebrune–Cap Martin

At Nice took car to Roquebrune where Cholerton waiting for me. Next day (Sunday) I got an idea of Chol's manner of life. For two hours or so daily he waters the garden, in that time, as he told me proudly, distributing some two tons of water. He likes to do the watering practically naked, gets himself covered with mud, and then plunges into the sea to clean himself. Also, he goes to market, greatly fancying himself as a shrewd marketer. Sceptical myself about this. Otherwise potters about, always seemingly in a hurry, but over nothing. Altogether, he's a period piece, down to trimmed beard, etc. – the Englishman who's learnt the pleasure of the table, etc., through living in France; who makes remarks like: 'the French are the most *adult* people in the world;' whose little ragged library contains all the old pornographic classics (*Lady Chatterley*, *Tropic of Capricorn*, etc.). The world which made such a life possible, which gave it whatever validity it ever had, has now passed away, with only a few residuary vestiges in places like the Riviera. This accounts for a queer wistfulness, even hopelessness in him; but he carries on – a fool persisting in his folly, and if not becoming wise, becoming at any rate rather lovable.

June 19–20, 1950

Car came for me at 1 o'clock, drove in to the Nice aerodrome. Plane landed, and out came Kitty carrying my old straw hat which she'd brought by hand. Got all her news; felt, as always everything fall into place in her company.

Next morning walked into Monte Carlo by the sea and had breakfast there. Noted, as before, astonishingly period figures – elderly Englishmen carefully dressed in white, lady with corrugated legs and with three English books tied together with string under her arm; fantastic ancient characters heavily rouged and quite mad. Casino now caters more for charabanc parties, each member of which is prepared to lose 1,000 francs, than for millionaires. It, too, has been brought into the Century of the Common Man.

June 20–23, 1950

Pleasant days in Roquebrune – in and out of Monte Carlo, Mentone. Went to see Prince's Palace in Monaco – little court all complete with protocol, curious survival from the past of set-up like Italian or German Principality in 18th century. Day in Nice, looked over Napoleon Bonaparte museum – the Emperor's uniform, swords, handkerchief, etc. piously preserved, but all redolent of commonness so characteristic of him; the important milestone in the progress towards ever greater vulgarisation of life, I reflected, comparing him and everything he stood for with Madame de Lafayette's *La Princesse de Clèves*.

June 24, 1950

Came along in the train from Mentone to Santa Margherita, long, slow journey along the coast. Noted the greater vivacity in Italy after France, which remains curiously dead, flat, bad-tempered. In Genoa squalid streets, crowded windows; later, by the blue Mediterranean, large American cars, top flats in waterside houses taken by rich, dolled up, roof gardens, etc. No solution in this situation, save bloodshed; no compromise possible between over- and under-fed when neither side accepts any possibility of duties, responsibilities to God or to man – only the fight to get near the trough, the Gadarene rush.

Auberon Herbert met us at the station; drove us terrifyingly to his house, chattering all the way about English staying at Portofino – Robert Graves, writing couple named Selwyn Jepson; Richard Hughes; Alexander Korda, Ingrid Bergman, Rossellini, etc.

Auberon's house, large, solid Victorian, built by his grand-father in 1860 of Portland cement specially imported for the pur-pose. Walls painted with quotations from Dante, one room hideously decorated with paintings by John Churchill – very 1920s, frail youth in armour with dragon at his feet; the T. E. Lawrence phiz. Auberon very properly going to have the whole thing painted out, replacing by more Dante quotations and flowers on the ceiling by local Italian.

To drinks with Alex and Jenny Clifford, who've got a house nearby. Alex dying of cancer, not likely to last more than eighteen months or so, but seemingly quite hale; face however, despairing. Party already assembled when we arrived – Korda, with Graves eagerly in his company. Graves interested me – a face with a kind of lost beauty in it; something about him that made me feel in-finitely sad – like seeing a ruined landscape, piles of rubble where once a city had been. Talked briefly with him. The Cliffords' house quite chic, St George flag flying, wonderful view, etc., but what desolation! Treasure on earth, I thought, very susceptible to moth and rust.

June 26, 1950

Went down with Auberon for early morning swim, necessitating rock climbing; slightly hazardous, but pleasant once in the water. Sat with Kitty on the terrace in the sun, and decided Portofino the most lovely place I'd ever visited – mountains in the distance, illimitable blue Mediterranean on one side and on the other bay with tall, coloured houses lining it.

Read report of Archbishop Stepinak's defence at his trial – most impressive defiance of Communists and Communism. Bought paper and noted that South Korea had been invaded. Wondered if this were the beginning of war, and if so how Kitty and I would get back to the children. What a rushing and scrambling of characters with their pockets stuffed with hard currency there'd be in such case I observed. Thought much about what might happen, with deep pessimism since Europe's resistance potential is very small – indeed, scarcely existent.

June 27, 1950

Again bathed from the rocks, and later from the boat. Went over by boat to Rapallo, met Auberon, and then he and Kitty and I took a cab to the Beerbohms' villa to have tea with them. As it turned out, cab exactly the right vehicle. Elderly servant waiting to show us in. Max and Lady Beerbohm on the roof, he in old-fashioned, elegant linen suit, black tie with tie-pin, no turn-up in the trousers; she in white dress, long, pretty old lady effect, in her manner of speaking very much the actress. Main road goes by the villa now, and conversation punctuated by hooting, noise of gear changing, braking, etc. Formerly secluded. Max has little workroom built on the roof, painted, as he said, in bright Rickett's Blue. His face very old, somehow shaggy, gentle, quite sad; affectionate, gentle, sad eyes; head bald, very browned from the sun. Speaks in a slightly tremulous way, but with perfect lucidity. No clouding of his mind, but a wearying, a slow fading out. He spoke of interior decorators, who, he said, were usually females, and operated in couples; dreadful to behold and in their works. Of John Churchill he said that he felt sure he could not be a particularly good painter because he talked intelligently about painting. In his (Max's) experience, those who could talk about painting could never paint, whereas great painters made only gruff, brief remarks about their own and others' works. Lady Beerbohm keeps her hand fairly heavily upon him – she bought inferior brands of cigarettes in the hope that he might give up smoking, but he kept on; an ant crawling over his coat received her attentions; when he made a slip in talking (American instead of Irish) she correct him. He calls her Florence, no abbreviation. Max talked about Auberon's house, and his memories of it. He said he had only twice been into Rapallo since he came back after the war. Before the war he had, he said, been one for walking about. Lady Beerbohm corrected him in this, and recalled a drawing someone had made of Max standing beside a milestone marked 'Rapallo 2 miles' with the caption: 'Is Rapallo near here?' He said that, in reading newspapers, he first read the headlines, and if it was bad news left it at that. In the case of good news, he read on, his principle being that it was absurd to worry oneself about matters which one couldn't influence. I heartily agreed, and pointed out that Johnson had taken this view. He was glad to know it was Johnson who, he said, was one of the few cases of a man of powerful intellect who was also sensible. So many others, he had found, were brilliant, learned, etc., but essentially silly in their attitude to life. In illustration of his point, I quoted Johnson's remark: 'Why is it that the loudest whelps for liberty come from the drivers of slaves?'

For tea we adjourned to the next house, also theirs, where a neat tea of frail sandwiches, little cakes, etc., was laid out under an arbour formed by a vine. For this business, Max put on an old-fashioned straw hat of the boater sort. Here, too, the noise of traffic constantly intruded on our conversation. Max said he was very sorry the Italians had got rid of their king because a monarch was much more stable a factor in society than a president or an elected head of State. He was, he said, now very deeply conservative, and hated all change. He spoke with true and delightful affection of 'dear Belloc', 'dear William Archer'. A recent photograph he had seen of Belloc had, he said, made him feel very sad. The face seemed so empty. Auberon gave him news of Belloc – that now he was better than he had been, that he's managed to forget the, to him, most lamentable happenings of recent years, and lived in happier times. How, Beerbohm asked, about money? Auberon said Churchill had got him let off income tax. This pleased Max very much.

He spoke of Mrs Shaw's will, which included a considerable legacy to establish institutions for improving the manners of the

Irish. This seemed to him quite extraordinary, but I suggested the
purpose was clear enough – to prevent any recurrence of Shaw.
My explanation vastly amused Max. Lady Beerbohm described
how, on one occasion, Belloc had come to see her, bringing with
him a large parcel of his washing for her to have done. She was, she
said, surprised, especially as he seemed to be about to open the
parcel in her drawing room. Even so, she had the washing done
and returned to Belloc, and had a most diverting letter from him
about it from Paris. Max's manners quite exquisite, and reflected
that manners a great mitigation of human life, being, essentially,
no other than consideration for others as distinct from eagerness
to assert the ego such as Graves and Co constantly indulged, thereby infecting others, including oneself. Trouble with G. B. Shaw,
Max said, was that he had no interest in art or poetry whatsoever;
not even in human beings. His best work dramatic criticism in the
old *Saturday Review* because he really did appreciate and know
about acting. Spoke of Chesterton also with affection. Said he'd
largely been dragooned into the Catholic Church by Belloc – as
with Maurice Baring, and, if he had lived, George Wyndham.
When, later on, he spoke about the ugliness of modern English
domestic architecture, he added: 'But don't let us spoil this charming visit by talking of unhappy things.' We returned to the roof of
the other house and went on chatting there. All the interior neat
and fragrant and careful.

When the time came to leave, Max noted that we had kept
waiting for us the ancient hired carriage in which we'd arrived.
'Carriage people!' he said, and explained that in late Victorian days
this was an honourable epithet – though not then with a hired
carriage. He asked how long we were staying in Portofino, and I
said that the next day we left for Monte Carlo. Again he went
through the motions of awed admiration – 'Carriage people going
to Monte Carlo!' He came to the door to see us off, and gallantly
waved his straw hat in the air. I felt a great affection for him. In
Hughie's phrase, he was 'mild and cured', and by remaining true
to his own world and times had remained true to himself.

June 29, 1950

Everyone frenziedly following Korean news, some panic beginning. Certain that France will in no circumstances offer resistance to anyone – a resistance-less people. Tried to get Monte Carlo radio news, but only succeeded in getting curious religious broadcast punctuated by lugubrious hymns put out by Mormons.

July 1, 1950

Took plane at Nice. Glad in a way to be leaving – after all, a rather sad playground. Love the blue sky and the sea and the warm sun; but a fearful nothingness about it all, a sense of unutterable futility – bodies indolently browning, self-absorbed, self-regarding.

London seemed very welcome, shabby houses friendly. Strong feeling as I returned to Regent's Park that it is now nearly zero hour; the last phase in our decomposition nearing, not much time left. In such circumstances, the only thing to do is for the individual to purify his own heart, establish his own true relationship with time and with eternity. Of earthly hope there is momentarily very little; this at least serves to make it relatively easy to realize the transitoriness and unimportance of earthly things.

July 2–3, 1950

Went into the *Daily Telegraph* and might have never been away. Collected books, wrote leader on French politics, picked up the threads again – such as they are. Pleased to find Italian publisher has taken my novel – though what an Italian reader would make of it Heaven knows.

July 4, 1950

To American Embassy for Independence Day party – vast crowd. Shook hands with Lewis Douglas, the Ambassador, who greeted me most genially. Saw Kingsley Martin, Editor of the *New States-man*. Ran into Ernest Davies, now Under-Secretary for Foreign

Affairs, who said he'd seen me at the Garrick seated 'so comfortably'. I wondered if he'd have felt happier if I'd been sitting on a drawing pin, or on a shooting stick.

July 5, 1950

In the House of Commons Cripps made statement on gold reserves, and then Attlee followed on Korea. In between an odd thin-legged character with a sword came and removed the mace and then put it back again. Attlee followed by Churchill, whole affair pretty unreal. My conviction that the forces of evil are temporarily going to be dominant in the world; they must be fought, of course, however hopeless the battle, but more important than fighting them is to maintain one's own contact with what is good and true, the principle of love in contradistinction to that of hatred. Such thoughts came to me particularly when, in response to an observation of Churchill's Tom Driberg stood up – a face quite full of darkness and spreading darkness before it. Churchill seemed very tired and old; even so, he stood out as immeasurably superior to the others, and remote from them in his greatness. It was, after all, the third time of asking, and the stoutest heart, submitted to such a test, might begin to falter. The Labour Party benches seemed somewhat dazed, as though they wondered what was happening, and why they should find themselves going in the opposite direction to what they had intended. ('We sing the Red Flag,' the Attorney-General said the other day, 'not because the words are in the least apt to the facts of the modern world, nor as a substitute for our country's National Anthem, but as a traditional song of our party. . .')

July 6, 1950

Dick Brooman-White, Julian Amery, another MI6 figure and I talked about yesterday's debate on Korea. Amery really rather impressive – quite tough, ambitious. Thought afterwards that it is encouraging that nowadays one finds the adventurous, alive, young men on the right rather than the left. Amery said (and I agreed) that the only sensible thing to do now would be to re-arm, which would necessitate cutting down expenditure on other things, but that no party government could possibly undertake this. He said that alternatives were 40 divisions and 100 Communist MPs or present parlous state and Conmunists out. Of the two, he preferred former. Something in this, though I expressed doubts about wisdom of his choice. MI6 man said Americans expecting next Russian move in Persia. Much concerned when Dick told me that young men in Foreign Office all anti-American and against Korean intervention. Afterwards thought that this another example of how leftism being, as it were, driven out of the system rightwards, and finding its last foothold in Eton, *The Times*, diplomatic service. No doubt last stand will be fought in White's and Pratt's.

Started reading Boswell's *London Journal* – quite fascinating.

Picked up P. J. Grigg at Whitehall Court. He was playing patience and had already made a sidecar for me. Said that he was getting fed up with his directorship because of 'managerial revolution'. Executives had all the power, and he and his fellow directors, supposed to represent the shareholders, were expected to be rubber stamps. Directors got £3,000 a year, but the managerial personnel £12,000 with £6,000 pensions. Managed, in spite of taxation, to get up to between £5,000 and £6,000. At the same time, he said, his only interest in life was to establish his own relationship with eternity, and he was quite ready to accept the inadequacy of all he'd so far done. Felt great affection for him as he said this looking out over the Thames, and at the absurd buildings being put up for the Festival of Britain on the opposite bank. We walked through St James's Park, and he said the flowers were just like those in his garden in Simla. 'We shall see strange happenings in the next year or so,' I said, 'and perhaps the light of our religion and civilization will be put out; but we who have known the light can try to be true to it until the end. That is worth doing, and, indeed, all we can look to do.'

July 7, 1950

Daily Telegraph. In the chair because Colin Coote at Wimbledon. Read *New Statesman*, and much enraged because at their usual game – H. N. Brailsford asking whether blood should be shed to maintain regime like South Korean one; Security Council a 'ramp' because Russia doesn't attend its meetings – in fact, the whole party line being put across. Some trouble over adjusting leader at last moment – printers all very friendly. One of the subs said to me that I didn't look as cheerful as before, and I replied that I'd great nostalgia for the days when I contributed my little piece of folly to the larger folly, and then pushed off. All the same, human beings mostly very dear as they struggle along as best they may along life's stony path.

July 8, 1950

Ate lunch on hill overlooking Coulsdon. Hadn't been there for thirty years. Now little trace of countryside, houses everywhere. Still, however, vague traces remaining of walks I went on with my father. How confident he was that his intelligence and will were sufficient to measure up against the universe! How utterly subsequent events have proved their inadequacy.

Went on to have tea with my mother and Ingrid, and as usual disturbed by them. Ingrid going to Berlin, but unsure whether she ought to go. Mother wanting to get her out of the house, and I wanting to get her out likewise for my mother's sake – this little personal contretemps projection of massive world conflict. My mother, at 84, told me she wanted to go on living as long as possible. Reflected that in the very old, egotism, the will to live, becomes quite vicious; suppose that in order to live to 80 such a development of one's ego is necessary.

July 11, 1950

I took 18B bus (which, as Tony said when I told him about this, was peculiarly appropriate) and was on top reading Cominform newspaper ('For A Lasting Peace and a People's Democracy') when suddenly a whisper came over my shoulder: 'It's a pity the movement isn't stronger in America'. Without looking round, I vaguely assented to this observation. Then the voice went on to say that,

seeing what I was reading, he'd felt impelled to speak to me; that
he'd just come from a holiday in Italy. He passed me a snapshot
of a streamer across a street calling for the abolition of the atomic
bomb. Still I didn't look round, and it was only when I got off the
bus in Shoe Lane that I saw what he was like – a little rat-faced,
pale man. Thinking it over afterwards, I felt that the whisper was
particularly abhorrent, an intimation of terrorism to come.

July 12, 1950

Dined with William Deedes, now a MP, and character named
Enoch Powell, member for one of the Wolverhampton divisions. He made great impression on me when we ran into each
other on an Army intelligence course in May, 1940 – Mongolian
features, very bright eyes, receding forehead, sprouting moustache.
In the war he determined to get into the Operations Branch, and
did, becoming a Brigadier. Then, he told me, he went to India,
became mad on the place, learned Hindustani, etc., decided that
British Raj was most wonderful thing in history and that to participate in it London was the place. On being demobilized, therefore,
made for London; looked up 'Conservative' in the telephone
directory, went along to Conservative Party Central Office, worked
there; was adopted for not very hopeful constituency, lived there
for eight months concentrating on candidature and to everyone's
amazement got elected by 600 votes. His great heroes: Newcastle,
who defended Rotten Boroughs; Curzon, who was last real Viceroy. Found electioneering very distasteful. I said this had been well
expressed by Shakespeare in *Coriolanus*, and he agreed, adding
that Coriolanus seldom out of his mind during election. If things
get really tough quite likely will hear of him.

July 13, 1950

Lunched at Macmillan with Harold, his brother Daniel, and Lovat
Dickson. The two brothers vastly different, but both rather nice,
Harold distinctly above average in intelligence. We talked about
politics and the present difficulties. Harold on the whole very
gloomy.

Went down to Southsea for BBC *Any Questions?* programme. Went to hotel and ran into Dick Crossman whom I hadn't seen for a long while. Began almost at once to argue with Dick, but in a friendly way. He looks extremely like an Indian Brahmin, and the temper of his mind more and more recalls one – singular facility for demonstrating a proposition, but the propositions themselves unconnected to any central point of view.

We went upstairs and there the others were including Quintin Hogg, plump figure wearing boots, also BBC producer and other personnel – not particularly friendly. Also present, Ralph Wightman, a standing BBC farmer who appears in many broadcasts to indicate that broadcasting is not the preserve of intellectuals.

Hogg and Dick talked rather loudly about Parliament over dinner, and then we all repaired to the Pavilion, large crowd assembled, and we went in one by one, announced beforehand like prize-fighters. Programme went reasonably well, argument over atomic bomb in which I said that one should be dropped with the other three dead against it. Also discussed strikes, commercial wireless, etc., nicer than the Brains Trust, but all the same pretty silly. Audience occasionally applauded, and once hissed Dick Crossman.

Went back to hotel, sat talking to Dick until about 1 a.m. By this time we had largely resumed our old relationship of agreeing about many things.

July 15, 1950

Went down to Bentley with P. J. Grigg, Monty waiting for us at the station and drove us back to his house. Noted Monty's keen face, sharp rather than intelligent; despite maniacal egotism, a certain sweetness, endearing simplicity as well. Usual very military lunch with two O.R.s waiting, bottle of Alsatian wine for P.J. and me. After lunch he showed me four papers he'd prepared in connection with Western defence, written in his own inimitable and unmistakable style, and pointing out that whole show had been a complete wash-out – 'une tromperie', as General de Lattre de Tassigny had said, and he, Monty, agreed. Particularly taken with paper describing interview with Dutch Defence Minister in the course of which Monty observes: 'He (Defence Minister) is a typical politician, always trying to evade the issue. I saw that it was necessary to stamp on him and be quite brutal.' Monty's conclusion – that 'the plain truth is there's no reality whatsoever in general defence structure of Western Europe. We've plans and committees and paper and talk, but nothing of any real value if a battle should develop in the West. . . We're not moving steadily towards the achievement of our aim, but going backwards.' Odd to sit in his room, with a pretty meadow and stream outside the window, and Monty himself standing leaning on the mantlepiece, with his pinched, lean features, while I read of this desperate situation.

Afterwards, we talked about it, Monty elaborating the various points, and describing interviews with Attlee and Shinwell. Showed me various notes from Attlee, his handwriting so variable that one wondered if they were all from the same person. This, I suppose, sign of indecisive character. Plenty of other symptoms of the same thing, God knows. Monty spoke of period when he was C.I.G.S. and how, during coal shortage, Shinwell had solemnly suggested giving only 18cwts for each ton of coal. Actually, he rather likes Shinwell. Also said that when he'd invaded Sicily he'd asked General Alexander what his objective was to be, and had had great difficulty in getting an answer; finally received half sheet of note-paper written in Alexander's own hand telling him to hold port on the Straits of Messina. Pointed out the fatal consequences of politicians' decisions taken in war, and how our troops could have taken Prague, Vienna, and, he considers, Berlin, and what a difference this would have made. Said that as Eisenhower gave no effective orders, he and Patton had no alternative but to go ahead, and that this situation was basis of famous controversy over attack on wide or narrow front. Spoke of recent lunch with Churchill at which he'd noticed Churchill's complexion now very puffy, and breathing heavily and noisily all the time. Thought he was cracking up – my own impression, too. Churchill, he said, was capable of being very little-minded and jealous – e.g. his jealousy of Monty's public ovations in the war. I made notes from his papers while he and Grigg strolled round the garden. 'What a mixture of greatness and littleness!', P.J. whispered to me. I wasn't sure in my own mind about this.

On way back thought much about this conversation, and the sombre events ahead. Glad to feel myself not afraid even though I know beyond any doubt that war must be expected. Read in absurd memoirs of General Carton de Wiart that when people are happy they don't fear death. Quite true. In other words, only those who want to die fear to die, and vice versa.

July 18, 1950

At Heinemann Frere described Noel Coward going off to Jamaica – 'the gentlest breeze sends that particular songster flying for cover'. Walked all the way home to shake off depression – succeeded. Natasha and Andrew Romanenko (now Ronalds) came to supper. Really delighted to see them again, and we reminisced much about Lourenço Marques, where I'd first met them – the Polana Hotel looking over the sea, the bathing, Campini, the Italian Consul-General. Romanenko had excellent Soviet story – music-hall performer in Moscow has performing flea which on the word of command jumps from one of his hands to the other. Then he pulls off the flea's legs, gives the word of command, and, of course, the flea doesn't jump, whereupon he says to the audience: 'You see, he can't hear'.

July 20, 1950

Finished defence article based on Monty talk.

Went on to party for Graham Greene at Heinemann. Saw Kitty waiting outside British Museum before she saw me – always delightful. Mixed literary–clerical company – Irish priest, rather congenial, Father Daniel, said he'd met me in Rome at some sort of Congress. Insisted that I wasn't there, or only in spirit; but he still seemed doubtful. Greene's two brothers present – the tall one in the BBC, and the doctor one. We chatted, and recalled eating sausages during the blitz when the raids were on. Also chatted with Lord Radcliffe, whom I knew at the Ministry of Information when he was Sir Cyril. Noted how becoming a judge had, as it were, stiffened him up. Said he liked it on the whole, especially trying to write clear legal judgments; said that style of such writings quite standardized, rather nice, and echoes of it to be found in Jamaican, Indian, etc. judgments. Often, he said, the style was caught more readily than the law it expressed.

Supposed also to go to Rothermere party, couldn't face it. Hate, in any case, wearing white waistcoat. Rang up Osbert Lancaster about this, and found he was already in white waistcoat at three in the afternoon.

Had discussion with Bill Deedes about Liberalism, which was, I said, an attractive doctrine, but which I increasingly abhorred because false. Its great fallacy, I pointed out, was the perfectibility of Man – i.e. the assumption that left to himself he would be humane, orderly, and industrious. My experience has been the exact opposite – namely, that, left to himself, Man was brutish, lustful, idle and murderous, and that the only hope of keeping his vile nature within any sort of bound was to instil in him fear of God or of his fellow men. Of these two alternatives, I preferred fear of God – an authoritarian Christian society to an authoritarian materialist society, fear of Hell as a deterrent to fear of human brutality. And, as a matter of fact, more potent and wonderful is fear of being cut off from the light of God's countenance and living in darkness – this fear the only deterrent which is, at once, effective and ennobling.

July 21, 1950

Went to Connaught Hotel to meet Robert Menzies, the Australian Prime Minister – large, sentimental, really quite impressive man. Later, he delivered a sensible address to those present about Australia's need for immigrants, and about defence problems, particularly in relation to Korea.

Went on to the Travellers where I picked up Tony, then dined at Pratt's. Joined by Evelyn Waugh, quite ludicrous figure in dinner jacket, silk shirt; extraordinarily like a loquacious woman, with dinner jacket cut like maternity gown to hide his bulging stomach. He was very genial, probably pretty plastered – all the time playing this part of a crotchety old character rather deaf, cupping his ear – 'feller's a bit of a Socialist I suspect'. Amusing for about a quarter of an hour. Tony and I agreed that an essential difference between Graham and Waugh is that, whereas Graham tends to impose an agonized silence, Waugh demands agonized attention.

July 22, 1950

Went in the evening with Kitty to dine with Antonia White. Also present Bobby Speaight, actor, Roman Catholic. Very egotistic like all actors. Looked him up afterwards in *Who's Who* – long entry listing all his parts, including 'Voice of Christ' in *The Man Born to be King* the radio plays by Dorothy L. Sayers. Long discussion of Evelyn Waugh whom Speaight obviously detests. Said that Waugh always pretends not to know him although they've been introduced innumerable times, and that when they're introduced Waugh always takes the line that it's most odd that he (Waugh) should consort with an actor. Another gambit of Waugh's is to assume that Speaight is acting in pantomime and to make remarks like: 'Christmas is coming along, so you'll be busy . . . Where's your false nose? . . .' etc. I said that Waugh was a man imprisoned in his own fantasy – the most terrible sort of imprisonment anyone could have to endure, and that it might well end in madness.

July 24, 1950

Dined in the evening with Camrose in his Dorchester suite. Other guests Michael Berry, Coote, and Lewis Douglas, the American Ambassador. Douglas obviously very worried about Korea. He'd been with Attlee that morning trying to persuade him to send British troops to Korea and going into the question of financial implication of British re-armament. Reflected how the essential reality was overlooked – viz. how many people prepared to die; everything else available – money, support, arms even, but the great strength of the Russians that they are lavish with blood, which others provide most parsimoniously. Money talks, but blood wins. Another factor difficult to formulate without seeming fantastic is that the British Government consists of men who, consciously or unconsciously, have invested in defeat. Really quite pleasant sitting there, but a bit like the talks with Monty – a sense of impending disaster, and of participating in its historical origins; of having a walking on part in the 'Decline and Fall of Western Civilization'.

July 25, 1950

Wrote leader on Formosa, largely based on conversation with Douglas. Then on to see Hesketh. Gladys now bedridden. While we were there had fit of coughing which she hadn't enough strength to master. Pitiable to see her struggling. Hesketh exceptionally gentle with Gladys and she quite serene – after many storms acceptance achieved; as Hugh Kingsmill would have said, modus moriendi if not modus vivendi. 'Men must endure their going hence even as their coming hither,' I thought.

July 26, 1950

Brilliant description by John of meeting his brother Pan and his fellow evangelists:

'I saw Pan "in action" on Tuesday. In the morning I received a telegram telling me to meet him "on the main road between X and X". At X an extraordinary sight met my eyes: six sun-burnt, unshaven youths, clad in khaki shorts and bush shirts, pushing the famous trek-carts, with the words "Jesus Saves" painted on the side. In front was the "trek leader" riding a very antique push bike conducting the chorus singing. What struck me from the start was their enthusiasm for the cause and their light-heartedness. In spite of the fact that they had just completed an 18-mile walk, in spite of the fact that they had a night in a Dutch barn before them, they laughed, they joked, they sang and anyone who passed them received six of the cheeriest good evenings they could sparkle. When someone accused Christ's disciples of frivolity didn't he say something like: "the very stones would break out into mirth, if these men were prevented from doing so"? It was the same with these students; one felt they just could not keep their happiness to themselves.'

July 28–29, 1950

Went to Victoria and met Philip Jordan. Travelled down with him to Pulborough, talking about Korea and the Prime Minister's broadcast on Sunday.

The next morning I went into Petworth with him, bought newspapers, waited outside shops, usual week-ending country pursuit. Many similar cottagers – Gerald Barry, Vernon Bartlett, etc., whole place rather redolent of multi-wived, high-thinking, deep-drinking, surtax-paying Liberals and hommes-de-lettres. Would find atmosphere this generated somewhat depressing – good terms with the Publican, time of day passed with farm labourers, corduroy trousers, coloured scarves, etc. Walked over downs with Philip in the afternoon, and we talked affectionately together. Told me about the Attlee household, Mrs Attlee, it appears, subject to sudden fits of rage which, embarrassingly, seize her sometimes in public. They worried the Prime Minister more than the prospect of atomic war, and are the real reason he's considering resignation. Said to Philip that I could quite understand Mrs Attlee's reaction – comparable to clergyman's wife whose rage kindled at husband's mildness, especially when, despite, or because of it, he achieved preferment.

In the evening discussed sabotage and how to deal with fifth columns. Said to Philip that there was now a world-wide civil war, and that increasingly, whatever might happen, whether we liked it or not, we should be preoccupied with it. Our side might on a short view, lose; but it had to be our side. Suggested point I thought ought to be made in Prime Minister's broadcast, and Philip asked me to scribble it down. This I did, and passage appeared unchanged following night when broadcast delivered, as follows: 'There are those who tell you that offers have been made by the Russians at the United Nations which would have made possible the disarmament we all so much desire. This is quite untrue. When it came to the point, the Russians have invariably envisaged the Security Council as the controlling authority of any scheme suggested. This means that the Russian veto would operate, and that, in practice, there would be no control.'

August 2–16, 1950

Gap in journal due to being Acting Editor of the *Daily Telegraph*. Whole day spent there – innumerable things to do, letters to answer, people coming in all the time; all the curious pushing, intriguing, obsequiousness and envy which goes, and ever must go, with the exercise of authority; hints about salary inadequacy, digs at others in terms of professions of friendship and admiration, and so on. Poor Stowell, Features Editor, in and out all the time, grey-haired, breathless – up to the fifth floor where Camrose and family function (the fifth floor being a generic term in the *Daily Telegraph*, personalized as, 'the fifth floor wants so and so,' or 'the fifth floor view is', etc.). He loves his servitude (human beings, collectively and individually, fall into servitude so often because they love it) and recounts in a high-flown loquacious way what Mr Michael said about this, and how he reacted to that. Such a job makes for an entirely different kind of life – no thinking, little reading; caught up in a kind of activity which fills the day.

Christopher Buckley was killed in Korea, which involved sending a lot of telegrams, writing a leader on him, etc. Often wonder what proportion of the feelings generated when a person dies are genuine. Felt really quite sorry about Buckley, and yet when he was alive he usually bored me, though in a way I quite liked him. Sent a long telegram to Cecilia.

August 23, 1950

Received unexpected call from Churchill's secretary to go down to Westerham to see him. Drove down in an office car accompanied by character named Emery Reeves, who has long acted as Churchill's agent. Churchill has the characteristic 18th-century nobleman's attitude that he should have a Jew to look after his financial affairs, and in this case there is no question but that the choice has turned out well. Driving down Reeves explained to me how he had first managed to persuade Churchill to let him look after his interests. He said that Churchill had an insatiable need for money and reckons to spend about £10,000 a year net. His family costs him a lot, and though he doesn't live luxuriously, he lives amply and travels with a great suite, which is very expensive.

Arrived at Westerham – large, not very attractive house, part of it old, much added to, like the residences of all power addicts (the Webbs, Monty) curiously impersonal, nothing individual about it at all, comfortable without being cosy. Through the window a really beautiful view over a little artificial lake. When we first arrived no one about. Finally a rather sulky secretary arrived and said that we were expected, but that Churchill had gone out into the garden somewhere. Then Bill Deakin appeared – one of those characteristic dons of this time, on the spot, obviously very capable but needing to attach themselves to someone, the don trying to muscle-in on the world of action.

Churchill walked in suddenly wearing his famous siren suit and smoking a huge cigar – a quite astonishing figure, very short legged, baby faced, immensely thick neck, and oddly lovable. I was expecting tea, but a tray of whiskies and sodas was brought in, and continued to be brought in at intervals. Churchill began by talking about his Memoirs and how he was getting on with them. I told him that he ought now to do the last volume before the intervening ones because it was so essential that he should write an account of Yalta. He agreed that it was essential, but said that to do so would involve so much criticism of the Americans that the political reper- cussions would be dangerous. Nothing, he said, would convince the Americans of the reality of the Russian danger. He, Churchill, had wanted Patton to take Prague, and had suggested to the Ameri- cans that there should be no Anglo-American withdrawal in Germany until a final agreement had been reached. He wanted a battle conference between himself, Stalin and Truman where the armies met, before there had been any disarmament, and he wanted German arms to be kept handy in case they were required. This proposal, he said, was entirely unacceptable to the Americans. It was not, he went on, the Yalta Agreement which was at fault, but the breaking of the Yalta Agreement; and the moment the Russians began to break it he had done all that lay within his power to induce the Americans to join him in calling them to order.

What has happened about his Memoirs, and why he was so troubled, is that in truth he has lost interest in them and has simply been stringing together masses of documents which he had written in the war. The Americans, who have paid a huge sum of money for the serial and book rights, have protested. In the course of conversation about them it slipped out that certain chapters had not been written by him at all, and I suspect that he is doing extremely little.

He broke off to speak about his conversation with Attlee concerning the advancement of the summoning of Parliament. Attlee, he said, now takes in at most 50% of what is said to him. He referred scornfully to the fact that Attlee had insisted to him (Churchill) that there was no possibility of taking troops from Hong Kong for Korea and that the Americans were not pressing for the British forces. Both these statements were contradicted the very next day. When I told him that the troops going from Hong Kong were going naked, with no proper equipment and, to all intents and purposes, unarmed except for ammunition, he was even more distressed. He spoke much about his broadcast and started reciting a few bits of it.

He then spoke about the Germans and said it was absolutely essential to re-arm them. He mentioned that he'd been invited to go to Cologne where he was to address a huge gathering, perhaps 30,000, and he believed he would receive a great ovation. He then began walking up and down the room and, in effect, giving the speech he was to give at Cologne – a bizarre spectacle, the great wartime Prime Minister, rather tight, walking up and down reciting his speech which he proposed to give to a German audience from whom he expected warm applause. He obviously still has a great affection for Stalin. 'What a pity,' he said, 'that he has turned out to be such a swine' and went on: 'Why, he and Truman and Attlee could have governed the world – what a triumvirate!'

He treated me with great respect, and kept on looking at me out of the corner of his eye to see how I was reacting to his performance. A curious mixture of cunning and animality in his face, as with so many of the very old. He obviously longs more than anything for power and therefore is only interested in the present rather than the past; in an odd way reminiscent of my mother-in-law, Mrs Dobbs, and, curiously enough, like her he has developed a passionate affection for a dog which follows him about everywhere.

He took me downstairs to look at his pictures which are really very striking, one room completely covered with them, remarkably vivid colouring. Here he was rather touching. Sitting humped-up in a chair looking at them, he pointed to one which he said was the last he'd done, and added, 'I expect the last I shall ever do.' I made the usual observations about being sure he would do many more etc., but he just paid no attention and sat there seemingly sunk in thought surrounded by these brilliantly coloured pictures. We then went into his study, the walls of which are covered with presentation photographs, and, still thinking about his German speech, showed me a picture of Bismarck which had been given by the German Chancellor to his father. He also showed me a printed notice offering £25 reward for his (Churchill's) capture dead or alive at the time of the Boer War, signed by Kruger. He said, 'It's more than they would offer for me now.'

We strolled out into the grounds, and he showed me the little waterfall he'd made, and explained the difficulty he has in getting sufficient water. He'd been draining his ponds, and had hoped to have the whole operation completed by the time his wife returned, but now she was coming back four days earlier and he feared she would be displeased with it all and that there'd be trouble. We went along to see his goldfish in a little pool. He sat down in a chair set there specially for him and began to shout, the supposition being that at the sound of his voice the goldfish would assemble. They showed no signs of assembling as far as I could see, but presently an attendant appeared and gave him some maggots which he threw into the water, whereupon the goldfish did come and started eating them. He said that his whole standing with the goldfish depended on their associating the sound of his voice with the provision of maggots, and he laughed heartily when I said that he was in very much the same situation vis à vis his constituents, that they, too, needed to associate the sound of his voice with a provision of maggots. Some of the goldfish, he said, were worth as much as £6 each. In a nearby pool there were a lot of little ones for which he had paid only a few shillings apiece, but as they fattened they increased in value. Here, he said, is the younger generation, and looked quite sentimental at the thought of these little fishes fattening up to be worth £6.

He then took me to a little pavilion which had originally been built for the first Duke of Marlborough and his wife, Sarah. The walls had frescoes done by his nephew John Churchill. Churchill seemed to think they were very good, but they were quite deplorable. Another characteristic of the power addict, I think, is to have no taste, since taste belongs to the individual soul and exists by virtue of its separation from, rather than identification with, the herd.

When he came to see me off he shouted to some odd characters who were waiting there, 'I'll be back soon' and suddenly I was reminded forcibly of King Lear and his conversation with poor Tom – the conversation in which he calls poor Tom 'my philosopher'. This sudden identification of Churchill with Lear made me feel full of pity for him, imprisoned in the flesh, in old age, longing only for a renewal of the disease of life, all passion unspent. He waved goodbye very cheerfully, and I waved back, and drove thoughtfully back to the *Daily Telegraph*.

August 24–31, 1950

Dined with the Griggs and C. P. Ramaswamy Iyer, aged ruffian whom I'd known years ago in Travancore, and afterwards in Simla: recalled most vividly last years in India, Viceregal Lodge, Willingdon, etc. Talked with C.P. about India's future. He is deeply pessimistic, convinced that civil war will come, and that for the next two decades at any rate Asia belongs to the Kremlin. Drove him back afterwards. He asked me about Churchill, and I said I thought all that was left in him now was a senile craving for power – like, I said, an aged and impotent lecher still given to womanizing. The observation made C.P. rather thoughtful, he being precisely in this case.

September 2, 1950

Drove P. J. Grigg to see Monty and had another long session on Western Defence. When we arrived Monty had opened the gates and was walking restlessly up and down the lawn. He had broken his holiday because he'd heard that things were brewing. Struck again by the clarity and simplicity of his mind and his complete concentration of purpose. He sits all day thinking about defence matters. Quite a different type of power maniac from Winston – more, perhaps like Cromwell than Marlborough. The moment he gets off his own subject his simplicity becomes apparent.

September 3, 1950

Walked in Hyde Park with Kitty and the children, then to the *Daily Telegraph*. Rather astonished when Winston rang up and embarked on a long conversation about Attlee's broadcast, etc., and asked me whether I thought he ought to issue a statement in answer to it. I said it would be very unwise and he agreed. He described Attlee's broadcast as 'ferocious bleating' – so attractive a phrase that I put it into Peterborough. The affairs of his Memoirs have been thrown into even greater confusion by the printers' strike.

I put all the Monty stuff into the *Daily Telegraph* as from the Diplomatic Correspondent; it made quite a good story. Colin Coote turned up from his holiday, and on the whole I was happy to hand things over to him.

September 14–October 1, 1950

The Daily Telegraph *sent me on a fact-finding mission to Trieste, Belgrade, and Vienna; and then to Germany where I visited principally Berlin and Dusseldorf.*

In Trieste 'what intimations of decay everywhere'. The society I found seemed to me 'a society sick unto death, just kept from dying by transfusions of US dollars'. In Belgrade I reported 'all the Muscovite manifestations – gimcrack buildings with painted slogans upon them. . . I have never felt such repugnance for a place, for this fearful proletarian megalomania which laid life waste'. In contrast, the centre of Vienna was 'wonderfully intact, quite delightful, shops flourishing. . . Occasional Russian soldiers – but even they more or less respectable, decently turned out, less villainous than elsewhere'.

In Berlin, did the British commandant think that the Russians intended to do a Korea? No, he did not. At the centre of the city vast desolation, 'the mountains of the moon'. 'In among the ruins shops well supplied; in contrast, went into Russian sector; blindfolded, really could have told by the smell when we passed into it – that sour smell I know so well, compounded of dirt and fear and propinquity – crowded streets, empty shops, people just walking along seemingly sightless.' In Dusseldorf a meeting of the Allied High Commission was in progress, 'all very like the League of Nations, unreal' but aiming to give Western Germany 'the chance to do what's going to be, got to be, done anyway'.

October 2, 1950

Usual *Daily Telegraph* Sunday. Got myself up-to-date with the news. Korea campaign going wonderfully, and nearing conclusion; Labour Party Conference at Margate, picked up the threads.

October 4, 1950

Lunched with Dick Brooman-White, spoke to him about my travels. Cocktail party at Tony's. Osbert Lancaster showed me an excellent drawing he'd done of William Morris, Jane Morris, and D. G. Rossetti on a three-fold lavatory which Morris had put in at Kelmscott. John Betjeman had now taken Kelmscott and Osbert saw this curious object there. Observed that it was very like John Betjeman to take the house, which must be atrocious – part of his whimsicality.

Photograph in the newspaper of Stafford Cripps kissing the hand of the lady who keeps the starving place at Zurich where he now is. There is a strong rumour going round that he has at last gone completely off his head.

October 21, 1950

Went down with P. J. Grigg to see Monty. As usual, he had various papers to show us – how he got the Dutch Defence Minister sacked, what he wrote to Moch, French Minister for War, about German re-armament, etc. Read all this, heard his plans. In the dining-room three new portraits beside large one of him – his great-grandfather, grandfather and father. Grigg remarked that the family hadn't improved in looks. Grandfather's face the most impressive – plump, intelligent, spectacled; he a Governor of the Punjab, decoration round his neck, star on his breast, etc. Father in Bishop's regalia, very grey and deathly-looking; then Monty. We went on talking about defence, and how really nothing whatever had been done in Western Europe. Monty's solution to give someone authority – a Supremo, himself. He ridiculed the idea of a 'democratic' Korea, and I tried to explain why the acceptance of such a ludicrous pretence was politically expedient, and how, in politics as in individual existence, the direct consequence of humbug is becoming entangled in it. Words like Freedom, Self-determination, Democracy – how easy to use, how ruinous have been the results of their usage. What we sow that must we also reap. Monty talked about John Gunther's book on Roosevelt, and I elaborated my favourite proposition – that authority, in the Century of the Common Man, requires a symbolic rather than a human setting. Thus, Hitler, Stalin, Roosevelt, etc. – men with immense power and no biographies. Monty much pleased with this idea (of which, to a certain extent, he is himself an exemplification). I've observed, with him, that such ideas he grasps readily, but that others which might seem to be simpler he quite misses. Where the imagination operates he can follow; where the mind, only with difficulty.

October 15, 1950

Bertrand Russell's *Unpopular Essays* please and irritate at the same time, like so many things. Consider his kind of mind and point of view, though in a way attractive, the most ruinous of all, the most destructive, the most cowardly, the most lamentable. His reason tells him to seek what pleases and to shun the disagreeable, and, obeying it, he becomes utterly selfish, indifferent to all forms of responsibility, personal and social – in fact, the precise opposite of what he intends. Tolerance in excess is as much a vice as any other virtue in excess.

October 16, 1950

Lunched with Richard Comyns Carr whom I enjoy seeing because he is unegotistic and with an odd kind of humour of his own. Said that at Broadway he was often humiliated by not being familiar with office gossip, and that when he'd tried to correct this by going round and collecting a bit, he'd found that eyebrows were raised. I said that gossip, like everything else, required a particular technique and also that when you got a little it was easy to get some more because you could give your little in exchange. We spoke about Russia, and I developed a favourite proposition that what is going on there is not so much a Marxist Revolution as a belated industrial revolution, which produces all the same outward manifestations in terms of sentimentality, etc., as in Victorian England.

I also met Alec Waugh, whom I hadn't seen for a number of years, now very bald and benign looking. Chatted with him about Hughie, with whom he'd been a prisoner-of-war in the 1914–18 war. Odd to reflect how his first book, *The Loom of Youth* made such a sensation. He mentioned with pleasure that he was often confused with his brother Evelyn, which delighted him because it so annoyed Evelyn.

October 17–19, 1950

Returned late to find that the Cholertons had arrived, and at once embarked upon interminable subject of finding Chol a job which he doesn't really want and wouldn't be able to do if he got it – he just the same, jabbering, plucking at his beard.

Came into the *Daily Telegraph* on the Thursday morning because Coote taking the day off – his birthday. 57. Reflected that he is ten years older than I am, and looks sick, and that if he conked out on the present form I'd become Editor – which I should both like and dislike.

Early in the evening Cripps' resignation was announced. Had to write article on him in two hours, each sheet taken away as I finished it. Result really quite satisfactory, confirming opinion I've long held that in journalism the quicker and more urgent the better. Such effort, however, involves getting very excited, and excitement has to wear off before sleep possible.

October 21, 1950

Went down with Kitty and Tony to Sevenoaks to look at Knole again. Taken through by female guide, whom I insisted was Irish Roman Catholic – anyway, someone who had been worked over by nuns. We strolled round the house looking at the pictures, etc. Pointed out to Tony that once anyone has news value it continues for ever – e.g. distinct reaction in the party when the Reynolds portrait of Johnson was pointed out – much more interest shown than in any of the other portraits. The same thing applies to Bernard Shaw today. At the Garrick his surgeon told me that when he came to after his operation and they told him he had a tube in him he asked to see it, and then, after looking at it, said that in his case it should have been made of silver. It appears that he is now so brittle that if he turned over sharply in bed he might break something. Strolled round the grounds with Kitty afterwards. Tony pointed out how a place having been lived in for a long time gives it a curious sort of atmosphere, to which one is immediately sensible. Though the grounds are large and open, they do not at all seem like open country. This is the spirit of long occupation.

Read an inconceivably boring life of Lord Dawson of Penn. Hughie and I had thought that the other Dawson, editor of *The Times*, should have taken the title 'Lord Dawson of Ink'.

October 29, 1950

In bed read Wells' *The Invisible Man*, and found it funnier than I'd expected, but less interesting. Been looking over Wells lately – *Autobiography*, etc., and the more I've thought of him the more pitiable he seems. Much preoccupied with indigestion – even in the case of *The Invisible Man* it is recorded that after he'd eaten bread and cheese this could be sensed by onlooker because not wholly assimilated. Likewise Mr Polly. Remembered the same thing with my father – indigestion tremendous factor in lives of turn-of-century utopians.

November 15, 1950

Went in the morning to look at exhibition of 18th-century French painters – Fragonard, Watteau, etc. – very delicate and charming, had again very strongly the feeling that all that is most exquisite in French art came before the Revolution.

Went to Old Vic to see *Twelfth Night*. Churchill in the audience, given tremendous ovation (in which I joined) when he arrived. Reflected that in his case, as in all others, the will doesn't get what it wants – i.e. he gets popular affection but not popular support. All the same, very charming to see the old boy bowing, smiling, and everyone applauding. Production, alas, not particularly good. Peggy Ashcroft magnificent, but too old for the part of Viola, all the clowning overdone. Recent discovery that Shakespeare is 'good theatre' involves getting more theatre than Shakespeare.

November 19–21, 1950

After conversation with Johnson about Swift and Addison, Boswell says: 'We then talked of Me'.

At lunch with Camrose we discussed Salisbury's speech in the Lords about making another effort to reach agreement with the Russians, and I expressed strong disagreement with any such project. One of the difficulties for me at the *Daily Telegraph* is that Coote really agrees with Salisbury, and we are always coming up against this problem. As I have just written to Peter Viereck: The conflict between East and West has become so fierce that there is now little possibility of being 'liberal' about it, one just has to be on one side or the other. MacArthur has done more to save Western civilization than any Salisbury or other enlightened protagonist of tolerance and reason. I am for MacArthur, just as I am for German rearmament, and even for De Gaulle. These are imperfect and perhaps dangerous instruments, but the situation is dangerous, and it is no good pretending otherwise.

November 22, 1950

Went with Kitty and the Cholertons to see Picasso exhibition, to me excessively depressing. Amused to overhear a French lady remark: 'Ou il est fou, ou il se moque de nous', which seemed to me a fair summing up of the whole thing. Ironical thought – the

Russians, who won't allow Picasso's works to be exhibited, enjoy his unquestioned adulation, whereas the British, whose behinds he constantly kicks, fall over themselves through organizations like the Arts Council in advertising and selling his pictures. It is all part of the pattern.

Streets packed with people watching Queen Juliana of the Netherlands go by on her State visit. Reflected how easy it is to get people into the streets and recalled excellent observation of Cromwell to Fairfax when they were met by enthusiastic crowds. Fairfax said to Cromwell, presumably hoping to please him, that clearly the people loved them, and Cromwell replied that they'd just as cheerfully turn out to see them hanged.

November 26, 1950

Everyone at *Daily Telegraph* somewhat mournful, big break-through by Chinese Communists in North Korea, looks like the beginning of the trouble that is coming. In an odd way, all working out to plan – even the Marxist plan, which doesn't mean that Marxism is right. The old phrase I always think of – in order that the prophecy may be fulfilled.

December 6–8, 1950

Went to look at three one-man shows at the Leicester Galleries. One, not too bad, an Australian (Russell Drysdale) – gave a good sense of vast, rather desolate landscape; reawakened in me faint desire to go there.

Lunched on Friday with P. J. Grigg and Monty at the Garrick. Monty interested in his quick, ferret way in the club, the pictures, the people there. Seemed very tired and old, I thought; wondered what was to happen to him when Eisenhower appeared on the scene shortly; glad to have got rid of De Lattre de Tassigny to Indo-China. Somewhat gleeful over MacArthur's reverses in Korea, convinced that the Germans will turn down re-armament offer. Saw him off, then went to pick up Auberon Herbert to drive down to see Hilaire Belloc.

Belloc's house fairly roomy, but shabby, rather desolate. His daughter received us wearing a heavy tweed suit. Auberon said that formerly she wore what he described as a 'Pixie Franciscan costume'. Grandson also there. Belloc came shuffling in, walks with great difficulty because he has had a stroke, inconceivably dirty, almost on the Mrs Dobbs level, mutters to himself and easily forgets what he said, heavily bearded, fierce-looking and angry. He saw some sherry on the table and said: 'Wine! Oh good! I want lots of it.' Actually very little available, and that of indifferent quality. Sucked on a pipe, said that he had been prevented from getting a Fellowship at Oxford because he was a Roman Catholic and against Dreyfus. This was sixty years ago, and it seemed very pitiful that such a grievance should survive so long. Wondered whether in old age I'd have such a grievance myself. Not at all a serene man. Although he has written about religion all his life, there seemed to be very little in him. Spoke about Cardinal Newman coming to distribute the prizes at his school when he was a boy. Reminded me oddly of Churchill, and even of Mrs Dobbs – the fearful wilfulness of the very old when they are not reconciled. The will still beating against the bars, and the strokes becoming more and more frenzied and futile as they become feebler. Again thought of King Lear. Belloc occasionally hummed snatches of old French songs, and then burst into what must have been a music hall song when he was young – 'Chase me girls, I've got a banana, oh what a banana!' This song pleased him hugely. He gave me one of his books and wrote my name in it with a shaking hand. When his daughter and grandson were out of the room, he turned to Auberon and me and said: 'They're longing for me to die,' and then laughed gleefully. When he quotes other people he changes his own voice, which is deep with the French rolled Rs, and talks in a curious high, almost piping, voice. Spoke with hatred of Lloyd George. Said that Lloyd George had no opinion of him because he thought he was done, and how he'd said to him: 'I shall rise again on the third day.' Then, chuckling, added: 'The blasphemy shocked the little Welsh Nonconformist.'

A sombre, angry, penurious household. Drove back with Auberon, talked about Belloc. Said that I thought the best thing he'd done were his satirical verses.

At home found Bridget Lunn – very sweet, the exact opposite of Belloc, truly religious and gentle, intends to be a nun.

December 9, 1950

In White's Club ran into Randolph Churchill whom I hadn't seen for more than ten years. He was very genial – now immensely bloated and rather absurd-looking, laying down the law to a little circle of fellow drinkers about politics, etc.: not an edifying scene, but, all the same, I like him in a way. White's very odd place these days, extraordinary mixture of broken-down military figures, hommes de lettres, nondescripts of various kinds.

December 12–13, 1950

Mrs Eleanor Roosevelt, the very type of maundering American do-gooder – liberal. As with F.D.R., her fabulous cynicism – e.g. incident in which Madame Chiang, when asked what she'd do in China with someone like John L. Lewis, the US miners' leader, passed her hand over her throat. This vastly diverted Eleanor.

December 13, 1950

Lunched with Coote, Johnstone and Hugh Gaitskell (Chancellor of the Exchequer). Gaitskell rather soft-looking character, large face which always looks slightly unshaven; amiable, and, in his way, intelligent, rather like a certain type of High Church clergy-man with a slum parish. He talked about the ending of Marshall Aid which he was going to announce in Parliament that day; quite clear from what he said that we hadn't chosen to relinquish it, but had been told by the Americans that we couldn't have any more. Much amused when Gaitskell said that at the London School of Economics they had a machine which demonstrated the economic system electrically by lighting up buttons in different colours so that if, for instance, inflationary pressure was increased other things happened. Gaitskell was dead serious about this, couldn't understand why it made me laugh so much. I told him that it re-minded me of the Island of Laputa which Gulliver visited on his third voyage. I also said that when, as had probably happened to all of us, I found myself an exile in America, I had long had the intention of founding there the First Church of Christ Economist, and that, though for this organization there were plenty of sacred texts and plenty of prophets, hitherto I had seen no possibility of a suitable ceremonial. His London School of Economics machine would, I thought, provide this lack. It could be used to demonstrate the sacred mysteries of the First Church of Christ Economist.

December 18, 1950

In the evening drove out with Kitty to Wimbledon to dine with Richard Comyns Carr and his wife. Old Comyns Carr there, now a KC. We talked about our previous meeting in Tokyo and about the war criminals' trial there, in which Comyns Carr had appeared for the prosecution. Agreed with him that although in our youth we had presumed that we were born into the most humane era in history, in actual fact there had been more inhumanity in the world in our time than for many thousands of years, perhaps than ever before. This old, desiccated Liberal extremely conscious of this, but not of course conscious that his liberalism had played so large a part in bringing about such a state of affairs. Liberalism is the greatest of all destructive forces, for its total moral vacuity almost inevitably leads to terrorist government. This theme should be worked out.

December 19, 1950

Lunched with Percy Cudlipp at the Garrick. He is obviously very under the weather, worried about the *Daily Herald*, the Labour Party, above all about himself, wonders what will happen to him, where he stands. Talked, as many Labour supporters do now, with great admiration for Churchill. Obvious nostalgia for his return. Said that Attlee once told him that the two people he (Attlee) got on best with in the Cabinet were Shinwell and Bevan. I said this obviously meant that he loathed and feared them both. Very typical of a politician to say that he liked people he dared not get rid of. Percy much nicer than he used to be now that he feels the ground shaking under his feet a bit.

December 22–27, 1950

Read life of Henry Newton, slave-trader and evangelist. Interesting how he took slave trade for granted even after he became pious. Most difficult to realize how human beings do take things for granted.

Great atmosphere of sadness everywhere, feeling that future Christmases very problematical; the sands running out. When Cholerton spoke of the vineyards in the Burgundy country felt sure I'd never see them again; imagined them as they'd be under Russian occupation – the litter, the awful pall of Slav hopelessness which would fall upon them. A sense of doom in the air.

Drove out with Kitty and the children to Windsor, tea with Alec Vidler. We all went to carol service in St George's Chapel. Rather disappointing – carols dolled up in a madrigal way; all the lessons read by 'a member of the Windsor community', etc. Felt the poison has now spread through the whole body politic. Whole affair somewhat threadbare and even macabre.

On Christmas Day listened to the King's broadcast. To my surprise it was really excellent, based largely on *The Pilgrim's Progress*.

At *Daily Telegraph* great amusement over theft from Westminster Abbey of the Stone of Scone, presumably taken by Scottish Nationalists. Reflected that portents of this kind quite comprehensible since regime so feeble as to allow such a theft clearly doomed.

December 31, 1950

Saw the New Year in with Kitty and the Cholertons. BBC well up to form, and finished up with Robert Donat giving recitation from *In Memoriam*. Future most menacing as race of Gadarene swine for the precipice grows faster. Curious sensation belonging to a dying civilization – like living in a house which is falling down – roof collapses, floor-boards give, rain comes in through the windows, but still some sort of shelter provided, and each new manifestation of decay, after initial shock, got used to. From my own personal point of view, more serene than hitherto because reconciled to this situation, more aware of its inevitability. Whatever is

understood, by being understood, ceases to be frightening. Only
the incomprehensible terrifies – which is why a powerful weapon
with all tyrants is bewilderment. A dying civilization is sad, but,
like a human death, not despairing. The most contemptible are
those who try to jump on other band-wagons; the most futile those
who manage still to persuade themselves that London Bridge
stands as firmly as ever it did – the rats who bow down before the
barbarians, and the Don Quixotes who attire themselves in rusty
armour and cardboard helmet.

January 14, 1951

During the day read Roy Harrod's Life of Keynes. Keynes and his
gang – Lytton Strachey, Lowes Dickinson, Leonard Woolf, etc.,
to me deeply unsympathetic: in a sense the true destroyers with
Ramsay MacDonald, Attlee etc., trailing rather pitiably along
behind. The politicians, in any case, at least take certain risks, but
these others, remote from the fray, demolishing by remote control.

   Wrote paragraph on sudden death of Lady Beerbohm. Thought
that Max would be slightly irritated at her stealing a march on him
and managing to die first, leaving him stranded.

January 16, 1951

Went on to see Monty at P. J. Grigg's flat. Monty, on the whole,
in excellent form – delighted that Eisenhower now has blood
pressure, some sort of pain in his shoulder, and has had to give up
smoking, and rather pleased that the Americans have done so
badly in Korea. Talked about his interview with Adenauer 'What
is your political aim?' (Herr Chancellor) in his inimitable way;
also about Eisenhower's plans, and how he (Monty) will have the
only important Command under Eisenhower. Asked me if I
thought there could be a coalition, and I said I fully anticipated
formation of one before the summer, and that, practically speaking,
all politicians would join in if they got the chance, including
Winston.

January 17, 1951

Monty very pleased with a letter he'd got from Eisenhower asking
him to carry on with Western Command while he (Eisenhower)
was in America – gushingly worded in the American manner. Told
me about his talks with Eisenhower etc. Looked very small in his
Dover House office, next to the Treasury – like a little, sharp, grey
ferret. Always nowadays wears rosette of Legion of Honour in his
button-hole as symbol of his Continental status. Reflected, driving
back, on how necessary it was for his type of person to have such
symbols, how they liked them.

Typed memorandum on talks with Monty; then lunched
upstairs with Camrose, guest of honour being Portuguese Ambassador – an ex-professor (like Salazar) now big business. We
spoke of Gulbenkian, Armenian oil magnate who lives in Lisbon
Hotel. Camrose slightly annoyed when Ambassador (named
Ulrich) said that Gulbenkian had £200–£300 million. 'Is he
happy?' Camrose asked eagerly, and Ulrich (to my delight) replied:
'Yes, I think so.' I weighed in to say that I never could understand
this business of the burden of wealth, being always myself in the
position of wanting to shoulder some. This also didn't please
Camrose, but did his son, Michael, sitting beside me, immensely.
The Ambassador got up to go saying he must attend his Atlantic
Pact talks. It was just like a cartoon from the *Daily Worker*; and,
of course there is much validity in the Communist diagnosis, but
not in the cure.

January 18, 1951

Lunched with the Israeli ambassador Elath whom I'd known in
Washington as Epstein – large, solemn, virtuous, man; his wife
really rather beautiful, giving an impression of purity and serenity.
Large house in Avenue Road; next door the Pakistanis, so even
here the two flags fly side by side, Jewish and Arab. Also present
Counsellor of Legation, Kedron, who turned out to be an im-
passioned student of ecclesiastical history. He was shocked when
I said to him that if I was a Frenchman I'd support General de
Gaulle. This led on to my developing my favourite proposition –
that now we have to take sides; no Liberalism, only the destructive

force of Marxist materialism and whatever can or will oppose it. He agreed on the whole, but said it was very wretched, that he'd like to contract out. 'Ah,' I said, 'so would we all, but it can't be done. And anything's better than pretence.' Thought about the Jews afterwards – how what is attractive in them is that they never quite make terms with life – which gives them their genius for religion and for humour, but also is liable to make them highly destructive – two great destroyers of Christian civilization Marx and Freud, the one replacing the gospel of love by the gospel of hate, and the other undermining the essential concept of individual responsibility; always and irretrievably strangers in a strange land – the terrible image of the Wandering Jew, Ahasuerus, always moving on, never assimilated, bringing woe with him. In a sense, therefore, Hitler's mania was justified – but he justified it. The prophecy is always fulfilled because the will which conceived it makes it come true.

January 19, 1951

Spent morning with another MI6 character, this time from Belgium. Whole proceedings had to be in French. However, got along, but found it distinctly odd sitting in a Hammersmith flat discussing what would happen under a Red Army occupation etc.

Usual drill at *Daily Telegraph*. Drove back with Ziman who suits a Sunday evening in January. The compositors suddenly produced a chap who, they insisted, was my double. They said he'd always wanted to draw attention to this fact, but had been too shy. Chap himself quite delighted, and so was I. Whole episode somewhat warming – as it always is when you find that human beings whom you pass in vacancy or indifference, or even embarrassment, are interested in you as an individual. Life warm and touching when it is personal; cold, inhuman, cruel, when it is not. God had to become a man to be a God.

January 22, 1951

Strolled round the terraces with Kitty after supper, and heard a woman scream. Went to see what was the matter and found woman with dog on a lead whimpering. Said she's been attacked. Man lurking nearby looked suspicious, but on closer investigation it turned out that he and woman, both more or less drunk, had had a row and she'd screamed to disconcert him. Altogether my knight errantry had rather a Don Quixote outcome.

January 24, 1951

With Christopher Chancellor of Reuters, and Philip Jordan discussed question of Communist infiltration of Press. Strongly urged that MI5 should make what information it had available thereby preventing the sort of thing that's recently happened to Chancellor in sending a chap to Korea for Reuters who turns out to be a Party member.

January 30, 1951

Stanley Morison talked about Alan Pryce-Jones, and confirmed that he's been received into RC Church and in the same week withdrawn again. Stanley said he couldn't understand. Told him that the key perhaps was to be found in Keynes's brief memoir: *My Early Beliefs*. Alan belonged to this galère, but uneasily. Thought it still might be possible not to take sides.

Dined with Kitty, and Natasha and Andrew Ronalds. Natasha perhaps has second sight, makes strange uncannily perceptive observations in the midst of wild chatter. She said that Pan was a saint to make up for all my sins.

January 31, 1951

Had a talk with Harold Macmillan who expects a war in May. He gave interesting description of de Gaulle, who said to him on one occasion – 'Les Anglais sont embêtants, les Americains sont fatiguants, et les Russes sont inquiétants.'

February 3–4, 1951

Drove down to Sevenoaks to lunch with Thelma Cazalet. We
talked a lot about the Wodehouses. Good remark of P.G.'s at the
zoo: he said of a baboon with a particularly flamboyant behind
that it was wearing its school colours at the wrong end.

Kitty went off to see John who's written in some distress. Much
moved by Kitty's reply – humorous, sympathetic, understanding.
One phrase stuck in my mind – 'Your slightest worry is my worry.'

February 19, 1951

Finished off article on Wells for *The Times Literary Supplement*
which rather pleased me. At *Daily Telegraph* started working on
article on Soviet Documents on Foreign Affairs. Looked in for a
drink with Douglas Jerrold who's very keen we should take a house
together in the country. Said his chief requirement was a large
garden in which he could lose week-end guests, and that he wanted
to be near Stellenbosch Generals. No Stellenbosch Generals left,
of course, and if there were Douglas wouldn't want to know them.

Tosco Fyvel described his recent visit to Austria; how at first
he'd felt, as a Jew, personally affronted, but after a while he'd
come to feel that individuals can't be held responsible for history.
Foolishly I asked him if he's still got any relations in Vienna, and
he said no; an old uncle who had gone blind was put in the gas
chamber, etc. It gave me one of those sudden turns of horror – a
sense one has sub-consciously all the time, but only now and again
consciously, that one is living through the total disintegration of a
civilization.

February 23, 1951

Kitty and I went to the ballet (*Sleeping Beauty*), Moira Shearer
dancing, but very icy. Rest of ballet not particularly good. Noticed
how female ballet dancers all get curious bird-like faces, almost
indistinguishable from one another. Men quite odious. Apart from
ballet always love Covent Garden Opera House, superb in its rich
and completely satisfying expression of what it is supposed to be –

which is the essence of all loveliness. Don't really care for ballet
as a form though – too abstract for my taste.

February 25, 1951

Went along with Cholerton to Trafalgar Square, where Com-
munist-inspired ex-Servicemen's Movement for Peace was holding a meeting. Watched the preparations with great interest – weak
faced character in a kilt arranging Union Jack; bagpipes rather
wheezily struck up ('the People's Republic of Scotland', Chol
remarked), other characters arriving; sellers of literature, mostly
female, circulating in the audience; clergyman, for whom I felt a
particular loathing. The proceedings began with recitation by
kilted character of Binyon's *For the Fallen* and a minute's silence.
Thought that such a pitiable proceedings represented, after all,
decrepitude even of the Communist Party, whose real mystique is
revolution, down with the rich, the mighty dethroned and the
humble and meek exalted in their place. This shabby, dog-eared
parody of a shabby ceremonial provided no effective substitute.
While the clergyman and the others were standing for the minute's
silence, felt nostalgia for Uncle Joe, who can at least be relied on
to sweep such canaille into oblivion.

February 27, 1951

Letter from Downing Street to ask whether, if a Civil List pension
was given to Dorothy Kingsmill in favour of her daughter, I'd
agree to act as trustee. After talking the matter over with Trelawny
Irving, he said that the other daughter had got a job in Paris dancing
at the Lido. Marvelled at such fulfilment of Hughie's determination not to be a Methodist; at the ultimate realization of Sir Henry
Lunn's suppressed desires; at how everything must work itself out
to its ultimate consequences – a stone dropped into Time's pool,
and the ripples widening out to eternity. Imagined just how
Hughie would have announced this item of news.

Amused to learn that American tie manufacturers had applied

for permission to reproduce fragment of Boswell's *London Journal* on one of their ties. Application refused by Yale University – which would have annoyed Boswell, who on one occasion put placard with legend 'Corsica Boswell' in his hat to indicate who he was. Which passage would the manufacturers have chosen?

March 7, 1951

Went to Ivy to lunch with Aneurin Bevan and Philip Jordan. Bevan very luxuriant person, rich voice, warm personality. Fancies himself as a political theorist. We talked about the Press, he most resentful of newspaper attacks, even very obscure ones. Said that he thought the Government should be entitled to two columns in all newspapers to present its case, and I indicated that I considered this impractical. Soon we were on Nye and Malcolm terms, talking away. After all, for me he's much easier person to get along with, more stimulating, than, say, Eden. He said he thought most despicable newspaper was the *News Chronicle*, with which I cordially agreed. Spoke of Beaverbrook, with whom at one time he's been very friendly. Knowing someone like Beaverbrook, he said, from his point of view, brought great advantage that he met all sorts of people – Lloyd George, Winston, etc. Once he was with Beaverbrook and noticed on the table a copy of *Ecclesiasticus*. Opened it at passage which, he remarked, exactly described his relations with Beaverbrook:

> 'Press thou not upon him (the rich man) lest thou be
> put back; stand not far off, lest thou be forgotten.'

Beaverbrook often offered him a highly paid job, but he wouldn't take it because he knew it wouldn't last. I aired my favourite thesis that, whether we like it or not, society is becoming monolithic, and therefore party government, free Press etc., are ceasing to have any validity and must wither away. He largely agreed. We inevitably talked about Russia, which, he said, like the Welfare regime in this country, had suffered through devoting an undue proportion of the national income to capital expenditure. Wondered about him afterwards, what he was worth, what he could be expected to achieve, and decided that, though intelligent and able, he was somehow soft, and so not capable of a major role except briefly.

All the same, parted from him with a sense of exhilaration, due to having communed with someone rather than no one. Most people shadows of shadows.

March 8, 1951

Lunched with Hesketh Pearson. Gladys now gone to hospital, and Hesketh in slightly hysterical state about it.

Later heard that Gladys Pearson was dead. Of course, a merciful release etc., yet these phrases, when it comes to the point, scarcely valid; death a fact about which there's nothing to say.

March 11, 1951

Dark, sombre day. Sat in *Daily Telegraph* office surveying the news and particularly conscious of the crack-up everywhere. Read account of rubber boom in Singapore – Rolls Royces etc. Plot in Pakistan, racial legislation in South Africa; demand for self-government in the Sudan, for 'nationalization' of oil production in Persia; here prices rising, everything getting scarcer; in Paris Ernest Davies (of all people) arguing with Gromyko; aged Count Sforza, decrepit de Gasperi, on their way to London . . .

March 12, 1951

Kitty low spirited, so I took her into town to lunch. We strolled up and down St James's Park, always interested in people going past. Among others noted Anthony Eden, as it were shrinking from being noticed, and at the same time asking to be noticed; quite white now except for a patch of yellow, like a nicotine stain on his moustache; somehow unco-ordinated, legs, arms, head at variance.

March 14, 1951

Monty very pleased with himself because he'd got a paper from Eisenhower specifying that he was to be Eisenhower's deputy as

Supreme Commander NATO with numerous vaguely defined duties and large but indeterminate responsibilities. He showed me this paper, already creased from much handling. His function, he said, was 'to binge things up'. Described Eisenhower's Head-quarters at Hotel Astoria – complete confusion, people coming and going, Eisenhower himself on the verge of hysteria. Monty said he didn't propose to be there much himself; he'd be 'travelling'; would work in his garden at Fontainebleau and have helicopter to go to and from Eisenhower's HQ when it was set up in Marly.

Started re-reading St Augustine's *Confessions*, one of the world's truly remarkable works. Thought of Augustine living at a time rather like ours, barbarians sacking Rome etc., and taking little or no account of these events; concerned rather with how 'I had grown deaf from the clanking of the chain of my mortality': his love of words, of expressing himself; his sensuality ('earth going unto earth'); his delight in success ('I loved the vanity of victory'); the wonderful picture of his childhood, his parents' poor circum-stances; their ambitions for him. All, to me, most moving and wonderful.

March 17, 1951

Drove down with the Jerrolds to look at houses. First one, at Brasted, near Westerham, just the house. Felt it at once – solid, large, light; former rectory, and, I guessed, connected with Oxford Movement. Drove on to Tunbridge Wells which Douglas had known as a child. Said that it now seemed much smaller. Took us to hotel for lunch which he recommended as largest and newest in the place. Laughed loud and long when it turned out to be miserable shabby little place. We were all very excited over the house, and Eleanor Jerrold and I were insistent we were going to live there. Said to Kitty afterwards that it would be possible to share a house with the Jerrolds because one was fond of them and respected them without liking their company.

Went on reading St Augustine, marvelling how a book can continue to shed light, actual radiance; how from centuries ago the plight of a fellow human can seem so precisely one's own, each word valid, each emotion comprehensible.

March 20, 1951

Went to Coliseum to see *Kiss Me Kate*. On the whole much taken with the show, especially *Brush Up Your Shakespeare, Faithful to you, Darling, After my Fashion*. Would personally, for these American musicals, exchange Anouilh, Sartre, T. S. Eliot, and throw in Christopher Fry for good measure. Love their humour, their vitality, and the authentic poetry of their lyrics.

March 22, 1951

American journalist, Williams, one of the editors of *Life* magazine, is doing a piece on Aneurin Bevan, and wanted to know my views, which I gave him. Said that Bevan was, essentially, a power-addict, and, like all such addicts (Hitler, for instance) greatly given to self-pity. Although, so far as the Conservatives were concerned, in the current political morality play he was cast for the role of villain, actually he'd mixed more with the upper classes than most Labour Party leaders. His refusal to wear evening dress was sound demagogic instinct, but in point of fact evening dress occasions were far more familiar to him than to, say, respectable Mr Attlee. All the same, he was the most interesting and considerable figure in English politics at this time. His greatest weakness was his mistaken belief in himself as a political theorist; his greatest strength his love of power, which would prevent him from ever in any sense being a fellow traveller or accepting stooge positions vis-à-vis the Kremlin.

March 23, 1951

Drove down to Hastings with Tosco Fyvel and Kitty; took a walk by the sea; then went to Beckley to see Gerald Reitlinger. Hadn't visited the house since before the war – Gerald himself shrunken. Sits in his study with an oil stove on either side of him writing a history of the annihilation of the Jews. No more visitors, spongers, parties, travels. Second wife has left him, first (Varda) lately committed suicide. Tosco said afterwards that writing the history of the annihilation of the Jews was an act of atonement for his efforts not to be a Jew.

March 26–27, 1951

Went on reading St Augustine. Interested to note that he left
Carthage, where he had been teaching, to go to Rome because in
Carthage his students were so undisciplined ('the licence of the
students is gross, and beyond all measure'). Convinced more than
ever that St Augustine, and those like him, alone have found the
answer to life, which is to 'slaughter our self-conceits like birds,
the curiosities by which we voyage through the secret ways of the
abyss like the fish of the sea, our carnal lusts like the beasts of the
field' in order that 'you, O God, you the consuming fire, should
burn up those dead cares and renew the men themselves to
immortal life.'

Walking round St James's Park I thought intensely of the
difference between Tolstoy and St Augustine. Tolstoy tried to
achieve virtue, and particularly continence, through the exercise
of his will; St Augustine saw that, for Man, there is no virtue
without a miracle. Thus St Augustine's asceticism brought him
serenity, and Tolstoy's anguish, conflict, and the final collapse of
his life into tragic buffoonery.

March 30, 1951

Lunched at the Savoy with Persian Press Attaché, Hamzavi.
Talked about present Persian troubles, and he was really very
shrewd and sensible. Very Anglophile, but worried. Said that
present Persian Prime Minister, Ala, was a great friend of his, and
that there had been some talk of his going into the Cabinet. It
seemed to me, however, that, in existing circumstances, he preferred humbler post in London. Obviously what he wanted was
direct British intervention in South Persia. Expressed considerable
contempt for Anglo–Iranian oil people. I said business men were
always foolish and short-sighted politically because as long as they
were seeking profits they assumed all was well – e.g. Shanghai
business men who now praise Mao Tse-tung. Added that this inherent foolishness and short-sightedness was what brought
Capitalism tumbling down much more than Marxist 'contradictions'. He agreed. Said that a member of Persian Parliament
(Majlis) was now in London, and he'd asked him why he voted for

nationalization of oil. Character replied that, just before leaving for that particular session he'd been visited by tough-looking personage who'd produced mauser revolver and intimated in no uncertain manner how he was expected to vote. Hamzavi said that arrangements under the old Shah were really happier. Then one man had taken bribes, now many, this representing, as far as Persian was concerned, difference between dictatorship and democracy. We sighed together over the incalculable damage done by pursuit of political mirages – the British and Americans self-righteously sending Riza Khan packing and creating this shambles. Laughed to think of how neatly history puts the pin in the butterfly drearily proclaiming infallible virtues of nationalization, and now, with the fag-end of British power in their hands, confronted with demand of Mauser-driven Majlis for nationalization of Persian Oil industry.

March 31, 1951

Much amused by Tony Powell's account of staying with Evelyn Waugh. House not very large with huge coat of arms, Herbert's on one side, Waugh's (from College of Heralds) on the other. Depressed manservant who wore morning coat in the evening. All the contents of the house Victorian, and, as Tony said, looking as though just bought. Waugh can't stand any of his neighbours except an old-fashioned leftist Etonian with whom he consorts. He said he wishes there was a Big House nearby where he would be patronised and a Little House with a 'nice young couple' living in it whom he could patronise.

April 2, 1951

Decided that whatever happened, every day I'd read something other than newspapers, books about contemporary affairs, etc. Read Hughie Kingsmill's introduction to his anthology *The High Hill of the Muses*. One sentence particularly evoked him – 'Byron was indissolubly bound to his ego in a three-legged race which brought the two of them crashing to the ground when barely half the course was run.'

April 4, 1951

Looked in to see Randolph Churchill in the London Clinic, where he's having his Korean wound attended to – immense figure propped up in bed, drinking and smoking, writing letters to newspapers, telephoning etc.; a sort of parody of a man of action; of his father, indeed. We talked about politics. Poor Randolph, who looks almost as old as Winston, still trying to be wild young man of destiny.

April 7, 1951

On the way back from visiting new house at Brasted had time to spare, so visited Croydon Town Hall in the expectation of finding there a photograph of my father. Asked the porter, who remembered him well, but no photograph. Large portraits beside stairway of past mayors, whose names I remembered – Trumble, Edridge, etc. Also Town Clerk, Newnham. Looked in at Council Chamber, which I hadn't seen since, as a child, I sat in the gallery and saw my father among the councillors below. Quite a small place, with elegant red chairs bearing Croydon arms, and large chair in which the Mayor presided. Asked at the library if there was a photograph of Mr Muggeridge and girl there said: 'You mean Malcolm Muggeridge?' Rather confusing, and destructive of my mood of filial piety. Had tea with my mother, who seemed very pale and forgetful and near the end of her days.

April 8, 1951

Read George Orwell's *The Road to Wigan Pier*, and thought much about him, especially in the light of the second autobiographical part. Odd manias – as that the poor are believed by the middle-classes to smell, and that this is the basic cause of class feeling; that Orientals have pleasanter bodies than Occidentals because they are less hairy. Many of his statements extravagantly false – as when he speaks of lower upper-middle-class families with £400 a year and two resident servants. The fact is he knew nothing about the ordinary life he specialized in describing – George Orwell, the unproletarian proletarian.

April II, 1951

Rung up at ten o'clock in the morning with the news that Truman had given MacArthur the sack, and so had to go straight to the office and do a piece on MacArthur. Altogether an extremely strenuous day, solid work.

Impressions of a busy week

Masses of news – Budget backwash, MacArthur back in America and addresses Congress, Persia sinking into chaos, Attlee Government disintegrating, Dockers tried and discharged, Mrs Braddock chaired, etc., etc.

Visit to Anthony Eden – little shabby-smart house in Mayfair, Chesteron Street off Curzon Street; seated with him talking and drinking rather stingily concocted martinis. Habit of getting up and straightening a picture, then standing back. Weak face, with protruding teeth, mark of vanity. He said he couldn't make up his mind whether he ought to go to the Foreign Office or to be Leader of the House (assuming, of course, the Conservatives get into power), and I said he should try and do both, with good deputies. This pleased him enormously. About Winston, he said gravely that his health was not as good as people thought, and that he could speak of this with an easy conscience because, as far as his own private inclinations were concerned, he'd vastly rather be Foreign Secretary than Prime Minister. The only funny remark was when he said, in answer to my question as to whether the Attlee Government was likely to fall soon: 'I don't think Winston can hold them together much longer.'

Curious Kafka-like dream, immensely vivid. I was under arrest for some crime, probably murder. Whether I was guilty or not didn't seem to trouble me greatly. Probably I was guilty of some crime or other, but that seemed far away and not to matter much. It appeared that I was allowed out of my prison from time to time, but I always had to return. I was always conscious of the prison, yet the prison itself was not a place of bars and locked doors but a small, bare house, of whose back rooms I was terrified. Once when I was out I saw a woman outside her house, and her husband

arrived and asked for food. She spoke to him shortly, and he
answered back sharply, and soon they were quarrelling, their
faces distorted with rage and hate. I rushed up to them and said
that hatred and anger were devilish and never in any circumstances
justified, and suddenly, in my dream, I had one of those moments
of comprehension when the universe and human life in it make
sense. This was accompanied by a feeling of inexpressible happiness. I went back to my prison quite cheerfully, though everyone
else was moving in the opposite direction, and thought how really
quite pleasant a place it was. I even looked at the dreaded back
rooms, and found that they, too, were harmless and clean. Then
I reflected: 'How lucky I am to be here. I might be in the town
prison with all the ordinary criminals.' At this reflection another
great burst of feeling seized me, and I thought to myself: 'The
ordinary criminals are no different from me. It might be a privilege
to be with them. I might be able to help them and they me.'

Lunching at Claridge's with the Israeli ambassador Elath – he
agreed with me that the trouble with our times was that things were
happening now which should have happened three or four decades
ago. He was very Jewish when he said that Israel was a poor country,
but that this circumstance had been advantageous because if it
had not been poor the Jews would never have been allowed to have
it.

Kitty described how she met a gipsy at the front door who said to
her: 'Buy something from a gipsy, smiling face.' She bought
something, of course, but it is a good description of Kitty.

A week of politics – April 22–29, 1951

Went up to Downing Street to see Philip Jordan – seemingly
almost deserted (Prime Minister still away in hospital, sipping his
gruel and reading Arthur Bryant), two or three uniformed mes-
sengers hanging around. Sat talking with Philip about Bevan
episode – was it a rebellion or a revolution? Suspected it might be
the latter, Bevan being angry and demented; a fit instrument.

Malaya, 1952

January 11, 1952

I went to see Oliver Lyttelton, Colonial Secretary. Decided to walk to Colonial Office, and then found to my horror I'd arrived at the Commonwealth Relations Office. Asked various people where the Colonial Office was, but no one seemed to know. Finally located it at Church House, in Great Smith Street, very provisional sort of set-up. Struck me that this decline, if not disintegration, of the Colonial Office from Arthur Dawe's time was highly symptomatic.

Lyttelton himself large man with thick neck and, I thought, a bit distraught. We talked about Malaya – and inadequacy of police, phoneyness of ostensible political organizations, difficulties of conducting political warfare when unnecessarily large number of local inhabitants detained without trial owing to police incompetence. Lyttelton tended to walk up and down as he talked. A change at the top, he said, might make all the difference, but administration itself paper-logged. Promises of eventual self-government had to be maintained, but actually it would be a matter of at least thirty years before anything of the kind would be possible. Great difficulty, he said, was that the police were largely Malays and the Bandits Chinese. Also that Chinese were liable to pay out money to bandits to procure protection against attack and to re-insure in case of British walk-out on Indian model. He defended Malcolm Mac-Donald, but tepidly. Not a very satisfactory interview.

At the *Daily Telegraph* was rung up by Monty who said he'd hoped to show me various papers connected with Malaya, and suggested I should come over to Paris to see them. It meant leaving at once without any luggage. One of the *Daily Telegraph* drivers got me to the Air Terminal just in time.

Found Monty waiting up for me in his Chateau near Fontaine-bleau with a large log fire burning – a draughty, majestic sort of place, very beautiful outside, as I saw in the morning, but inside not in particularly good taste, more like one of those royal or ducal households preserved as a museum, than a present residence. He took me up to my room, also vast, with canopied four-poster bed, and we sat talking by the fire. As I had no pyjamas he fetched a pair of his, thick, flannel, which he rather touched me by laying out in front of the fire to warm. He told me all about Malaya, his conversations with Churchill and Lyttelton, and left me to read various documents, which I did by the fire and drinking whiskey which he insisted on providing.

January 12, 1952

Lay in bed thinking about Malaya, Monty, Western defence. No possibility really of staying the dry rot. To Monty it seemed possible, and perhaps because of that, for him it would be possible. Not for a Lyttelton, or Anthony Eden, however. They were themselves part of the rot.

After another long talk with Monty drove into Paris; RASC driver said he didn't like living at Monty's Chateau, too lonely, and in the summer nowhere to bathe. As a matter of fact, I shouldn't myself much like living there; *morne* unreal, except for Monty himself, who, however bizarre, is real and alive, a good man who understands much in essentials but little in detail; the precise converse of an intellectual.

January 15, 1952 – Singapore

Met at airport by Bill Dobbs, who took me to press conference at which Malcolm MacDonald, the Governor-General, announced General Templer's appointment as High Commissioner for Malaya.

Reflected that any world crisis developed rival passions – blood-thirstiness and money-thirstiness. The pattern is the same everywhere. Here rubber and tin, like oil in the Middle East, pro-ducing a wild abundance of money, which is itself invalidated by the uses to which rubber, tin, and oil are put – mad money cupidity and mad power cupidity growing apace.

January 16, 1952

Had long talk about Malayan economics with official named Brennan, shrewdish, of the Treasury sort. Went over the economic consequences of the Emergency:

1. Costing locally about £20m. but some of this non-emergency expenditure. Costing British Government probably about £50m.

2. Emergency building requirements such as additional police stations have prevented other desperately needed building such as housing and schools.

3. Rubber and tin production maintained but much thieving, probably largely on behalf of the bandits.

4. In the case of tin, no new prospecting; in the case of rubber, not as much new planting and usage of better plant breeds as there should be.

Went on to Sir John Hay, the Managing Director of big rubber company, Guthrie's. We talked about why no leadership, futile handling of Malayan emergency, etc. Also, inevitably explained that Guthrie's profits were not particularly high, and that welfare on their estates was impeccable. All the same, by no means a fool, and indicated awareness from time to time that he knew the game might be nearly up. Struck by immense influence of Maugham on British in Malaya, so many of them either trying both not to be, and at the same time to be, like the characters he describes.

January 17, 1952

Talked with chap named Rayner about psychological warfare in Malaya. Tried him out on difficulties of psychological warfare to which he produced cogent answers.

(a) How to fit in Nehru as part of the 'free' Commonwealth and as public supporter of Mao Tse-tung and Dr Mossadeq?

(b) What about the Korean War?

(c) How to fit in British today and recognizing Peking with bandit war in which the enemy look to Peking for direction and support?

(d) How to extol merits of free society when, partly owing to bandit war, Malaya isn't a free society?

Drove out to Malcolm MacDonald's house for lunch, former palace of Sultan of Johore, highly ornate, wonderful view. Largeish party, mostly officials. Talked to Mrs MacDonald about Bedales and asked her if she intended to send her children there, and she said with great emphasis 'not for anything'. Stayed on to talk to MacDonald who takes his tone and such from his company, and quickly realized that his usual line of talk wouldn't go down with me, so became cynical – Machiavellian. He'd say things like: 'With great difficulty we got the Malay and the Chinese to agree . . .' Asked him who were 'the Malay', 'the Chinese', and of course it turned out to be two corrupt politicians, a Chinese and a Malay, meeting at his table and hiccuping out acceptance of some formula imperfectly understood by both. I said it reminded me very much of his father Ramsay, at the Indian Round Table Conference, which he didn't much like.

January 18, 1952

Went to see General Keighley, C-in-C, East Asia. He had the usual large map and gave the usual explanations, waving his hand about. All very unreal, I thought. Anyway, what can he do with his division missing in Hong Kong and bandit war in Malaya? Felt once more how unrelated his set-up and the war already being fought. Quite polite, answered questions – was there really any point in keeping troops in Hong Kong when the Chinese could take the place any time, and only didn't because, for the time being, it suited them that it should keep its present status? I asked. Questions, as usual, not really designed to get information, but formality convenient to both sides.

Drove afterwards into Jopore, met resettlement officer named Thompson who'd been with Wingate. Went out to look at re-settlement areas; barbed wire round them, guards not very formidable looking. Chinese squatters brought into these re-settlement areas with the idea of keeping them out of contact with bandits. Scheme hasn't worked, and end-result bears uneasy resemblance to concentration camp.

Climbed up wooden tower with Thompson and looked around – easy to see how little security the re-settlement areas afforded; jungle so near, wire perimeter so easy to get under, etc. Thompson said that concern for agriculture and for security incompatible; he pointed out small pepper field which police had wanted to remove because they considered it provided useful bandit cover. But compensation to owner would be some thousands of dollars. The other side wouldn't have cared.

On the way back, looked at Chinese School, rather charming. Chinese genuinely keen on learning, and so school impressive. Thompson said that he often wondered how Wingate would have reacted to Malay situation, and thought that probably he'd have got fed up with Malay incompetence and fecklessness and have inclined to build everything on the Chinese. I agreed, and knew that if I stayed in Malaya I'd go the same way.

Talked with influential Chinese named Tan about getting Chinese cooperation in fighting bandits. Very softly, almost music-ally, he said that it was difficult to present the matter in terms of freedom when the Chinese weren't free to become Malayan citizens. Shouldn't there, he whispered, be more idealism? Shouldn't it all be put on a higher plane? Something a little devilish even frighten-ing. Tan could so easily have been right in the bandit show; probably was – likewise putting that on a higher plane.

January 19, 1952

Went off in the early morning by plane to Kuala Lumpur. Drove very fast out to Taneh Mareh, Snoxhill's estate, seventy miles distant, especially where bank was high. Incidentally, arrange-ments for meeting not made over phone, as this considered insecure. Snoxhill produced a bandit's cap, found near body of his assistant, murdered three days ago. Embroidered red star, very small. We passed it from hand to hand – factory made, not improvized. Mrs Snoxhill said she'd seen a dead bandit in the jungle, a woman with tiny feet. The minuteness of her feet had given a moment's pity. Then the conversation proceeded – how they might well all have been murdered when the bandit war began; how it never need have begun at all if the advice of those who knew had been heeded by Government.

January 20, 1952

Drove to club at Port Dickson. Talked with planters, some quite intelligent, but basically dispirited – the two shocks, first of being so easily captured by the Japanese, and now this bandit war, too much for them; oddly old-fashioned in their ways and costume (more than one monocle to be seen) – for *Cherry Orchard* read *Rubber Plantation*.

January 21, 1952

At Army HQ, Kuala Lumpur, chatted with Information Officer who showed me map of bandit order of battle, but agreed that constitutional set-up made effective action impossible. He pointed out that bandits, fortunately, not very efficient, bad marksmen, etc. Otherwise, they might have cleaned up.

Lunched with Louis Heren of *The Times* and character named Jack Brazier, Trade Union figure who is in Malaya to organize 'respectable' Trade Unions. Brazier gave long dissertation on necessity for Trade Unionism, and how he'd been along to very dangerous spot to help organize a strike. Propaganda value of such a strike extraordinary, he said, as indicating that 'good' Trade Unions were genuine. In the same way holes blown in synthetic gryère cheese. Not bad chaps, I suppose.

Drove to airport, took plane to Ipoh. Met there by Ian Patterson. He'd been terrified that I'd get caught up in what he called the 'party line', but I soon reassured him on this score. He considers that Templer represents last hope of saving Malaya. As it is, the corruption and muddle is almost overwhelming. Honest, conscientious civil servants have had just as much as they can stand in the way of strain, and if now the change of Government at home, Lyttelton's visit, etc., doesn't mean a new start, they'll pack up.

January 22, 1952

Went along with British Adviser's Personal Assistant to see Mentri Besar, Prime Minister of State of Perak. We talked about the Federal Constitution, and I said I couldn't understand it, and in any case considered it ought to be suspended. To my surprise, he agreed with this, though he took it a little hard that I couldn't understand the Constitution because, he said, he'd been largely responsible for drafting it. Again and again given the feeling that this Malayan affair is Indian repeat performance, with touring company and small inferior stage and lighting, but same lines and cast.

Points which emerge in every conversation as essential to any serious effort to bring Chinese into anti-bandit effort: (1) Malayan citizenship,.(2) Land ownership.

1953–1957

'Punch' Diary, 1953–1957

Towards the end of 1952, when I was deputy editor of the
Daily Telegraph, *Christopher Chancellor, then head of*
Reuters, asked me if I would be interested in taking on the
editorship of Punch. *I have always been all too ready to*
entertain suggestions of this kind, and, in fact, apart from
the seven-and-a-half years with the Daily Telegraph, *have*
never stayed in any job for more than four years – which, I
suppose, indicates a restless and unstable disposition; also an
incapacity to take any gainful employment as other than a
passing convenience. So I told Chancellor I would be interested,
and shortly afterwards found myself editor of Punch. *The*
only qualification I had for editing a humorous magazine was
a great love of laughter – if, indeed, that was a qualification.
Otherwise, I was quite at sea, and continued so to be throughout
my editorship, even though I inveigled on to my staff old friends
like Anthony Powell, Christopher Hollis and John Betjeman.
It was the only time in my life that I could be said to be part of
the Establishment apparat, *in the sense that Lear's Fool was*
part of his court.

January 1, 1953

Dined last evening at the Garrick with the Chancellors, the Agnews and Lady Chancellor's sister, Lady Glenconner. All very hearty, and talked about *Punch* under my editorship. Agnew senior very sold on me at the moment, very certain that I'll made a success of the job. I feel doubtful and uneasy about it myself, but attribute this mainly to the change of job.

Went along to *Punch* printing wotks where Kenneth Bird and H. F. Ellis were reading proofs. Later saw Percy Cudlipp at Garrick. Suggested to him that *Punch* should publish a Diary of a Somebody in which Mr Pooter has become Lord Pooter, Labour peer. Who better than the Editor of the *Daily Herald* to do it?

Then to the *Daily Telegraph* for the last time. Went up to see Camrose and Michael Berry to say goodbye. Both very genial. Delighted to be leaving without ill-feeling. Then over to Falstaff for presentation. Practically everyone there, office quite denuded. Colin Coote made usual speech, and I followed, truly moved. Presentation was silver inkstand of Punch and two Judies, majestic object, formerly in Royal Horse Artillery mess. Much pleased with it. Went back to *Daily Telegraph* and into composing room, where printers all banged their machines in token of goodbye.

January 4, 1953

Pakenhams came to dinner. He talked rather well, with vivid sense of absurdity of things. For instance, good description of Attlee, how conversation languishes. Awful moment recently when, at a party given by Gaitskell, he got wedged against a wall with Attlee and couldn't adopt his usual practice of escaping before conversation, bravely begun, died on him. Another occasion at Downing Street when he, Pakenham, had delivered an ultimatum about German policy, and Attlee came breezing in with: 'Hullo, Frank,' and then, when sternly reminded of Pakenham's letter threatening resignation, went on to say the whole matter at issue (continuance of dismantling of German industrial plant) would be reconsidered. Good additional touch was that decorators were working in Cabinet Room, so that this encounter, so momentous in Pakenham's eyes, took place in a small adjoining room in front of two secretaries.

In Kingsley Martin's book on Harold Laski a long letter from Attlee quoted (May 1, 1944) in which following passage occurs: 'I am sorry that you suggest I am verging towards MacDonaldism. As you have so well pointed out I have neither the personality nor the distinction to think that I shall have any value apart from the Party which I serve.'

January 5, 1953

Went to *Punch* for the first time. Office very strange. Lit fire, dictated some letters, etc.

Lunched with Osbert Lancaster and John Betjeman. They will do series on Public Schools, beginning with Winchester and Gresham's and to be illustrated with Old Boys of Distinction. Felt very lost still.

January 9, 1953

Feliks Topolski looked in, and we discussed possible contributions.

Lunched with Kitty and Ian and Ann Fleming (former Lady Rothermere). Ian gave me a slight pang by saying there had been talk of making me Editor of the *Sunday Times*. Ian definitely a slob, and difficult to see why Ann fell for him.

January 10–11, 1953

Stephen Spender came down in the morning. His observations about his friends quite diverting. He says, for instance, of Cyril Connolly that he would have looked well in 18th-century costume which 'showed up grease spots so admirably'. Of Sonia (Orwell) that her camp bed has been used by a whole succession of decamping wives. Our talk floated round a projected magazine, connected with the Congress for Cultural Freedom. Stephen, of all things, wants to run a magazine.

Learnt with apprehension that Kitty is to have operation, about which I feel abnormally apprehensive, though doubtless because of memories of when she was last operated on.

January 11–12, 1953

Ionesco, formerly a Rumanian diplomat and now in exile in London, came over for tea. Somewhat embarrassed when he said he'd read all through last number of *Punch*. Tried to explain that it'd be a matter of months before I had *Punch* under control. It seems that in *The Listener* my discussion with Bertrand Russell on television is highly praised. Can't but think of him as vainglorious, ape-like. The true destroyer of Christendom isn't Stalin or Hitler or even the Dean of Canterbury and his like, but Liberalism.

Discussions about new arrangements for going to press, etc. Osbert Lancaster came in, and I then took him off to lunch at the Savoy with Russell Brockbank, Art Editor of *Punch*, very nice Canadian and a great standby for me. Everything beginning to get a bit more manageable.

January 13, 1953

At *Punch* presided over the Table* with greater ease than hitherto. General reaction to first piece I'd ever contributed to *Punch*, on Kingsley Martin's book on Laski, quite favourable.

Arthur Koestler told me that one of the accused at the Prague Trial (Simone, real or former name, Katz) in his confession actually quoted some sentences from *Darkness at Noon*, presumably as a signal to the West, or even because these sentences alone fitted his case. In the beginning was the word . . .

January 14, 1953

Beginning to get used to going to Bouverie Street and to forget the *Daily Telegraph*. People come in all the time, and I try to get to know the staff and to suggest more topical articles and drawings. Tell everyone, and indeed believe, that my chief purpose is to make *Punch* again social history. This would be worth doing. John Betjeman came in with the piece he's written on Winchester.

[1] Weekly gathering over lunch in the office primarily to discuss the main political cartoon for the next issue. On the table on which lunch was served previous editors had carved their initials. Participants in this function were known as Members of the Table.

I dined with A. P. Herbert. He's oddly broken-down, uneasy figure considering how ostensibly successful he's been, and, I think, resents finding himself as it were under me. Tells anecdotes well, sympathetically jovial. Joined later by Tony Powell who, to my great delight, has agreed to become Literary Editor of *Punch*.

January 15–18, 1953

Usual routine at printing works. Colm Brogan full of good ideas. Put him on to doing *The Diary of a Somebody*. Much pleased with Illingworth's drawing of Eisenhower taking over Atlas role from Truman.

Dined with Pudneys, also present Lionel Hale. Didn't take to me, nor I to him. Said almost at once how he hated Carlyle. Like one of those opening gambits which, with really good chess players, make all the rest of the game, up to checkmate, inevitable.

Went on to Thelma Cazalet's where Compton Mackenzie was celebrating his 70th birthday. Remembered reading his *Sinister Street* thirty years ago when it seemed very gaslit and terrible in its alluring implications.

January 20–21, 1953

Usual *Punch* Table, discussion of cartoon. A. P. Herbert gave imaginary Churchill speech on subject of MP who has been arrested and charged with importuning men in West End lavatories applying for Chiltern Hundreds. 'Why should the innocent and blameless Chilternian be subjected . . . etc., etc.' *Punch* already becoming familiar routine.

January 21, 1953

Lunch for what Alan Agnew calls 'Heads of Departments'. Discussed advertising, sales, etc. Advertising Manager, Verrinder, presented statistics. Long discussion with Topolski and James Laver about series under consideration on subject of Clothes and the Welfare State. All moving along. Cummings has started doing political drawings.

January 23, 1953

Looked through proofs of next *Punch* number. On the whole thought it improved, especially Cummings' political drawings.

Gave lunch at the Garrick to Israeli ambassador, Elath. Told me that Soviet Ambassador, Zorubin, had once telephoned him to ask whether he'd received invitation to some function or other at which dress was optional, either white tie or dinner jacket. Zorubin furious about this; said it was a 'trap', and that in Moscow they were always specific about such matters. As Elath pointed out, under Soviet or any other totalitarian system discretion intolerable. What everyone wants is orders.

January 24, 1953

Went with Kitty to see my mother. She was just up, and came walking slowly into her sitting room muttering: 'I'm done for, I'm done for.' She makes me feel tormented with pity, but impersonally, as though she had nothing to do with me at all.

Drove on to pick up Val at Banstead, where she's doing her nursing training. Came running out when we arrived in her nurse's uniforn and red cloak to show us what she looked like.

January 29–30, 1953

Full days at *Punch*. Alternate between despondency and confidence. Probably on the whole, in the end it will suit, and I'll make something of it. Concerned now, nearly fifty, to evolve a routine, continuing work instead of sport and collapse. I must do much, much more.

E. V. Knox, at the Garrick, insisted on having a bottle of champagne. Reminisced about *Punch*. Said that Owen Seaman hadn't wanted him to become Editor. Seaman, he said, was strong Baldwinite, who'd destroyed *Punch*'s 'radical' tradition. Whispered to me as a great secret that Max Beerbohm's *Maltby*, the first of his *Seven Men*, was perhaps based on Seaman. Evoe great oddity, gives an impression of being unhappy, but defiantly so; complicated as to religion with background (and fears) of oppressive Evangelicalism.

February 2, 1953

Suggested to Ronald Searle he should do some satirical work in Hogarth manner.

In the evening went to see Randolph Churchill. He was in his usual state, walking up and down; much exercised over *Times* treatment of visit Queen had paid to house of Douglas Fairbanks, junior, for dinner. Randolph particularly indignant because of descriptive jibe of Fairbanks coming into Whites in all his medals and someone saying, 'Captain Hornblower, I believe.'

February 4, 1953

Like everyone else, sick of the winter and dispirited. Floods image of prevailing mood.

Tony Powell looked in and we laughed long over the drawings of André Francois, French (or rather Rumanian) artist. Another good drawing in from Paris. There's a vein here which I mean to exploit.

February 5, 1953

Self-pity, I decided, the cause of all despair. Eliminate it, and nothing to despair about. Walked in the bitter cold to the printing works at Mount Pleasant. Quite exhilarating. Had to get another cartoon done on the floods.

March 2, 1953

Long period of worry. Kitty in hospital, but now all well, and she, to my inexpressible relief, looking much better and coming home from Barts on Wednesday next.

*   *   *

January 1, 1954

First day of New Year, about which I feel personally exhilarated, but otherwise utterly pessimistic. Intimations of senile decay in institutions, etc., of Western Europe most marked. Went along to work and looked at proofs, everyone very cheery. Then to Heinemann, where much laughter over piece in *The Times* headed 'Dylan Thomas's Last Work'. This, it reported, was first published in Italy under the title *Lareggub*. Wanted to put this in *Punch* with the heading *For Backward Readers*.

January 2, 1954

Went shopping with Kitty in Brewer Street – street market, large crowd on a Saturday morning. Kitty loves anything like this, and steers her way around with relentless determination. Had great difficulty in keeping up with her, but fortunately she had red hat which I managed to keep in view.

Read Dostoevsky's *The Possessed* in new Penguin edition entitled *The Devils*; also looked at life of Dostoevsky and some of his letters. Wrote brief piece for BBC Critics. Strolled along to Marble Arch to see film – *From Here to Eternity*. Frank Sinatra in it, and surprisingly good actor. Mood of film Kiplingesque – which is what we'd been expecting from America for some time. Walked back, noting how nowadays much of West End oddly deserted on a Saturday evening.

January 3, 1954

Looked in on my mother, in bed and looking absolutely minute; at last, to my infinite relief, serene, even cheerful. Miss Roffey said she'd lost interest even in the wireless.

January 4, 1954

New number of *Punch* not too bad, but long for it to be better. Miss Dorothy Sayers being troublesome over her article – bad-tempered, large, grey old geyser, but basically a good soul.

Auberon Herbert rang up, and he'd just come over on the special plane with Diana (Cooper) and the coffin containing Duff Cooper's remains. As so often, I marvelled at his odd practical utility; imagined him dealing brilliantly with officials, etc.

January 5, 1954

Bad night full of dark fears. While shaving suddenly thought with infinite longing how, of all things, I'd most love to live a Christian life. This the only wish now I'd ever have. And yet other satisfactions, known to be spurious, still pursued. Discussed next week's *Punch*, had a row with Lady Rhondda on the phone because I'd agreed to write piece on Duff Cooper, and then said I wouldn't. A foolish rich old woman, but all the same I was upset at quarrelling with her.

Later Tony Powell agreed with me that the death of Duff Cooper removed linchpin in particular social set.

January 7, 1954

Duff Cooper's memorial service at St Margaret's. Great turn out of brass. Winston Churchill leaning heavily on stick; lesson read by Salisbury; combative address by Bob Boothby, many attractive women in congregation who'd fluttered round Duff Cooper circle, and perhaps, I reflected, been in taxi cabs with Duff. Hymns 'old favourites' – *Onward Christian Soldiers*; *For All the Saints*, and then at the end, *The British Grenadiers*. As ever, all this truly reflected Duff's inward character – sentimentality, charm of a sort, vulgarity.

Walked afterwards to BBC for Critics. Then in Graham Greene's flat great MI6 gathering, including boss, General Sinclair, who was very flattering about *Punch*. Graham's brother Raymond had mysterious telephone from Paris, and innocently asked if anyone present knew anything about ciphers. A deadly hush.

January 8, 1954

Press day for *Punch*. Gave lunch to Stella Gibbons, author of
Cold Comfort Farm; highly intelligent, and, what's more, sensible.
Megan Lloyd George at nearby table. Mentioned to her that I was
debating the introduction of commercial television on BBC with
her arch enemy Lady Violet Bonham-Carter who is against it. She
said first technique in debating with Lady Violet was to by-pass
Maginot Line.

Visited by two Czechs, Levitt and Wise, who do wonderful
colour for, particularly, Schweppes advertisements. Getting them
to do cover for *Punch* Summer Number. They said they'd heard
in New York that *Punch* had become revolutionary. I said correct,
and that *Punch* now critical of all authority, including revolutionary.

January 10, 1954

Drove down to Sevenoaks to lunch with Thelma Cazalet, picking
up Megan Lloyd George on the way. Megan said she always contended that the two essential qualities in politics were courage and
patience, in that order. She is fantastically like her father, L.G., in
a way; just the same shape of body. I told her that what she'd miss,
if she switched from the Liberals and joined the Labour Party, was
radicalism. 'They're a subservient lot,' I told her. This was more
to worry her in her projected apostasy than because I believed it,
though there's something in it. Later discussed the famous Lloyd-
George–Asquith row, now carried on between her and Lady Violet
Bonham-Carter. Said that it was important in that it reflected two
basic trends in those who were pushing upwards in society –
Asquith towards incorporation in the upper classes; L.G. towards
personal power and, ultimately gangsterism. (I didn't put it quite
like this!) The Labour Party, I went on, were by and large
Asquithian in this respect.

January 11, 1954

Bored stiff with all the manuscripts, etc., at the office. Looked
listlessly out of the window into Bouverie Street and the *News of
the World* opposite.

Lunched at the Garrick with Patrick Dickinson, poet and

also high-grade golfer; formerly of BBC. He lives at Rye, next door to Alec Vidler's old house. We talked about a programme he's done on A. E. Housman. He said he'd had a lot of trouble with the BBC over mentioning Housman's homosexuality. Of Frank Pakenham he said that he was the baldest man he'd ever known. Almost passionately bald, I agreed.

In the evening listened to the Housman programme. Quite interesting except for sententious reading of verses. When it came to the point, however, there didn't seem much in Housman. I thought of him trudging about Cambridge (or was it Oxford?) roads and lanes in the afternoons trying to overcome his boredom and to work off the beer he'd drunk at lunch. Thus his poems were born, and they show it. Agreed for once with Cyril Connolly – 'Housman will last as long as the BBC.'

January 12, 1954

Spent the evening turning over press cuttings on R. A. Butler, about whom I've to do a piece in *Life*. Reflected how the Treasury's the place for getting on; the Foreign Office (which they all like because of the publicity, the travelling) a tomb of reputations. How it fires them on – that dream of pulling off a 'settlement'; what a will o' the wisp it is! Whereas currency meddling. . . .

January 13, 1954

At the office wrestled with the Agnews over circulation, which looked good, except that, as anticipated, a lot of American subscribers haven't renewed. Reflected there was no greater fallacy than current conviction that figures are final. Then the *Punch* Table. These functions decidedly sombre, but relieved by my beloved Fougasse (Kenneth Bird) who, happily, sits next to me. Like so much else, the whole show is an afterglow, the shadow of a feast.

January 14–15, 1954

André Laguerre (London Editor of *Time-Life*), Pamela and Michael Berry came to dinner. Pamela in excellent form. As Kitty and I agreed afterwards, she's not witty, but immensely droll; not clever, but shrewd and tough. Dresses always exactly like a gipsy with heavy, glittering metal on her dress.

Long talk with Michael Cummings about future drawings, *Daily Express*, etc. He's not set in a mould, not (like Osbert Lancaster for instance) trying to be something he thinks he ought to be. Fougasse said people who draw well must think clearly. Cummings a good example. Great clarity, even luminosity, in him.

January 16, 1954

Quiet day with Kitty. Walked across St James's Park in winter sunshine to Tate Gallery to look at new Picassos. Find such art incomprehensible and sad. Glad, on the way back, to go to street market and buy vegetables. Its non-abstraction refreshing. Only like sensuality or mysticism; all the rest, to me, a darkening of the spirit. Over the hills and far away, or the hills themselves, but not those grey, cold, solitary unearthly peaks.

January 17, 1954

Looked at *London Magazine*, *Encounter*, two new highbrow magazines, one edited by John Lehmann, the other by Stephen Spender. Dead fruit on the whole. Wrote speech for debate with Lady Violet Bonham-Carter on commercial television. Rather sick of the controversy by now.

Looked at volumes of *Punch* for 1938 and 1939. Pont really wonderful, far the best thing in them. Otherwise decidedly depressing – politically, feebly Baldwinian (Chamberlain flying to Munich bearing olive branch with caption *Still Hope*); socially, still upper classes who change for dinner, have pretty whimsical children in nurseries, and lower classes who speak illiterately (hobjets dart) and dress as proletarians. Thus *Punch*, too, fulfilled

the Marxist prophecy and announced a class-war line-up. At outbreak of war in 1939 several pages of reproduced drawings from
August, 1914. This too, characteristic.

Max Reinhart at The Bodley Head wants me to write a defini-
tive book on the Windsor Story. Large sums of money involved
for serial rights, etc. Wouldn't mind doing it.

January 18, 1954

Furious blast from Dorothy Sayers through agent. Lost my temper
and said I wouldn't be bullied by my contributors, however good.
She's a ferocious old thing.

Lunched with Campbell Moodie of Canadian High Commissioner's office to discuss my trip to Canada in March when I
am to address Canadian broadcasters in Quebec. He suggested
Toronto, Montreal and Ottawa. Reflected afterwards on deep
resentment those from Dominions who are strongly Anglophil
always seem to have. Their sycophancy turns sour in them. He
spoke bitterly of speech by Lord Ismay (Churchill's Chief of Staff
during the war) to Canadian Institute of Foreign Affairs, of
Churchill's present senility, etc. Then, to impress me, told how
Mackenzie King had asked him (Campbell Moodie) whether he
should resign the Canadian Premiership, and how he'd advised
resignation on the ground that Mackenzie King's health of para-
mount importance. To everyone's amazement, Moodie went on,
this advice taken, and Mackenzie King resigned.

January 19, 1954

Took Tony Powell home, and there were Conradine Hobhouse,
and her daughter Libby and son-in-law Michael King. Speaking
of Michael being on the *Daily Mirror* (which his father Cecil
controls) Conradine said she wouldn't allow it in the house, but
had felt bound to get it for the servants, though, she added, she
feared it was read above, before going below, stairs.

January 20, 1954

In the evening went to see *Twelfth Night*. Wonderful production, and acting all good except for Claire Bloom as Viola. Fancied she bore traces of association with Charles Chaplin – electric smile like his exposing teeth. Reflected that it was lucky Barrie was dead or else he'd surely have written a play for her. Struck by melancholy of Sir Andrew Aguecheek. Very poetic character altogether, with a touch, perhaps, of Shakespeare in him; even more in the Fool (Feste). Last curtain, with Feste left behind on the stage, the happy lovers all gone, and then the song – *A long while ago the world began*, wonderfully moving. Came away full of delight. *Twelfth Night*, I should say, best comedy ever written, or likely to be written. Reflected on the difference between good and bad entertainment, the one uplifting one, making one feel somehow differently about one's fellows, all the world, and the other somehow depressing, making everything seem a bit meaner and cheaper, shoddier. Again the same conclusion – that life revolves round each individual like planets round the sun.

January 22, 1954

Lunched with the editor of *Burke's Peerage*. He explained how *Burke* had been acquired before the war by rich American named Zimmerman, who had wanted to put in American section. He (the editor) had prevented this on impregnable ground that so far no American nobility. He told me about his lecture to rotary clubs; great interest in peerage – greater than ever before. For instance, hundreds of copies of *Burke* bought by private individuals. I said that, inevitably, the more egalitarian a society became the more snobbish.

Went to see *The Boy Friend*. Play burlesque of musical comedy of early twenties, delightfully done. Phase of nostalgia about this period now, I suppose, begins.

January 23, 1954

Robin Mount, brother-in-law of Tony Powell, arrived for weekend. Full of intelligent observations – e.g. after bawling at deaf aunt, that one gets angry because one shouts, not vice versa. He and I went to see ancient silent film *Battleship Potemkin* directed by Eisenstein. Not much good, rather to my relief; sentimental. Imagine it couldn't be shown in Russia now because bad for naval discipline. Crowd scenes good. Robin amused us greatly by account of Siegfried Sassoon, who told Robin that, one evening, following his cook, he'd found she'd gone into various hutments with tape measure to measure organs of inmates. As Robin said, episode gave one a remarkable insight into Sassoon's own idea of how to spend an evening.

John Fernald, theatrical producer, looked in later. Learnt from him that *The Boy Friend* put on against pansy opposition. According to him, first successful Resistance operation for a long time.

January 24, 1954

Somerset Maugham dinner (in honour of his 80th birthday) at the Garrick. Maugham made brilliant speech, but as he said afterwards when we talked it over, he lacks human dimension. Very clever of him to pause in middle and say: 'Now I want to think for a while.'

January 25, 1954

Some doubts about a cartoon I'd had done showing Churchill, as Illingworth put it, sightless, and to have caption indicating that it's time he went. It's true, but there'll be accusations of bad taste.

Listened in the evening to the radio play by Dylan Thomas about a day in the life of a small Welsh town (cf. January 1, 1954). Some of it quite good, and even funny (*She Couldn't Say No to a Midget*), with flashes of true poetry here and there along with much affectation and sentimentality.

January 26, 1954

Punch Table. Kenneth Bird had splendid idea of showing, by way of comment on Berlin talks, just four gramophones on a table.

Dined at the Beefsteak with Alan Herbert. Walked out with him into bitterly cold night. Saw him to Green Park Station – duffle-coated, grey scattered hair, hatless. Just before he'd called youthful Admiral 'Sir'. Left him with a pang.

January 27, 1954

Met Lady Violet Bonham-Carter at Manchester station and drove to Midland Hotel. After tea wandered round town, went to look at *Manchester Guardian* offices which I hadn't seen since 1932. Still bitterly cold, but town seemed prosperous and friendly. Returned to Midland Hotel and had a drink with BBC character who later took Lady Violet and myself to place where debate was to take place. I delivered my speech, I hope effectively. Then Lady Violet. Then discussion, mostly against me. I weighed in once or twice, and spoke impromptu as well, but, I fear, not too well. Felt vaguely dissatisfied with the whole show, although no complaints of BBC conduct of it.

January 28, 1954

Very pleased with Ronnie Searle's drawings, after Hogarth. Looked at final proofs of *Punch*. Very taken with joke drawing of man who's gone through cafeteria, arriving at pay desk with empty tray, and remarking: 'I couldn't see anything I wanted.'

January 29–30, 1954

Caught Cornish Riviera express for St Ives. Later joined by Freddy Grisewood, BBC *Any Questions?* question-master, A. G. Street, farmer, and Mrs Mary Stocks – whom I hadn't seen since Manchester days, former principal of Westfield College. She was very hostile to begin with, but gradually we became friendly. St Ives rather beautiful and much milder than London. Coast looked good for walking.

Usual preliminary discussion before *Any Questions?* programme. Fourth member of team Wilson Harris, lately fired from being Editor of *Spectator*. Little politics, happily. Note new mood of being utterly sick of politics. Good sign. All the same, thought afterwards that constant appearance on such programmes would be degrading. One would be forced to build up synthetic, vulgar personality, as Street has, and Gilbert Harding on such programmes as *What's My Line?* etc. Understand exactly why Harding has to stay drunk.

Travelled back to London the following morning with Mrs Stocks. She was reading Kingsley Martin's life of Harold Laski. I asked about Mrs Laski, and she said she'd gone out to India to do 'birth control work'.

February 6, 1954

Received rather touching letter from Randolph Churchill about the cartoon of his father in which he said that at least twenty of his friends had drawn his attention to it. Robin Mount expressed doubt as to whether Randolph had twenty friends.

Went to Crazy Gang. Some of the members quite good, particularly Bud Flanagan, who holds the whole show together with his personality, still *News of the World*, very traditional in his coarseness – skirts blown up by wind, etc. Audience's immense enjoyment adds to one's own; but, at same time, it is the kind of show one tends to over-praise in order to show one isn't highbrow – merely, of course, showing one is.

February 10, 1954

Much perturbation in office over strong reactions to Churchill cartoon. Pretend to be less perturbed than I really am, even pleased about it. Usual Table. I'd brought in Christopher Hollis, *Punch*'s Parliamentary reporter. In the afternoon talked with Michael Cummings who's again under pressure at the *Daily Express* to stop working for *Punch*. Tried to stiffen him up.

February 11, 1954

Protest letters about Churchill cartoon still pouring in.

February 12–14, 1954

Dwye Evans at Heinemann very excited over manuscript by woman, Roberta Cowell, formerly man – RAF officer, DFC. It appears that operation was successfully performed by gynaecologist of repute and that story's confirmed in every particular. Bit sliced off nose, etc. to complete new surgically constructed female parts. *Picture Post* are to run series of articles. Doubt if Dwye would have been as excited if I'd brought in hitherto undiscovered work by Shakespeare.

Stephen Spender and Nicholas Bentley and his wife came to supper. We discussed parasiticism, with special reference to Cyril Connolly.

February 15, 1954

Still in black mood. Walked much about the streets – Embankment, round by Covent Garden, streets I knew so well. Tried to write but couldn't. Went on signing letter answering those protesting against Churchill cartoon. Felt suddenly angry about them – silly, angry abuse. Thought how hateful this particular class. *Punch* readers *par excellence*. George Malcolm Thomson and Derek Marks, *Daily Express* man in Parliament, both said I was entirely right about Churchill.

February 19, 1954

Often wake up in the morning haunted by the idea of work undone, of time slipping by with so many projects unfulfilled. Delighted when post came, to get card from John in Kenya saying he'd be home on last day of month.

February 24, 1954

Dragged myself to *Punch* for Table, but after lunch decided to pack it in and cancel everything I'd got to do in rest of this week. Felt conscience-stricken. Got on with Butler article steadily, and found, as always, that steady writing suits me best. Other activities basically against the grain.

Read with a kind of fascination autobiographical volume *Friends Apart* of Philip Toynbee, his relations with two friends – Jasper Ridley and Esmond Romilly – both of whom were killed in the war. The last progeny of Gilbert Murray; the fag-end of all that highmindedness and enlightenment. One scene described particularly memorable – rich Liberal country house, everyone fairly tight, out on the lawn; then singing 'revolutionary songs'. Effect on me is, at once, to see point of Senator McCarthy and of Communists, and to long for the total destruction of a society no longer entitled to exist. This longing likely to be satisfied.

February 25, 1954

Still lying low with a guilty conscience. Butler piece now taking shape. As I write about Butler succumb to one of those moods when whole idea of politics, of power, becomes anathema. Long to be shot of any part of it; to concentrate thought and effort on a more distant horizon.

Gerald Bullett came to supper. Hadn't seen him for ages. 'The trouble with me and Priestley,' he said, 'is that we've amused the company long enough.' He's sick of writing novels, but has to earn; no other way.

February 26, 1954

René McColl just back from Berlin Conference, and full of good stories about it. Very diverting account of British Press briefings by Con O'Neill. René quoted good music hall line – 'I'm the only Jewish Scotsman in the Irish Fusiliers.' Twitted René about his story in the *Express* of Molotov phoning Mao Tse-tung in Peking – 'Is that you, Mao; speak up. I can't hear you well. This line is very weak!'

Tottered down to dine with the Priestley's. He very battered after week of drubbing for his new novel *The Magicians* and his play. Says that everyone's against him because he's 'got under their skin'. While we sat together confided in me that, though everyone thought he was rich, actually he was very broke.

February 27, 1954

Rounded off Butler piece. Decided not to go out during day. (Curious feeling these days of lack of interest in earthly life. Even so, still, it must be admitted, grab morning papers to see what's happened. This a kind of nervous reaction. Anyway, no feeling whatsoever that contentment or delight can ever again be derived from any sensual experience, and I'd be enchanted to be removed, in spirit, and even in flesh, from all sensory experience.)

Dined with the Grigg's. P.J. had immensely long letter from Bridges, head of Civil Service, in most circumlocutory way asking him if he'd undertake enquiry into possibility of getting some proportion of BBC monitoring service paid for by other departments. We laughed long over ludicrous phraseology, and planned suitably contemptuous answer.

March 1954

Birkenhead's Party to meet Sir Gladwyn Jebb

This was the first Berry invitation since the Churchill row, so I was glat to get it and to go. Huge gathering in Camrose's house in Carlton House Terrace. Like all Camrose's residences, much more like a club than a private dwelling. Freddie Birkenhead looking frozen and unhappy, Sheila radiant. Went over and had a word with Pamela Berry. She said she'd given me up for Lent, but missed me and I said I'd missed her. So all was repaired.

March 19, 1954

Flying between Goose Bay and Montreal at the start of my Canadian trip. Usual lost feeling up in the clouds, but not melancholy. Reflected that, if plane crashed, my regrets would be passive rather than active. Have no wish to stop living, but often feel I've had enough of life. Seen off by Kitty and John – misty, rainy day; Kitty more than usually depressed at our parting. Not cheerful myself. Going off on a journey, I said, is an image of dying, and therefore disturbs and saddens. How soon, she said, one begins to think enviously of others, with homes to go back to etc. when one's own home is being temporarily disbanded. Kitty and John going off themselves to Roquebrune to stay with Cholerton.

John has written account of his stay in Kenya, which both Stephen Spender and I think most capably done. Stephen came to lunch on the day I left and we talked in the usual way about Connolly, Sonia Orwell, etc. I broke off to say that really such things alone truly interested me – I mean individual human beings and their inter-action from one another, and that it was a delight to talk about them, particularly as so much of one's time was taken up with politics and administration, essentially without interest. Stephen said I recalled Isherwood to him, and I said I didn't mind this comparison at all.

April 12, 1954

Punch office again, after trip to Canada and New York. A lot of letters to answer. Everything going along well enough, but took little part in bringing out new *Punch* issue.

Read Attlee's autobiography *As It Happened*, quite fabulous work, completely flat, but so flat, so fabulously flat, as to be fascinating. Thus he retired to hospital with 'prostate trouble', and while there some people tried 'to get rid of me as leader', but this 'met with little support'. It would be interesting to consider how he'd describe the Day of Judgment.

April 20, 1954

Everyone still full of enthusiasm over *Punch* parody of *New Yorker*. Gave dinner party to Osbert Lancaster who was amazingly got up in neat suit with double-breasted waistcoat, yellow boots. Delighted to learn that he has now started doing some things for *Punch*.

Particularly pleased because, he being quite worldly individual, it's very good sign that he should want to appear in *Punch*. He's waited eighteen months to see how the wind was blowing.

April 21, 1954

Punch Table and day in office; everyone coming and going. Beginning to admit to myself that really I'm bored often with whole show.

May 15, 1954

Staying here near Cork with Claud Cockburn – ramshackle Irish house, everything broken and disorderly, but agreeable. By air from London to Dublin – Kitty, as usual, very nervous of flying. Then long train journey, stopping and shunting everywhere. Claud met us at a place called Limerick Junction with hired car and we drove back through marvellous country – first plain of Tipperary, then bare hills. Put in for drinks twice – wonderfully friendly bars. Mrs Cockburn, Patricia, is mad on horses, formerly travelled much in Africa, etc. Talked sleepily by peat fire. Claud explained how what he calls 'Retreat from Moscow', i.e. British coming over here after war to escape income tax and revolution, now in reverse. All over and houses again, after fantastic inflation, now to be bought cheaply.

May 16, 1954

Slept in ramshackle room, no plaster on walls or ceiling, in oldest part of house, allegedly once occupied by Walter Raleigh. Wonderful bright day, with a kind of gleam in the countryside. After breakfast drove in by gig to nearby town of Youghal; very pleasant bowling along country roads, no smell of petrol, air pellucid. Youghal itself small town of 5,000 on estuary; perfect little 18th-century quayside, shortly to be used for filming of *Moby Dick*. In afternoon drove to Cork, then on to Blarney Castle. Climbed up tower and precariously kissed stone which, as I said to Claud, particularly honorable to journalists. Planned bringing over big party of journalists to honour Stone. Then walked in sacred Druidical wood, eerie place with trees thousands of years old. Dined in Cork and after dinner listened to Prime Minister de Valera making election speech after arriving in triumphal procession. Realized that Irish politics have provided essential pattern for American politics – convention, etc. De Valera tired looking, almost blind, not very eloquent, but still, in the dogged way politicians have, holding on.

June 21, 1954

Went early to Lime Grove for *Panorama* programme. Saw two films of eclipse of the sun – one from Harvard and the other from USSR. Latter very well done, but inevitable Uzbek peasants, etc. all looked like actors. In the end life itself becomes propaganda. Returned to *Punch* with guilty truant feeling. However, looked over dummy, etc. and everything in order.

Went with Kitty to see Griggs, where we talked about discussion I'm to have on Friday with a Scottish minister, George MacLeod, on Billy Graham and of interview with him. Tried to express basic feeling – that if Christianity identifies itself with causes of this world, however enlightened, it is sucked into this world and thereby destroyed. We all agreed in essence. Always in two minds about TV – half pleased, half disgusted, though, must confess, tickled to be described in *Tribune* piece as TV star.

*   *   *

March 12, 1957

Resume journal after long interval during which I was ill, troubled, etc., etc. Have decided that climacteric now passed, and henceforth my life must be quieter, more industrious. After being ill, gave up drinking, smoking and am gradually giving up taking dope for sleeplessness. Most of the time this makes me feel very well.

All day in office. Visited by Danish writer who said that in Denmark everyone prosperous, hygenic, but no one happy, and suicide rate highest in the world. Induced me, by this observation, to pour out favourite propositions about fallacy of materialism.

Dined with Kitty and Patrick Kinross at his house. Patrick is doing profile of me for *Atlantic Monthly* and questioned me about views on religion, etc. Envious of my abstemiousness, attributing it to my advantageous lower-class upbringing.

March 13, 1957

Christopher Chancellor said he'd been asked by Father Trevor Huddleston to decide whether he (Huddleston) should go on with his anti-Apartheid campaign, or return to his monastic duties, i.e. training novices. What should he recommend? I strongly urged monastic duties, if only because, in my opinion, as far as apartheid's concerned, he's shot his bolt.

March 14, 1957

With Val to see play *Look Back in Anger* by John Osborne, whom I once interviewed on television without being able to get anything out of him. Play quite execrable – woman ironing, man yelling and snivelling, highbrow smut, 'daring' remarks (reading from Sunday paper; Bishop of . . . asks all to rally round and make hydrogen bomb). Endured play up to point where hero and heroine pretended to be squirrels.

March 15, 1957

Caught train to Isle of Wight where I had to take part in *Any Questions?* radio programme. Sat in carriage with Lady Barnett, quite fascinating TV figure (*What's My Line?*) also on programme. She seems to belong to TV screen. Decided that, if seduceable at all, it could only be on television. In life, passionless, odourless, tasteless. Neatly dressed, with wonderful faculty for producing banalities with eagerness, even a sort of animation. Only tuned in to this world. No connection with any other. A Laputa Girl.

March 16, 1957

Went on to Robertsbridge with Andrew Miller-Jones and discussed with him programme on *The Thirties* that BBC are thinking of doing. Most uncanny that television critic of *Sunday Times*, Maurice Wiggin, wrote that BBC ought to use newsreel and other material to do contemporary history, and that suitable script was available in my book *The Thirties*. Another example of what I've so often remarked – how ideas make waves and can be picked up like light and sound ones.

March 18, 1957

Horrible lunch with my agent, David Higham. His head, Hughie used to say, might well be mounted and hung on the walls of the Authors' Club after he's dead.

TV programme with booming Hugh Dalton, former Labour Minister, and Francis Williams. Dalton, as ever, white, egregious, as Philip Jordan said, his eyes blazing with insincerity. Said to me: 'We haven't seen each other for such a long time.' Actually, never had seen each other before. Very political.

March 20–21, 1957

Table. Cartoon idea on strike situation – sheep-like strikers chivvied along towards dark forest by 'Sheep Stewards'. Long talk with Claud Cockburn who's not in best of form – flushed, unshaven, crumpled. Thinks, as I do, that we may now really be for it – strikes becoming general strike, possibly civil war. On the other hand, perhaps not. Anyway, sooner or later, crack-up inevitable.

Annie Fleming tried to persuade me to look in on Fionn's 21st-birthday party. Declined as being too old. Ann rather quarrelsome with Ian, who complained that she was packing her daughter's party with oldsters like Rose Macaulay (this did seem a bit hard), and her gang – Paddy Leigh-Fermor, Lucien Freud, etc. She in turn complained that Ian had been bitten by one of his girl friends. All a kind of elaborate show, legendary, set for a long run.

March 22, 1957

Drove down to Robertsbridge in the early morning with Illingworth – glorious morning with mist gradually clearing as we drove along. Spirits rose as we got further from London, clearing at last the interminable suburban belt and into the country. Described to Illingworth how, the evening before, I'd kept my spectacles on by accident, and looked down at plate of beef, all bloody, like an animal's platter; how terrific reaction against such food had seized me. Spoke of growing desire to escape altogether from senses – not in itself admirable; indeed, possibly the opposite if dictated by will to self-denial; but admirable if governed by awareness of more subtle, spiritual sensibility released by eschewing the grosser, material form. Also said that my own present trend towards asceticism related to deep conviction I had that troubled times were coming – a sort of training derived from mood very like one I'd experienced in years before 1939. (Very like life that shortly after this seized by happily fugitive, gross, fleshly desire.)

Reflected later that concept of dying in the flesh in order to live in the spirit most profound of all. Ah, how I long and long for this.

March 23, 1957

Long walk in sunshine along road I know so well from Vinehall to Battle. Glad to renew acquaintance with it. Found that I remembered each turn and bend perfectly, and felt odd resentment at houses built beside it since my time. Drove back with Kitty and Val who had been to meet Claud Cockburn. Claud very crumpled looking. All the same, he's very sweet and touching. Lives much in the past, in his Communist Party days when he was running *The Week*. This the high point of his life. I always feel that at some point in his life he's made some vital sacrifice which can never be recovered.

Read Dalton's book, *The Fateful Years*, which I have to review. Seem to hear, as I read, the old boy's booming voice. Like all politicians he's full of venom, and manages to find something disagreeable to say about many of his associates. Much diverted by his account of going to see Kingsley Martin just before outbreak of war and finding him quite hopeless and defeatist, advocating that we should give way, but as discreetly as possible.

March 24, 1957

To tea, reluctantly, with family named Harding in the neighbourhood, but he turned out to be fascinating character – little man with bright quick eyes. He told me that in 1914–18 war he'd been engaged in chemical business in Eccles near Manchester. Made first smoke screen for Zeebrugge operation. Then he'd decided he couldn't stand Eccles and went to Cambridge to do research. Looked into problem of sugar substitutes, but constitution of sweetness eluded, and eludes, him. Made two saccharine molecules coalesce, but result wasn't sweet (mentioned this with comical disconcertment). Then got on to some process connected with milk production. Went to New Zealand in connection with it. Finally sold out to United Dairies. Loved his zest, humour, good sense. Now he's taken to painting and making pottery.

March 26, 1957

Dined with Christopher Hollis and Johnson Society in Johnson's old house in Gough Square. Paper read, after abstemious dinner, by character named Tillotson on *Rasselas*. Somehow very moved to be sitting there thinking about Johnson in very room in which he'd produced the dictionary. Of all Englishmen he appeals to me most – the best, the greatest. Taken with quotation referring to his publisher – 'Cave has no relish for humour, but he can bear it.' Felt this referred to readers of *Punch*.

March 29, 1957

Quiet day working, reading and gardening. Not much work done. Very mystified by life these days, almost indifferent; conscious that strange happenings are occurring, and that my personal implication in them slight. Therefore unanxious and rather happy. Often find myself muttering prayers, lines of verse – e.g. Milton's 'Let us with a gladsome mind . . .' Find this Spring particularly delectable – blossom beginning to appear; the green valley up and down which I walk; everything waking up without reference to politics or other like considerations. Long above all things, with an intensity of longing, to be delivered from the self, from the will and the passion which clothes it. Long for the peace of God which passeth understanding (a phrase I also mutter). Long to find some means of expressing this, and so saying: 'Be of good cheer.' Nothing to worry about, no cause for fretfulness. It is true that to die in the flesh is to be reborn in the spirit. There is an inconceivable joy in not desiring – a joy which makes even food, the basic necessities, seem of passing and slight urgency – like children gulping down food and drinks because they are so eager to get out into the sun. How clear it all is at times! How clearly one understands. And then, suddenly, the clarity goes; the clouds roll up again, and all the old unprofitable desires assert themselves. The air is darkened, and in the shadows comes a chill – like a cruel hand shaking one from sleep.

March 30, 1957

Rae O'Rourke and his enchanting Hungarian wife, Matya, came for the week-end. Inevitably discussed Hungary and recent happenings there. Matya heart-broken, the same doom here. Very much my own view. Ever since Moscow I've always felt that what happened there in one form or another was bound to happen everywhere. The regime of the individual over for the time being – burden of being an individual too heavy to bear. So now the collectivity, the Leviathan. Of course the individual will emerge again. Someone else will convince men that the hairs of their heads

have been lovingly counted and that no sparrow falls to the ground
without intent.

April 1, 1957

Looked in on Kingsley Martin, whom I found more distracted
than ever – pacing up and down muttering and grimacing with
keen satisfaction at disasters threatening. He is the quintessence
of British leftism; himself our own fever and pain – tousled grey
hair, lined sallow face, beak of a nose and peering uneasy eyes.

At Lime Grove old familiar scene of *Panorama* programme –
camera moving, Richard Dimbleby pronouncing, all the fatuity of
an age in the compass of a single scene. I had to talk about Cyprus,
and the release of Archbishop Makarios, to Labour MP Philip
Noel-Baker and Conservative MP Paul Williams – which I did
rather   drearily.

April 2, 1957

Lunched at the House of Commons with Ian Gilmour and Francis
Noel-Baker. Gilmour tall rich young man who's bought, and now
edits, the *Spectator*. Noel-Baker strongly urged him to join the
Labour Party on the ground that they were 'desperately short of
good men'. Smiled wryly over this remark, remembering my father,
early days of Labour Party. Noel-Baker in his dry way talked about
Makarios, the echo of his father – echo of an echo, that's to say.
Gilmour walked back with me to Bouverie Street, quite a characteristic type – wanting to be enlightened, a reformer, and pumping
this zest into strong feelings about capital punishment, imprisonment and homosexuals, clergymen who secrete dirty postcards
among manuscript sheets of his sermons.

April 3–4, 1957

Long talk with Maurice Richardson of *The Observer* etc. about
necessity for abstemiousness as one grows older. Maurice has a

bashed-in nose, and is fairly mad and at times exceedingly funny. Inventor of 'Idiot Lanter' as description of TV. Calls Claud Cockburn the 'Chevalier'. Was once Communist, even now not so very far off being one. Considers that if only Communist Party of Great Britain had taken Titoist position at time of Nazi–Soviet Pact all would have been well.

Gave lunch to special party – Sir Ian Jacob, Director General of BBC, Sidney Bernstein, Kenneth Clark, Michael Foot, Dr Charles Hill and Leonard Miall. I sat between Bernstein and Jacob. Bernstein very excited about his Granada TV activities. Jacob typical staff officer, with spectacles, and a good deal of intelligence of rather limited sort. Comes of long line of soldiers, administrators (India). He rose to glory by being able to make brief, clear military appreciations for Churchill. What a contrast with Bernstein, typical Third Programme client and show-business tycoon combined. When I said I was going to New York he asked: 'Will you be going to the Coast?' The Coast is Illyria, Never-Never land, the hills to which we must lift up our eyes. Odd chance that has put them both in the same line of business.

April 5, 1957

Worked, mowed the lawns, thought about abstinence and of three talks I want to prepare on the fallacy of materialism. Not, I want to stress, that sensuality is disagreeable, or even bad, in itself. Only it's an inferior product – like reproduction, however skilled, in relation to original. The senses only a shadow of another reality, and this other reality precious, wonderful, even in glimpses the only possible pursuit. Sometimes the green valley of the Rother in the evening makes me jump for joy, and words roll about in my mind like vaguely heard music. Afterwards, alas, it often happens that I can't remember them – strain after them like straining after a tune. Almost everything's forgotten, and how is it possible to believe that the needs of the flesh and the exigencies of time really matter? And yet, from such a mood, one switches over to thinking about money, or a girl, or a dent in a motor car.

April 8, 1957

Came up to London early to see Duncan Sandys, the Minister of
Defence. Sandys good-looking in a way, but with a mirthless
smile. However he greeted me very affably, and we proceeded to
consider topics for TV interview in the evening. He tried to induce
me to commit myself to asking specific questions, but I refused.
Said this would make interview a bore. Decided on the whole
Sandys was more formidable than most of his colleagues. Spoke
to him about Eden, now in pitiably sick state. Said Eden had no
gift for leadership; under Macmillan as PM everything better,
Cabinet meetings quite transformed.

Went on to lunch with Gaitskell out at Hampstead. Also present
Ian and Annie Fleming, Roy Jenkins and his wife. Gaitskell not
finding leadership of the Labour Party quite as he'd hoped and
supposed. In fact, in a decided muddle over H Bomb, etc. He said
to me that as party was hopelessly split it was impossible to have
sensible or coherent policy. Such is politics.

Sandys interview went off quite well. He said to me on set:
'I see you're going to make it as difficult as possible,' always with
mirthless smile. I said, 'not difficult, as interesting and genuine as
possible'.

April 10, 1957

Visited in my office by Austrian named Flesch from German
section in Overseas Service of BBC – came to this country in 1934
as refugee from Nazis. Asked me various questions for purpose
of doing profile of me, but talked mostly about himself. If it hadn't
been for Hitler he'd now be famous writer, he said. This possible,
I suppose. Most impressed when I told him I was tactical pessimist
but strategic optimist. Wrote it down. Haunted after his visit by
his lean oval face and desolate eyes. Exile always sad, as is change.
The world overflowing today with strangers in strange lands.

April 13, 1957

Vividly yellow primroses on bare wintry bank. Feel deep, almost physical, longing to write and write. Yet when I sit at desk my thoughts wander and I soon desist. Resolve to make myself overcome this reluctance and acquire habit. Habit's the thing – so many things I want to get done. I may only have, say, 12–15 years of active writing. Nothing will be done unless I start soon. Perhaps early morning work a solution. Even with present commitments I could do minimum of 1,000 words a day. Once this habit was established all would be well.

Read David Low, the cartoonist's autobiography. Usual Antipodean mixture of hatred of English upper classes and inferiority before them. Colonel Blimp, as a creation, a wonderful piece of sabotage. A majestic line, but mostly commonplace ideas.

April 16, 1957

Tidied things up preparatory to going to New York.

Lunched with Kenneth Adam, old acquaintance (back to *Manchester Guardian* days), now No. 3 at BBC, Lime Grove. I'd always assumed he was hostile. On the contrary, he was most forthcoming. In character moralistic, earnest, with cynical, self-interested under-current. Quite a creature of this age, I believe a clergyman's son – anyway ought to have been; no good as journalist but with some talent, at any rate for getting along. Now that he's gone out of his way to be appreciative to me, I feel there's good in him. Before I didn't. Alas, judgments so subjective.

April 20, 1957 – New York

Arrival in New York. Came to the University Club where I'm staying, changed and sallied forth into Fifth Avenue with that immediate exhilaration New York ever produces. Dropped into St Patrick's (RC) Cathedral and sat listening to the singing and watching the worshippers come and go. Drove out with Alex Faulkner of *Daily Telegraph* and his family along the rolling parkway. Always love the suspension bridges – delicate this time against the misty sky. Thousands and thousands of cars, all, seemingly, new, all huge; a rolling petrol-driven procession. Reflected that American life exactly like the advertisements, whereas elsewhere advertisements a fantasy.

April 21, 1957

Went out to 93rd Street to lunch with Mary McCarthy and her husband, Bowden Broadwater. Mary looking very pretty in her odd rumbustious way. Spoke of dancing with Gaitskell in Milan, said he was giddy – Giddy Gaitskell. Much diverse gossip. Long account of odd circumstances of Dwight Macdonald and two wives, two families; said that generally when anyone turns in a wife he goes for a newer model, but Dwight got an older one.

April 24, 1957

Went along to Simon and Schuster office for chat with Peter Schwed about *Punch* publications. Told me as all publishers do, about success of books he'd chosen. Long discussion about America. Made my point that for the first time in history of the world 99.99 per cent of mankind want the same things – viz: American way of life. This is what American century means.

April 26, 1957

Gave tea to Richard Gordon, author of the 'Doctor in the House' books, and his wife. He's decided to try his luck over here – nervous-looking sharp. Taken a house, brought his family; his wife also a doctor. It seems, as immigrant, he's liable to call-up. We laughed, he wryly, at possibility that he might find himself drafted back to American forces in England.

Saw *My Fair Lady*, fantastically successful musical here. Not really very good, and in so far as Shaw's *Pygmalion* comes through, abhorrent. How Shaw despised the poor and hated them. What a fabulous snob! Success of show nostalgia of Ascot, amusing cockney working man, Alfred Doolittle (played by old trouper Stanley Holloway), etc. Americans nostalgic about what they've never had or experienced; nostalgia one degree removed.

April 27–28, 1957

Lunched with P. G. Wodehouse at the St Regis and drove back with him to his house on Long Island. P.G. just the same – a little older, a bit distrait, but in good order. Driving away from New York we talked about writers, income tax, the torture of pleasure and the pleasure of work. Some sort of procession passing down Fifth Avenue, Hungarian flags draped in black. On the big roads the cars all rolling along – as P.G. said everyone in Jacksonville making a trip to Johnsonville and everyone in Johnsonville making a trip to Jacksonville. P.G.'s books continue to do very well in England, and, under *My Fair Lady* dispensation, beginning to do well here. Latest to be made into a musical. Ethel Wodehouse awaiting us, just the same, domestically on the move all the time, many additions to the house. I asked P.G. if she meditated any more, and he said he had the feeling that she was crouching to spring.

Woke next morning, made breakfast, in ecstasy at having tea again in the early morning. Walked by the sea with P.G., exquisite weather, Atlantic breakers sparkling as they broke on the shore. Struck by the complete isolation of P.G. and Ethel. Might be on another planet. No contact anywhere with anyone or anything – P.G. sitting so many hours at his typewriter, then taking the dog to the post office for the letters. He doesn't really care much for the world or for his fellows. Told with relish story of man who, when someone said to him that the H bomb, if exploded, would bring the world to an end, replied: 'I can't wait.' Ethel moves restlessly all the while about the house, heavily made up, crouching forward. Somehow I love her dearly – something tough and wonderful about her. More real, more admirable, than P.G., who's also dear, but occasionally so strangely like their old dog Bill – waiting for his food, padding about in the garden.

Meditated on extraordinary survival of these two – wars,

revolutions, etc., but somehow they've managed to maintain their way of life, now here, in the last redoubt.

April 29, 1957

Lunched with William Shawn, Editor of *New Yorker*. He took over *New Yorker* from Ross, who founded it. Not much clue, I fancy, as to what to do with it now. We jointly bemoaned difficulties of editing allegedly humorous magazine. Also people who come up to us and say they can't stand *New Yorker* or *Punch* when it's quite clear they never even look at the magazine. Like Shawn very much, he's very eccentric. Boiling hot day, and he had overcoat and umbrella with him. Apparently can't bear lifts; so overcome by them that he has to travel alone when one's unavoidable.

May 2, 1957

Awaited Dorothy Olding, for lunch – no one ever had a kinder, sweeter agent. Owing to absent-mindedness mistook female connected with restaurant for Miss Olding, began to lead her to bar. All ended in laughter instead of embarrassment. Miss Olding at last arrived, and we chatted about business – CBS programmes, *Saturday Evening Post* piece, etc. Dropped in at Overseas Press Club and chatted with various characters there. In this mood much delighted by American enthusiasm – 'Very happy to meet you.' On to dine with Ionescos in little flat near Columbia University. Then on to party they'd arranged in friend's larger flat. Gathering of egg-heads – Lionel and Diana Trilling, etc. Diana very bitter about intellectuals having their fares paid to go abroad. I said I thought more lamentable things than this going on in the world. Guessed that her annoyance due to possibility this provided for Trilling to escape occasionally.

May 4, 1957

Day of departure. On flight read Alger Hiss's book. Didn't think I would get through another volume on the subject, yet did – every word. Nothing much in his apologia except clever analysis of Chambers' evidence. Didn't seem to me at all to establish Hiss's innocence. He's guilty – but what of ? I don't know. Incidentally, day before departure Joe McCarthy died – news of death whispered to me at Trilling party. Flags at half-mast, somewhat equivocal tributes in press. This and Hiss's book went together.

May 6–7, 1957

Back without much enthusiasm to my office. Pile of letters cursorily read. Peter Agnew low-spirited. Advertisements down, circulation slipping. I ought to care more, at the moment I don't. All the tedium of a job resumed. Stewart Maclean, *Daily Mail* boss, told me *News Chronicle* and *Daily Herald* both dying. Present project to amalgamate them, but, in his opinion, amalgamated newspapers would likewise die. Should suppose he's right. Also *Picture Post* near its end.

In the evening took Kitty to Australian play – *Summer of the Seventeenth Doll*. Decidedly good, full of vitality, humorous, good theme – two men who come down to Brisbane each year for a spree from cutting cane sugar; this year one of their girls has got married, the whole thing soured. It's over.

May 8–9, 1957

Increasingly bored by *Punch* routine. Ought really to give up job, sometimes think of doing so; then hesitate because it's easy way of earning money, and, by virtue of being Editor, other things turn up.

To Broadcasting House for *Frankly Speaking* sound programme with Robert Graves. Though I don't like him, glad to see him again. He's got a kind of almost physical charm – large face, white, with broken teeth, unshaven, hair without a parting; altogether very like the Roman Emperors he writes about so well. Talked much about mushrooms, which, he contends, connected with religious origins. Asked him which Caesar of Suetonius's twelve he liked best. He said, 'Caesar'.

May 10, 1957

In the evening took Mary McCarthy to Lime Grove for *Press Conference*. Usual form at Lime Grove. Aneurin Bevan arrived and drew touching picture of his victimization by four clever questioners who'd already made their plans. I said that if he went on I'd burst into tears. Programme wasn't very good. Bevan evaded all questions, and talked pretty good rubbish. Mary McCarthy said afterwards that on TV I was quite different from in life. Glad to know this. Awful when, as with Lady Barnett, the two coincide.

May 11, 1957

Down to Robertsbridge early, read Halifax's memoirs for *Daily Telegraph* piece. Halifax old-fashioned figure with all the cynicism and frivolity of one-time governing class. Remembered so well conversation with his successor as Viceroy, Willingdon, about him. Sitting with Willingdon, frail, cunning, *fin du régime* man, after dinner at Viceregal Lodge in Simla. Willingdon, slightly tipsy, said: 'Halifax was very bad viceroy, I'm quite a good one. Yet he'll be remembered and I'll be forgotten because he's managed to persuade people he's GOOD.' Quite true, especially with the English. Spoke to Frank Pakenham about Halifax. He said Halifax, next to Salisbury, dominated House of Lords. (Not difficult to do, I reflected.) Mentioned his sense of humour, odd, but authentic. It's apparent in his memoirs. Surprised to find myself reading the parts about India (especially Simla and Ootacamund), somewhat nostalgic. Saw it all clearly. Must write about it.

May 12, 1957

Went over to Sidney Bernstein for luncheon. He's got just the house you'd expect – neatly converted farmhouse, very hygienic, neat American wife rather like Claire Bloom, time and labour saving devices. Bernstein looks rather benevolent and cheerful nowadays – tall, grey, a lean Ben-Gurion. His TV, he says, is now beginning to pay. Appears that he inherited music-hall from his father, and that he and his brother built up present Granada business on this foundation. Sidney is very left-wing, attends Labour Party conferences. What does he want? He doesn't know. Perhaps answer is that he's found it so easy to become rich that he'd like a more difficult system to be introduced – contract instead of auction bridge.

May 13, 1957

Two lives nowadays – in the country and in London. Much prefer the former, and often plan how to make it the whole instead of a part. Actually, very tired indeed of parties, theatres, clubs, talk, etc. Had enough. Doesn't amuse me any more. See with desolation the grimy buildings through railway carriage windows telling me I'm back in London.

Dinner party at Libby King's with Selwyn Lloyd, Foreign Secretary, and Hugh Cudlipp and his wife. Much noisy argument. Poor Selwyn Lloyd took insults, everything, on the chin without flinching. Never met, even among politicians, such a poor little soul.

May 17, 1957

Read in piece on famous lawyer Sir Edward Coke that soon after he married he put his head on his wife's belly, heard a child stir, and remarked: 'A child in the pot.' To which she replied: 'Otherwise I wouldn't have married a Cooke.'

May 20, 1957

I was at Riverside Studios for hours, only to do a brief two minutes into camera on the difficulties into which contemporary journalism is running. Also in the studio Dick Crossman who was discussing his pensions project. This is universal suffrage at its lowest and worst – a straight bribe, with the Conservatives hurriedly trying to cook up a rival dish. Crossman very complacent, and says we're bound to win – meaning the Labour Party is bound to win, and he to get office. I said there was a God in heaven, and that to punish him he'd be made Minister of Pensions.

May 22–23, 1957

Wolf Mankowitz was interested in a piece I'd contributed to a series called *What I Believe*, said he'd reached more or less the same conclusions, was trying to bring them out through the medium of a novel about a totally amoral trickster. Love his Jewish vitality, sudden flashes of realism, sentimentality.

Took early train to Robertsbridge. Blue sky, but biting wind. Always upset by raging wind. Seems to get inside one and tear one to pieces. Unable to work, or even read much. Walked in the teeth of the wind without much refreshment. Wondered and wondered as so often, what I was supposed to be doing; what it's all about; why? Remorse over so much time lost in foolishness or nothingness. And so on. The mind goes over these old paths again and again. Shall I ever know what it means? If not, how to go on? How to go on anyway? One cries restlessly aloud – to whom? For what? I survey my activities, such as they are – TV, articles in papers, fragments of writing, unfulfilled projects – with contemptuous despair. Yet there's no escape from one's life being so because one is so. I don't believe in anything, or care about anything or anyone. All I have is the memory of some happy moments, and most, if not all of those were dubious. God is really there for everyone? I suspect it may be, with only fantasies propelling along. The only thing to long for is that it should be over and done with, and this will come, not so very long hence. I said to Kitty that anyway two-thirds of the journey is done.

1958–1962

Chinese Diary – 1958

After my statutory five years as Editor of Punch, I was glad
to relinquish the role of Lear's Fool which I had never enjoyed
and return to my natural habitat, the media maquis. This
now, of course, included the growing power and pervasiveness
of Television.

After leaving Punch, I was asked to go to Australia and
write a series of articles for the Sydney Morning Herald on
my impressions of that huge, ungainly continent, and to interview on television some of its more eminent or bizarre citizens.
On my way home I stopped off in China for a few weeks and
then went on to Moscow where I found everything exactly as
it had been in 1933, leading me to reflect – which may be why
I wrote no entries in my diary there – that the best safeguard
against future change is to have a revolution, thereby freezing
the status quo it creates.

June 1, 1958—Canton

I came through here by train from Hong Kong. Refugees from China have swollen Hong Kong's population – four teeming millions in a minute area, mostly very poor; some homeless. It's almost the last, if not the last, old-fashioned colony, with His Excellency in command, and the usual trappings.

My only contact with the establishment was an expensive lunch with the Information Officer, Jock Murray. Otherwise, I mooned around, dreading that something would go wrong over my Chinese visa. Actually, it didn't, and I caught the train and soon came to the frontier. There's a gap in the railway line, along which one walks, and then goes through formalities. I felt a great lightening of the spirit – although the first thing I saw in Communist China was a poster showing some idealized workers looking at television. However, I thought, it's only a poster. They haven't actually got it. There was a little group of Europeans travelling across. Among them, an Englishman, vaguely familiar. It turned out to be Joseph Needham, whom I'd known at Cambridge, a scientist who certified that the Americans used germ warfare in Korea, etc.

At Canton I was met by a young woman who looked about fifteen and was in reality twenty-five. After dinner, we strolled out together to the local Park of Culture. There were two games of chess in progress, whose course was shown on boards, round which there was clustered a large, intent crowd. The Chinese have the great advantage of being infinitely charming. The intentness of their faces, a kind of youthful wisdom, even innocence, makes it a pleasure to watch them. They are very eager and polite, and like smiling. As it was Saturday night, the Park was crowded – masses of people drifting about, small children strapped on the back; sometimes carried by the other children not much bigger than the passenger.

June 2–3, 1958—In the Peking Train

The South China countryside was exquisitely green – beautifully cultivated paddy fields, smooth as a billiard table. At dawn, peasants with large hats such as Riviera ladies wear, were at work, with the water up to their knees sometimes. At dusk we watched them turn homewards. This irrigation system has gone on for thousands of years quite unchanged. The scene from the carriage windows would have been the same before Julius Caesar came to Britain – the same soil tilled in the same way with the same patience. I did not feel that the Communist regime had laid a very heavy hand on this part of China.

Of course, the regime soon came to occupy most of our thoughts, and conversation. Chip Bohlen, former US Ambassador in Moscow, once said to me that no one could have contact with a Communist regime without being permanently maimed thereby, in the sense of being obsessed, distracted, by it. Certainly, he was a good example. This is a smiling revolution compared with the sour-faced Slav one across the way in Russia. Everyone smiles and looks happy, or at any rate serene. They bustle cheerfully on and off the train, into and out of the restaurant car. There are no signs at all of a food shortage, though of course there may be one in the interior, for all I know, or can know. This is, so far, a truly proletarian state – without a bourgeoisie or apparent provileged class. They are, in dress and bearing, up to ninety-nine percent the same.

From the rice lands in the south we moved into the wheat lands in the huge central plain. Here the crop was decidedly poor and the peasants were working in gangs, usually with a gang-leader wearing a red armlet. I saw one file of peasants moving to work with a man with a gun bringing up the rear. This looked like collectivisation in the bad Stalinist sense. We went over a new bridge across the Yang-tse. Very well designed, and completed, apparently, in record time, into a large industrial area. Here a lot of the houses looked squalid, but again the faces bore no signs of oppression. I still remember very vividly the fear which permeated faces in Russia – the grey, shrinking fear. I have not seen that here.

Peking

We arrived in Peking in the evening, dead on time. I had an idea of Peking as a sort of place like Xanadu, with magic domes and caves of ice. At first glance, in the dark, it seemed quite ordinary, with subdued lighting, little traffic and few people in the streets. We drove to the hotel, lately built, in Intourist style, with a large bas-relief of toilers toiling, and two unspeakable statues of a proletarian youth and maiden, scarcely Chinese, belonging to the Festival School which is standardized throughout the world – dedicated to the Unknown Common Man. Jack Gee of Reuters whisked me off straightaway to join a party at the British Embassy. It was like a strange dream. We drove through a massive red gate into the large Embassy Compound – a little, bizarre world all on its own, sealed – shut off. Our host was the Counsellor, Cedric Mabey. The men were sitting at table still, in white dinner jackets, brandy and coffee before them. Later, we joined the ladies underneath a tree in the compound outside. A Norwegian lady whispered that social life in Peking was very tedious because they all saw each other each day, from time to time showing one another their cine-camera films of the last May Day Parade. As though to give point to her remark, Mabey herded us all inside to look at cine-camera films of his travels in China and Cambodia. There were humorous interludes of his children skating. His companion in Cambodia was Malcolm MacDonald, who appeared several times in the film, bandy-legged and agile. Mabey's patter flowed on along a well-worn groove and when the showing was over we all thanked him and took our departure. No image that I could have invented would have conveyed better than this Embassy party did, what I conceive to be the present attitude of mind of the remnants of Western European bourgeois society. Had I invented the scene it would have seemed exaggerated.

The next day I telephoned to the Foreign Press Department of the Foreign Office and made an appointment there. It carried my mind back so vividly across twenty-five years to when I was a Correspondent in Moscow – the same set-up translated into Chinese. Then I went with the Gees to see the Forbidden City. It was very exquisite – the gleaming roofs, the bizarre shapes, the bright colours, but too strange and outlandish to move me much. For buildings, or any art, to make my heart stand still (as, for instance, Salisbury Cathedral and Chartres did) it has to be connected with what I understand and belong to. The wall and the massive gates and the towers were most impressive, but even then I could not populate the place, as I could, for instance, the ruined

Roman cities in Transjordan. I could not bring this place to life, at all, and so, for me, it remained just a curiosity. In any case, I have never had much interest in the past. I find the present too absorbing.

In the afternoon I tramped about Peking. Peking streets are decidedly ramshackle, but still, as on the train, people are smiling and amiable and orderly. They are very innocent. Most of the filth that used to be in China was foreign imported. Now it's all gone – no opium, whore houses, gambling dens, drunkenness, strip-tease; nothing of that sort at all now. At nine o'clock everything closes. Never have I seen such propriety. I like it – no eroticism at all; total absence of coloured filth and sadism, which is to be seen wherever Freedom reigns and Western Values prevail. The curious thing is that this orderliness seems to be maintained without evident supervision. There are very few uniformed police about, and one is not aware (as one is so constantly in the USSR) of the presence of secret police personnel. There is no ostensible terrorism; rather, it would appear, an elaborate and ingenious organization of surveillance based on the street, the residence, the floor, and, finally, the individual apartment.

The next day I presented myself at the Foreign Ministry. At Chinese Government offices no one askes you your business. You are expected, led to a waiting room invariably furnished in red plush, provided with tea and cigarettes and then the door opens and in comes the person you are to see. In this case it was two Chinese ladies, both of whom I called Miss Chang. They sat down side by side on the sofa, and I explained the sort of things I wanted to see in China. They nodded sympathetically and in unison, and then one of them went off to get me a press card. It was like having an interview with a Mother Superior and one of her assistants. From the Foreign Office I went on to the Post Office to get collect telegraphic facilities. There just the same thing happened. Then I looked in at the Russian Embassy about my visa to Russia. Two jovial, almost uproarious, figures there assured me there would be no difficulty. While he was speaking, one of them flicked over the pages of my passport. It was very unlike any previous contact with Soviet authorities.

Travelling around in China one comes across quite a lot of Russians. The Chinese put them into the European category.

For instance, they stay in the European hotels, sit with Intourist guides at public entertainments as we do, and at the University live segregated in a hostel with other foreigners. This makes them seem more 'European' than they do at home. One is, as it were, aligned with them. The attitude of the Chinese towards them seems to me to be almost identical with our British attitude towards the Americans – outwardly affable, inwardly irritated and touchy. They find them expensive, sometimes offensive and boorish, and, by comparison with the subtleties of Chinese intelligence, rather stupid. For the British, on the other hand, they have a sort of nostalgic affection, which, however, they seldom risk showing.

British businessmen are a great feature of Peking. They come and go silently, mysteriously. Towards the regime, they are well disposed, if not obsequious. At a gathering I was chatting to a Dr G, head of the Chinese Foreign Trade Department, when up came an Englishman with a glass in his hand who said to Dr G: 'I want to drink to the future prosperity of your great country.' His accents were rich and fulsome, his expression deeply solemn. He turned out to be the representative of a major engineering firm. It was, I thought, a rather fascinating little vignette! So, I believe, did Dr G. There was a decided twinkle in his eye as he responded. One of the great strengths of Communist regimes is that they can safely count upon the full approval, if not adulation, of foreign capitalists who hope to sell them things.

In fact, these latest travels of mine have convinced me more than ever before that a money system is inherently weak and vulnerable. It works all right if everyone is in on the game, but when a large part of the world has contracted out, those who continue to play are at a great disadvantage. To believe in money is to be weak; to accept money as the yardstick of human endeavour is to belittle, confuse, and ultimately render it unavailing. To take one small example. Reuters, to maintain its revenue, feels bound to stay on good terms with the Communist regime in Peking. For the sake of this revenue, it will, in effect, make propaganda on behalf of a regime which aims to encompass its ruin. The trouble with capitalism is, not that it is ruthless and unscrupulous, but that for the sake of a shilling today it will advance causes which will destroy it tomorrow. Trade Unions come into this category, just as much as Trusts and individual capitalists. The huge investment of the oil companies in the Middle East rather than in Canada provides another example. Within a decade at most all that investment will be lost, but it was irresistible because of the large, immediate return it offered. Greed is not so much wicked, as stupid and short-sighted. If we continue to base our society on it, we are lost.

Shanghai

I caught the plane in the early morning. As we were getting on to the plane a Frenchman travelling with me pointed to two Chinese ahead of us and said in awed tones: 'High Party officials'. It is rather sad that the former arrogance of the Europeans in China has turned into obsequiousness. Here, as in India and Indonesia, the generation which knew the former set-up will have to die off before normal relations can be established.

My Intourist man gathered me up and we drove to my hotel. He was a genial youth with immense teeth, which he constantly displayed by smiling. It was a relief to be away from Peking's antiquities. From my hotel window I looked down upon the familiar scene of a large, congested city. Our first call was at the Foreign Office – the usual drill, the wait in the red plush chairs, tea and cigarettes, the opening door, and the entry of two officials, one to talk and the other to take notes. The talker was a small, smiling man with whom I discussed the things I would like to do while in Shanghai; the listener was a spare bald man. We paid the usual compliments – I was so happy to be in China; they were so happy to welcome foreigners there from the West, etc. The politeness was terrific and pleasing. We took our leave, my custodian and I, and decided to take a drive round Shanghai. Though only a tiny European community remains, European influence is still all-pervasive, if indefinable. It is something about the buildings themselves, the way people walk. Ten years ago, we decided, the office buildings all round us would mostly have housed European firms; there would have been private motor cars for business executives, mostly European; there would have been hordes of beggars trailing after us, and men importuning.

That evening I visited a sort of amusement arcade – crowds

wandering from one entertainment to another. There was opera, a play of sorts, juggling, contortionists, etc. The place, apparently, had been a sort of vice den (according to my smiling interpreter). Now it was just males and females in blue trousers with their curious intent, innocent expressions. Up and down stairs, along galleries, moving.

On Sunday morning I went to an Anglican service in what had been Shanghai Cathedral. Quite a large congregation; Service in Chinese, including hymns, psalms, lesson, collects. The Red Flag was largely in evidence behind the pulpit. Next to us I found a youthful, polite clergyman in a neat grey suit and black tie. He talked to me through the service, explaining the situation of the Anglican Church in China – quite autonomous, self-supporting, permitted to conduct services and minister to its own congregation, but not to evangelize outside. My clergyman a bit too smooth to please me. We adjourned afterwards to a room and there went on discussing. He purported to know nothing about the situation of the Roman Catholics. Though neat and smiling, he seemed vaguely uneasy.

I went on to spend the afternoon with one of the few remaining Chinese capitalists – at least so he was billed. His house was in hideous taste, but affluent. He had been at Cambridge (read Economics) and purported to be highly contented with his present circumstances. His most frequent expression was 'I don't mind telling you'. What he had to say amounted to a kind of apologia – how his father had been a millionaire and lived by speculation; how he could have made a get-away to Hong Kong, but decided to remain and make his terms with Mao Tse-tung; how now he managed a family mill with a Communist associate, and found this more rewarding than any of his previous activities, though, he didn't mind telling me, at first he had been very doubtful. His face was oddly tormented – but the torment below the surface. On the surface he was embarrassingly ingratiating and unctuous. I felt sorry for him and drawn to him. He went on and on telling me how happy he was, and thereby conveying his truly appalling unhappiness. There is no truth to be learned from peering over the wall at this different sort of human society. Only lies can pass across the wall – on which my Chinese Communist-Capitalist had got impaled, cutting a truly woebegone figure.

On my way back to the hotel I looked in at a Roman Catholic

service. It was very different from the Anglican – much less
prosperous, no Red Flag, a kind of tatterdemalion defiance about
it. I fancy the Catholics have put up some sort of fight, whereas
the others have totally surrendered. They cannot win though.
Christianity has no roots at all in China. It just belonged to the
concessionary regime, and must disappear with it – unless a tiny
flicker manages to survive. A Buddhist temple I went to after the
Anglican service was even deader – polished, silent rooms and
scriptures neatly stowed away.

The hotel dining room was on the twelfth floor – quite small
and most frequented by foreigners. Russians are the sahibs or
Herrenfolk. They throw their weight about considerably. Then
come the Eastern Europeans, and then the Westerners. I have a
feeling that the hotel servants don't like the Russians much. To me
they have been exceedingly attentive.

I visited the docks – dock labourers doing gymnastic exercises;
a curious sight; dropped in at one or two houses, followed by a
horde of children; then joined by a man who was obviously the
local Party boss – quite youthful, pleasant, but in charge. Next on
to the inevitable new workers' housing estate – creches, kinder-
gartens, etc. An election going on. Rather disconcerting for my
interpreter when someone arrived at the polling station with a pile
of completed voting papers. Anyway, I reflected, all voting fairly
absurd; this just more so. Went to traditional opera – story of a
student who visited an island and fell in love with lady there.
Lady's brother, who was dissident, was engaged in trying to
abduct a virtuous Miss Wong, who fled pursued by abductor.
They all arrived at small town. Abductor told his men that when
Miss Wong got into her sedan chair they should whisk it off to his
sister's house. Actually student, unable to get into hotel, took
refuge in sedan chair, and then was carried away to the lady he
most wanted to see. All very delicately done – the singing beyond
me, but not unpleasing. All parts taken by women.

Interesting conversation on Monday with C. C. Tan, a
biologist at Shanghai University. Spoke about Lysenko controversy, about which he had very gloomy views as he'd worked
with Morgan. He said this controversy was 'unfortunate' and that,
though he had little regard for Lysenko's work, he told his students
to read it without prejudice. Talked to Tan for three hours, going
into the whole question of creative freedom. He was obviously

on my side, but argued the other, not unconvincingly – a powerful, attractive man, highly intelligent and unrattled. We started off with him insisting on answering me in Chinese, but as our conversation proceeded the interpreter got forgotten. I spoke about the rectification campaign whereby students and staff stand up in the form and make searching criticism of one another. I said that to me this procedure was exceedingly distasteful. 'I don't blame you,' he said.

I looked over a newspaper – the same old smell and noise; the same doorman smoking the same cigarette. Gather that information funnelled in from on high through China News Agency, and procured editorials. The Peking *Peoples' Mail* sets the tune, and the others (like the Shanghai *News Daily*) faithfully pipes.

At the hotel fell in with Quaker lady, who was concerned to justify everything that went on in Russia and China. I asked her if she'd like to accompany me that evening to meet some Protestant Churchmen. Along we went, finding the YMCA, where our rendezvous was, with some difficulty. There were four clergymen – the chap I'd met at Trinity Church, a Baptist, a Methodist and the YMCA Secretary. We got into a row immediately when I asked whether there was any possibility of conforming Christianity and Marxism. Yes there was, they said, and off we went. Without any question, they were the four most unpleasant Chinese I have met – venomous, untruthful and arrogant. I could so easily imagine them in the concessionary days sucking up to their English superiors – probably more horrible then because more outwardly wormish. Probably, I reflected afterwards, the clergymen were only getting their own back for past subservience. If only they had not called themselves Christians! All the same, I reflected, it would probably be easier to be a true Christian in China today than in concessionary times.

Russia Revisited

I left in a Soviet jet airliner on Friday, June 27. At the airport a 'youth' delegation had just arrived from Moscow – rather elderly looking 'youth', clutching bunches of flowers, and making fraternal gestures to non-existent welcoming crowds. Our plane at last loaded up, and it shot off into the sky, very smooth and impressive.

I was sitting next to a General in uniform whom I took to be Russian, but who turned out to be Czech. He spoke English reasonably well, had lived a number of years in America.

The first spot in Russia where we touched down (after crossing the Gobi Desert) was Irkutz. It was quite extraordinary to be back in this country after twenty-five years. I had never really expected to see it again, and now there I was, walking about, looking. The first impression was of incomparably greater affluence. That awful grey look of being famished, of having nothing, was nowhere in evidence. Also, the emergence of a bourgeoisie was apparent everywhere – officers, their wives in relatively elegant dresses, their children looking around them with that slight disdain of the offspring of the well-to-do. Between a quarter and a third of everyone one saw was in some sort of uniform. It all reminded me irresistibly of illustrations in old editions of Chekhov or Turgenev – much gold braid, soldiers with their uniform caps rather on back of the head, with hair flopping out in front.

At Omsk the same thing. Met there by Intourist girl, very amiable and ebullient. She was an English student at the local Institute of Foreign Languages. Again, a very different type from the Intourist girls of my time. We talked laboriously for about an hour, and then she saw me off. A nice rather sad man, also working in the Intourist office, said he'd been given a copy of *The Man Who Never Was* by one of the members of the Covent Garden Opera whom he'd shown round Omsk. He spoke of this book as though it was a rare classic.

The plane was supposed to go on to Moscow, but actually came down at Sverdlov because the weather was bad in Moscow. There we stayed the night. I settled into a chair in the waiting room, but the Czech General sought me out and woke me up, and told me he had arranged for me to have a room. I was most touched, especially when he brought me his razor in the morning.

We spent the next day hanging about in Sverdlov because the plane was out of order and we had to wait for a spare part. I played three games of chess with an unshaven man in the airport. He was hostile at first, but afterwards very amiable. Also, I watched the planes coming in. Almost all of them had at least one General aboard.

U.S. Lecture Tour, 1960

September 24, 1960—New York

I went to see Ed Murrow and Fred Friendly at CBS. Ed now much ravaged, like a decayed prima donna. Spoke about John Kennedy, Democratic Presidential Candidate who, Ed said, was utterly cold and self-confident; not in anyway like traditional politician, no flamboyancy, panache, humbug even. This, I said, was a new type of leadership (Iain Macleod, the British equivalent), seeking power for power's own sake – an abstract pursuit, with television its perfect instrument. Interested to learn that Kennedy goes to barber to keep his crew-cut going despite some thinning out on top, and Nixon to give him a loftier forehead and air of maturity.

Drove out next day, with Peter Schwed of Simon and Schuster and his wife, to see P. G. Wodehouse. Plum rather stouter and a little comatose, Ethel immensely ancient, but still bustling about. We sat in the sun in the garden. Ethel told Plum to take his tie off because it didn't match his coat. This he obediently did. He was delighted when Schwed told him that a congratulatory letter to him on entering upon his 80th year had been signed by more than 100 writers. We strolled down to the Sound at the bottom of their garden – quiet water, very peaceful. Plum very annoyed because a TV serial he looks at every day – *Love and Life* – was interrupted by Khruschev's speech at the UN.

September 25, 1960

New York Times Sunday edition bigger than ever. Reflected that American pursuit of happiness involves everything getting bigger and bigger – cars, steaks, newspapers, etc. Satiety the enemy of this pursuit, the doom which haunts American life. Lunched with Michael King and K. S. Karel, *New Statesman* Paris correspondent. Karel had been to see Castro, said Americans ought to be nice to Castro, who's no Communist; all his ministers young and eager, no striped pants. How often one's heard this! For me, the exit, or at any rate the bar. King and I went on to Staten Island ferry, past the statue of Liberty and former Ellis Island (now, it appears, for sale). Coming back I marvelled once more at the Manhattan skyline, misty in the autumn light, exquisite in its unique, original way. The only architectural achievement of our time. The cathedrals of Western Europe were built to be eternal, and convey the idea of eternity. The skyscrapers of Manhattan are shaped in the image of their own ultimate destruction. They convey the idea of time, not eternity.

In the cab, returning to my hotel, the radio was on. A little, tinny-voiced girl, asked what she'd like to be, said, 'a missionary in England.' I wondered what she envisaged converting us to.

October 5, 1960

Started lecture tour with Colston Leigh who's the agent who arranged the tour. Pumped him on his other clients. Mrs Roosevelt the most lucrative; Attlee, of English lecturers, the best from Leigh's point of view. Interested to learn that Attlee no good in Canada. Canadians, presumably, still nourishing romantic ideas about Britain, find the little, desiccated Earl a let-down. Americans, on the other hand, quite prepared to accept him as an authentic peer and statesman. He reassures them.

October 7, 1960

Took evening train to West Chester, Pennsylvania. As always found complete detachment of being alone in railway compartment most peaceful and pleasing. Had what's called here 'roomette'. My destination Paoli (named, I afterwards learnt, after Boswell's hero), where I was met by three ladies on the staff of the West Chester College and taken to my hotel. After breakfast I was collected by a bearded Professor of English smoking a pipe, and we went along together to the college. There were, he said, two styles of academic architecture in America – what he felicitously called nineteenth-century Hamburg gothic, and sham mediaeval. West Chester College was in the former style. On the whole I prefer it to the other, which I remember at Harvard, particularly the library – like a huge church, looming and twilit. Someone told me that the process for making the stones look weather-worn had been applied too vigorously, and had to be checked by means of a wax treatment to prevent the whole edifice falling down.

The large auditorium in which I was to speak was packed full of students, the females on the two wings, the males in the middle. This arrangement, it was explained to me, was not segregation, but for choral purposes. The proceedings began with a massed rendering of *My Country, tis' of Thee* to an organ accompaniment. Human beings singing together, particularly when they're young, seem to express in the purest, simplest way the yearning of all human hearts. It always moves me deeply. The bearded Professor was, it appeared, a devout Anglo-Catholic (in fact he intends shortly to take Episcopalian Orders) and he much resented legislation which forbade religious services at State educational institutions. I said this was our version of Communist godlessness. Step by step, in a kind of collective trance, we were going their way.

Student audiences in America are probably the most receptive and appreciative in the world. They exude the spirit of youthfulness; laugh with the gay abandon of children, and accept any old dog-eared epigram as though it had come straight from Jonathan Swift – as, indeed, in my case it often has.

The next day I drove out from New York to address a Garden City Ladies' Club. My hire car was a large Rolls-Royce. Passing the Waldorf Astoria Hotel, we got caught up in Harold Macmillan's cavalcade. At one point, his identical Rolls-Royce drew level with mine, and I fancied that he peered in at me with distaste.

October 8, 1960

Such ladies as these are enormously 'English' even when their political activities suggest the contrary. They complain, like their

English equivalents, of there being no servants, and of how sad it is to see the large estates being sold up. Although they are mostly unattractive physically, they create an impression of sensuality, even animality. This makes them a little frightening. When their faces fall into repose, they might be absorbed in some lewd dream, so loosely do their lips fold, so greedy is their expression. I suppose they are just rich, and, as such, self-indulgent, over-fed, and indolent. One easily imagines them in bed, wearing extravagant night apparel, and grimly waiting for reluctant, but ultimately docile, husbands. The nearly good-looking among them are, in a way, the most abhorrent. One knows quite well that in particular circumstances one might mistake the varnish for the glow of living flesh.

After the lecture, we adjourned for tea. One of the ladies came up to me and thanked me for my 'message'; then hastily corrected herself, and offered thanks for the lecture. 'Message' is, I imagine, the usual term. I was glad to be regarded as not having one. During tea they circulated about, ageing birds with rare plumage. The one I liked best was an immensely old, wrinkled bright-eyed lady who was pouring out. She pulled me down to her, and whispered: 'I thought you were going to say, as you did on television, that you didn't believe in anything. That with the cathedral so near wouldn't have been right. It would have upset them'. I assured her that I shouldn't have dreamt of saying anything of the kind in that place. 'You're quite right, of course,' she said. 'We can only keep searching.' I was greatly touched.

On the way back, the driver of my Rolls told me the approximate cost of the houses we passed. Americans love this sort of thing. To know the price of anything gives it existence. I earn, therefore I am.

Went in the evening to *The Best Man* by Gore Vidal. The play's a typical egg-head presentation of politics, quite amusing and ingeniously constructed, but completely wrong. Politicians are not cynical, but extremely sentimental and credulous. They will believe anything, of themselves or anyone else. If Julius Caesar had been cynical he would not have been murdered. Likewise, if Hitler had been cynical he would have won the war. Shakespeare, unlike Vidal and all the other egg-head camp-followers of power in this country, understood exactly the sort of man who becomes a power-addict. Shaw, another egg-head with an itch to get into, or at any rate near, the seats of the mighty, complained that Shakespeare's Caesar was such a trivial and absurd character that he could never have got where he did. On the contrary. Shakespeare's Caesar is to the life; Shaw's, good in the classroom and on television, but quite hopeless in action. The audience all enjoyed the play. It made them feel that their politicians are cynical, but funny, and ultimately serve the public interest in a sort of way. Actually, they're infinitely worse than this – self-righteous, earnest, and only concerned with the public interest in so far as it's identified with their own. If either of the present contenders for the Presidency, Nixon and Kennedy, thought that publicly kissing Khruschev's behind would ensure his election, he'd do it without the slightest hesitation, and, what is more, having convinced himself that it was a noble, disinterested and public-spirited act.

Left the next morning very early to catch plane at Newark Airport, New Jersey, to catch plane to Lancaster, Pennsylvania. Airport misty, dreary place at that hour. Everlasting self-service coffee bar going. Joined the queue myself for coffee and toast; toast; then, consuming this, watched the others. Thought how it would make an image of our time – such varied humans collecting their viands, and then passing through the wicket gate, where they paid. This a freely constructed concentration camp; first, through a long tunnel with a snake hiss, then the cook-house, then into the sky. Where's the world? We've lost it – not too much with us, but too absent. There's no escape from here. We're caught. Perhaps the only thing is to atomize it all into radioactive dust. No other solution but to blast our way out, even though we die in the process.

At Lancaster met by another Professor who drove me amiably and loquaciously to the campus. These smaller towns, to outside eyes, are indistinguishable one from another, even though they have their particular antiquities – in the case of Lancaster, President Buchanan's house, and the most ancient tobacco shop in the United States. I think of them always as neon signs shining in the darkness, and offering the basic essentials for the pursuit of happiness, which are: Food, Beauty, Drugs, Gas, or, in other words, the means to sustain life, to reproduce it, to protract it, and to achieve mobility. These are our Four Pillars.

October 9, 1960

Saw an American businessman at Lancaster airport with *Time* magazine and a book called *The End of American Innocence* under his arm. Did his innocence ever begin, I wondered? After lecture, rested. Then my Professor collected me, and we did TV programme about books including recent volume, interminably drawn out, on Max Beerbohm. Professor, like the writer of the book, took the line that Max the type of perfect English Gentleman. He was able to be so, I suggested, because he was a German. All types are fraudulent, otherwise they wouldn't be types. I thought of old Max, his straw hat on one side, in his horrible Rapallo villa. Sweet, indolent old fraud, with his red rimmed eyes and anguished mouth. Life caught up even with him in the person, first, of his wife Norma, a really terrible American lavendar and old lace; then of Frau Jungman, a German lady who'd looked after some elderly German man-of-letters. I hoped, when Max died, it would have been possible to move her on to look after T. S. Eliot. Alas, she died in her bath shortly after Max's death, and anyway Eliot married. I passed the villa the other day. It's still empty and for sale. No one wants it.

October 10, 1960

Following morning wandered about campus a little; then sat and wrote in my room, feeling for once well contented. Professor came for me, and we went together into cafeteria. At my table surrounded by students, all wanting to talk, and even to listen. All this ought to make me very tired, but doesn't. Perhaps I was meant to be campaigning politician.

At Albany loquacious elderly American waiting for me. He turned out to be some sort of steel tycoon. Insisted that in his car we should fasten seat belts. Said that if all did this great number of accidents would be avoided. He talked and talked. This, I have found, is nervous complaint which afflicts some Americans. It's not that they want to say anything. They just want to keep talking. The only protection against them is to detach one's mind and not listen, which they don't seem to mind.

Met at hotel by English journalist, formerly on *Mirror*.

Fellow-countrymen, for some reason, dearer to one in this country than in more alien places. Chatted with him until I left for drinks and dinner at some sort of club. Among the company there, a greying, obviously once attractive, affluent woman who was decidedly tight. This relatively common phenomenon – women, probably the nicer sort, who've pursued happiness so far that they've as it were, come out the other side. Dear alcohol. It was one of the creator's more kindly after-thoughts. Now-a-days, rich Americans mostly Anglophile. They so desperately want us to be as we seem in the advertisement pages of the *New Yorker*. Oh, if Britannia really did rule the waves still! When I say she doesn't nowadays even rule the Serpentine they only think I'm joking.

Watched Nixon–Kennedy TV show. Spent my time wondering what Khruschev would think of it. Decided it would confirm him in his view that our sort of elections as much a fake as his – two matching candidates instead of one. Abraham Lincoln perhaps surprised if someone had told him that a century or so hence grease-paint might be more decisive in electoral contests than soft soap.

Val came down from Toronto to spend the week-end, very self-contained and happy. It's more difficult to speak to one's own children than anyone; not because of reticence, rather because of basic similarities which make speech unnecessary. In the evening to her friend Polly Grant. Other guests mostly English – a sort of expatriate Chelsea set. Mostly rather tiresomely complaining about America and Americans. As the disparity in power and wealth between England and America becomes more marked, the English are the most inclined to take a patronising attitude towards the Americans, and the Americans to revere and emulate English attitudes. Understand that now an English accent, once derided, is an asset in America. Jobs can be got just on the strength of it.

Lunched with Alex Faulkner, and discussed with him curious way in which news of America sent to England acquires anti-American slant by the time it appears there. Admitted to being myself affected and then always surprised, on coming to America, not to find all youths juvenile delinquents, everyone smoking marijuana, taking bribes, being hauled before Congressional

Committees, and otherwise living up to American way of life as projected abroad. Distortion is, of course, instinctive rather than deliberate. With the aid of modern communication media, anywhere and anyone can be presented in any guise. Photographs, for instance, are infinitely varied, and can be chosen as required. Since they are all, in principle, true, this involves no overt tampering with truth. Art, which is supposed to be fantasy, conveys reality; reproduction processes like photography and television, which are supposed to convey reality, lend themselves to everlasting fantasy.

October 11, 1960

Left in the evening for New Orleans on huge jet, which rode vaingloriously into the sunset. Sat next to coffee planter in San Salvador – Spanish, with English father. Asked him about Castro. He intensely disliked Castro, and said he anticipated a counter-revolution in Cuba shortly, which would have covert American help.

New Orleans sultry, southern. I sniffed the warm air happily, noted the languid movements, the slowing down of everything – the whites a little strained, unduly white; the blacks at ease, as though they know inwardly that here, in these regions, they will one day be the masters. It always seems to me that the negroes in the South, where they are segregated, disenfranchized and otherwise deprived of civil rights, are happier, even more at ease, than those in the North, where they suffer so many fewer disabilities. This is perhaps because human beings are most uncomfortable when their ostensible circumstances differ widely from their actual ones. In the South the whites' public attitude to negroes expresses their true attitude. In the North it doesn't. For the same reason, it may be, the Jews have always loved Germany, and, for that matter, still do.

U.S. Lecture Tour, 1962

September 27, 1962

Coming over Triboro Bridge, as always, the lift to one's spirits. Thought of the car-load in *The Great Gatsby* making for New York. A misty evening; huge cars bumper to bumper, hugely powered, and crawling along. America.

At about three in the morning I looked out of my hotel window; drizzling, some lights still on, a few cars, steam rising from the pavement as though the city were on fire. Perhaps it is. Sleepless, I watched the awakening; garbage men noisily at work, more lights coming on, traffic gradually increasing. In the grey light, it was like being in a prison; walls everywhere, no escape.

Clark, my dear old friend, a Negro chauffeur, met me at the airport. He laughs and laughs with abandon. This unrestrained laughter of American negroes may in the end subdue the wry-faced whites. They begin to look a little furtive even here.

N.B. Great distinction of Americans in menial employment, like lift men and waiters. They have none of the dejected resentfulness of their European equivalent. They might be professors or diplomats. A lift man said to me that he liked his work. It brought him into contact with a lot of people. Happiness can be pursued as well in one job as in another. I never feel with Americans (outside teachers, non-best-selling writers, etc.) that they're eaten up with a sense of missing things.

October 2, 1962

New sort of isolationism – inward, of the spirit. Americans retreating into America and Americanism despite treaties and commitments. In some ways, out of the *Zeitgeist*. The Kennedy set-up somehow malodorous. He's an IBM equipped to speak and gesticulate, particularly to move his forearm up and down with mechanical dead emphasis.

The sweetness of Americans – 'You're welcome!' 'May I shake your hand?'. Later, in Cincinnati, feeling full of distaste for America and Americans, a waiter brought tea and cookies to my hotel room. 'It's a double portion today,' he said, 'because it's pay day.' He showed me his cheque. We both began to laugh uproariously.

Beaver – an American girls' college near Philadelphia. The college is a preposterous castle, built at a cost of $2m. by some Philadelphia tycoon at the turn of the century; dark, massive, unspeakable. Talking about this abomination aware, just in time, that it was taken seriously. The girls preferred the dormitory in it to the modern ones. They found it romantic, almost hallowed. Walked round the campus reflecting on the perfection of this false castle as a symbol of the American dream, of the American attitude to Europe. A folly; a joke in its sham, ponderous antiquity – massive, expensive, preposterous, phoney. Yet, to them, an authentic castle. Thus are Americans involved in Europe's decay, but unaware of the perils of their involvement because they had vested it with a seeming solidity. Everything reconstructed, down to the smallest and most abject details. The Europe the Americans imagine themselves to be defending is, in fact, a nineteenth-century, transatlantic model.

One of those dry, agreeable Americans, head of the English Faculty at Beaver, and the only other male besides myself around the place, told me how the Ford Foundation had decided to entrust the design of their pavilion at the 1964 World Fair jointly to a talented Japanese architect, Minoui Yamasaki, and Walt Disney, thereby, as they hoped, combining good taste and popularity. A pity Yamasaki wouldn't accept the collaboration. As my informant said, like breeding from Arthur Miller and Marilyn Monroe with the idea of producing some combination of their talents – a literate sex symbol, a third force. 150 million Americans can't be wrong, Disney has said. But they can.

October 3, 1962—Potsdam near Messena

Exquisite autumn day, flying low up the Hudson Valley, leaves gloriously autumnal. This part of America, towards the Canadian frontier, once much more prosperous than now (wood-pulp industry now derelict); has an air of decay. The affluent society is not really affluent at all; only flushed in places, with the blood draining away in others.

The inconceivable boredom that can overwhelm one in these American towns. 'Miss K has done a lot for America – culture – elegant turn-out.' I downed my fifteenth cup of coffee, and said that I wished Miss K wouldn't smile so much but spent just half an hour a day scowling.

The town waking up. Noisy gear changes, the crowing of the cock; soon a roar of passing automobiles. The St Lawrence River seen out of my window, with the mist dissolving in the morning sunshine. Students variously attired going willingly to school. Education a mighty endeavour, a booming industry; the Gross National Mind ever soaring upwards.

October 14, 1962—Indianapolis

Another metropolis of lights, shimmering, moving, changing. Neon lighted faces somehow look very weary. Only the cars glisten with new life. Driving them, American faces fail into repose and serenity. They are not only the index of American prosperity; they are that prosperity.

October 15, 1962—Chicago

The business Americans are constantly seen in hotels, and travelling about; in a black alpaca-type suit, trim white shirt with starched cuffs and collar; hair fairly close cut, well-shaved and well groomed. They're quite indistinguishable from one another, like Guards Officers.

Chicago Lakeside Drive a solid throng of motor cars coming into town in the morning, and returning in the evening. By the lake's edge practically no one. I stood there for quite a while, feeling detached from the town looming up in front of me, and the roar of the cars going by.

October 16, 1962—Oshkosh

Tiny churches and chapels in lonely places, strangely named – Chapel of the Birthright; rather touching, a tiny, bizarre gesture of faith.

At Oshkosh, as at Beaver College, large Elizabethan style residence constructed by pulp tycoon; new art gallery, mostly dedicated to nineteenth-century American painter, Innes. Ghastly edifice. Shown round by curator, in authentic Harris Tweed deep brown jacket, who pointed out with pride the various styles in the house's architecture, and in interior decoration. The death-watch beetle is at work here, too. Not by Communism, or its own internal violence and nationalism, will America die, but through a mania to participate in our dry rot. The immigrants were cheated. They did not escape from Europe, but took Europe with them.

October 22, 1962—Colorado Springs

The lush motel, carpeted, full of sounds, sweet airs. A blue, warmed pool, with wreaths of steam rising from it. All under steam heat, all neon-lighted; all hermetically sealed against the elements, against life.

President Kennedy on the screen, perhaps announcing the end of the world; pudding-faced, and reading from a paper like a child, knowing the words, but not always making sense out of the sentences. His appearance was preceded by an ad for some sort of jet-toy – a little boy firing, and triumphantly saying: 'Got it!'. (Which was the ad and which the Presidential broadcast?)

October 26, 1962—Salt Lake City

Met at airport by Mormon youth with gentle eyes who'd been missionary in England. 'We can at least be perfect in abstinence and in talking'. In other respects – like living up to the Gospel, perfection is unattainable. Took a walk towards the mountains, reflecting (Cuban crisis still going) that perhaps one might get cut off in Salt Lake City and spend one's remaining days among the Mormons. If this happened, they'd claim, plausibly enough, that Brigham Young foresaw it all, the nuclear holocaust, also he said 'This is the place!' A prophecy fulfilled. No support among

Mormons, however, when I hopefully suggest signs and portents
presaging the world's end. No more than usual, they insist. 'Life
is too marvellous,' I say in my lecture, 'to be taken seriously, and
truth too stupendous and luminous to be solemnly propounded,'
and mean it, too.

October 29, 1962—San Francisco, California

Everyone says San Francisco nicest town in US. I often say it,
but doubt if it's true. In most moods, secretly, prefer the straight
American product. Walked up and down the hills. Heard that
Khruschev had seemingly climbed down over Cuba.

Lunched at the Pacific Club with Scottish business man and
two of his cronies. All very rich. English-style club. Americans
of English origin like sahibs, but the others coming up – coloured,
Porto Ricans, Mexicans, etc. Will they ultimately, perhaps, get
self-government, like the Indians and Africans? Anti-semitism
prevalent, but rarely admitted.

October 30, 1962—Modesto, California

Caught Greyhound bus – cheapest form of travel. Queuing for
my bus with poor people, coloured, etc., felt a mounting blissful
sense of relief at being with them. Great truth in saying that the
poor are blessed. All the manifestations of riches contain misery,
implicit if not explicit. Joyousness comes from below. In bus, all
windows sealed, glass blue-tinted. Once again the governing
American passion to exclude the world – air, sound, light, food,
sensuality. Everything wrapped, packaged.

After my lecture sat with several Faculty figures and listened
to record of Canadian radio satire on McCarthy hearings. Quite a
conspiratorial air. We were like an underground company daring
to listen to clandestine broadcast, glancing anxiously over our
shoulders to make certain we were unobserved. Actually, the satire
was harmless enough, and in some respects distorted. Milton and
Cromwell appeared as champions of freedom. Tried to explain
that they had been on the other side. Liberalism, I reflected,
always wrong whichever way it's played.

October 31, 1962—Los Angeles, California

Los Angeles probably most horrible town in the world, enveloped in hurtful smog, all roads; a truly corrupted distorted place. One feels it at once on arrival. My hotel room at Pasadena had a balcony on which I could breathe, and from which see nearby mountains. I looked out with delight, and enjoyed the soft warm night.

At UCLA great gathering, good lecture, uproarious laughter and applause. Afterwards, taken off by weird disorderly woman who said she wanted to take my photograph. Drove back with her and her son to what was obviously rather affluent house at Santa Monica, which should have been overlooking the sea, but actually only overlooked smog.

November 6, 1962—San Diego, Rancho Santa Fe

San Diego naval base. Place full of sailors who all fell asleep with that touching, rather exquisite abandon of the very tired and the very young. Lady (Mrs Ames) met me and showed me the sights of San Diego before leaving for Rancho Santa Fe. The 300 affluent housing area, etc. A doubt seized her. 'Are you really interested?' I said I was. The Rancho turned out to be an immensely lush little pocket of life; no poor, no Jews, all very elegant. Stayed at the Inn, full of golfers, ageing executives with the faces of boys; weirdly youthful under their grizzled hair and wrinkles. Evening of the Congressional elections. The ladies solid for Nixon.

November 16, 1962—Cincinnati, Ohio

Journalist telephoned to my hotel room to say: 'Winston Churchill said Cincinnati one of the most beautiful inland cities in the world. Do you agree?' 'No,' I replied. Typical politician's remark, with the qualification 'inland city' to provide a sort of justification for the outrageous lie. Spent the day, as many another, walking about the streets. On the city's outskirts saw small shop with, on the window: 'Eternity, eternity, how will you pass eternity?' These

American towns indistinguishable from one another. All one remembers of them is some trivial occurrence; yet I know that whenever I meet an American who comes from Cincinnati I shall say I've been there, and he'll be enthralled.

November 18, 1962—Chicago

In the evening, sat rather gloomily in a bar. Woman perched next to me mentioned that she was fond of opera, looking forward to *Samson and Delilah*. I bring this out in people. Americans, in their happiness, keep together, excluding outsiders. This is why, alone, we can be so lonely in American cities. Strolling, in such a mood, after the meal, I noticed that Lenny Bruce was appearing at a sort of cabaret place; went in, was recognized by a girl at the ticket place, who arranged for me to see the show, though packed out. Bruce dressed in a kind of swami's suit. Act consisted of a monologue, disconnected in theme; a sort of whimpering, spiteful, petulant complaint against the times and man's lot today. Not particularly funny, but the audience laughed in a nervous sort of way when he used an obscene word ('shit', for instance), or at some sally against nuclear war, etc. Occasionally used Yiddish word, which aroused easier laughter. At my table married couple – mother-in-law, she from New Orleans, wife former air hostess, and her husband. Mother-in-law said she'd been married forty years, wonderful husband, wonderful son-in-law, wonderful home. All wonderful. Somehow, from there, got on to the subject of mistresses. Ex-air hostess said American women liked to be wives and mistresses in one. Large assignment, I said.

November 19, 1962—Pittsburg

Met at airport by Monsignor Ryan, large, amiable, talkative man. Confirmed opinion I'd long held that Roman Catholic clergy are having a Reformation of their own now, possibly at the wrong time and in the wrong way. Anyway, they're very evangelical, hearty, anti-ritualist and Italianate. Ryan drove me round the town, talking away. We looked in at Catholic cathedral to see modern statue of St Joan. Reminded me of 1914–18 war memorials; touch of T. E. Lawrence and of Sybil Thorndyke. (I've often wondered what Joan of Arc was really like; probably more in the genre of Edith Sumerskill or Sitwell than of Peggy Ashcroft).

Joined at dinner by characters from the university and art gallery. Talked about education (Pittsburg University's budget $38m). Was it any good? Ryan talked all the way back to his college about how celibacy of clergy now out of date, as Latin Liturgy was.

Always, when I'm with Catholics, I realize I could never join them. All the same, happy day here. Ryan told me rather scornfully how the nuns had set up a shrine to St Philomena, who, he said, probably never existed. 'All the same, it's a pretty name,' I said. He wouldn't have it. The shrine has been deactivated, he said. Even so, I saw a party of nuns visiting it.

November 21, 1962—Richmond, Virginia

One is less conscious of racial hostility in the south than in the north. All the negroes seem to be smiling. Perhaps the warmer climate suits them better. Or maybe the admission of segregation as distinct from its practice without being admitted, as in Chicago, makes for easier relations.

At Richmond airport got into conversation in cafeteria with substantial citizen who turned out to be some sort of clerical salesman. Americans love selling. It brings out all their ardour. Far from regarding it a demeaning occupation, they glory in it, love to talk about it. Case I heard of – motor car salesman so successful that he became highly paid executive. Used occasionally even then to slip out and sell a car to a difficult customer just for the sheer joy of it.

Everywhere I went, everyone I met, however casually, on this tour for some reason fixed photographically in my memory. Even, in some cases, people I passed along airport corridors. Perceptions heightened.

Plane late in starting, and arrived New York in drenching rain; road into town dense with Thanksgiving Day traffic, lights liquid and wavering in the watery air.

Farewell America

Driving over the Triboro Bridge, on arrival in New York, is always an exhilarating moment. This is especially true if one arrives in the evening. The lighted skyscrapers acquire a particular elegance as darkness descends, like a sluttish woman when she has dressed and got herself up for a dinner party.

Equally, the moment of departure is exhilarating. One loves to leave.

Almost everything that has been said about America is both true and false. It is enormously monotonous, and infinitely varied. Its pace is fast to the point of exhaustion and slow to the point of exasperation. Americans are kind and generous, and, at the same time, hard and demanding. They tell you everything about themselves in the first half hour of a casual acquaintanceship, and retreat behind a wall of impenetrable reserve.

The same man whose husky grace sems to fit him to climb Mount Everst sucks down vitamin pills to keep up his strength, and anxiously weighs himself each morning like a ballerina or jockey fearful of putting on weight. No enterprise is too difficult and extensive to be attempted, some of the most trivial remain unattempted. Highways with six lanes a side half unprotected over open railway level-crossings. Huge plates of food fail to nourish, newspapers as big as an encyclopedia fail to inform.

A sense of being the world's arbiter is combined with an agonized need to be reassured about whether the rest of mankind take this pretention seriously. Dr Gallup is a statistical physician whose services are in constant demand. Cuba pulverises America with fright; they can survey, unafraid, Russia's formidable battery of nuclear weapons. They love to get into Burke's *Landed Gentry*, and pride themselves on calling the boss by his Christian name.

Of all countries, America is the one where a stranger may enjoy the most open-handed and affectionate hospitality, and also the one where he can be most lonely. Affluence and dread of penury exist side by side. The millionaire fears that he will soon be penniless; the bum is sure that he will soon be a millionaire.

Virtue is highly regarded, irregular lives are no impediment to public adulation. The Gabors and Mrs Eleanor Roosevelt alike enjoy public esteem. A twelfth marriage is as romantic an occasion as a first one, and college students, in the same breath, ask questions about Chaucer and Jack Parr.

Any gadget which procures leisure is sure of a ready appeal. Yet leisure is abhorrent, and needs to be filled extraneously. On Sundays, as P. G. Wodehouse said, everyone in Jacksonville drives to Johnsonville, and everyone in Johnsonville drives to Jacksonville. Even crossing the Arizona desert car radios are turned on, and the few moments of a lift's ascent or descent requires piped music to be bearable.

Juke boxes play as assiduously in Alaska as in Brooklyn. The fight against silence is assiduously waged. Dentists drill decayed molars to music; and the commuters, as they homeward plod their weary way, are assailed in the terminal stations by pop songs, and, at Christmas time, carols. Afternoon papers appear in the morning, and morning ones in the early evening. Protest processions of unemployed make their way to Washington in a motorcade, and outside one of the largest atomic missile installations appears the notice: 'Our Profession Is Peace' – a slogan which uncannily recalls the Ministry of Peace in Orwell's *1984*.

I decided to make my farewells to a country, not of humans, but of mechanical brains. Though it was a Sunday, several of them were thinking hard, with lights flashing, and bells ringing. As some interesting thought occurred to one or other of them, an attached pointer sprang into sudden activity. Hoping to share its moment of truth, I looked over its shoulder. Alas, they all seemed that day to be wholly preoccupied with figures. There was no divine revelation. I should have liked to ask them about an after-life, and when the end of the world was to be expected, but felt it would be discourteous to intrude upon their cogitations. One of them was ready to play draughts with me, but was, I gather, unbeatable. Another was struggling to translate *Little Red Riding Hood* into English.

It might have been permissible to try a joke on them if only to see whether they could laugh. Unfortunately, I could not think of a suitable one. So I just waved a cheerful good-bye. Afterwards, I asked one of the keepers whether their many accomplishments included laughter. It appeared not, yet.

Diary 1961–1962

April 5, 1961

Just now I am in love with abstemiousness. Walking in the early morning, uplifted by it; not, however, because sensuality is bad, but because it clouds a further-reaching and more perceptive vision. Thus the ardours of abstemiousness are like the longer and more arduous way taken because the view is better. One should not give up things because they are pleasant (which is Puritanism) but because, by giving them up, other things are pleasanter.

April 6, 1961

I am very happy these spring days. Each morning I wake between 4 a.m. and 5 a.m.; then make tea, read for a while, work until 7.30, when I go for a walk. Through the window I watch the day begin, from first grey light to full sunrise, as, in the evening, I watch it end. It is a great joy to see each day's first and last light. After breakfast I read the papers, then work until lunch time. After lunch, I lie down with a book, and usually sleep for an hour or so; then walk or do gardening, mostly mowing the grass; followed by a late tea, work until about 7.30, another short stroll, supper, a game of cards with Kitty, and bed. This quiet and serenity set one apart from public affairs. The newspapers, which I still avidly devour, seem to be about another world than mine. I continue to want to know about it, but not to visit it.

A paperback series of religious books has, for its first volume, St Augustine's *Confessions*, and for its second *Sex, Love and Marriage*. In contemporary terms, anything about fornication is religious, as anything about raising the standard of life, and ameliorating its material circumstances, is Christian. In this sense fornication can be seen as sacred, an act of Holy Communion – which, as Euclid says, is absurd.

April 8, 1961

As always, deeply distressed by seeing myself on television – interviewing Sir Roy Welensky, Prime Minister of Central African Federation. Decided never to do it again. Something inferior, cheap, horrible about television as such; it's a prism through which words pass, energies distorted, false. The exact converse of what is commonly believed – not a searcher out of truth and sincerity, but rather only lies and insincerity will register on it.

Read Edmund Wilson on the Dead Sea Scrolls. Faith and its sacred texts are of the desert, not of affluence; on sandy wastes and rocky mountain tops men think of God; in the lush, sheltered plains, forget Him.

Everything we do, say, wear, think; set of a hat, drop of a trouser-leg, creases of a face, gestures of hands, lips' turn and eyebrows' curve – everything, large and small, important and trivial, expresses us. We cannot hide by falsity; what is buried soon stinks, and camouflage may disguise in one direction only to be more obvious in another. Thought of this when I saw a pretty girl I knew who works on a women's magazine, running beside a train, in shoes with long, projecting toes and tall stiletto heels. Those useless, foolish toes were all her dreams and aspirations; all the fiction she's ever chosen for her magazine, accumulated and secreted in them. She wears her heart on her toes.

Almost the only thing the English never lose their faith in is hymns. If the National Anthem had been set to a different sort of music, we should long ago have become a republic. The 'Red Flag' and the 'Internationale' are both hymn tunes, and so permissible. After the Civil War, the English decided never to have another, and invented hymns to prevent its recurrence. The arrangement has worked excellently. Whatever has a hymn is secure. Rationalism, ethical societies, all the various organizations which sprouted out of Darwinism, fertilizers of the decay of the Anglican Church, have ceased to be because they failed to produce hymns. Societies like the Salvation Army survive because they have hymns. Popular poets like Tennyson, Kipling, Betjeman, invariably use hymn metres. So did A. E. Housman, whose dreary, arid, homosexual pessimism was acceptable because hymnal in form. Imagine if he had written it in Alexandrine couplets. It would probably have been banned. 'Abide with me' provides an umbrella for anything from a Cup Final to a hunger march. Wilde should have written hymns of Reading Gaol, not a ballad. Then all would have been well.

April 11, 1961

Talking with John Boulting about my *Heavens Above* film story, I realized that the producers didn't understand the theme at all. They're caught up in almost universal fallacy that the good Christian is one who tries to behave in what he supposes to be a Christian way, not the 'changed' man, the man who's put away the old Adam, and tried in the flesh to be reborn in the spirit. Dropping the conversion from my story (which they propose to do in their film treatment) is St Paul without the Damascus Road, or a story of adolescent love without adolescence – the *change*.

April 13, 1961

On television news, Professor Bernard Lovell said that getting a man into space was the greatest achievement of human history. By comparison with what? – presumably, Christianity, Shakespeare's plays, Chartres Cathedral, etc. Considered his observation probably the most fatuous I'd ever heard. One line of Blake is greater than getting to the moon. Believing so, I felt rather lonely, with everyone else, seemingly, taking Lovell's view. Feat presented to the world like woman's magazine fiction – handsome cosmonaut, suburban love, wife and two children, factory worker, etc.

April 18, 1961

Lindemann (Lord Cherwell, Churchill's scientific adviser during the war) insisting on saturation bombing of German working-class residential districts because people packed closer together. (See C. P. Snow's *Science and Government*). Thus the Class War probably fulfilled. So in division of Germany, Russia given the slums. Met Lindemann once with the Birkenheads at dinner. White-faced, unwholesome-looking, cold and Germanic. Special vegetarian dishes brought in for him. Abstemious in the cruel way – to have more energy for the exercise of his hate.

The question was brought up of how Churchill came to be so strongly under this malign influence. Suggested that it was because he was a German. Churchill had a respect, almost veneration, for the Germans. The only time I saw him he went on and on about how he would visit Germany, and be given a stupendous reception. He, who became famous for standing up to the Germans, most wanted to find himself on their side.

April 21, 1961

Watching film of Stalin, Roosevelt, Churchill, Khruschev, etc. noted that the only authentic human in this menagerie was Harry Truman. Felt enormously drawn to him.

April 23, 1961

Oswald Mosley's household – at the top of a block of flats in Onslow Square, with a long corridor suitably conveying the idea that it's a place of mystery, a headquarters, the centre of an *apparat*. Mosley has a deformed foot, I imagine of the same nature as Byron's. His wife, Diana, still attractive, with that upper class air of vagueness, of not quite understanding what everything's about. Expensive clothes, soft and mystifyingly alluring. All, Mitford-wise, exaggerated, exploited. Mosley himself, at 65, still being boyish, eager. 'We're going to live through the most exciting days there have ever been. Isn't it wonderful!' Surprised to hear from him a panegyric of Asquith. All rather macabre – the electric smile, the fitness, the energy. Actually, he's a terrible bore, as all power maniacs are. The fact that he's a failed power maniac makes him more touching, to the point that one feels a sort of affection for him. That's all.

May 4, 1961

After Tate Gallery Brains Trust sat talking with Sir Robert Adeane, Henry Moore, Victor Passmore, and Stephen Spender about why Rembrandt was a great painter. Good old-fashioned stuff. Quite enchanted with Henry Moore – small luminous man, with great gentleness and humility, and, underlying these qualities, the artist's passion, ardour and audacity, erupting like an impudent choir-boy. Moore said he watched schoolgirls' legs, and one would be more beautiful than another, not because better proportioned or presented; just because it was a more beautiful leg. So Rembrandt a greater painter than other painters. Passmore observed that the difference between abstract and representational art was that the abstract artist had to invent his painting and then paint his invention, whereas the representational artist painted from life itself.

June 7, 1961—Hamburg

Flew from London yesterday to Hamburg; then to office of *Stern*. The usual chaos. Editor large, rather attractive, humorous man – Henri Nannen. All speak English, usually with marked American accent.

Later proceeded to visit Hamburg night life. A street with lights, Montmartre, Moulin Rouge, all the old, familiar names, but singularly joyless; Germans with stony faces wandering up and down, uniformed touts offering total nakedness, three Negresses and other attractions, including female wrestlers. Not many takers, it seemed, on a warm Tuesday evening. Had the feeling that all this had been set up in place of the rubble out of habit. It was there before, so put it back.

Dropped into a teenage rock-and-roll joint. Ageless children,

sexes indistinguishable, tight-trousered, stamping about, only the
smell of sweat intimating animality. The band were English, from
Liverpool, and recognized me. Long-haired; weird feminine
faces; bashing their instruments, and emitting nerveless sounds
into microphones. In conversation rather touching in a way,
their faces like Renaissance carvings of saints or Blessed Virgins.
One of them asked me: 'Is it true that you're a Communist?' No,
I said; just in opposition. He nodded understandingly; in opposition himself in a way. 'You make money out of it?' he went on.
I admitted that this was so. He, too, made money. He hoped to
take back £200 to Liverpool. (As it happens it was the Beatles just
beginning.)

June 10, 1961

Saw Public Relations Officer at *Bundeswehr* Army headquarters.
Usual wall diagram showing HQ organization. Arranged to go by
helicopter to manoeuvres following day, when flew over Luneberg
Heath where Monty took German surrender. All marked and
filled with military vehicles. As soon as one exercise over another
begins, like a raddled old whore taking sailor after sailor.
    Then off to watch the manoeuvres. Thought of cavalry exercises
before the 1914–18 war. One of few certainties about any future
hostilities is that these weapons won't be used. *Bundeswehr*
ostentatiously citizens' army. Badges of rank obscure, no heel-
clicking or ostentatious saluting; easy conversing between officers
and men. (Does this suit the German temperament? Will they
ever be able to make an army on these terms?) Talked to some
artillery personnel perched beside their guns, which were mounted
on a vehicle. 'What were they at?' Youthful officer replied, the
others all, German-fashion, accepting him as their spokesman.
Rather sweet boy who spoke about freedom, (what was it! I asked,
and like Pilate did not wait for an answer), atomic warfare, future
plans for studying. On to see General Muller, commanding whole
exercise, an optimist. In Wales, once *Bundeswehr* training began
there, everyone would settle down and be happy. I felt it was all
the third serial rights of an old war, and looked into the sky, where
a new one, if it came, would explode strangely, tragically, raining

death on us all. Muller laughed heartily when I said, of Franco-German rapprochement, that the French hated the Americans so much that they even liked the Germans. His laughter the first authentic sound made. Suddenly overwhelmed with sadness at these stiff-jointed, threadbare manoeuvres of antique panzer divisions on the same training ground as had served those others which swept so suddenly and disconcertingly over Europe in 1940.

Looked in on Belsen, now a shrine, dignified and quiet. An exquisite evening, quiet and still, in the evening light. Peace here at last, I reflected, and was overcome with emotion, summoning up a picture of the other scenes, which tombstones marked; some individual and some mass graves. Bert Hardy who had photographed it, recalled how the imprisoned guards were being fed, and he couldn't restrain himself from snatching the food of one of them and throwing it on the ground. An English family, presumably an officer and his wife and children, taking an evening stroll. An odd place to choose in a way. Someone had thrown down a bunch of flowers on a stone. I was happy to have seen the shrine and its present peace.

Drove to Hanover, passing through Celle, lovely little town with Gothic inscriptions on the antique houses. These little towns which escaped the war's holocaust dotted about here and there, seeming more and more museum pieces, pleasing relics of another time now immutably past. Hanover all rebuilt, and belonging to the neon present. It might be anywhere.

A rally of refugees from the East beginning in Hanover. Start the morning wandering about the city, others so doing, mostly aged. Surveyed their faces. Something very sad about this re-built country. Not an active sadness, a leaden absence of happiness—in some taking the form of energy, of just doing, doing, doing; in others, a kind of inert contentment or acquiescence. How can it be otherwise? Such a nightmare that has lately passed, and such present dangers.

In the afternoon went out to meet some of the people assembling for the rally of the people from the East. Talked with a little group who had come in, at great risk, from the Soviet Zone. When they saw Bert Hardy's camera they were terrified. 'No picture!' So they could not be photographed, which was a pity because they had good faces; some of the best I saw. As is mentioned in *Doctor*

Zhivago the front line has the advantage that there is less fear there than elsewhere. Above all, fewer lies. It was like talking to people who had been in the French *Maquis*. They described their struggles to lay hands on food and clothing, their encounters with authority and occasional opportunities to get the better of it. Authority was the enemy – a sound, and, to me, sympathetic attitude. They were very poor. Perhaps, after all, the New Testament is right when it says the poor are blessed. They cheered me up. It is sometimes difficult to resist the conclusion that the monstrous apparatus of collective power can snuff out the little light of individual men, which alone can illumine life. Yet they cannot be snuffed out, as these assuredly were not. I detected in them no envy of their relatives and friends in Western Germany, where, of course, they might have stayed had they cared to. They had families left behind, and duties, and considered themselves, it seemed to me, as being a battered and thinning garrison in a beleaguered fortress, which could not hope to hold out indefinitely, but still must be defended to the last.

August 14, 1961—London

Berlin crisis. Disputation now pointless. Resolved, in all circumstances, to live and die a free man. No tyranny, however odious, no warfare, however destructive, can prevent this. It is what I will do.

August 29, 1961

May I be guided to eternity with my senses unclouded, my mind unafraid, and my soul full of love.

September 7, 1961

We, the English, too small for our boots.

* * *

January 1, 1962—Roquebrune – Cap Martin

Still very tired from shingles, etc. Death will be like this only more so; a great tiredness. I've never really been ill before for a protracted period. Illness the greatest of all misfortunes, the only one that's quite defeating, itself destroying the energy which might overcome it.

Lunched with Willie Maugham and his secretary, Alan Searle. Maugham now very frail, and barely holding on to life, but, as Kitty said, in his frailty more real than ever before. He's shed all dross, and now comprises only his tiny integrity. Felt very drawn to him. He'd put a coat over his pyjamas, and dragged out of bed because he was excited over seeing us. He's worried about his pictures (valued, he said, at £600,000); no pleasure in them now because of worry over them being stolen. He and Alan Searle went to Switzerland with a view to settling there to escape taxation. Said he'd had 'very attractive offer' from the Swiss authorities, so, presumably, they write to ageing rich men explaining the fiscal advantages of Swiss domicile. One can imagine the brochure. After a dismal two weeks in Lausanne they homed to Cap Ferrat. Some sacrifices, Maugham said, are too great even for money. His face is very ravaged, and he's almost too tired to stutter, let alone talk. Also, he's very deaf. He looks more than ever like an old mandarin. Acting on an impulse, I said: 'We don't care about your pictures or anything. We just want you to be happy and serene.' I think he was pleased.

January 2, 1962

Reading Sherman Adams' book, which, in its flat way, gives excellent picture of US administration under Eisenhower. Tasteless, colourless, odourless, as we used to be told of gases in chemistry lessons. No bite in it. Poor old Eisenhower, the original 'Innocent American', conscientiously getting through the Presidential day buoyed up by the hope of taking his niblick out on to the White House lawn at 6 p.m., and then having drinks and canapés with his cronies. Adams refers to how they 'solved' various problems like Korea, etc. In fact, none of them solved.

Colin Coote received knighthood in New Year Honours. Thought of that sleepy, grey old head munching sandwiches evening after evening, seated in sham Chippendale chair, hideously uncomfortable, with portraits of previous *Daily Telegraph* editors, a sad lot, staring down at him. Now rewarded. I was glad.

January 3, 1962

Maugham said the only happy exile he saw in Switzerland was Charlie Chaplin. Though over seventy, he had a child a year. This, he said, gave his wife something to do, and him, too.

Hesketh Pearson and his wife Joyce arrived. We prattled away as usual, repeating old stories and laughing a lot.

January 5, 1962

Suddenly felt better, and believed in possibility of functioning normally again. Went up to old Roquebrune with Hesketh and looked over the sea, again delighting in the scene. Somewhere or other there is a true balance between bodily appetites and spiritual ecstasy; an exquisite serenity which is neither complaisant nor anguished. I seek it always. Hesketh and I agreed that, apart from mysticism, no expression of truth can be satisfactory unless it has some element or flavour of humour. Thus, *Hamlet*, of all Shakespeare's plays, is for that reason beloved of actors. They slaver at the mouth over it. Hughie Kingsmill used to say of *Hamlet* that it was not a masterpiece, but contained material for a dozen masterpieces.

January 6, 1962

Now really no longer sick, and resolved to resume full work routine. Apropos Byron, discussed with Hesketh how romantic, narcissistic characters of Byron type make a play of their lives, with themselves in the main part. Thus Byron's going to Missolonghi was just the last act, which he had to play. Likewise, Wilde's trial. Perhaps this is in a sense true of all lives. Christ, for instance, had such a feeling about Gethsemane. All the same, there's a difference between fulfilling a personal destiny, related to that of a diety's purpose for mankind, and shaping the play itself to give one's own ego maximum scope. It's the difference between a dramatist's and an actor's view of dramatic art. Byron and Wilde both players who, because of their performances, captured and held the audience's attention.

January 7, 1962

I remember my father saying to me once that he had imagined that growing old would mean becoming sagacious, serene, and immune to the follies and hurts of the ego. Not at all. He was the same man as he had ever been. The Old Adam did not tire with the years. But for the convenient circumstance of having grizzled hair, decayed teeth, short breath, wizened flesh, etc. he would behave accordingly as the costume and the make-up changed, necessitating a different performance; not the part itself.

January 8, 1962

Laughed with Hesketh about Boswell's visits to Voltaire and Rousseau. Though Voltaire and Rousseau spent quite a time in England, the English only interested in sojourn among them of royalty and VIP's – Empress Eugénie, Talleyrand, Lenin. Typical of their whole attitude. We spoke about Lincoln and his weirdly poetical sayings. For instance, when someone, wanting to ridicule his long legs, asked how long legs should be, he replied: 'Long enough to reach the ground'.

Kitty pointed out that Lincoln one of rare cases of a tall man making a mark. I said also de Gaulle. Something in common between de Gaulle and Lincoln. Quoted de Gaulle's remark about Pétain when he was pleading for his release from imprisonment – 'It was necessary to condemn him because his person symbolised the capitulation. But now there is just an old man in a fortress who once did great things for France. Is he to die without ever seeing a tree again, a flower or a friend?'

January 10, 1962

Couldn't sleep, read short story by an Italian. Excellent theme – the first night of an opera by a German at the Milan Scala. All the top people, dressed up, jewelled, there. Rumour begins to spread that there's been a revolution, and that the streets outside are in the hands of an angry mob. Finally becoming panic. No one cares to leave the Scala. They stay there all night, getting more and more dishevelled, panic-stricken. Some prepare for making terms with the revolutionaries. Finally, morning breaks. Nothing has happened. It's all been an illusion. Feeling silly and ashamed of themselves, they make off. Cowardice and spinelessness of rich well conveyed. How easy it is to make a revolution!

January 13, 1962

Feeling at last fully restored. A picnic up in the mountains, strong fresh wind, pretty green young fir trees bending to it, and, in the distance, the sea. Keep thinking, in a rather asinine way, of my 'The Titans' television programmes, and the success the first one, on Russia, has had. Illingworth writes, 'a smash hit'. Charles Wintour, Editor of the *Evening Standard*, writes: 'I really thought it was about the best TV programme I have ever seen'.

Hesketh and I recalled visit we'd paid to A. A. Milne, after he'd had brain haemorrhage. We went to see him in a nursing home at Tunbridge Wells. His face dazed, and rather sinister, we thought. He picked up scissors lying by him, and, opening and shutting them, made some scarcely comprehensible remark about the nurses. The sense we got was that he'd like to slit open their clothing, if not their bodies. A reaction, we assessed, to all the syruppy Christopher Robin stuff spilling over from his unconscious which, before his haemorrhage, had been buried away and lightly sealed there. The curse of *Punch* was upon him.

January 23, 1962

Went with Hesketh, Joyce and Kitty in quest of Frank Harris. First to Napoule, where he put Oscar Wilde in a hotel soon after he came out of prison. A rather sad little place on the coast just beyond Cannes. Wilde very bored and wretched there, it seems. Used to stroll in pine woods, which we located. Once, strolling there, encountered Sir George Alexander (who first played 'Earnest'), who cut him, Alexander on a bicycle. Had a clear picture of Wilde, large, shambling figure; in poor condition; blear-eyed, mooning about, bored and inert; finding no comfort in the sea coast, or the view of the snowy alps.

January 26, 1962

Alleged remark by some Soviet Top Person in Africa: 'We still have the personality cult. What we lack is a personality.'

De Tocqueville – 'le moment le plus dangereux pour un mauvais government, c'est lorsqu'il commence à s'amender.'

January 27, 1962

On our Harris expedition, we went on to look at a house he'd occupied in Nice – Villa Edouard VII, Boulevard Edouard VII. It turned out to be block of flats, rather like Whitehall Court, high above Nice, in what had obviously been once an affluent suburb. At the Villa Edouard VII we found a concierge who remembered Harris. He was, she said, *très gentil*, and, when she was having her first child sent down a bird and a bottle of champagne to her. Mrs Harris she obviously didn't care for. When I mentioned that she was younger than Harris (in point of fact, 25 years), she sniffed, and said 'very little' (*très peu*). Harris, she said, sweated a lot ('*il a transpiré beaucoup*'), and used to hang his shirt out on his balcony to dry in the sun after he returned from a walk. He had left the Villa Edouard VII about a year before he died (in 1931), but she didn't know where he'd moved to. She'd heard vaguely that he'd moved twice in that year. It was pretty obvious, from the tone of her voice, that Harris was flitting because he was broke. The concierge must have been quite attractive thirty years before when Harris was around. I suggested that there had probably been a bit of behind-pinching and other amorous interludes, which, added to the poulet and champagne, gave her voice its nostalgic tone in recalling Harris. This might also account for the hostility to Mrs Harris, who anyway, according to Harris, was a prize bitch. We drove back over the top corniche, picturing to ourselves Harris in that last place, desperate for money, setting his autobiography under the counter, dyeing his hair and moustache (the latter sustained by pegs at night), writing his book on Shaw; still with his deep voice and roving eye, but pretty broken and forlorn inside. Shaw, against his wife Charlotte's wishes, visited Harris when he was staying in Nice during the last year Harris spent there. I asked Hesketh why Charlotte didn't like Harris. 'She didn't like his work,' Hesketh said. We laughed inordinately over this as a sublime under-statement.

February 11, 1962

We watched de Gaulle on television – an astonishing performance, quite unreal, but still impressive. Rambling on about France in the 17th century, and the Revolution; alleged quotation from Shakespeare about a man who found a pearl in the sea so beautiful that he threw it back. Haunted for the rest of the evening by this weird, forceful Don Quixote, with all France sheltering behind him; the voice summoned up from a vanished past to provide momentary reassurance in a shifting present.

February 17, 1962

Reading Pascal after Balzac (which I did) is like breathing mountain air after an evening in a night club. That lucidity! Oh, if I could capture it. Pascal died at 39. He was in pain almost every day of his life. Yet his life was triumphant, one of the most triumphant ever lived.

February 22, 1962

Tadeusz Horko, editor of the *Polish Daily*, and his wife, arrived. Tadeusz, to me, the Exile – intelligent, dear, amusing, and, just below the surface, infinitely sad. Walking along the path to Gorbio, with the coast delightfully spread out beneath us, he said, à propos his exile status: 'We poles can hold out best because we've had most experience of being over-run'. Poland now, in his opinion, virtually without a Government. The Gomulka Government exists, and is likely to go on existing, precisely because it has no contact with the country at all or its people. Tadeusz with his sallow face and soft eyes and Gauloise cigarette, now English, but for ever Polish – the more so because English.

February 23, 1962

Woke up with that feeling of being a castaway which Cowper so exquisitely expressed in his verse. The night still in my head; a sense of being lost and alone in an inhospitable universe. No refreshment from the troubled night hours. Then started reading the *Pensées* (Pascal), and, miraculously, the clouds all cleared away and my fears dissolved. Such is the power, across three hundred years, of one clear, true mind on another which, however inadequately, is striving after clarity and truth. No other specific can work this transformaton; no pill, potion, headshrinker's incantation, etc. I felt a sense of inexpressible happiness, and met the sun, when it came up, with joy and gratitude to have its light and heat for another day. The communion with Pascal was greater than I have ever felt on any previous occasion in reading, or dwelling upon those who went before. As I read I had a quite fabulous awareness of Pascal strolling one evening by the Seine, and this thought coming into his mind: 'Les rivières sont des chemins qui marchent.' A short, spare figure, with those luminous eyes, and that sensitive, suffering, gently ironical and ample mouth. The awareness was so strong that I felt certain he could not be dead, or I ever die. The only uplifting I ever want is from ecstacy. Nothing else will do.

February 24, 1962

I have known some outstanding liars. Their distortion of truth is
not merely fantasism, or egotistical – a desire to present themselves
in a good light, or to shelter themselves against an inconvenient or
hurtful reality. It is also malignant; a deliberate distortion of life
out of wickedness – like that deliberate sullying and destruction of
Abwehr quarters before a withdrawal I remember so well in the war;
excreta about the place, windows broken, furniture and pictures,
even the very walls, hacked and soiled. This is exactly what lying
does. It is a kind of madness, and, indeed, often leads to actual,
certifiable lunacy – itself a form of lying.

Johnson felt that if he did not hold undeviatingly on to truth
madness would overtake him. Truth was his sanity's lifeline. Also
Pascal, who said truth was all his force, and that if he lost it he
would be utterly lost. There is no great man who has ever lived who
has not loved truth, and no liar who has not been despicable. Over
the face of a liar a shadow hangs, with fear lurking round the eyes –
fear of truth. A liar, in lying, often sweats visibly, and gives off a
stench. This has been a great age for lying. It is lies, rather than
mushroom clouds, which hang so ominously over our heads.
Truth lights the way through life and is therefore always symbolized as some form of illumination – a candle, a torch, a lamp.

February 27, 1962

I want to live as far as possible now outside my body, so that when
I come to leave it, which will be soon, the departure will be easy.
No possessions to regret, no keys to hand over, no agonized
partings. Just to go – like leaving a furnished lodging, rented by the
week, where one had been temporarily housed. That is all I want
my body to be to me now.

March 2, 1962

Tadeusz Horko described how a friend of his was once in a
Marseilles brothel when a pornographic film was being shown.
The friend couldn't stop himself laughing at it, to the great

annoyance of the management, who finally had him thrown out. Excellent example of how laughter anathema to the will, whether exerted collectively through power, or individually through sex. The film, it seemed, showed some whores absurdly attired as schoolgirls, whose Professor assaulted them one after the other. As he related it, Tadeusz also fell into paroxysms of laughter. Quite see that, from the management's point of view, mirth was ruinous. One cannot feel randy and laugh, any more than one can exercise absolute power and laugh. D. H. Lawrence and the Marquis de Sade are as humourless as Hitler and de Gaulle.

The Polish Ambassador in Moscow during the war, a certain Kot, asked at a diplomatic gathering to be introduced to Beria. When the presentation had been made, Kot said to Beria: 'I'm happy to meet you. I've heard so much about you from the Poles'. Beria furious, thinking this bad taste joke. Kot bewildered because he had intended no joke at all. After all, he *had* heard a lot about Beria from the Poles.

March 14, 1962 – Robertsbridge

It is a good thing to have ringing in one's mind at the beginning of the day words that are true and pure, like Pascal's. This acts as a sort of filter through which the day's deluge of false and corrupt wards can pass.

April 9, 1962

Curious encounter yesterday. Distracted woman arrived at the house in the afternoon, wet through from having walked from the station. She asked to see me privately, to which, with some reluctance, I agreed. Then embarked upon long rigmarole about how in America she'd been chased by the FBI, probably as a result of friendship with East European Jew, who may well have been a Communist, though she didn't know it. Said she was British subject, though long resident in USA. Had, in fact, strong American accent. Came to England, and there also subjected to police persecution. Described this vividly, and quite crazily. Everyone watching her – ticket collectors on underground, bus conductors, etc. Telephone tapped, letters opened. What was she to do? Rather a beautiful woman in a way, sallow, with an oval face, rather like Mary McCarthy; but, of course, crazy. At least, I suppose so.

When she had finished, I said that I thought she was imagining a lot of this surveillance. Quite understandable, but still a victim of persecution mania. 'Paranoia?' she asked, almost hopefully. 'No,' I insisted, 'persecution mania.' I tried to explain that this whole odious business of investigating people's views and contacts a Kafka-esque nightmare, and calculated to induce morbid state of mind among the investigators and the investigated. Then, to my surprise, she suddenly got up, and said that, if that was my view, she'd try and look at the matter differently. She professed to be very grateful, and Kitty took her to the station to return to London. On the way, she went on saying how grateful she was. Whole episode left me dissatisfied and troubled. Was there anything in it? Or was she just a nut? Had she even, perhaps, some hidden motive for coming to see me? I don't know, but her ravaged face, her halting, inconsequential narrative, continued to haunt me through the evening. She was not unpleasant or unappetizing, as mad people often are. Just, I expect, yet another victim of these evil times. Somehow the poison had got into her, as it has into so many. Some instinct led me not to ask for her name or address. If I displayed any sort of curiosity, I thought, she'd think that I, too, was in the game. I just listened attentively and sympathetically, and then told her, as truthfully as I knew how, what I thought. It seemed to work, if only momentarily.

April 21, 1962

Gerald Reitlinger all alone in his house, and pulling down the blinds ever earlier in the day. Now the early afternoon, soon before lunch, until the time comes that they are never pulled up at all. Gerald, in the shadows, with his collection of Ming china, accumulating sale-room information about the shifting price of pictures. A kind of tragic figure, all alone. He spoke to me yesterday from his solitude, with a note of desperation in his voice, like a man desperately breaking out from a prison in which he knew he was incarcerated for ever.

Pascal points out that if an artisan dreamed each night that he was a king he would be in precisely the same situation as a king who similarly dreamed each night he was an artisan. The only difference between sleeping and waking dreams is that the former lack continuity. Otherwise the two are indistinguishable. We have to look for a reality which transcends both sleeping and waking dreams. This is the pursuit to which I should like to devote every second of the time remaining to me on this earth. Then at least I should come into Pascal's second category – of those who seek God without finding him. This is better than the third category – those who neither seek nor find God, and who are 'fous et malheureux'. The second category are 'malheureux et raisonnables', and the first, who, having found God, serve Him, 'raisonnables et heureux'.

June 2–6, 1962

Freud said he preferred to think in torment to not being able to think clearly. Therefore took no drugs, and only with difficulty was persuaded to take aspirin at the end of his life.

Freud's basic discovery was that anxiety and neurotic conditions are due to sexual repression. Deduction from it more dubious – viz: that by eliminating sexual repression, taking off the lid, as it were, anxiety and neurotic conditions likewise automatically eliminated. Would seem to be the case that since application of Freudian methods, more, not less, neuroses and neurotics around. It might be contended these existed before, and have simply been uncovered thanks to Freud. Doubt this. Consider that fleshly appetites, and the ill-consequences of checking and indulging them, will disappear as a result of spiritual ones. The eye looks further afield for its preoccupations. Frustration is hurtful, and so sometimes is control exerted through the will, but the higher appetite drives out the lower as good money drives out bad. If I force myself to eat less than I want by an act of will I may damage my inner self, but if I cannot be bothered to linger over a dinner table because I want to get in good time to hear

Beethoven's Piano Concerto, there is no deprivation and no consequent neurosis. In such circumstances, it is abstinence, not indulgence, which appeases the demands of appetite. These pleasures of the senses are inferior to those of the spirit. Who stuffs himself with pickles and cheese when a soufflé awaits him? Who wants to look at magic lantern slides when the bright landscape spreads out before him? The senses are only what Pascal calls *divertissements*. They cease to trouble, whether eschewed or indulged, when they are seen as such. More serenity has been caused by dying in the flesh in order to live in the spirit than the other way round.

Diaries, like old soldiers, never die, they simply fade away; as a life comes to an end, so does writing them, not so much because there is nothing more to say as because there seems little point in going on saying it. Experience continues, but has become too habitual to require comment; events go on happening, but they no longer contain any element of surprise. As a commentator one is in the same case as a child who has been taken to see the sights of London, but dozes off on the way home. Thus, my last diary comments are largely ruminative; the curtain has come down, the play is over, and such thoughts as I have about it relate only to its message, if any. In any case, I have come fully to realise that here truly, as the Epistle to the Hebrews tells us, we have no continuing city, and find myself increasingly preoccupied with seeking one to come – a pursuit that belongs to Eternity, whereas diaries belong to Time.

Epilogue

It would be agreeable, of course, to look back on the unedifying selves recorded in my diaries as belonging to a vanished past. Alas, in old age, as I have found, the despicable ego is as liable to lift its cobra-head as heretofore, though perhaps more cunningly, and, contrary to what the young believe, carnality can still stir in ancient carcasses. Nowadays, to be conscious of one's own wickedness is commonly regarded as mental sickness; it is the fashion to diagnose feelings of guilt, and the penitential longings that go therewith, as a sick state of mind that needs to be treated by psychiatrists. On the contrary, I am convinced that awareness of sin is a necessary precondition to any regeneration, not to say sanity. The Apostle Paul, St Francis, all the most holy men and women, have seen themselves, not just as run-of-the-mill sinners, but outstanding in their wickedness. For that matter, Jesus himself would not accept the appelation 'good', which, he insisted, pertained only to God.

This is not mere affection; the clearer the vision of goodness, the more insistent the sense of failing to measure up to it. Similarly, the more ardent the longing to walk with God, the more agonizing the separation from Him. It is the greatest artists who are most conscious of the inadequacy of their colours and lines; the greatest writers who are most aware that words with a beginning and an end cannot possibly convey the sublime mysteries of our earthly existence which never began and cannot end.

The fourteenth century mystic, John Ruysbroek, tells us that we should keep three books constantly before us – the first old, worm-eaten, musty, written in the blackest of characters; the second white and beautiful, with blood-red writing; the third golden and glittering. We are to begin by reading the old musty book, which involves contemplating our past life, and finding it 'black in guilt and sorrow' – as it might be, reading my diaries. Then we are to 'reflect on the evil of our ways, on how indifferent we have been in words, works, wishes and thoughts', and finally to 'cast down our eyes with the publican and say: "God be merciful to me, a sinner."' Having thus purified ourselves, we may turn to the other two books – the white one which tells of the Incarnation, and the golden one that tells of Heaven.

Seen as Ruysbroek's black book, the day-by-day record of a life, mine or anyone else's, becomes, as it were, the scenario for a documentary on our human condition – as Dante saw it, a Divine Comedy; as Bunyan, a Pilgrimage; as Milton, a Paradise Lost; as Shakespeare, a tale told by an idiot, full of sound and fury, signifying nothing; an infinite variety of concepts, but the same essential theme – of mortal men peering into the Cloud of Unknowing that lies between them and their creator, sojourning in an earthly city on their way to a heavenly one where they belong.

Confronted with my own sorry record in my diaries, I turn for comfort to the Sage in Dr Johnson's *Rasselas*, who expresses so cogently the hopes of a great soul greatly humbled as he approaches the end of a long life, 'whose retrospect recalls to my view many opportunities for good neglected, much time squandered upon trifles, and more lost in idleness and vacancy.' Now he composes himself to tranquility, 'endeavours to abstract my thoughts from hopes and cares which, though reason knows them to be vain, still try to keep their old possession of the heart; expect with serene humility that hour which nature cannot long delay, and hope to possess in a better state that happiness which here I could not find, and that virtue which here I have not attained.'

Index